The S&M Feminist

* * *

Clarisse Thorn is a feminist, sex-positive educator who has delivered sex-related lectures and workshops to a variety of audiences, including New York's Museum of Sex, San Francisco's Center for Sex & Culture, and universities across the USA. She created and curated the original Sex+++ sex-positive documentary film series at Chicago's historic feminist site, Jane Addams Hull-House Museum. She has also volunteered as an archivist, curator and fundraiser for that venerable S&M institution, the Leather Archives & Museum. In 2010, Clarisse returned from working on HIV mitigation in sub-Saharan Africa. Her writing has appeared across the Internet in venues ranging from *The Guardian* to *Feministe*. She blogs about feminist sexuality with a focus on S&M at clarissethorn.com, and tweets @clarissethorn.

* * *

Also check out Clarisse's awesome book
Confessions of a Pickup Artist Chaser!

* * *

There's a huge subculture of men who trade tips, tricks, and tactics for seducing women. Clarisse Thorn, a feminist S&M writer and activist, spent years researching these guys. She observed their discussions, watched them in action, and learned their strategies. By the end, she'd given a lecture at a seduction convention. This is her story — and her theories about feminism and seduction to boot.

Paperback copies: https://www.createspace.com/3830583

* * *

* * *

The S&M Feminist:

Best of Clarisse Thorn

* * *

* * *

clarissethorn.com
@ClarisseThorn

* * *

This book is copyright 2012 Clarisse Thorn, although I have mixed feelings about modern copyright law. Check out the Electronic Frontier Foundation at [http://eff.org], a nonprofit that protects free speech on the Internet and does lots of awesome work around copyright issues.

Cover image copyright 2002 Clarisse Thorn.

* * *

* * *

If you're afraid of pain, you have to find out what pain is.
~ Marina Abramović

* * *

I'd like to thank all the brave pioneers of the BDSM community, for exploring the reaches of human sexuality, and coming back with maps.
~ an unsourced quotation offered by one of Clarisse's blog commenters

* * *

I think of Clarisse as the John Stuart Mills of sexuality.
~ one of Clarisse's ex-boyfriends

* * *

People's ability to understand their own emotional and physical experiences and sensations is limited by what is safe to ask or know, what systems of interpretation they have received for screening that raw material, and whether they find it possible to connect with anyone who thinks differently about these matters.
~ Pat Califia

* * *

Abuse of power comes as no surprise.
~ Jenny Holzer

* * *

* * *

Notes, Acknowledgments and Resources

* * *

I had a privileged upbringing. My education and safety nets are the biggest reasons I'm able to do the work that I do, and I try not to forget that. I have been blessed with parents, friends, and lovers who have supported me both emotionally and intellectually. Since this is a "Best Of" my blog, I want to particularly acknowledge the commenters who have contributed their perspective to my blog, and the other bloggers who have responded to me and cross-posted my work. There are too many to name, but thank you all so much.

Special thanks to Brenda Errichiello, a guerrilla editor-for-hire. Brenda has been very generous and helpful to me; errors and weirdness in this book should be blamed on me and not her, because a lot of the time she tries to convince me to fix those things and I refuse out of writerly arrogance. If you need editing for your self-published book (and you do), then you should totally contact her. Her website is [http://www.bee-editing.com/].

I try to keep my writing as accessible as possible. One way I do that is by avoiding jargon and by using terms that I think most people will recognize. I often write "S&M" instead of "BDSM," for example; and when I'm using technical S&M language like "top" or "bottom" or "scene," I try to define the words as I go along. But sometimes I slip into jargon by accident. Also, plenty of S&M terms are super useful, and giving a quick overview of S&M language can go a long way towards describing S&M culture. Hence, I have included a Glossary at the end of this book. Many of the terms in the Glossary aren't terms that I use in this book, but you might find it useful or interesting anyway. (I also included a few terms that come from other subcultures, such as polyamory or queer studies.)

I've received a lot of feedback over the years informing me that I'm the "gateway drug" into feminism for some readers. That's kind of cool, but I want to make it clear that if you're just now getting into feminism, there's lots of other stuff to learn before you draw any conclusions. Feminism is a huge, varied, rich movement with lots of history, schisms, and discontents. Also, in case it needs to be said,

I'm not the only feminist who does S&M. There are others, some of whom love my work and some of whom disagree with me frequently.

One advantage of the blog format, as opposed to more traditional formats, is that each post can contain tons of hyperlinks — and each article has comment space, so there can be fascinating discussions that explore each topic more deeply. (Of course, there can also be silly, boring, or offensive discussions.) As soon as a blog becomes moderately successful, it develops its own community of regular commenters, and mine is no exception. Facilitating and moderating these discussions can be amazingly fun and interesting. It can also be stressful and exhausting. As a commenter community evolves, it shapes how other people read the blog's articles and comment on them; sometimes the community will develop norms or tendencies that make certain people feel more comfortable — or less comfortable. I've tried to control this with my blog so that it's a welcoming environment for most people, but I have such a diverse range of commenters that it's sometimes quite difficult.

I bring all this up because, if you're intrigued by some of the articles you read in this book, I encourage you to check out the original post. In this book, I've made a lot of hyperlinks into footnotes, but not all of them. More importantly, if you look at the original post, you can read the comments. But my commenter community has changed over time. Sometimes it's more feminist, for example, and sometimes it's less feminist. So just be aware, if you read the comments, that the range of opinions may not reflect any group that would assemble elsewhere on the planet; that a different community might produce really different comments; and that other articles might have really different discussions.

If you've already read my incredibly awesome book *Confessions of a Pickup Artist Chaser,* then thank you! (Bonus points if you can pick out all the parts of *Confessions* that I pulled verbatim from articles included in this book.) If you haven't read *Confessions,* then please check that out, too. Paperback copies of *Confessions* are available through CreateSpace: https://www.createspace.com/3830583

* * *

BDSM Resources

BDSM is a 6-for-4 deal of an acronym that stands for Bondage, Discipline, Dominance, Submission, Sadism, and/or Masochism. Some people call it S&M, B&D, leather, fetish, or kink. BDSM can mean very different things to different people, and there are a lot of activities that can fall under the BDSM umbrella; such activities might include spanking, Master/slave role-playing, handcuffs, cages, rape fantasies, razor blades, or all kinds of other things.

I mention a lot of resources in the articles that I've included in this book, but I wanted to include an overview at the beginning, too.

Hands down, I believe that one of the most important resources within the BDSM community is the Kink Aware Professionals list. If you are seeking medical, legal or other professional help for a problem that is influenced by alternative sexuality, there is probably someone on the list who can help you. When I was going through my own complicated and difficult BDSM coming-out process, I tried two therapists from the KAP list. One of them didn't really get me, but the second was wonderfully helpful — so, if you're looking for a therapist, don't be afraid to shop around until you find the right fit. The list is here: https://ncsfreedom.org/resources/kink-aware-professionals-directory/kap-directory-homepage.html

Books

My personal favorite beginner BDSM books are *The New Topping Book* and *The New Bottoming Book,* by Dossie Easton and Janet W. Hardy. If you look for those books on Amazon.com, you will also see a lot of interesting related books in the "Customers Who Bought This Item Also Bought" section. I remember liking Jay Wiseman's *SM101,* although I know some people who have mixed feelings about it; a number of people recommend *Screw The Roses, Send Me The Thorns* by Philip Miller and Molly Devon, but I've never read it myself.

If you're thinking of coming out to a loved one, I recommend the book *When Someone You Love Is Kinky* by Dossie Easton and Catherine W. Liszt. I've also heard good things about the "Parents of Alternative Sexuality" pamphlet by Dr. Amy Marsh.

If you, like me, are particularly attracted to the idea of needle piercing, there's a great book called *Play Piercing* by Deborah Addington.

If you're more interested in getting a feel for common BDSM philosophies and what the BDSM community is like — an anthropological perspective, one might say — then there's a book by Mark Thompson called *Leatherfolk,* and a newer one by Staci Newmahr called *Playing at the Edge.*

Online

I usually direct total newbies to this BDSM 101 page by Franklin Veaux: http://www.xeromag.com/fvbdsm.html

As it happens, the same writer has a good Polyamory 101, too: http://www.xeromag.com/fvpoly.html

There are a lot of websites on BDSM, and they aren't all carefully edited or moderated; so if you can manage it, then I suggest you try to get hold of one of the above how-to books. That said... overall, one of the best online BDSM resources is FetLife.com, the kinky social networking site. Once you have an account, you can join a huge variety of discussion groups about BDSM. FetLife is not a dating site; it's more like a kinky Facebook (seriously). I think that there are important problems with how FetLife is structured. For example, there's no way to search for past topics, which is ridiculous; this means that the research process for finding discussions is incredibly weird. The BDSM activist maymay has written intelligently about many issues with FetLife: http://maybemaimed.com/2011/03/20/fetlife-considered-harmful/

But the fact remains that FetLife is a huge gathering place.

Another good online resource is the amazing sex education site Scarleteen.com. Scarleteen offers a ton of advice on a ton of sexual topics, and has its own message boards.

The site KinkAcademy.com has received some good reviews, and features video tutorials by some people who are pretty well-known in the community. You have to buy a membership, though.

The BDSM writer Ranai from Germany has labored long and hard to make an amazingly comprehensive, international, multilingual directory of kink resources. I haven't gone through it extensively, but every time Ranai comments on my blog she's brilliant, so I'm sure her directory is brilliant too. Here's the directory: http://ranai.wordpress.com/kink-resources/

There are so many BDSM blogs that I could never count them all. I want to direct special attention to Kink Research Overviews, an abandoned but still excellent blog that profiles the sparse and scattershot research on BDSM: http://kinkresearch.blogspot.com/2009/10/welcome-to-kink-research.html

In Person

If you've decided that you want to start attending workshops, discussion groups, parties, or other BDSM events in person, please keep in mind that not everyone is going to mesh well with their local

BDSM groups. If you don't like your local BDSM group, then don't force yourself to participate! That said, I generally encourage people to get into their local community, because it truly can be an amazing resource — it's way more than just a place to meet partners.

If you make an account on FetLife, you may be able to join groups for your area (for example, if you live in Chicago, then you should look for Chicago groups), where local issues or events will be discussed and publicized.

For those aged 18-35, many major cities have branches of The Next Generation, a.k.a. the local "kinky youth group."

Otherwise, just Google around. It's much easier these days than it was for our parents.

* * *

* * *

Table of Contents

* * *

Remember that there's a Glossary at the end! Page 349.

I write both personal narratives and cultural analysis. Almost all my writing mixes the two, but most of my pieces incline more towards one than the other. Accordingly, I've tagged all the articles in this book as either [storytime] or [theory].

* * *

SECTION 1:
The Basics
In which we explore the foundations of S&M, feminism, and sex-positive feminism.

* * *

S&M [storytime]:
Love Bites: An S&M Coming-Out Story ... page 3

Education [theory]:
Liberal, Sex-Positive Sex Education: What's Missing ... page 16

Communication [theory]. **Sex Communication Tactic Derived From S&M: The Annotated Safeword** ... page 24

Communication [theory]: **Sex Communication Tactic Derived From S&M: Checklists** ... page 33

Communication [theory]: **Sex Communication Tactic Derived From S&M: Journal-Keeping** ... page 35

Communication [storytime]:
Sex Communication Case Studies ... page 38

Feminism [theory]:
Towards My Personal Sex-Positive Feminist 101 ... page 44

S&M [theory]: **S&M Superpowers** ... page 55

S&M [theory]: **BDSM Can Be "Love Sex" Too** ... page 58

S&M [theory]: **Body Chemistry and S&M** ... page 60

S&M [theory]: **Going Under** ... page 64

Orgasmic "Dysfunction" [storytime]:
A Unified Theory of Orgasm ... page 68

Boundaries [storytime]:
I'm Not Your Sex-Crazy Nympho Dreamgirl ... page 88

Boundaries [storytime]: **Orgasms Aren't My Favorite Part of Sex, and My Chastity Urge** ... 93

Boundaries [theory]: **Anger, Fear and Pain** ... page 98

Evolution [theory]:
Sexual Openness: Two Ways To Encourage It ... page 102

Relationships [storytime]:
Fear, Loathing and S&M Sluthood in San Francisco ... page 108

S&M [theory]: **BDSM As A Sexual Orientation, and Complications of the Orientation Model** ... page 116

S&M [theory]: **BDSM "versus" Sex** ... page 122

S&M [theory]: **BDSM Roles, "Topping From The Bottom," and "Service Top"** ... page 133

Feminism [theory]: **"Inherent Female Submission": The Wrong Question** ... page 137

Manliness [theory]: *Fifty Shades of Grey, Fight Club,* **and the Complications of Male Dominance** ... page 142

Abuse [theory]: **The Alt Sex Anti-Abuse Dream Team** ... page 147

Section 1 Study Guide ... page 155

* * *

SECTION 2:
Activism and Allies
In which we explore activism and other topics tangentially related to S&M feminism — from sex work, to community organizing, to the nature of masculinity.

* * *

Activism [theory]: **Grassroots Organizing For Feminism, S&M, HIV, and Everything Else** ... page 159

Activism [storytime]: **Interview with Richard Berkowitz, Star of *Sex Positive* and Icon of Safer Sex Activism** ... page 164

Abuse [theory]: **Social Responsibility Within Activism** ... page 171

Boundaries [storytime]: **Taking Care Of Each Other** ... page 175

Manliness [theory]:
Questions I Want To Ask Entitled Cis Het Men ... page 178

Education [theory]:
Sexual ABCs in Africa, Part 1: Abstinence ... page 188

Education [theory]:
Sexual ABCs in Africa, Part 2: Be Faithful ... page 194

Education [theory]:
Sexual ABCs in Africa, Part 3: Condoms ... page 200

Activism [theory]: **Colonized Libidos** ... page 207

Vegan [theory]: **Confections of a Pickup Artist Chaser** ... page 210

Polyamory [theory]: **In Praise of Monogamy** ... page 217

Polyamory [theory]: **My Top Questions About Dealing With Multiple Lovers** ... page 223

Sex Work [storytime]: **One Blurred Edge of Sex Work: Portrait of a Sugar Baby** ... page 227

Sex Work [theory]: **A Sugar Baby Leaves The Business** ... page 234

Section 2 Study Guide ... page 239

* * *

SECTION 3:
Making It Complicated
In which we really get into it.

* * *

Relationships [storytime]: **Chemistry** ... page 243

S&M [theory]: **Start From A Position of Strength** ... page 259

S&M [storytime]: **Predicament Bondage** ... page 263

Relationships [theory]: **Relationship Tools: Monogamy, Polyamory, Competition, and Jealousy** ... page 269

Evolution [storytime]:
You Don't Always Know What You're Thinking ... page 275

Abuse [theory]:
Thinking More Clearly About BDSM versus Abuse ... page 280

Communication [theory]: **What Happens After An S&M Encounter "Gone Wrong"** ... page 286

S&M [theory]: **Aftercare or Brainwashing?** ... page 292

Communication [theory]: **Feminist S&M Lessons From the Seduction Community** ... page 302

S&M [storytime]:
The Strange Binary of Dominance and Submission ... page 316

Feminism [storytime]: **My Mom's Rape Story, and A Confused Relationship with Feminism** ... page 321

Section 3 Study Guide ... page 329

* * *

Clarisse's Lectures, Workshops and Events ... page 331

Footnotes ... page 333

Glossary ... page 349

* * *

* * *

SECTION 1:
The Basics

*In which we explore the foundations of
S&M, feminism, and sex-positive feminism.*

* * *

When I think of this section, I think of:

If you're afraid of pain, you have to find out what pain is.
~ Marina Abramović

*I'd like to thank all the brave pioneers of the BDSM community,
for exploring the reaches of human sexuality,
and coming back with maps.*
~ an unsourced quotation offered by
one of my blog commenters

* * *

The S&M Feminist — Clarisse Thorn

* * *

S&M:
[storytime] Love Bites:
An S&M Coming-Out Story

The events of this story took place between 2005-2008; I wrote it in fits and starts over the span of 2006-2008. I started blogging as Clarisse Thorn in 2008, but my coming-out story wasn't published until early 2010, when Time Out Chicago *picked it up. I look over this piece today, in 2012, and I think about what I would have written differently if I'd had the hyper-focused feminist sex educator instincts that I have now. I would have written differently about consent, and I would have written differently about the communication that happened with my partners about my consent. I would have talked about how the S&M subculture isn't always welcoming for everybody, though it feels welcoming for me. Plus, I'm no longer practicing monogamy; I'm polyamorous these days.*

But at the time, my goal was to do two things: (1) write out how S&M stigma felt for me, as a young feminist, and to talk about how I was overcoming it. And (2) show that sometimes a partner just isn't good for you, even if he has a quality that you really really want — and you can always walk away.

* * *

I was very drunk. My perceptions had a frame-by-frame quality, and the evening didn't seem immediate: pieces of it were foreign, disconnected as a dream. I was being bitten very hard on the arm. It would leave marks the next day.

I was so muddled by assorted things that even now I can't sort out how I felt at that moment. When Richard's nails scored my skin I gasped, but I didn't ask him to stop. I flinched away, but he kept a firm grip on me. "Beg for mercy," he said softly.

Frame. Skip. I discovered that a mutual friend of ours had seen us, stopped, and was sitting on the grass across from Richard. "Hey," he said. "You shouldn't do that."

"It's okay," Richard said, "she likes it," and pulled my hair hard enough to force me to bow my head. *I do?* I managed to think, before thought vanished back into the blur of alcohol and pain. Our friend's face loomed over me, concern sketched vividly on his features.

I closed my eyes.

"Mercy," I whispered.

* * *

Later, Richard reminded me of something I said that night: "I wish I'd met you years ago." Thinking hard, I could only recall the evening in broad strokes. We'd gotten drunk at an outdoor party; he'd hurt me a bit; I'd said that; and then I'd staggered off to help clean up.

"A lot of crap comes out when you do this stuff," he now said. A few weeks had passed. I was lying on my stomach across the foot of his bed. Sitting perpendicular to me, he leaned back and propped his feet on the small of my back. Thin and pale, he tended to wear black, and had intense dark eyes. It was summer in 2005. I was twenty years old.

He'd asked me why I wanted to be hurt. I couldn't work out an answer — wasn't certain the question was valid — so I asked him why he liked to hurt people. He'd half-laughed, with a tone that I couldn't evaluate. Ruefully? "That's a long, dark road," he'd said.

"How do you know?" I asked, irritated by his presumption, nervously curious. I wasn't sure I was what he thought I was — wasn't sure **what** had been going on that night, beyond alcohol dulling my reactions and feelings. But I knew I hadn't been abused or violated. I hadn't asked him to stop, and I wanted to figure out why. "How did you know about me?"

"I can tell," he said, and grinned. "With you, it was obvious." He paused, added quietly, "You were begging for it."

A couple of hours later, we remained fully clothed, my face was buried in his pillow, and I was crying. He'd pinned me down so I couldn't move, and was raking his nails across what was exposed of my tank-topped back. When Richard first spotted the tears, he'd asked if I wanted a break. I'd said that it was okay, that he should continue, that I was fine.

I felt myself fragmenting, desperation and terror and pain pouring through me in an unbearable, necessary torrent. I told myself over and over that it didn't hurt that much, but I couldn't stop myself from tensing, crying out. After a while, I found myself saying, "No."

I felt him check himself, shifting his weight from my back. "Can we clarify something?" he asked gently. "Do you really want me to stop when you say no?"

No, I realized, *I don't,* and something vital in my psyche seemed to snap. The tears overwhelmed me. I couldn't get an answer out through my sobs, but even if I could have, I haven't the faintest idea what I might have said.

"We should take a break," he decided, and moved away. I'll never forget the relief — and desolation — I felt as he did.

* * *

It was a long time later that I remembered: I **had** met someone like Richard, years before. It had been in spring 2003; the guy was thin and pale, dressing mainly in black. I hadn't once thought of him in a romantic light.

I'd counted him a friend, but had only been alone with him once. We were in his living room, seated next to each other on dun-colored carpet. I couldn't recall how it started — we'd been sitting playing video games? had he tickled me as I shouted invective at the screen? — but it ended with him holding my wrists, me lying back on the floor and wondering how to get him off me.

I'd thought he might kiss me, so I turned my head away. Instead, he bit my neck. "No," I said aloud, more in startlement than anything else, and he gave me a searching look — as if he wasn't sure I was serious. "Please let me up," I said, and he asked, "Why?"

I didn't feel panicked, but strangely at a loss: he didn't seem to take my objection seriously. Yet he wasn't particularly threatening me, and I wasn't afraid. I explained that I was in a committed, monogamous relationship I didn't want to disrupt; I carefully didn't react when he bit me again, although it hurt.

I didn't say I wasn't getting anything out of my powerlessness or his apparent desire to hurt me, that it left me cold. Maybe I wasn't sure it would register: he hadn't appeared to **believe** me when I first told him to let me up. And maybe something in me agreed that such a response was incorrect.

Eventually, I got away. Stupidly, confused, I mentioned the incident to my boyfriend. Of course he was furious; I had to calm him. For my part, it hadn't occurred to me to be mad. That didn't feel as bizarre as it sounds — on some level, I felt that the whole incident was reasonable, even if it hadn't turned out to be what I wanted.

Not then. Not with him.

* * *

After I cried my heart out in his bed, Richard was very kind. He brought me a glass of water and listened as I said a lot of bewildered things. When I finally ran down, it was late; he invited me to sleep over, but didn't put the moves on me. The next morning, he told me he had work to do. Straightforwardly, I asked when I could see him again. He smiled, said to email him, that we'd work something out.

The next few days — weeks — time, I don't know; however long it was, it felt like being put through a shredder. I couldn't think about anything but that night and how, through my turmoil and tears, I'd found a kind of exultation. I had been sober, prepared and clear-headed. I couldn't find a way around the brutal, uncompromising revelation that apparently, I wanted nothing more than to be subordinated, used, hurt. I actually **wanted** to be a victim.

I wanted to talk to someone, but wasn't sure how to frame my words. I was positive it would help to talk to Richard, but he was busy, and busy, and busy. I had a number of friends who I suspected were into hardcore BDSM; I could have called any of them. But it was one thing to be fine with other people doing it, and quite another to discover such a desire in myself. In another situation, I would have thoroughly deconstructed my obvious double standard — but just then, it was a minor irrationality on top of one big chunk of insanity.

I considered asking my loving, liberal parents for advice and tried to imagine how it would go.

Mom. Dad. I love you, and I'm so sorry. I know you've tried to give me an independent, rational, feminist outlook, as well as self-esteem and integrity. Sadly, none of this appears to have taken; I guess I'm a broken mockery of everything you tried to instill. I don't want you to worry, or blame yourselves, but have you any advice on where to go from here?

No.

* * *

My mental images of that summer are hazy with remembered anger. As Richard remained occupied, I felt fury building within my fascination. I'm sure I felt like the classical woman spurned: he was nice enough when he ran into me and told me he was there to talk if I needed it, but the evidence contradicted his words. For weeks after that night, if I tried to see him he didn't have time.

It didn't help that he reacted very badly when I went after him aggressively — too aggressively, I knew, but couldn't help it — and told him honestly how vulnerable I was. He backed off fast, leaving me more confused than ever. (Though not too confused to think: *How stereotypical.*)

It went beyond being a woman spurned, though. Especially since I believed, intellectually, that he didn't **owe** it to me not to be busy. He wasn't required to sort me out. And — since it seemed to be what I was after — he wasn't obligated to continue hurting me. We'd just met, after all.

It was more that I was enraged by how desperately I wanted to be hurt — and infuriated that someone, **anyone**, could have such power over me. I had always thrown myself into infatuations; like most people, I'd been known to get angry at the object of my affections. But this was different. Not only was I infatuated, I was aching for something I couldn't reconcile. Even if Richard had been the perfect counselor I had no right to expect, I might have hated him. As it was, I felt toyed with, and found as many other reasons to dislike him as I could. As long as I could focus on wrath, I didn't have to think about my other feelings.

It kept me from falling apart.

He was away for most of the summer. I went to a few trusted friends for reassurance and validation; giving few details, I allowed my anger to calcify. But Richard ended up surprising me. On a visit to Chicago, he called me every night for a week. The bruises he left took weeks to fade, some of them bleeding and leaving scars. I raged as I covered the worst of them — but felt also a low-burning fulfillment. One close friend, Andrew, caught sight of a bruise on my leg and cast me a worried look. "That looks pretty bad," he observed, and I could only say, "Yes."

By then, I'd well and truly internalized the belief that Richard didn't want to deal with emotional vulnerability, and my furious resentment remained. This feeling was not helped by society in general; men hate emotions, right? Still, the more time I spent with him, the more I had to admit that he made an effort to be sensitive. Most of our failures to understand each other came from how different our relationship paradigms were, not to mention my unevenly-repressed identity crisis. I know I tried to warn Richard that I wasn't doing well at expressing myself and that what I thought, or felt, or believed I was might change on short notice; but I doubt I got even that concept across.

He identified fairly publicly as a BDSMer, and made it clear that he considered me superficial and cowardly because I was unsure about doing so myself. He was also polyamorous, a lifestyle that I had some experience with — but though I respected others' choices to engage in it, I'd decided against polyamory for myself. It felt strange to draw the parallel, but it **was** somewhat like dealing with a difficult boyfriend. Still, I didn't trust him, and our relationship didn't particularly involve sex.

Just pain.

Towards the end of one night, wan light filtering through my curtains, Richard inquired unexpectedly, "Are you happy with the way we are now?"

"What do you mean?" I temporized, sighing inwardly. Now I'd have to come up with a rational, coherent answer that would satisfy him. In those days, rationality and coherence felt like improbable dreams.

Richard explained that he hadn't particularly been satisfied with how he'd dealt with me before he left, but hadn't had time for anything better. Now, he thought the situation was "healthier." "What do you want from this?" he asked seriously.

I want the strength to walk away from you, I thought unclearly. *I want you to actually care about me. I never want to see you again.* I hugged my arms to myself, resting my hands gingerly on swelling skin. "Um," I said slowly, "nothing in particular?" I took a breath and gathered the one overriding fact: *I want you to keep hurting me.* "I don't expect anything from you," I told him, "and I don't want you to expect anything from me."

I knew from his smile that my answer was the right one. I could only hope it was accurate.

* * *

The summer passed, Richard away again for the end of it, then returning in September for the beginning of the school year. I, however, was leaving the city soon, and would be gone for some time. Those days were my last chances to see him for a while, and I was acutely aware of his nearness: I felt oriented towards him, as if I were a compass and he was North.

But I still felt the rage, lurking under the surface of my mind like a submerged monster. And though I ached with disturbingly intense thoughts of violence, it seemed that I was staying away from Richard, closing him out when I ran into him. He finally confronted me and asked, blunt as ever, if I was avoiding him. I denied it reflexively. How could I avoid North?

"I'm still figuring out how I feel about you," I told him as we walked late one night on the waterfront. I'd started to come to terms with being a masochist, had begun to assimilate that into my self-image, but that didn't explain why it had taken him to force the knowledge on me. The man I'd known in 2003, for instance, made no impression — though he'd obviously seen exactly what Richard saw, and had taken almost exactly the same approach. And I'd known heavily, formally BDSM-identifying folks for years. I'd even experimented with light bondage in previous relationships — being gently tied up, for instance — though I hadn't found it especially compelling.

Was it that I'd been drunk the first time I encountered Richard, my careful rational mind turned off? Was it that nothing less drastic than the bruises he'd left could have forced my understanding? Was it simply that I'd been romantically unhappy at the time, whereas I'd been content when that other man pinned me to the floor? Even in the midst of my now-constant confusion, I couldn't stop myself from analyzing it all to bits. Now I concluded that I ought to know how I felt about Richard if I wanted to get to the roots of myself.

It had taken me a while to call my openly-BDSM friends for advice, but — maybe around the same time I really started acclimating — I had. One of their offhand comments came to mind. "I guess there's no reason you would know this," she'd said, "but it's fairly common for people to have one person who's their lover, and a separate person for inflicting pain."

I thought about that, and about Richard saying, "A lot of crap comes out when you do this stuff." I considered the maxims that tell us that the opposite of love isn't actually hate, and how much time I'd spent encouraging myself to hate him. Finally, I admitted that the only term I had to cover this depth of emotion was "love"... but that couldn't make it **feel** like the right word. Then again, it wasn't exactly "hate", either.

He was a demon, an idol. He hardly felt like a person to me.

I didn't vocalize any of this. Coming back from the waterfront, we arrived at the intersection where Richard would go to his apartment and I'd return to mine. An awkward pause ensued: I was leaving in a few days, and wouldn't be alone with him again. Watching him, I wondered if he was thinking about asking me over, or was looking for an excuse not to. I looked away.

"Goodnight," I said. Walking home, I wished I felt strong.

* * *

It was after I left Chicago that I really started piecing myself back together. My anger drained away quickly, as if an infected wound had been lanced. Perhaps I found my strength under the scab. I figured that maybe all this did identify something about my personality, but it didn't tell the whole story. Even now, I could be independent, rational, and feminist, with self-esteem and integrity. Right? Right.

It was impossible to deny that the desires were real — and when I allowed myself to focus on them, I didn't try. Ruminating on my past, I recalled heart-twisting details that put everything in a certain compelling context. It wasn't just the man who'd gone after me in 2003. Wincing, I remembered childhood fantasies: I'd compulsively written and drawn brutal dreams until, at some confused middle-school point, their horror came home to me and I recoiled. In those long-repressed fictions of slavery and pain, I recognized my newly-acknowledged desires.

One conversation I'd had with an early boyfriend rang in my head. "There's a dark current inside me," I'd told him. Self-consciously, I'd averted my eyes at my own melodrama. "I don't know how to be with you, when I feel it." I hadn't exactly been trying to leave him, but I'd needed something **more**.

The last dream I remember of Richard didn't involve any pain at all: he just kissed me. Awakening, I felt a melancholy pang. Richard invested a lot of self-conception in being a sadist, and he was so distant — I couldn't imagine relating to him as a lover. And I knew our relationship (such as it was) would never have started without BDSM as a focus. Previous to that night at the outdoor party, he'd hardly registered on my romantic radar, and we had little in common in terms of how we dealt with relationships.

Still, for a moment I wished — unreasonably, I knew — that I could have fallen straightforwardly in love.

* * *

I was gone for six months, and I returned in heartbreak. A relationship more important than words can encompass had become — after years of attempts — impossible. I think it was obvious. One friend told me vulnerability was all over me; *like a scent,* I thought, and wondered if Richard could smell it. In worse shape than ever, I saw Richard and laughed with an edge to my voice. I gave him doe-eyed looks, but deflected his interest with doublespeak and icy tones. I wanted him, and I felt the rage returning. I hated and sheltered behind the unclear verbal games we played. Furious and despairing, I refused to chase him, yet I felt him everywhere. North.

I had to do something. My identity had somewhat solidified: I was into BDSM. I believed it, I even accepted it, but I couldn't go on feeling like I did.

In looking around the Internet, I came upon a directory of Kink Aware Professionals, including therapists who provided their names for people who needed to talk about BDSM but feared judgment. [1] I visited two. One listened to me silently, with a vaguely sorrowful expression; he offered no feedback, and left me wondering why he'd listed his name in the directory. He obviously didn't know what to do with me, and I got the uneasy feeling that I worried him. Naturally, that didn't help at all.

Luckily, the other was everything I could have asked for — open, patient, clearly knowledgeable about BDSM. He looked straight at me and nodded understandingly when I confessed the whole trail of events; he explained how common my experience was; he gave me ideas about where to look for more information, but didn't try to put his own preferences into our talks. "Most people in your situation feel that they've broken a major taboo," he said. "A lot try to get away from BDSM. But I'm not hearing that from you. You want to adjust, not escape." I nodded, and arranged to see him regularly.

Still, I don't think I could have put myself together again without two other things.

My close friend Andrew went after me at a drunken party. *Shades of Richard*, I might have thought, but I never did. Andrew pinned me to the floor, laughed as I fought back, hurt me, finally kissed me. When I asked in bewilderment what brought this on, he confessed. "When you were gone, I missed you," he whispered, "and I've never missed anyone like that before." He was as afraid of the darkness of BDSM as I had been, yet he'd thought of me and found himself fantasizing. He wanted to try it with me, but first he wanted to be sure that he and I would remain close — wouldn't lose what we already had.

In everything Andrew told me — everything we said to each other, laughing, almost in tears, burying each other in embraces, happily drunk and clear-eyed in the morning — I found the things that were missing with Richard. Uncertain about BDSM, guarding his and my boundaries, Andrew wanted to commit to me and to a devoted monogamous relationship. Part of me counseled caution and withdrawal, but as my therapist laughingly put it, Andrew was as tempting as an ice-cream factory. It was my chance to fall straightforwardly in love.

Soon after that, I had to explain to my parents why I wanted a psychiatrist who was out-of-network for my health insurance. I closed my eyes as my father asked why I needed this specialist, what his focus was. "S&M," I said shortly.

Why had I worried? I knew my parents had striven to give me an independent, rational, feminist outlook. Self-esteem and integrity. I was so lucky, I understood as my father said nothing but, "All right." It was a blinding realization: my father might have judged me with all the worst things I thought of myself — but instead, he trusted me to do my best.

When I called my mother (long separated from my dad), too many of my flatmates were around for a private conversation indoors. I banished myself into a warm summer storm, cradling my cell phone away from the rain. There was a pause after I said the fateful words — then she said, "Have you talked to your father about this?"

"Yes," I said hesitantly. "Why?"

"Well, I think it was an issue in our marriage that I was more into that stuff than he was."

Fat droplets soaked my hair. The tight knot in my chest — familiar for nearly a year — loosened as I caught my breath. I turned my face up to the sky and let the tilted world resettle around me; my mother's faraway voice helped me through a hundred things that had torn my heart. "You aren't giving up your liberation," she reminded me, and emphasized my continuing right to a partner who respects me. She even noted mildly that she'd "wondered" about me when I was a child.

I'd feared that I was damaged, that there was something deeply broken in me. I'd wildly guessed that I'd suffered trauma and repressed the memories. But if my mother — one of the most independent, feminist women I've ever met — could reconcile BDSM, then I knew I could. And if she was into BDSM herself, then rather than viewing my proclivities as damage, I could see them as something intrinsic we shared.

Over the next hour, my mother told me I could retain rationality, self-esteem and integrity. For the first time, I found myself believing it.

My therapist laughed when I told him. "I swear," he cried, "it's genetic!"

* * *

There was one loose end to a conclusion that felt like a fairy tale. Though we had some unfettered conversations, tension remained between me and Richard — perhaps it even worsened. At one point, observing us, Andrew said mildly: "Settle down, you two."

Worse, Andrew and I were going in different directions. I finally felt somewhat at peace with BDSM, but he couldn't gain that comfort, and started backing away from it. It was impossible not to think of Richard and shiver, remembering how uncompromisingly vicious he could be. When Andrew and I broke up over a year later, I knew: *I shouldn't see Richard.* My therapist warned me to be careful with BDSM when my heart was in pieces.

Of course I wasn't.

It was the first time I'd explicitly pursued Richard since he'd told me, so long ago, that he was busy. I emailed him straightforwardly, sat down on his bed shortly after Andrew and I broke up. When Richard set his fingernails into my skin, he murmured, "It's been a while," as if he'd always known he'd see me here again. The tears came more quickly than they once had — I'd fought them then, unwilling to break down in front of him. I'd been successful, too. Richard had only made me cry once, before.

This is what I want, I reminded myself as Richard wound his hand in my hair and pulled my head back. His teeth bruising my shoulder felt familiar and wrong. A kiss on my neck sent me rigid. Sobs nearly choked me. *Why now,* my heart cried, *why not when you were who I dreamed of, Richard?*

I couldn't fault his empathy — he pulled away. "No," I said unwillingly, "I'm fine," but he wouldn't continue. Uneasily, he pointed out that I'd never reacted like that. I said he'd never kissed me like that, and he asked, "Really?" as if it were a surprise.

Yes, I thought, forcing my tears away. *I was desperate for it. I know.*

To get him to keep hurting me, I had to convince him that I was fine. *This is what I want,* I coached myself. I was nearly composed when Richard mentioned Andrew, and I felt grief rip me open.

He watched me cry, got me a glass of water. *Shades of two years ago,* I might have thought, but I never did. I apologized; he said only, "I thought this might happen." On some level, I knew that I had, too — for all my self-reassurances that I would be fine. *What was I thinking?* I asked myself, and the answer came instantly. *I had to know.*

When Richard asked if I wanted to sleep over, I said I didn't. "Then don't go yet," he said softly, putting his arms around me where I lay. I rested my head on his chest. *I won't tell Andrew about this,* I decided, wondering if he and I would be together again. *Even if I've learned that I don't want Richard anymore.*

* * *

In retrospect, it seems surreal that I reacted so badly to my BDSM orientation. The agonizing memories of my adjustment have lost their emotional flavor. I've learned a lot about how to practice BDSM safely — physically and emotionally. I've had multiple BDSM partners, and I've had positive experiences in the welcoming BDSM subculture. In recent times, I've even begun to switch: occasionally I'll be the dominant partner, though I feel submissive masochism far closer to my core.

Still, I remember the unease I felt at first — and I recognize stronger unease in others. I certainly wouldn't describe this orientation to, say, an employer. I believe BDSM needs a liberation movement, just like homosexuality, but I'm not (yet?) ready to be a public spokeswoman. And I definitely wouldn't consider dragging others out of the closet. I write about BDSM under a pseudonym, and I have changed the names of Richard and Andrew.

I fear that others will read this narrative as describing an assault, a near-rape — and a woman who tried to rationalize her experience by embracing it. That's not what happened. When Richard first pulled my head back and hurt me at that drunken outdoor party, I could have said no. The word was echoing in my mind, waiting on my lips, and I didn't say it because I didn't want him to stop. I was certainly intoxicated, but I wasn't helpless. I was threatened, but I was not afraid. I may have fought self-actualization like a caged animal, but I could not deny it. I have always been this way.

Conversely, I'm afraid that some conservative will read this and say: "Look how the feminist movement has failed us!" That's not what happened, either. I identify as feminist, and I don't believe that to be at odds with being a submissive masochist. Indeed, I believe that the feminist movement helped my practice of BDSM: it's one of the factors that gave me the strength and self-assurance required to figure out and discuss my sexual needs.

Andrew and I did get back together; then we broke up again. Richard and I have had other nights together. I wish this narrative ended cleanly. I wish I could say that I've found a fairy-tale lover, that I'm now with a man who both hurts me till I cry and gives me the relationship I want. (Why stop there? He could be rich and handsome and a great cook, too!) But this is my story, not a fairy tale. Just as well; that means I still have space to learn. I believe I've gotten better at communicating clearly. I believe I've gotten better at sorting out the harsh emotions inspired by BDSM, working with — and enjoying! — those feelings in the context of a loving relationship. And I hope I no longer objectify my sadistic partners to the extent that I objectified Richard. Still, I know I've got a ways to go.

I see BDSM as a continuum — similar to the theory that homosexuality is a continuum — and sometimes I think that everyone's on the continuum to some degree. I don't think Andrew is as far into the continuum as I am, and not as far as Richard, either. But there are reasons I was with Andrew for nearly two years, yet never let myself fall completely into Richard.

A certain kind of devoted relationship is important to me. I felt strongly about Richard, and he was a good fit for BDSM, but he couldn't give me the relationship I want. I went back to Andrew, though he was far less into BDSM, because I was able to love him. I wonder, though: if I ever fall for a completely vanilla man, will I be able to compromise that far? It seems unlikely. Maybe if that happens I'll have to remember my friend's words and find a separate person, a non-lover who inflicts pain.

I'd rather not do that, but I can't imagine giving up BDSM. The idea feels equivalent to a vow of celibacy. As my therapist said, I'm not looking to escape — especially not now that I've finally adjusted. It wasn't easy, but I feel that today I am triumphant. And I believe, I hope, that knowing what I want is the surest path to falling straightforwardly — happily — in love.

* * *

This can be found on the Internet at:
http://clarissethorn.com/blog/2010/06/30/love-bites-an-sm-coming-out-story-mirror/

* * *

***

EDUCATION:
[theory] Liberal, Sex-Positive Sex Education: What's Missing

I originally wrote this in 2009, then reposted it in 2010 as part of a group drive by sex-positive bloggers to solicit donations to Scarleteen.com. Scarleteen is an amazing sex education site run by the equally amazing sex educator Heather Corinna, and it can always use donations! You should totally go investigate that site — after you're done reading my work, of course.

When I first published this piece, the sex-positive film director Tony Comstock commented on Twitter, "I think that post of yours might be one of the most important things written about sex-positivity in the last 10 years." I was really honored by that, because he does excellent work.

My parents occasionally read my blog, and I also got some interesting feedback from my mother. She wrote to me: " Speaking from where I sat when you were growing up: I wish I could have taught you what you eventually learned on your own. But I felt there was this unchallengeable wave moving and I didn't have a place to stand to counter it. I kept thinking I was leaving you to learn the hard way exactly what I learned the hard way, and was still learning, and was despairing of ever learning."

I wrote back: "For what it's worth, I remember you trying to stem the tide with small comments, and I think that those comments later helped me center myself in a place where I could reach my own conclusions rather than blindly sleeping around." I hope it made her feel better, because it's true. I'm not a parent, although someday I would like to be... but I think one of the hardest things about parenting must be knowing that your kids will learn terrible things from the surrounding world, and the best you can do is try to be there while they process those lessons.

***

I am fortunate. I was born in the eighties and I received a great sex-positive upbringing. The public school I attended taught students how to use condoms; middle school health education included a section on sexually transmitted diseases. My parents didn't throw their sexuality in my face — but they were almost always matter-of-fact, understanding and accepting when they talked about sex. (I'll never forget how, at age 12 or so, Mom sat me down and gave me a long speech about how it would be **totally okay** if I were gay.) I was raised Unitarian Universalist, and the Unitarian Sunday School teen program included a wonderful sex education curriculum called About Your Sexuality. (I understand that the sex-ed curriculum has been changed and updated, and is now called Our Whole Lives. [1] I haven't delved deeply into the Our Whole Lives program — maybe it addresses some of the issues I'm about to describe.)

So I think I'm in a good position to describe the problematic signals we face in liberal sexual education. Yes, I've experienced the overall sex-negative messages that drench America, and they're terrible — but so much is already being said about those. I also received lots of sex-positive messages that are incomplete, or problematic, or don't quite go the distance in helping us navigate sexuality — and I think the sex-positive movement must focus on fixing them.

I'm so grateful for my relatively liberal, relatively sex-positive upbringing. I think it did me a world of good. But here are **my five biggest problems with the way I learned about sexuality:**

1. I wish that I hadn't gotten this message: "Sex is easy, light-hearted — and if it's not, you're doing it wrong."

Do I believe sex can be easy? Sure. Do I think it can be light-hearted? Absolutely! But do I think it's **always** those things? No, and I don't think it "ought to" be.

I think we need to teach that sex can be incredibly difficult. It can be hard to communicate with your partner. It can be hard to learn and come to terms with your own sexual desires. It can be hard to understand or accept all your partner's sexual desires. And just because it's hard, doesn't mean that you're with the wrong partner — or that you're missing some vital piece of information that everyone else has — or that you're doing it wrong.

And as for light-hearted, well — sure, sex can be "happy rainbows joy joy!", but it can also be serious... or dark. And there's nothing wrong with that!

I recently talked to a friend, who also identifies as a BDSMer, about our stories of coming into BDSM. Both of us had sadomasochistic fantasies from a very early age (mine, for instance, started in grade school — seriously, I actually did tie up my Barbie dolls). I told my friend about how I'd always had these intense, dark, violent feelings — but when I made it to middle school, I remember a change. I had a series of vivid BDSM-ish dreams, and I freaked out. I closed it all away, I stopped thinking about it, I repressed it all as savagely as I could.

Before that, I had also started thinking about sex. I imagined sex at great length; I read about sex. I had long since filched my parents' copy of *The Joy of Sex* and examined it, cover to cover — not to mention many other fine sexuality works, like Nancy Friday's compilation of female sexual fantasies *My Secret Garden.* I was totally fascinated by sex. I talked about it so much that one of my friends specifically searched out a vibrator as a birthday present for me. I actually pressured my first major boyfriend into some sexual acts before **he** was ready, which I suppose is an interesting reversal of stereotype (but to be clear, it's not okay that I did that). As I started having sex, I found that I liked it okay, but knew a lot was missing — and couldn't figure out what.

It took me years and years to connect sex to BDSM — to figure out that the biggest thing I was missing was BDSM. Why? Because BDSM was horrible and wrong, and I'd shut it away; BDSM (I thought) couldn't possibly have anything to do with the bright, shiny, happy horizon of sex! Coming into BDSM was a crisis for me partly because — although I knew other people practiced it, and had never thought much about that — my own need for those dark feelings totally shocked me. This wasn't me. This wasn't **healthy sex**. Sex was light-hearted, happy rainbows joy joy!... wasn't it?

In contrast, my friend — who had an extremely sexually repressed upbringing — never had any trouble integrating BDSM into his sex life. Sex, for him, was already wrong and bad... so as he got in touch with his sexuality and began having sex, BDSM was involved from the start. After all, there was no reason for it not to be.

As glad as I am that my upbringing was not stereotypically sexually repressed, I have to say that I envy my friend his easy personal integration of BDSM.

2. I wish this point had been made, over and over: "You might consider being careful with sex."

I recently read an excellent *New Yorker* article that reviews the new version of *The Joy of Sex*. [2] It talks about the time when *The Joy of Sex* came out, as well as a similar contemporary feminist book, *Our Bodies, Ourselves,* and it points out that "both books espoused the (distinctly seventies) notion that sex could be a value-neutral experience, as natural as eating."

"Value-neutral": that's a great way to describe the overall attitude about sex that I absorbed. As if sex were something I could do as an amusing diversion, with anyone, at any time, and it would always be fun fun fun! As if there was no need to be overly careful or sensitive — sex was just a game I could play, like a sport — where the worst that would happen if I screwed up might be a skinned knee.

I wish that there had been an emphasis on how emotions can really **matter**, when it comes to sex. I wish that there had been acknowledgment of the fact that we can really hurt ourselves, and others, when we're cavalier about sex. (Not that we always do — but we can.) I wish I had understood sooner that sex is not always value-neutral; that everyone has all manner of different sexual needs and hangups, anxieties and strong emotions. I think maybe there are people out there who can have "value-neutral" sex — where it's totally about physicality and nothing more — but I am not like that, and I suspect that most people are not.

Which isn't to say that I think there's anything **wrong** with people who can have sex that's "value-neutral." (And maybe "value-neutral" is not a great term for it; I worry that I sound like I'm judging when I use that term.) I just don't think it's a good model for everyone, and yet I think that it has somewhat been promoted as if everyone "ought to" be that way.

I think that there are lots of people out there who feel as though the sexual liberation movement "failed" or "betrayed them," because they convinced themselves that sex is value-neutral and then got hurt. You see a lot of assertions along these lines in the conservative media — for instance, here's a quotation from a synopsis of the book *Modern Sex:*

The 1960s sexual revolution made a big promise: if we just let go of our inhibitions, we'll be happy and fulfilled. Yet sexual liberation has made us no happier and, if anything, less fulfilled. Why?... sex today is increasingly mechanical and without commitment — a department of plumbing, hygiene, or athletics rather than a private sphere for the creation of human meaning. The result: legions of unhappy adults and confused teenagers deprived of their innocence, on their way not to maturity but to disillusionment.... These beautifully written essays — on subjects ranging from the TV show

Sex and the City to teen sex to the eclipse of the manly ideal to the benefits of marriage — add up to the deepest, most informative appraisal we have of how and why the sexual revolution has failed. [3]

I disagree with most of their attitude. We don't need innocence. We don't need sexual mystery. We don't need to eliminate teen sex. We don't need to re-establish some limiting, patriarchal "manly ideal." But they've got one thing right: we do need to start talking about sex as something that is **not** mostly mechanical — as something that, yes, can be "a private sphere for the creation of human meaning."

3. I wish I'd learned this: "Good sex doesn't just require two (or more) people who like sex. It requires desire — and desire simply doesn't work the same way for everyone."

I've said before that I went through a period — back when I was first becoming sexually active — where I simply **could not figure out** why sexual acts with people I didn't care about didn't seem to turn me on. Or rather — they turned me on a little, but not... much. It took me a while to understand that sex requires more than just two eager people. It requires attraction and desire.

When I was fifteen or so, and at summer camp, I remember making out with a boy. I didn't really want to make out with him, but I wasn't sure how to reject him (more on this under point 5). And I figured: he seems nice enough, so I might as well make out with him. Afterwards, I felt angry at myself, and I felt like I'd wasted my time — and I felt confused. I'd been bored at best and repulsed at worst, and I wasn't sure why I felt that way, or why I'd done something that made me feel that way.

So why **had** I done it? Because I'd thought: "Sex is value-neutral." Because I'd thought: "Making out is fun, right? — that means I ought to do it when I get the chance!" Because I'd thought: "My preference not to make out with him is probably just some silly repression that I need to get over." Because I didn't understand that desire is complicated, that you can't just make yourself feel desire when it's convenient, and that you don't need a reason for your attractions — or lack of attraction. This situation was to reprise itself in various forms over the next years, until I finally learned that sometimes you simply want or don't want things, and that you aren't required to justify your desires.

4. I wish I'd gotten a list of suggestions: "Here are some places you might go to start figuring out what turns you on."

I was told that sex was fun. I was even told to explore! But I still spent years with very little actual idea of what I wanted. No one ever told me how or where I might be able to learn more about my needs, or what exploring my needs might look like. And no one ever explained that people are turned on by different things, that some people like some sex acts and don't like others, and that's okay.

I went into sex with a buffet-style attitude, thinking that I must naturally enjoy sex equally in all ways. I was so surprised when I found out that I like some positions better than others! I remember how confused I was when I dated a guy who didn't like fellatio, and how hurt I felt — like his lack of enjoyment meant that I must be doing it wrong, because **everyone** likes oral sex, right?

And of course, while I had a pretty comprehensive idea of the vanilla sex acts I could experiment with, I had very little idea of what else was out there. In retrospect I find this hilarious, but I remember — back in my vanilla days — I had two boyfriends who tied me up. They tied me up and were nice to me, and I suppose it was amusing enough, but didn't drive me crazy with lust or anything. And — this is the kicker — **because I did not understand that there's a lot more to BDSM than light bondage, because I did not understand that there are many separate BDSM acts that people can enjoy and many ways to flavor them, I assumed from this experience that I didn't like BDSM.** I went through my old journal entries the other day and uncovered one in which I, confused, am speculating about what's missing from my sex life: I write, "I've tried S&M, so it can't be that."

What a learning curve I had ahead of me, eh?

I wish someone had tried to explain to me the vast cornucopia of human fetishes out there. I wish someone had explained that erotica and pornography are both actually really good ways to learn about your turn-ons, and — more importantly — had told me that **not all erotica and pornography are the same,** so the fact that I wasn't into mainstream stuff didn't mean I automatically wasn't interested in all erotica or porn. I've mentioned that I had lots of conversations with friends about sex, but — until recent years — those conversations were never framed as "This is what I like," or "I've found something new that turns me on," and I wish I'd realized sooner what a great resource conversations like that might be.

5. *I wish I'd gotten a list of ideas: "Here are some ways you can try communicating with your partner about sex."*

Lastly, but certainly not least — I was never taught how to communicate about sex. No one ever gave me even the first idea. In all my sex-positive, liberal sexual upbringing, I was told over and over that "relationships require communication", but no one ever said: "And here's some ways in which you might communicate sexually with your partner."

One big benefit of teaching sexual communication strategies is that it helps people learn to say "no" when they don't want to do something. Teaching people how to set boundaries is massively important, and I think a lot about ways to do it. I saw this adorable video about cuddle parties recently that really struck me — these people create parties where everyone basically just cuddles, but everyone also specifically has the power to say "no" to any given person or act. [4] The reporter who made the video talks at the end about how she found the whole experience to be empowering — how she felt like it gave her space to say "no" that she hadn't had before. Perhaps these could be used to teach people to set boundaries?

But you can't really use cuddle parties in a school or workshop setting, more's the pity. When I developed my first sex education workshop, it was all about describing good communication strategies. I listed questions that all sex partners could benefit from asking each other, including "What do you like?" and "What do you fantasize about?" and "Is there anything you really don't want me to do?"

And I talked about ways that you can make communication easier, if the two partners are uncomfortable having this conversation. I took a page from the BDSM community by creating checklists of all kinds of sexual acts and weird fetishes and gender-bending craziness, and I put it all on a 1-5 scale (with 1 being "not at all interested" and 5 being "I'd love to try this"), and I told people that they could try filling out those checklists and giving them to their partners. (The amazing sex education site Scarleteen later implemented the same idea, in a much more comprehensive way than I had! [5]) I suggested that partners write out their fantasies and email them to each other, or write out descriptions of their mutual sexual experiences — long accounts, describing how they felt about everything and what sticks out in their minds — and send those to each other, too, so they can get each others' perspectives on what they've done.

(By the way, I still offer a much-improved version of that workshop on my list of events, lectures, and workshops, just in case you're interested in bringing me in....)

God, it's so **hard** to talk about what we want. It's even hard to talk about talking about what we want. I mean, it's hard enough to figure out what we want in the first place — but communicating it... eeek! And it's worth noting that this is not just a problem of having good sex. As was pointed out recently on the blog for the wonderful sex-positive anthology *Yes Means Yes!*:

[There is a] need to demystify and destigmatize communication about sex. If we can't talk about what we like and what we want, we will always have problems making clear what it is we're consenting to. If we can't be frank about what we do want, we put a lot of weight on the need to communicate what we don't. [6]

Giving everyone great sexual communication skills doesn't just give us all better sex — it fights rape. There's a noble cause for you!

... So, that's my five-pointed analysis. And that's what I'm pushing for. My goals are not just to get people thinking that sex is awesome and sexual freedom is important. It's going to be hard, and it's going to be an uphill battle, but I'm hoping that I can not only help out with sexual liberation — I'm hoping to **improve** it.

* * *

This can be found on the Internet at:
http://clarissethorn.com/blog/2010/11/11/classic-repost-liberal-sex-positive-sex-education-whats-missing/

* * *

* * *

COMMUNICATION:
[theory] Sex Communication Tactic Derived From S&M: The Annotated Safeword

As soon as I started researching S&M and thinking critically about the communication tactics promoted in the S&M community, I realized that there were a lot of really important lessons wrapped up in those tactics — lessons that could be deconstructed and applied to all kinds of sexuality. From the beginning, I planned to do a series of posts on Sex Communication Tactics Derived from S&M, but I only got around to it in 2010.

The post about safewords caught the attention of Thomas MacAulay Millar, a feminist blogger and S&Mer who is older and more established in the blogosphere than I. Thomas asked if he could annotate the article, then post it on the blog where he usually writes — the blog for the excellent sex-positive anti-rape anthology Yes Means Yes. *Of course I agreed. The final product looks something like a conversation between me and Thomas, although I wrote the post before he added his input.*

* * *

Thomas MacAulay Millar:

Clarisse Thorn's post about safewords is so good I'm just going to repost the whole thing and annotate it.

Clarisse Thorn:

Everyone knows about BDSM safewords... or at least, everyone thinks they know about safewords. But one of the initial moments that really impressed me about my current boyfriend was when I asked him, many moons ago, if he knew what a safeword is. He paused, then answered, "I think I'm familiar with the idea, but I probably don't know much more than a stereotype, so I'd like to hear you define it." Humility and open-minded curiosity are so **incredibly** hot!

Righto. Hot boyfriend aside, I'm here to explain safewords and check-ins, and how those concepts can exemplify excellent sexual communication for everyone — not just S&Mers — in a world that doesn't do a good job teaching anyone how to communicate sexually.

When two (or more) people have a BDSM encounter together, generally they set a safeword — a word that anyone can say at any time to stop the action. (Sometimes people don't use safewords. This is their choice and I totally respect it. I would not recommend going without safewords for anyone who doesn't know their partner **extremely well**, and I would be seriously sketched out by anyone who pressured a partner to go without safewords.)

Thomas MacAulay Millar:

A word on origin: safewords are only strictly necessary in one circumstance — where the participants want words like "no" and "stop" not to have their ordinary meaning. One can do BDSM for a lifetime without a safeword, if words have their ordinary meanings. As former porn star and kinkster Ona Zee once put it (I'm quoting an interview from memory here), "our safeword is 'that hurts.'" Folks can even do heavy play depending on how they react to things, without a safeword, simply saying "stop" or "too much" or "fuck, I can't handle any more of that!" when the play gets too intense. Any BDSMer who would tell you URDOINITRONG if you use ordinary words to communicate in scene is not someone you need to listen to.

Safewords are essential for roleplay where "no, please don't, I'll do anything!" should not stop the action. It's also essential for any bottom who will involuntarily shout "No! Stop!" while actually wanting more. Other than that, it's an optional tool — a very, very useful one, for many reasons. Clarisse mentioned that some people "don't use safewords." From the context, she's talking not about people for whom no means no in scene, but people for whom there is no definitive way for the bottom to stop the scene. And perhaps readers can tell from Clarisse's tone that that's... the advanced class. You'll find the safety police in any BDSM space or community that finger-wag about it, and the swaggering more-kinky-than-thous that brag about it. But what does it mean?

I can only tell you what it means for me. There are times I give up my safeword: only to my spouse. We've been playing together for about a decade and a half. If I give up my safeword, and that's something we do rarely, it doesn't mean I don't have limits. I have limits! Yes I do! There are things I can't handle, mentally or physically, and things I never want to handle! There are "hard limits," things I've said I'm just not willing to do. And there are soft limits, things I don't think I'm ready for but I'm willing to bump up against them and see what happens. If I give up my safeword, it means I have limits, but instead of telling her when I've reached them, I'm going to trust her to listen to me and watch me and make that decision. I may say, "I can't, I can't, I can't," and she may decide I really can't. Or she may decide I've got more in me than I believe I do. There's a lot of risk associated with that. But there's a trust in those moments and a closeness that does not go away when the scene is over. Or ever, really. Risk and reward: we set our own tolerances.

Some folks may have come across the term "consensual nonconsent." It's one of those terms with multiple meanings. Some people use it to describe any situation where the bottom is saying "no, don't" but has not yet safeworded — a usage I find less than useful. Others use it to describe roleplays of nonconsensual situations. The last common usage, though, is that which I like to describe using Hunter S. Thompson's phrase, "buy the ticket, take the ride." It means that the bottom consents to be in a situation I've just described, where the top decides if the bottom needs to stop, often but not always around specific activities, and usually (wisely) heavily negotiated.

Clarisse Thorn:

When I give advice about setting safewords, I usually offer the following:

A) Some people like to say that it's good to use a safeword that's jolting, and is likely to make your partner feel totally unsexy. Isn't there a *Family Guy* episode in which Lois & Peter's safeword is "banana" or something?

Thomas MacAulay Millar:

Not a fan. The more obscure a safeword, the harder it is for a bottom who is spacey or flying on endorphins to access it. It's easy to remember "banana" in the calm before the storm. At the moment when it's most needed, that can easily become a muddle of "yellow? was it a fruit? Shit, what do I do?" That's not a place bottoms want to find themselves and a top never, never, never wants to have a bottom who is at a limit but can't communicate about it.

Clarisse Thorn:

B) In my experience, the generally accepted safewords in the S&M community are "safeword" and, more commonly, "red." I consider it useful to go with the "public standard" because that means that in the future, you're likely to be attuned to the correct word if you practice BDSM with other partners as well. (It also means that if you ever do S&M in a public space such as a dungeon, everyone in the place will recognize your safeword if you scream it.)

C) At first wasn't excited about this, but I've grown to love how the safeword "red" also sometimes encompasses "green" — and "yellow." That means that if I'm in the middle of an S&M encounter, I can say "red" and my partner will stop; I can then catch my breath and say "green," which means "by God keep going!" Or, if I'm a little uncertain about the territory but don't actually want my partner to stop — if I just want my partner to be a little bit cautious — then I can say "yellow" (and, of course, I can move to "green" if I become really psyched, or shift to "red" if I really want my partner to stop).

Thomas MacAulay Millar:

My spouse and I use the "stoplight system." It's simple, it works, and "yellow" option is really useful for things that are getting hard to handle. Also, a lot of bottoms are either submissives or masochists with more pride and stubbornness than is good for them — the former out of an overdeveloped desire to please, the latter sometimes out of a desire to impress or even just a pitbull-stubborn urge to push themselves as hard as they can go. Take the personalities that finish an Ironman and collapse and need IV fluids, and put them on a spanking bench with big welts from a prison strap, and you've got someone who won't safeword when ze probably should. In those and other circumstances, giving the bottom an easy option to say, "I'm struggling here" without feeling like they're quitting is a very useful thing.

[Editor's Note: "ze" is the gender-neutral pronoun, and it's in the Glossary. Clarisse tried to use it regularly for a while, but ultimately concluded it made her posts less accessible to non-gender nerds.]

Clarisse Thorn:

I know that this probably doesn't sound sexy at all, but it totally can be! Consider the following example: during my last vacation to

America, I had an S&M encounter with a dude I'll refer to as Klark. (It's not my fault. He requested the pseudonym.) At one point, Klark was experimenting with hurting me, and I had my eyes closed and was whimpering / crying out in a totally glorious way. (The poor overnight desk clerk. He was only one short flight of stairs away from us.) I think Klark was legitimately having trouble detecting whether I was enjoying myself, though — understandably, because we had only just met, and I enjoy sinking myself into dramatic masochistic misery — so he leaned over me and said, in a low dark voice, "Red, yellow, green." Immediately, I gasped back "Green." Because he spoke in a gritty and dominant voice, and the check-in was quick, we were able to maintain the mood — and it was actually kind of hot in itself.

Which brings me to the other thing: check-ins. Sometimes, you want to check in with your partner. Which can be easy: you can just say, "Hey, how does this feel?" or, as a more precise example, "Give me a rating of 1-10 on how good this feels (or how much this hurts)." But if you want to do it quickly and without shifting the mood, you can do it as I outline above in the Klark example. Or even quicker, as for example with the hand-squeeze system, where the participants agree ahead of time that you can squeeze another person's hand twice and expect two squeezes back — and if there aren't two return squeezes, it's time to stop and figure out what's going wrong. (Squeeze system: also very helpful when gags are involved.)

Thomas MacAulay Millar:

There are all kinds of safesigns when nonverbal communication is necessary; one being to give the bottom an object to hold and to drop when at a limit. It has the disadvantage of being binary, so it loses the middle step that the stoplight system provides.

Clarisse Thorn:

Sometimes submissives will have a hard time safewording — whether out of pride, inexperience, or eagerness to please — and that's another reason check-ins can be good even when there's a set safeword. If you aren't sure how to read your partner's reactions and you suspect ze may be uncomfortable with what you are doing, then you might consider checking in even if ze hasn't safeworded, because **your suspicion may be right**.

Thomas MacAulay Millar:

This can't be emphasized enough. **Tops Can Never Be On Cruise Control!** A safeword gives the bottom a tool to communicate, but it does not ensure safety. The top has at least as much information that the bottom doesn't have, as the bottom has information the top doesn't have. Therefore, the top has to be a full participant in making sure the scene is working and the risks are under control at all times. Anyone who thinks ze can ignore safety as long as the bottom has a safeword is dangerous.

This post was edited to add: In the comments on this article, Dw3t-Hthr made a powerful point that for some people, safewords are unavailable in scene. She said, in part:

[I]f I am in a place where a safeword might be necessary, a safeword is not possible. Not just because I am someone who is regularly nonverbal, but because the altered consciousness state that I achieve makes processing those sorts of questions at best difficult and at worst unachievable...

But I'm not a bottom, I'm a submissive, and this isn't about "wanting to please," it's about a psychological incapacity to recognise when I might be doing myself damage in certain situations. If I'm not in that state, I can say "Oh stop doing that it's wrenching my shoulder" or whatever is appropriate. If I am in that state, I cannot indicate and have to place complete trust in the judgement of my partner.

I happen to know that I'm not the only person like this. I think it's important to recognise that safewords are not always possible. It's important, I think, to communicate to the person who resembles me in this that while their brainwiring is not morally incorrect, that they probably ought to think of themselves as Advanced Subjects and try to do their thing in a context where the trust and competence required to do it safely is demonstrated.

Also, a note on terminology: Clarisse used "submissive" there in a way where it's not clear from the context whether it's meant as an umbrella term like "bottom" or as a specific term. The use of "dominant" and "submissive" as the default terms seems to me to have started in the mid 90's, and I've never liked it because of its imprecision. Not all bottoms are subs; some people like to bottom but don't have a submissive bone in them. Some bottoms are wisecracking smartassed masochists only in it to play the pain game and ride the endorphins; some bottoms don't see themselves as giving up power in any way to the top. And I top my fair share, but I certainly don't think of myself as a dominant. I think the change in terminology arose with a small but vocal minority of kinksters who believe that everyone who does BDSM is really looking for a deep power exchange, ultimately even a 24/7 relationship. I still see people make this argument. They're still wrong, and they're still few in number. Using "submissive" and "dominant" when one means to include folks who are just topping and bottoming may be misunderstood; saying "top" and "bottom" is almost always correctly understood as the inclusive term. ("Sadist" and "masochist" are specific terms that shouldn't be pressed into general service either; there are submissives that really, really don't like pain at all and dominants that would prefer never to inflict it.)

Clarisse Thorn:

What I love about safewords and check-ins:
1) Hypothetically, mainstream society acknowledges that anyone could say no at any point during sex, but in practice, this is really hard. A variety of forces — girls socially pressured not to be so-called "cock-teases," boys socially pressured to supposedly "prove their manliness," and everyone anxious to please their partners — work against people's capacity to say no; and while there is a vague understanding that "no means no," that vagueness is as far as it gets. There's no explicit framework in place for how to say "no," and no understanding of how to continue an encounter (or relationship) after one's partner says no. Even worse, there's an assumed linear progression of sexual activity — the best example is the "base system," which places sexual interaction on a metaphorical baseball diamond where "first base" = groping and "home base" = penis-in-vagina sex. Have I mentioned that I hate the base system?

So anyway, the biggest moral of the story with safewords and check-ins is that consent does not only happen once. **Consent is always happening, and can always be renegotiated or withdrawn**. Adapting my understanding of sexuality to reflect this — even in my non-BDSM sex — might have been the best thing that ever happened to my sex life.

Thomas MacAulay Millar:

What can safewords do for non-kinky people? Permission communication. In a culture that delegitimizes communication — especially women's communication of limits or needs — this is

huge. Safewords permission "no." That which permissions the free exercise of "no" also, necessarily, creates space for the free exercise of "yes."

Clarisse Thorn:

2) On a related note: **Good sex is not about entitlement**. If we acknowledge that anyone can safeword out of any sexual act at any time, then we acknowledge that no one is entitled to any kind of sex from a partner — ever. If your partner loves you but doesn't want to have sex with you? That's a respectable choice. If you're really turned on, but your partner can't stand the idea of having sex right now? That's a respectable choice. Those two are easy, I think, but how about these?

+ If your partner used to do something with you a lot, but doesn't want to do it anymore? That's a respectable choice.

+ If you are married to your partner, but ze doesn't want to have sex? That's a respectable choice.

+ If your partner performed a sexual act with another partner but would prefer not to do it with you? That's a respectable choice.

+ If you know your partner likes a certain kind of sex, but they don't want to do it right now? That's a respectable choice.

+ If you think a certain act is "mild" and "taken for granted," like kissing or tickling, but your partner doesn't want to do it? That's a respectable choice.

By the way, if you (like I once did) feel as though your partner is entitled to sex of any kind, I encourage you to re-examine that feeling. Ditto if you've got a little voice in your head telling you that you "ought to" be up for sex all the time just because you don't get it very often... or that you "ought to" be up for sex if you've done it with your partner before... or whatever. The other best thing that ever happened to my sex life was when I finally, finally, finally internalized the idea that my partners don't ever "deserve" sex for any reason — that there's no reason I ever "should" be having sex — and that the only reason I should ever, ever, ever do anything sexual is because I legitimately want to.

Of course, if you truly believe that you need a certain kind of sexuality in your life, then you're absolutely entitled to **ask** your partner to consider it — and you're entitled to leave the relationship if ze isn't up for it. But this doesn't mean that you "deserve" to do that act with that person, or that your partner "owes" you a certain act.

And hey, if your partner isn't down with one specific sexual act, then that means you've got the chance to explore all kinds of other sexuality. Another other best thing that ever happened to my sexuality? Quite possibly, it's my current boyfriend — whose religious adherence has drastically limited our physical sexual options.

Thomas MacAulay Millar:

We're each entitled to our own identity, but not to our own partner. Our partners are people, with thoughts and desires and limits of their own, and they don't have to do what we want them to do. This goes for tops, too! Tops have limits! Because of my blogging covenant with my spouse (what I do as a bottom is personal to me and I decide how much I reveal; what she does as a bottom is personal to her and she prefers that those stories not be blogfodder) I don't have any really good stories to share about hitting my limits as a top. But they exist. Tops are not required to be into everything a bottom is into, and they damned sure are under no obligation to do things that make them uncomfortable just because the bottom wants it — whether the reason for the discomfort is risk tolerance, ideology, squeamishness or anything else. Tops can say, "no, I won't suspend you from that eyebolt because I don't trust it", "no, I'm not interested in doing that roleplay because I wouldn't be comfortable with it", or "I don't do play piercing because blood is a hard limit for me." We all have a right to say no to sexual acts we don't want; even if we're topping.

* * *

This can be found on the Internet at:
http://yesmeansyesblog.wordpress.com/2010/07/07/the-annotated-safeword/

Clarisse's original post on safewords can be found on the Internet at:
http://clarissethorn.com/blog/2010/07/03/sex-communication-tactic-derived-from-sm-2-safewords-and-check-ins/

* * *

* * *

COMMUNICATION:
[theory] Sex Communication Tactic Derived From S&M: Checklists

This is part of the same 2010 series as the previous article — in fact, it came first.

* * *

S&M checklists are long lists of different acts that sexual partners can use to discuss different acts and measure each others' interest in those acts. [1] Each act on the checklist usually looks something like this:

FLOGGING — GIVING _____ O O O O O
FLOGGING — RECEIVING _____ O O O O O

Each partner rates each entry by filling out 1-5 bubbles, with 1 darkened bubble meaning "Not interested" and 5 bubbles meaning "I crave this!"

I think this concept is brilliant because:

1) Too often, it's assumed that "sex" encompasses certain acts, and if you're interested in a sexual relationship you must be interested in all those acts. Or there's assumed to be a kind of linear progression, as exemplified in the "base system," where "first base" is groping and "home base" is penis-in-vagina sex. Talking about each sexual act as its own self-contained idea short-circuits those problematic ideas about sex and makes it easier for couples to turn down some of the "assumed" acts (e.g., if I don't want oral sex but I do want penis-in-vagina...).

2) It provides an easy way to communicate desires — if a person is nervous about saying, "Hey, is it okay if I flog you?" then the couple doesn't even have to talk about it right away. They can just sit down, fill out their checklists and compare results without getting too worried about how to bring up certain desires. I mean, at some point of course they'll hopefully talk about it, but hopefully the checklist framework makes it easier and lower-pressure.

3) Concurrently, it provides an easy way to **turn down** acts — it's much harder to reject a lover's proposition when ze says, "Darling, can I flog you?" than it is when you simply fill in one bubble on the "Flogging — Receiving" section. In the past, I've certainly felt a lot of anxiety when I wanted to turn down partners, and it's nice to imagine a set-up that would have made me feel less anxious.

In fact, I love the checklist concept so much that when the University of Illinois at Chicago had me design my sexual communication workshop, I created a "vanilla" version of the checklist that had entries ranging from "oral sex" to "sex in public" to "tying up / being tied up." (Okay, maybe it wasn't **entirely** vanilla... I wanted to encourage people to voice things they weren't sure about!) Then I later found out that the amazing sex education site Scarleteen has created its own non-BDSM checklist, and theirs is way better than mine. [2]

I just love the **principle** of the thing — the principle that a couple can have a lot of fun just by sitting down and talking about every conceivable sex act, being presented with some options that they maybe haven't thought of before, and honestly describing how into each idea they each are.

* * *

This can be found on the Internet at:
http://clarissethorn.com/blog/2010/06/14/sex-communication-tactic-derived-from-sm-1-checklists/

* * *

* * *

COMMUNICATION:
[theory] Sex Communication Tactic Derived From S&M: Journal-Keeping

This is part of the same 2010 series as the previous two articles. In this piece, I mentioned 24/7 Master/slave relationships, which I had just learned about. Since then, I've learned a lot more about those relationships. I have never been in one, although I have occasionally had partners order me to do long-term submissive things. But I've read and heard a lot of tales about 24/7 M/s.

24/7 Master/slave scenarios are rare — and I will say that there are some awful horror stories floating around about them. Some BDSMers say that 24/7 Master/slave relationships are always a terrible idea and should never be done. I am unwilling to condemn them so thoroughly, but those relationships obviously require a lot of respect and care from each participant. I would advise a person interested in such a relationship to only consider it with a partner they know very well; to establish pressure-free channels of communication; and to ensure crystal-clear understanding of how, exactly, the relationship can be ended if anyone involved truly wants it to end.

* * *

Some BDSMers play with really, really strong power dynamics. A good example of this is couples who choose a "24/7 dynamic": one partner is dominant and the other is submissive... **all the time**. I attended a workshop once with Sir Top and slave bonnie, two wise BDSM educators, where I learned that slave bonnie was only ever allowed to disobey orders of two kinds:
* Suicidal orders,
* Orders that would cause financial ruin.

The rest of the time, bonnie obeyed Top — **all** the rest of the time.

Obviously, relationships like this are totally cool with me as long as they are — say it with me, everyone — **100% consensual**! Such relationships can also encourage the use of interesting communication tactics, because many of the usual tactics don't feel right to the participants. For example, these relationships often take place between people who feel such a strong power dynamic that it would be almost impossible for the submissive to feel comfortable safewording — safewording can feel disconcertingly like a form of resistance.

One way of dealing with this problem is for both partners to keep journals that are open to the other partner. (With some couples, only the submissive keeps an open journal.) They talk about their romantic feelings, they process their sexual encounters, they articulate anxieties, etc. Sometimes a partner will give the other one journal prompts to answer. [1] The idea is that it's easier to express these things when there's a designated space for it outside the relationship; the journals mean that partners (especially submissives) can talk about what they need without fearing that they're undermining the power dynamic.

I find the concept of simultaneous journals intriguing for a number of reasons. One is that I've used similar tactics myself; I kept a private journal for many years, and once in a long while I'd give entries to my partners when I needed to explain something complicated about my feelings. I only did this a few times, ever, but it was really effective when I did.

Later, I took to writing love letters that I noticed were very similar to both my journal entries, and to the simultaneous relationship journals suggested for Master/slave couples. I realized that I was writing letters because, at the time, I felt more comfortable writing about my desires than talking about them. I've gotten a million times better at talking about my sexuality honestly and shamelessly since then; but back then, there were definitely things I wrote to my partners that I couldn't have said aloud. I also wrote because — just like Master/slave couples — I wanted to communicate my feelings outside the anxiety-inducing frameworks of the "serious discussion," the bedroom, etc.

So when I developed my sexual communication workshop, I encouraged love letters. I gave two suggested points of departure for a love letter:

1) Describe what happened during a sexual encounter you had together, with particular emphasis on what your partner did that you really liked — and what you liked about it. ("I love it when you fuck me" is a great thing to say, but you give much more information to your partner if you say "I love it when you fuck me from behind," or

even better, "I love it when you fuck me from behind and it feels amazing when your balls hit my clit." [This blog does not necessarily reflect the desires or encounters of Miss Clarisse Thorn.])

2) Describe a fantasy you have. Bonus points if you explicitly put your partner in it. ("I like to imagine you sinking your teeth into me until I scream." This blog does not necessarily... oh, who am I kidding.)

Postscript: In the comments on this piece, a reader noted that they might feel anxious and pressured if a partner described them doing something specific. I hadn't thought of this, but I totally believe that it could be a problem. Certainly, I've sometimes had experiences writing to a partner where I described him doing something and he thought it was ridiculously hot... but I've also done it and had partners dislike it. I guess my final advice is that — as with all communication — you'll want to consider the audience, and be ready to apologize.

* * *

This can be found on the Internet at:
http://clarissethorn.com/blog/2010/07/30/sex-communication-tactic-derived-from-sm-3-journal-keeping/

* * *

***

COMMUNICATION:
[storytime] Sex Communication Case Studies

I wrote this post in 2011, years after the events in my coming-out story, and a long time after I'd done all the above research into communication tactics. By 2011, I'd picked up lots of sexual and BDSM experience with a variety of partners. I had just written a post about my most destructive past relationship; the post got a lot of readers and was eventually cross-posted to Jezebel. [1] I wanted to do something positive with all the attention, so I decided to offer a productive counterpoint.

***

In the wake of my last post, which was basically a meditation on one relationship with bad sexual communication, I want to offer some positive examples of sexual communication from my life.

***

1) **Low pressure and leather belts.** Years ago, when I was pretty inexperienced in the community, I had a single BDSM encounter with a gentleman in his home. We met at a BDSM discussion group, arranged to meet later at a café, and went home from there; as we exited the café, I took his driver's license and texted his full name and license number to a friend. (I think more people should do this, frankly — in fact, more non-BDSM people should do this when they go home with strangers from bars.)

We sat together on the public transit and quietly discussed the upcoming scene: he asked me many, many questions about what I was okay with and not okay with. Questions like: "What do you have experience with?" "Could you go into that more?" "What do you like?" "What makes that fun for you?" "Is there anything you really don't want me to do?" He asked a lot of the questions twice, too, which I think is a really great strategy especially with new partners. People don't always have their heads together enough during these conversations to answer an S&M question properly the first time, especially if it's a broad and open-ended question like "What are the things you really don't want to do?"

I made it clear that I just wanted a BDSM encounter, that I wasn't up for oral sex or vaginal sex or anything like that. He'd never had a BDSM encounter that didn't involve orgasm, so it was a new concept for him, but he was cool with trying it.

After our long discussion of boundaries and limits, we made it to his apartment and settled in. He got out some equipment, including a collar, and he said: "While you're wearing this, you will obey everything I say. Do you have any final boundaries to set? Anything you really want me to do? Anything else you don't want me to do?" I said no, and he snapped on the collar. (We did have an agreed-upon safeword, though — so I had a way of interrupting the proceedings if I really needed to.)

It was an interesting encounter, partly because he was looking more for dominance (giving orders) than sadism (inflicting pain), whereas at the time I was looking more for masochism (receiving pain) than submission (accepting orders). So we started out with him giving me a bunch of orders (primarily to fulfill his kink), and then in the end he hit me a lot with a leather belt (to fulfill mine). At the time I was still figuring out where the boundary was for me: whether I identified as a submissive or only a masochist; how much submission and masochism were intertwined. That night showed me a lot about how one can create submissive energy within a pre-defined space, even with someone you barely know.

Afterwards, when I was done crying, he took off the collar and we went to bed. (By that time of night, I didn't have a way back home from where he lived, so I had to sleep over.) We chatted about random things, neither of us quite tired enough to sleep. Within half an hour or so, he realized that there was no way he was ever going to get to sleep unless he had an orgasm, but he also understood that I didn't want to have sex with him, so he didn't try to push that. Instead, he said: "I really need to have an orgasm before I can get to sleep. I can either take care of that in the bathroom, or I can do it here. If I do it here, then you can help me along, or not. I'd especially appreciate it if you could talk dirty while I jerk off, but it's your decision."

Talk about low pressure! Yeah, I learned a lot from that guy.

* * *

2) **Scripts and Lists.** I had one brief relationship last year with a gentleman who is really, really awesome — but we have very different approaches to S&M. We had a hard time communicating about it... honestly, if he hadn't been such an awesome guy, I would probably have given up on the relationship after a couple nights together. We were great at having extensive theoretical conversations about sexuality, but when it came down to actually having sex with each other, things got puzzling. We had difficulty predicting, understanding, and initiating with each other.

I'm not sure what made it so hard. I think, mostly, we just brought really different assumptions to the table. I tend to take an "improvisational" approach to my encounters, whereas he tends to take a "scripted" approach. He's into doing stuff like rearranging the furniture, taking on specific roles (e.g. teacher and student), using costumes and props, and knowing exactly what will be said beforehand.

Me, I like going free-form. I talk to my partner about hard limits (things we absolutely don't want to do); I talk to him about things we really like; and we set a safeword. I'm usually okay with diving in from there. If he wants a more structured conversation, I'm glad to have one (and sometimes, especially when I'm dominant, I'll ask for more conversation myself). But generally, I like seeing how things go based on a very loose set of guidelines, and making minor adjustments during the encounter, then evaluating the situation afterwards.

One of the reasons I like doing this is that unexpected things happen. On the flip side, there's also more room for experiences that aren't very exciting. I think I'm more likely to have disjointed or confusing encounters than a lot of other BDSMers I know, although maybe I'm just falling prey to the bias of assuming other people are doing better than I am. And Scripty Guy in particular really doesn't like disjoint and confusion — he likes knowing what's going to happen.

Late in the relationship, I suggested that we try going through a checklist. When people use these checklists, a lot of the time they just write their rating for each act, and give them to each other to read. What we did instead was go through the checklist together and discuss what we found hot, what was not, and whatever else came to mind.

This worked amazingly well — it totally bridged our theoretical gap and it was a turn-on in itself! (Seriously, by the time we were done going through the whole list, I **could not wait** to have sex with that guy.) The conversation also helped me figure out the scripted vs. un-scripted difference between us.

We stopped seeing each other for unrelated reasons soon afterwards, and they were good reasons, but it seemed like a shame; I felt like we'd only just started figuring things out. I'm not sure how well our S&M styles would have ultimately meshed, but I was curious to try. Oh well... win some, lose some.

* * *

3) **Transparent as Glass.** Very rarely, I'll end up with a BDSM partner where our brief in-the-moment communications — you know, like groans, or physical shifts, or facial expressions, or even jokes — function very well. We can get into intense, intimate S&M in a way that seems almost instinctive (although it helps future encounters if we talk it over and process what we did afterwards). This is really exciting when it happens, but I recognize it as unusual. A gift.

The person I'm about to write about is totally going to get a swelled head because I write about him so much, but he's such a good example, I have to. The first time I went home with him, I knew he wasn't in the public BDSM community. We'd had one really vague conversation about BDSM previously, and he'd read a small sample of my work. I didn't expect anything much.

He kissed me, and then I think he gave me some kind of mild signal like a bite on my shoulder. It was a gentle bite, by my standards. So I took matters into my own hands and removed my shirt, preparing to give him some feedback. He leaned back and said, "Whoa," and I thought, *Oh damn, I'm totally going too fast for him, he's probably not accustomed to a high degree of sexual directness,* so I said, "Sorry, is this okay?" and he laughed and kind of threw up his hands and said, "Sure."

That made me a tad nervous — if me taking off my shirt surprised him, what else would surprise him? — but I figured I'd see it through, see what happened. So I explained to him what kind of biting I really like, and showed where I like it on my back and my arms. I think I gave him a couple of other tips, too, but I honestly can't remember; it didn't take more than five minutes. I certainly didn't give him an exhaustive rundown of my preferences before I said, "Does that all make sense?" and he said "Yes," and put his hands on me.

Which is why it was so surprising that within a very short time, both of us were breathing hard and confused and maybe slightly dizzy and looking at each other with very wide eyes, and he was saying in an amazed tone: "I just — I'm a little shocked. That was **really good**," and I was saying: "Yes. Yes it was."

It went like that for a while. He'd go for it, and then pull back, and I'd drag myself out of my BDSM headspace long enough to explain one or two ideas, or reassure him that I felt fine. And then he'd go for it again. And by the end of it, I was — blazing.

Sometimes, it just works. You've never met this person before, you've talked for half an hour about something completely irrelevant like science fiction novels, yet it only takes five minutes of discussion about preferences and safewords, and then it just **works**. I don't know why, and I don't know how, but sometimes you find a partner who can just — **read** you, like an open book — or who seems as transparent as glass to you; or, if you're really lucky, both.

(But I write about this with some hesitation, and I'm putting it at the end of this post after two other examples for a reason: because I don't think it's the standard, and I don't think it ought to be seen as standard. Especially because, paradoxically, this kind of instinctive connection will sometimes throw me off guard, make me unlikely to communicate when I probably ought to, because if he can read me that well — it's so tempting to assume that "he just knows" everything. But of course he doesn't. I later had a couple rough moments with that particular guy, where I didn't tell him about boundaries that were actually pretty important, because I thought he could just tell — and of course he couldn't always "just tell." Sometimes he could, but sometimes he couldn't.)

The overall moral of the story is this. Even with him, even with this guy, who totally blindsided me with his ability to read me despite the fact that he barely knew me: even with him, I had to be able to talk directly about what I wanted. Our connection was established because I was able to say, "Okay, that bite was a tad gentle, here's how I really like it, and here's what not to do with your teeth on me." **All my most extraordinary sexual connections have benefited from everyone involved taking ownership of their desire, and talking about it directly at least a little bit.**

I occasionally come across people who ask me how they can get their partners to do BDSM without talking about it directly. While I appreciate and sympathize with both their need to do BDSM, and their anxiety about talking about it — I just can't get behind the premise of the question. The fantasy of a sexual relationship that is totally instinctive and perfect without any effort is just that — a fantasy. And moreover, while you might be able to get some BDSM experiences without actually having a conversation about BDSM, direct sexual communication is not a threat to your sexual experiences — it can improve them.

Do what you want, really, as long as it's consensual. If you want to have sex that's not communicative, that is your prerogative, as long as it's always consensual. (It's worth asking, though... are you so sure you can tell that it's consensual, if you don't talk about it?) Still. Learning how to talk about sex more directly and exactly might be hard or embarrassing or complicated, **but it is seriously worth it**. Not just BDSM; all sex.

It's so worth it.

* * *

This post originally appeared at:
http://clarissethorn.com/blog/2011/03/11/storytime-sex-communication-case-studies/

* * *

* * *

FEMINISM:
[theory] Towards My Personal Sex-Positive Feminist 101

I wrote this in 2011, when I realized that I couldn't find a good Sex-Positive Feminist 101 anywhere on the Internet. The original version contains a lot more links, including an evolving set of relevant links at the end.

* * *

There's an aphorism from the early 1900s literary critic Andre Maurois: "The difficult part in an argument is not to defend one's opinion but to know it." Even though I identify as an activist and genuinely want to make a real impact on the world based on my beliefs... I often think that much of my blogging has been more an attempt to figure out what I believe, than to tell people what I believe. And sometimes, I fall into the trap of wanting to be consistent more than I want to understand what I really believe — or more than I want to empathize with other people — or more than I want to be correct. We all gotta watch out for that.

But I'm getting too philosophical here. (Who, me?) The point is, I am hesitant to write something with a title like "Sex-Positive 101," because not only does it seem arrogant (who says Clarisse Thorn gets to define Sex-Positive 101?) — it also implies that my thoughts on sex-positivity have come to a coherent, standardized end. Which they haven't! I'm still figuring things out, just like everyone else.

However, lately I've been thinking that I really want to write about some basic ideas that inform my thoughts on sex-positive feminism. I acknowledge that I am incredibly privileged (white, upper-middle-class, heteroflexible, cisgendered etc [1]) and coming mostly from a particular community, the BDSM community; both of these factors inform and limit the principles that underpin my sex-positivity. I welcome ideas for Sex-Positive Feminism 101, links to relevant 101 resources, etc.

* * *

Some Central Sex-Positive Feminist Ideas, according to Clarisse Thorn

1) **Desire is complicated, and people are different.** These ideas both seem basic and obvious to me as I write them, but I wanted to put them out there because I think they're useful anchors for all the rest.

2) **Gender is not a binary, and gender cannot be determined by a person's outer appearance or behavior.** Different people experience and display gender in a galaxy of ways. No woman in the world is perfectly submissive, perfectly hourglass-shaped, perfectly kind, etc, although these are stereotypes commonly associated with women. No man in the world is perfectly dominant, perfectly confident, perfectly muscular, etc. While many people reduce the idea of a person's gender to whether they have a penis or a vagina, the existence of trans people and intersex people proves that this isn't a valid approach. Individual people have all kinds of qualities that are attributed to the "other" gender... and the concept of an "other" (or "opposite") gender is weird in itself, because why does one gender have to be the "other," and what does that imply?

All this having been said, gender is frequently perceived as a binary, and many people fit themselves into the possibly-arbitrary system of gender that currently exists. There are ideas of "men" and "women" that are culturally understood, widely adopted, and socially enforced. Feminism has its roots in women resisting men's violent and social dominance, and in women resisting the cultural emphasis on stereotypical men's desires.

3) **Historically, sex has usually been defined in terms of two things: (a) reproduction, and (b) the sexual pleasure of stereotypical men.** Cultural sexual standards are based on these things. For example, the sexual "base system"; if you've read my work before then you'll have seen me talk about it a lot, because it's such a perfect example. It's commonly discussed among USA schoolchildren and describes kissing as "first base", groping as "second base", oral sex as "third base" and penis-in-vagina sex as "home base." Why should this hierarchy exist? It only makes sense if we think of sex as being centered around reproduction. If we think of sex as being about pleasure and open exploration in ways that are different for everyone, then having a "home base" — a standardized goal — makes zero sense.

Another example: penis-in-vagina sex is often seen as "real" sex or "actual" sex, with all other sex considered "less real." How many arguments have you had over the course of your lifetime about whether oral sex "counts" as sex? (Hint: more than the subject deserves.) For a recent example, there's the Kink.com virgin shoot, wherein a porn model publicly "lost her virginity" notwithstanding the fact that she'd already had plenty of oral and anal sex on camera for years — she'd just never had vaginal sex. [2]

As for sex being defined by the pleasure of stereotypical men: one example is how people usually think about orgasms. In my experience and that of people I talk to — and in the vast majority of porn — it seems commonly accepted that sexual activity ends with a man's orgasm, whereas women are commonly expected to continue engaging in sex after having an orgasm... despite the fact that many women seem just as tired and less-interested in sex post-orgasm as many men are. In part, this goes back to defining sex in terms of reproduction: men have to orgasm in order for reproduction to happen, so men's orgasms must (supposedly) be central to sex. It's all influenced by these other constructions, like how penis-in-vagina sex is "real" sex, or "home base": many people are confused by the idea that you'd shift sexual gears to (for example) manual stimulation if you've already "made it to home base." But it also arises from centering stereotypical men's desires — from a culture that just generally sees them as more important, more driving, and more necessary than women's. (Note that the majority of women don't achieve orgasm from penis-in-vagina sex in itself. [3])

When sex is defined in terms of reproduction and stereotypical male pleasure, the following things result:

+ People who aren't men have a harder time understanding their sexuality, because there are fewer models (for example: it's fairly common for women to figure out how to have orgasms much later in life than the average man — like 20s or 30s, if ever)

+ Men who don't fit masculine stereotypes have a harder time understanding their sexuality (for example: there's a great essay by a former men's magazine editor in the anthology *Best Sex Writing 2010* in which he talks about how hard it was for him to come to terms with his desire for heavy women)

+ Even men who do fit masculine stereotypes feel limited from other types of exploration, and may derive less pleasure from sex than they would in a less broken world

+ Sex acts or sexual relationships that aren't reproductive are devalued, are seen as weird, or aren't even defined as sex (for example: stigma against gay sex, lesbian sex, many fetishes, etc)

4) **Women are expected to trade sex to men in exchange for support or romance.** Women who don't get a "good trade" (e.g. women who don't receive a certain level of financial support or romance "in exchange for" sex) are seen as sluts. Men who don't get a "good trade" (e.g. men who don't receive a certain amount of sex "in exchange for" a relationship) are seen as pussies. (Yes, "pussies"... don't you just love that a word for female genitalia is a commonly used insult against so-called "weak" men?)

What this also means is that many people have trouble examining motivations outside this framework: women are always expected to be looking for more emotional or financial investment from a guy, whereas men are always expected to be looking for more (or more so-called "extreme") sex. Women who actively seek sex, or men who actively seek intimacy, are shamed and hurt and confused for it — often even within their own heads.

5) **Since stereotypical men have historically been much freer to explore their sexuality than people of other genders, the desires of stereotypical men have formed the pattern for "liberated sexuality."** As women have won freedom to act, work and explore outside the home more, we've been following patterns created mostly by men, and those patterns might look extremely different if women had created them.

When we talk about sexuality, I think that leads us to examine what "liberated sexuality" looks like. "Liberated sexuality" is often stereotyped as promiscuous, for example. "Liberated sexuality" is also stereotyped as being unromantic, never involving any of those pesky pesky feelings, etc. I write about this cautiously: I have no intention of telling anyone what "real" men do or feel, or what "real" women do or feel. However, it seems conceivable to me that most men are generally more likely to enjoy promiscuity and emotionless sex than most women are — if only for hormonal reasons. Here's a quotation from the brilliant trans man sex writer Patrick Califia on the effects of testosterone:

It's harder to track psychological and emotional changes caused by one's taking testosterone than it is to notice the physical differences. But I think the former actually outweigh the latter. It isn't that testosterone has made me a different person. I always had a high sex drive, liked porn and casual sex, couldn't imagine giving up masturbation, was able to express my anger, and showed a pretty high level of autonomy and assertiveness. But all of these things have gotten much more intense since I began hormone treatments. During the first six months on T, every appetite I had was painfully sharp. A friend of mine expressed it this way: "When I had to eat, I had to eat right fucking now. If I was horny, I had to come immediately. If I needed to shit, I couldn't wait. If I was pissed off, the words came right out of my mouth. If I was bored, I had to leave." My body and all the physical sensations that spring from it have acquired a piquancy and an immediacy that is both entertaining and occasionally inconvenient. Moving through the world is even more fun, involves more stimulation than it used to; life is more in the here-and-now, more about bodies and objects, less about thoughts and feelings.

... Casual sex has changed. When I want to get off, my priority is to find somebody who will do that as efficiently as possible, and while I certainly would rather have a pleasant interaction with that person, I don't think a lot about how they were doing before they got down on their knees, and I don't care very much how they feel after they get up and leave. It's hard to keep their needs in mind; it's easier to just assume that if they wanted anything, it was their responsibility to try to get it. I always preferred to take sexual initiative, and that has become even more ego-congruent. (pages 397-398, Speaking Sex To Power)

A trans woman friend once told me that not only did she get turned on more frequently pre-transition; also, she now has to feel more emotionally connected to her partner in order to enjoy sex. And she noted that she has to "take care of herself more" in order to feel turned on now — not just in the moment, but in life, and in the relationship.

If we accept that there is, speaking generally, a difference in sexual desires between men and women (although individuals will always be unique), then it leads to new questions. If women were socially and culturally dominant, what would so-called "liberated sexuality" look like? If people of all genders are following patterns set by stereotypical men, then what does that mean for attempts to think around those patterns?

6) Communicating consent is complicated, but consent is the only thing that makes sex okay, so we have to make every effort to respect it. All sex is completely fine with me as long as it's consensual. Seriously, I really don't care what you do — as long as it's consensual. (Try to find a consensual sex act that shocks me. I dare you.)

Communicating consent can, however, be complicated, and there are lots of different ways to do it. Many BDSMers are eminently familiar with this, as you can tell by the fact that some parts of the BDSM community have developed an extensive array of tactics for discussing consent. For example, the most famous BDSM communication tactic is safewords, which gives everyone involved a clear word that they can invoke to stop the action at any time.

Most people don't communicate directly about most things, and the stigma and high emotions around sexuality make it even harder for most people to communicate directly about sex. Hence, most sexual communication is highly indirect. Even among people who are accustomed to direct sexual communication — like many BDSMers — a lot of communication ends up being indirect and instinctive anyway; there's just no way to discuss every possible reaction and every single desire ahead of time. Everyone fucks up sometimes. No one in the world has a perfect track record on creating a pressure-free environment for their partners to express what they want... or asking their partners for what they want... or even knowing what they want in the first place.

So, yes, I acknowledge that communicating about sex and getting what you want consensually can be really hard. However, it's most important to not violate people's boundaries. No matter how hard it is, it's necessary to make a serious and genuine effort to measure and respect a partner's consent every time sex happens. Feminist ideas of enthusiastic consent are designed to help this process.

Here's my attempt at a quick definition of enthusiastic consent:

The basic idea is simple: don't initiate sex unless you have your partner's enthusiastic consent. Not a partner who says, "Okay, I guess," in a bored tone, but doesn't actively say "no." Not a partner who is silent and non-reactive, but doesn't actively stop you when you start having sex with them. Not a partner who seems hesitant, or anxious, or confused. Enthusiastic consent means an enthusiastic partner: one who is responding passionately, kissing you back, saying things like "Yes" or "Oh my God, don't stop"... or a partner who talks to you ahead of time about what will happen, as many BDSMers and sex workers do, and knows how to safeword or otherwise get out of the situation if you do something they don't like.

It's worth noting that there are critiques within feminism of the concept of enthusiastic consent. For example, some feminist sex workers point out that when they have sex for money, their consent is not exactly "enthusiastic," but they still feel that their consent is real consent, and that their choices must be respected. The same goes for some asexual people. Asexuality is commonly defined as "not feeling sexual attraction to others," but some asexual people have romantic relationships with other people in which they have sex entirely to satisfy their partner, and some of them have said that they don't feel included by feminist discussions of enthusiastic consent. [4]

Hey, even some of my non-asexual, non-sex worker friends have problems with the idea that they aren't "really" consenting unless they're super-enthusiastic about the sexual act at hand. A married friend once commented wryly that if she and her husband always demanded 100% enthusiastic consent from each other, then the marriage would fall apart. But as we continued to discuss it, she and her husband both agreed that they have zero problem with the situation as it stands.

I don't want to sweep those critiques under the rug. I figure that as long as everyone's communicating about the situation openly, and working to keep things relatively low-pressure, then consent is likely to happen, even if it's not perfectly "enthusiastic." I've had extensive debates on the topic with other feminists, though, and I often seek more, because honing consent theory is one of my favorite things!

All this having been said: the concept of enthusiastic consent has been very helpful for me personally. I know that it's also been helpful for an enormous number of other people who are trying to understand boundaries in their sexual relationships. I absolutely believe that enthusiastic consent is an important and useful standard, and I do my best to observe that standard as much as I can in my own relationships. So, while I think some critiques are reasonable, I also think that the idea of enthusiastic consent is the best baseline assumption to start these conversations... if not to end them.

7) **In practice, as long as everyone involved is having consensual fun, criticism is secondary.** Practically speaking, consent is the most important thing; from a pragmatic standpoint, the question of whether sexuality arises from biology or culture doesn't matter nearly as much. (I find the question of whether BDSM can be categorized as a sexual orientation to be more politically and theoretically interesting than practically important.)

Understanding sexual biology or culture may help us grasp some of the complexities of consent. For example, people often have trouble saying "no" to things directly: when was the last time you explicitly said "no" when you didn't want to do something? Which of the following exchanges is more likely:

Person A: Hey, want to come over tonight?
Person B: You know, I'd love to, but I'm so exhausted from work,

I really need to get some sleep.
or
Person A: Hey, want to come over tonight?
Person B: No.

People of all genders really don't like saying "no" to things directly. Grasping this important cultural concept is one step on the path of learning how to communicate effectively about consent. But in my book, it's really not as important to understand why people hate saying "no" directly, as it is to understand that people hate saying "no" directly. It's necessary to understand that because it means that pushing someone until they say "no" can mean pushing them further than they wanted to go.

I believe that the most important role of social criticism — including sex-positive feminism — is not to tell people what to do. If you have sex that appears to be in line with ridiculous and oppressive stereotypes, I really do not care as long as everyone involved is consenting and having fun. I reserve the right to occasionally have consensual sex where a gentleman friend beats me up before fucking me, and I reserve the right to enjoy it.

But I want to offer sex-positive feminist analyses in order to help people understand themselves and their desires... and also understand their partners and their desires. I think that many people have sex they don't like, sex that's in line with ridiculous and oppressive stereotypes, because they haven't been exposed to anything they like better. I think many people have sex they don't like because they don't feel like they can look for something different — they think it's the best they can get. I think many people have sex they don't like because they think it's what their partner wants — and I think those people are frequently wrong, and I think most partners would genuinely prefer that everyone be having fun.

Which is why I try to deconstruct sexual norms and stereotypes. Which is why I encourage people to look for what they like. Which is why I always emphasize talking about it.

8) Awesome, respectful, joyful, mutual sex means approaching sex as collaborative rather than adversarial. Aside from solo sex (i.e. masturbation), sex always involves another person. And at its best, it's about having a good time with other people — understanding their reality, accepting it, playing with it. The best metaphors I've ever heard for sex were all about collaborative art, like a musical jam performance. Here's a bit from Thomas MacAulay Millar's totally brilliant essay "Towards a Performance Model of Sex" (please do read the whole thing someday):

The negotiation is the creative process of building something from a set of available elements. Musicians have to choose, explicitly or implicitly, what they are going to play: genre, song, key and interpretation. The palette available to them is their entire skill set — all the instruments they have and know how to play, their entire repertoire, their imagination and their skills — and the product will depend on the pieces each individual brings to the performance. Two musicians steeped in Delta blues will produce very different music from one musician with a love for soul and funk and another with roots in hip-hop or 1980s hardcore. This process involves communication of likes and dislikes and preferences, not a series of proposals that meet with acceptance or rejection.

... Under this model, the sexual interaction should be creative, positive, and respectful even in the most casual of circumstances.

("Towards a Performance Model of Sex" was first printed in *Yes Means Yes,* edited by Jessica Valenti and Jaclyn Friedman, the brilliant sex-positive anti-rape anthology that I want everyone in the entire world to read. It was also reprinted in *Best Sex Writing 2010,* edited by Rachel Kramer Bussel.)

9) **All people deserve equal rights, including sexual minorities.** As long as people are having consensual sex, they do not deserve to be stigmatized, harassed, or otherwise harmed for their sexuality. Period. No one should be fired for their sexual or gender identity. No one should have their kids taken away for their sexual or gender identity. Rape is still rape, even when it's perpetrated against a sex worker. I support decriminalizing sex work for a lot of reasons; for example, I'd love it if the law would quit harassing and jailing sex workers for having consensual sex, and I'd love it if sex workers could organize for better workplace safety. The bottom line is that people — all people — have rights. It's time to treat them that way.

* * *

In terms of actual ways to be sex-positive in everyday life, here are the three ways I usually encourage people to spread the sex-positive love:

A) **Avoid re-centering.** Sexuality shouldn't be societally "centered" on any particular norm, idea, or stereotype (except consent). It is frequently tempting to re-center "objective" ideas about sexuality onto ourselves, if we're different from the norm, or onto people we admire. But the truth is that — on a societal level —

queer sex is just as awesome as straight sex; that BDSM sex is equally admirable as vanilla sex; that cisgendered people are not any more or less amazing than trans people. The decision to have sex is no better than the decision to avoid sex, and asexual people are just as great as hypersexual people who are just as great as anyone with any level of sex drive.

In alternative sexuality subcultures, one often encounters a kind of superior attitude, perhaps because we have to push back so hard against the norm. In polyamory, for example, some of us use the sarcastic term "polyvangelist": a person who insists that polyamory is "better" or "more evolved" or "makes more sense" for everyone, everywhere, than monogamy does. Neither monogamy nor polyamory is better than the other; they're just different. Polyvangelists are trying to re-center onto polyamory. Not cool.

B) **Start conversations.** One of the most damaging problems around sexuality is the overwhelming and constant stigma. It hurts people with certain sexual identities, preferences or pasts. It hurts them spiritually. It can hurt them societally, like when LGBTQ folks have difficulty adopting children, or former sex workers are not allowed to work at other jobs. It can even hurt them physically: 40 years after doctors started noticing the HIV pandemic, too many people are still refusing to talk about sex openly, or give healthcare to sexual minorities directly affected by HIV. To say nothing of people who are attacked or killed for their sexual minority status, like trans people who are murdered in the street, or lesbians who are raped in order to "fix" their sexuality. Sexual stigma kills.

So when someone says something icky about sex and gender, or stereotypes a certain sex or gender identity, it's so great to challenge them — or at least to question them. ("Really? What makes you think all gay people are abuse survivors?") And some of the most powerful sex activism out there involves starting discussion groups, creating venues for discussion, hosting sexuality speakers or sex-related art, etc.

C) **Be "out" or open, without being invasive.** This can be tricky, because I don't want to encourage people to aggressively talk about sex at totally inappropriate times — and again, I'm against re-centering. On the other hand, the most powerful tool for destigmatizing sexuality appears to be coming out of the closet — whether a person is queer, BDSM, or whatever. Openly acknowledging, owning, and discussing your sexual preferences can help others respect those preferences — and can help others who share those preferences respect themselves. (Can you tell that I cried when I saw the movie *Milk?)*

* * *

This post can be found on the Internet at:
http://clarissethorn.com/blog/2011/05/08/towards-my-personal-sex-positive-feminist-101/

* * *

* * *

S&M:
[theory] S&M Superpowers

I wrote this post in 2011, but I encountered the "superpower" framework for fetishes in 2008, before I started blogging. I was telling one of my first S&M partners about how broken and anxious I felt, and he said: "Why talk about it that way? You haven't lost anything. You've gained a superpower!"

* * *

I've gotten so bored of the biases and stereotypes against S&M. It's like, "Hey, another person who implies that those of us who do consensual S&M were all abused as children? Sweet! That person is wrong, and I consider those views highly stigmatizing and sometimes damaging. So, can we go for a swim now?"

(For the record, the biggest and best-designed study ever done on this topic surveyed 20,000 people and found that S&Mers "were no more likely to have been coerced into sexual activity" than the general population. [1] But — also for the record — an S&Mer whose sexuality was associated with being abused would not be "less legitimate" than the rest of us, as long as that person practiced kink consensually. Because what makes S&M okay is consent, right? Right. S&M isn't okay or not okay because of its "source," whatever that might be — it's okay only when it's practiced consensually, right? Right. So this is all actually kind of a silly conversation to have in the first place, right? Right. It's too bad stigma tends to make zero sense, isn't it? Stigma loves to trick you into debating on its own terms. [2])

It's much more entertaining to imagine how people would talk about S&M, if we lived in a culture where S&M wasn't wildly stigmatized. In fact, **what if S&M were admired or seen as a great thing**... instead of being repressed and forced underground and seen as a dark, evil, disgusting thing? I've known people who called S&M and other fetishes "superpowers," in a kind of ironic twist on this concept.

Many people have written about how S&Mers can offer lessons in sexuality that we gleaned from our outside-the-box perspective (there's a whole paper on this topic for clinicians, written by psychologist Peggy Kleinplatz and titled "Learning from Extraordinary Lovers" [3]). I myself have talked about how S&Mers tend to use much more careful and precise sexual communication tactics than the mainstream (examples include checklists and safewords). But these lessons are hardly **confined** to S&Mers — there are lots of vanilla people out there who are awesomely careful and precise about communicating sexually.

The superpower framework is a bit different....

+ For example, I already noted that it's been demonstrated that S&Mers are not more likely to have endured non-consensual acts — so we know that despite what Freud would have had you believe, all S&M does not arise from childhood abuse. But maybe it does arise from a childhood experience... an **awesome** childhood experience. Maybe the Missing S&M Link is that something totally wonderful happened to S&Mers in our childhoods.

Hey, vanilla people? I'm so sorry you all had such bad childhoods. Really, you have my sincerest sympathies.

+ For example, some folks will say that we S&Mers have a wire crossed somewhere; some genetic inferiority. But maybe we are totally way superior. Maybe average dominants and sadists are, say, more empathic than the norm. (There is, after all, actual research showing that consensual S&M increases intimacy. [4]) Maybe average submissives and masochists are better at processing pain and enduring challenges, both physical and emotional, than the norm.

Sorry vanilla people, but we're going to have to start screening for your gross vanilla genes in the womb. Nothing personal.

+ For example, one of my exes has a story about how he was down in Latin America and he only had access to incredibly cold showers. So he gritted his teeth, stepped into the shower, and told himself that a dominant woman was forcing him to take it. "Actually it made the shower a million times easier to deal with," he said later. "And I had a raging erection the whole time."

Aren't submissives awesome? I pity those of you who lack submissive tendencies.

Just because anything on the Internet can and will be misread, I will conclude this post by hammering down the point that **this is all a thought experiment, and I do not actually think vanilla people are any less wonderful than S&M people**. It's okay vanilla folks. I love you just the way you are.

* * *

This post can be found on the Internet at:
http://clarissethorn.com/blog/2011/06/21/sm-superpowers/

* * *

***

S&M:
[theory] BDSM Can Be "Love Sex" Too

In early 2011, my fellow sex blogger Rachel Rabbit White asked me to participate in her initiative "Lady Porn Day." [1] There's a list of relevant links at the end of the online version of this article.

***

I'm not a big porn consumer, but I have no problem with porn in itself. When I have a problem with porn, it's because I have a problem with how it was made: because there are labor issues, or questions of the actors' consent. Sometimes, I get frustrated with the context in which porn exists or the stereotypes it expresses — but there, the problem is with the context and the stereotypes, not with porn in itself. I think most anti-porn anxiety arises from irrational grossed-out reactions and stereotype-created fears, and I try to open up conversations about the ethics of making porn whenever I can.

This isn't to say I don't get angry because many people in our society are pressured to have sex that doesn't work for them — but that's not the fault of porn. I certainly get frustrated by sexual stereotypes, but I don't think porn created those stereotypes.

One stereotype I've been thinking about a lot lately — one that I see expressed over and over in BDSM porn — is the idea that BDSMers don't love our partners, or that love can't be part of a BDSM relationship. Here's a quotation from Pat Califia's *Speaking Sex To Power* that touches on this (note: contains **spoilers** about the endings of three famous BDSM novels — *Story of O, Return to the Chateau* and *Nine And A Half Weeks*):

I still remember how crushed I was when I read Story of O *and* Return to the Chateau *and came to the ending, where Sir Stephen loses interest in O and tells her to kill herself. I can also remember being furious with the way* Nine And A Half Weeks *(the book, not the movie) ends. The submissive woman has a public breakdown. She begins to cry hysterically, and is abandoned by her master, so that strangers have to obtain help for her. One of the cruelest stereotypes of S/M people is that we don't love each other, that there is something about our sexual style that makes our relationships mutually destructive and predisposes us to suicide.*

This quotation came to mind during a conversation I had a few days ago: I was talking to a girl who really likes BDSM sex but referred to non-BDSM sex as "love sex." Because, you know, love is just not an ingredient in BDSM sex. "Everyone knows" that — the same way "everyone knows" BDSM always arises from childhood abuse, or dominant sadism is for villains, or everyone who likes BDSM is damaged and miserable and irresponsible, or....

Not to put too fine a point on it: fuck that.

I'm not saying there's no BDSM smut out there with love in it. Anne Rice's Beauty series ends with Beauty riding off into the sunset with her loving sadomasochistic partner (although of course the characters deal with all kinds of uncaring brutality first). But even nuanced BDSM erotica seems to fall into this trap more often than not — for example, Jacqueline Carey's *Kushiel's Dart,* which is so consciously written that it includes safewords, also portrays a main character whose most compelling BDSM relationships are with her enemies and whose love relationship is with a man who can't stand to hurt her. (Carey took a very different tack later in the series, with other characters; I've always wondered whether she did so as a reaction to criticism.)

It's easier to criticize than create. And all my porn critiques could come back and bite me soon, because I plan on releasing my own BDSM smut sometime... and I'm sure that what I produce won't even be close to perfect. Yet one thing I really want to ensure I represent in whatever I write is love. There are plenty of BDSM fantasies that partly operate on the absence of love — that even **demand** it, perhaps because the fantasy is all about a vicious and emotionally distant dominant, or because much of the erotic tension is derived from how much the partners hate each other, or for lots of other reasons. And yeah, they're hot in their own way....

But it'd be so great if those weren't the standard.

* * *

This can be found on the Internet at:
http://clarissethorn.com/blog/2011/02/22/ladypornday-bdsm-can-be-love-sex-too/

* * *

* * *

S&M:
[theory] Body Chemistry and S&M

This was originally published in 2011. I don't normally write basic "how-to" posts like this, but every once in a while I see a gap I just have to fill.

* * *

I often think that good physical health is a widely-ignored element of good sex. I am obviously not saying that people in poor health can't have good sex (and in fact, I certainly hope they do — more power to 'em). But it consistently amazes me how much my physical health factors into my sexuality, especially S&M. I am by no means an expert on this topic, but here are some examples:

* **Food.** I am both less interested in sex and in S&M when I'm hungry; ensuring that I've eaten well before I take some punishment is especially crucial. I try to eat well in general, but if I'm planning to have a heavy S&M encounter, I don't cut myself any slack. I try to specifically ensure that I eat enough protein before the date and I try to include some vitamin-heavy foods like beets, leafy green vegetables, etc. Eggs are a good source of protein; nuts, beans and tofu are my primary protein sources. If I don't have enough protein available for whatever reason, I at least eat enough food that I won't be hungry when I see my partner.

Part of the reason I'm writing this right now is that I've had trouble finding useful resources on the Internet for what people recommend as good pre- or post-S&M food, especially during aftercare. "Aftercare" is an S&M term for how people end their S&M encounters. One excellent page on aftercare describes it thusly:

Aftercare is the last act of the SM drama. It is the culmination, the pulling together of all loose ends, the finishing touches, the final communion between sharers of the SM ritual, the phase where the participants (usually the tops) formally give the fantasy scene a context in everyday reality. Its technical purpose is to transition both players from the elevated states created in a scene [i.e., an S&M encounter] back into normalcy, returning to the motor control and awareness they will need to drive home once the scene is over. But as any good SM practitioner will tell you, it's much more than that. It is the time after the action when the participants come together in mutual affirmation that something special was created and shared. It is when affection and closeness is offered and sought. It is, at very least, the proper time to express thanks to the person who has shared this tiny segment of your life with you. It can be, and often is, the most beautiful part of a scene, and it is part of the scene. To skip it altogether is as rude as having dinner at a friend's house and then bolting once you've eaten your fill. [1]

A lot of tops keep food and water on hand to give bottoms at the end of a scene, which I think is probably a good idea. (Eating post-scene doesn't feel necessary for me as a bottom, but it might if I weren't so careful about what I eat beforehand.) Some people say that fruit or fruit juice is the way to go — and indeed, it will give the bottom's system a sugar boost and may make them feel better for that reason — but I would personally rather eat a protein bar, and I have some friends who feel the same way. Dungeons usually serve snacks, although the snacks aren't always very healthy.

A final note on food: I know there are people who specifically include food deprivation as part of their S&M. Obviously, this is totally fine by me as long as it is consensual, but I'd encourage people not to expect themselves — or their partners — to react the way they usually do to S&M, as long as they're hungry.

* **Weight.** I used to be much scrawnier than I am now, and as my health has improved, I've gained weight. Sometimes this freaks me out (it's impossible to be female in our society and not daydream about having cheekbones that can stab people), but it has been worth it. One time, after I'd been having a lot of anxiety about weight gain, my then-boyfriend emailed me the image of an art piece printed with the words, "I gained 30 pounds... & sex has never been better!" He perceptively wrote: "Maybe that's why it's easier for you to have orgasms now? I think you should investigate this if you try to lose weight."

I am not in a position to comment about whether being overweight affects sex. But I can definitely assure you that being underweight is not good for your sexual well-being.

* **Sleep.** I much prefer to have S&M encounters on days when I've gotten a lot of sleep the night before; this is at least as crucial as eating well before an encounter. There are approximately a billion studies that show the far-reaching effects that getting enough sleep can have on our health, and they seem to usually recommend around 7-8 hours as a good amount per night (more for teenagers).

As with food, I know there are people who include sleep deprivation as part of their S&M encounters. Again, this is obviously fine by me as long as it is consensual, but I'd encourage people not to expect themselves — or their partners — to react the way they usually do to S&M, as long as they're tired. I don't know about you, but exhaustion certainly makes **me** erratic and overly emotional. If you're going to be doing something like S&M that can specifically create an crratic and overly emotional state... well, when overlapping that with exhaustion, it just seems like a good idea to be careful.

* **Alcohol.** Alcohol definitely decreases my pain tolerance (quite dramatically in fact), and it definitely makes it harder for me to get turned on. There is only one bonus to alcohol, and that's the famous "social lubricant" effect. I personally prefer to limit myself to one glass of wine, maaaaybe two, if I'm planning to hook up with someone; in general, stone-cold sobriety is my preferred state to go into S&M. Good S&M makes me high enough on its own.

I get the impression that some people get drunk before they do S&M because otherwise they feel too anxious to do S&M. As always, I'm not going to tell other people that they shouldn't do consensual things... but drunkenness frequently makes it hard to communicate and hard to know what's going on in your head, which means that drunkenness makes consent hard. Not impossible, just hard. Be careful.

A lot of people say that mixing substances and BDSM is always bad. Personally, I figure that if a person has a lot of experience with a given substance, and a lot of experience with a given BDSM act, and a lot of experience with their partner... then I kind of doubt they're taking a huge risk by doing a familiar BDSM act with a familiar partner in a familiar state of mind. It's a lot to deal with at once, and again, it's worth being careful. And of course, substance abuse problems are a whole nother ballgame. But if a person has been drinking a glass of wine with dinner every night for 10 years, then I'm not going to tell her that I consider her incapable of doing BDSM after dinner.

I am not qualified to comment on non-alcohol drugs because I, of course, never do anything illegal. But for all your drug-related questions, the website Erowid.org is often very useful.

* **Illness.** I don't have any particular observations about how being sick changes my experience of S&M, but it definitely does. When I get sick and I have the option to reschedule a date, I always do.

* Aaand finally, **menstrual cycle.** I haven't tracked my cycle

with enough care to know exactly how it affects me S&M-wise, but I'm pretty sure it does. As one of the good people at EduKink once observed, "The great part about playing with a woman is that you have 28 different partners, one for each day of the month!" [2]

* * *

This can be found on the Internet at:
http://clarissethorn.com/blog/2011/01/30/body-chemistry-and-sm/

* * *

* * *

S&M:
[theory] Going Under

This was originally published in 2011. People have asked me whether there's any actual research out there on the altered states that some people access through S&M; as far as I know, there isn't. It's also worth noting that a lot of dominant partners go into another kind of "zone" that's sometimes called top-space.

* * *

"Come back," an S&M partner said softly, the other day, pushing my hair out of my eyes. I blinked and shook my head in a futile attempt to clear it.

"That's weird," I said. "Someone else used to say those words to me when I was coming out of subspace. I... that's weird."

"I'm not surprised," he said. "It's a natural thing to say to you. You go under so fast, and so deep. You're so far away."

"Not all the time," I said. "And not with everyone. You're good at putting me there."

He smiled. "You bring it out in me."

Subspace is so hard to describe. I've written about it before, in passing, so many times, because it's so important, but I've never come up with a good description for it; and when I Google for it I can see that other people have the same problem. When I'm starting to go into subspace it's just soft and dark and slow. But when I'm really far under, I'm totally blank. Falling. **Flying.**

Somewhere else.

Come back.

What is it, where do I go? It's just submissive, masochist headspace. But I don't always get into subspace when I submit, and I don't always get into it when I take pain either. I'm not sure what the other ingredients are: some amount of trust, of course. And strong feelings about my partner make everything more intense... way more intense. Orders of magnitude more intense. Still, I've had new partners put me under with surprising thoroughness.

It's a lot like deep sexual arousal — hard to think, hard to process, hard to make decisions — but the deepest sexual arousal does not put me anywhere near deep subspace. Deep subspace is. More. Than anything else.

Some S&M teachers tell people not to drive after an S&M encounter, not for a while; not until you're over the subspace. They compare it to an altered state, like being drunk. Some S&M teachers caution that it's dangerous for the dominant partner to suggest a new activity in the middle of an S&M encounter — something that wasn't negotiated beforehand — because the submissive may not be able to think clearly enough to consent. (And because in those moments, the submissive will have a harder time than ever saying no.)

I sometimes think that when I was younger and less experienced, I abandoned myself to subspace more easily. I'm better at pulling myself out of subspace now, but I think the cost may be that it's harder for me to really get into it. (Safety first?) I trained myself to be able to say, "Don't stop," when I wanted my partner to keep going. (Sound easy? Trust me, it took a while.) Playing with unfamiliar partners, I trained myself to be on guard. (One of my sex worker friends told me once, "I don't care how deep the subspace is, I can always come out if the client tries to fuck me without a condom.") I got better at calling my safeword **before** I had to — asking my partner to do something else or give me a break, rather than suddenly stopping everything once I hit my absolute limit.

I am nowhere near perfect, of course. In particular, I can rarely answer complicated questions, and sometimes my partners literally can't get me to answer **any** questions when I'm subspaced. Sometimes it takes me a long time to come out, and partners may get nervous while I'm surfacing. But I'm not sure these aspects can actually be eliminated from subspace. And I've gotten better.

I'm sure that in an emergency, I could talk and function straight out of heavy subspace. I doubt I would be optimally intelligent and thoughtful, however.

When I was younger, I'd get frustrated with my partner if he tried to ask me questions or clarify things or otherwise check in with me when I was in subspace. *Damn it, can't you see I'm not here? Can't you see I'm under? Don't drag me back* — Intellectually, I understood that my frustration was unreasonable, and I did my best to train myself to deal with the check-ins. To surface quickly, slip back under afterwards. But I had to experience subspace from the dominant side before I understood **how** hard it was to deal with

I remember sitting with my arms around the submissive and occasionally asking him how he was; in response, he would murmur and snuggle up to me. Ten minutes. Twenty minutes. I was processing my own dominant experience, and I had questions; I'd occasionally ask one. He'd murmur something softly. After a while I really wanted a glass of water and I thought he'd basically fallen asleep, so I said, "Hey, I'm going to go get a glass of water, okay?" and tried to move away.

"No," he cried, and grabbed me. *Holy shit,* I thought, *so that's what surfacing from subspace can look like from the outside.* Suddenly I understood exactly where his head was at: barely any time had passed for him at all, and he was still drifting up through velvety layers of consciousness. When I tried to leave, he'd felt sudden panic, a shot of pure abandonment, *no no **no** you can't, you **can't** leave me alone when I'm like this, please I need your arms around me, I need you —*

I knew exactly what to tell him. "Shh," I said, "I'm here."

A dominant friend once told me that he always informs his partners ahead of time that he has to move after a good scene, he has to go for a run, and he won't stick around to guide them out of subspace. I've always wondered how his partners deal with it. Maybe it's easier if you know it's coming.

There are questions of consent, of negotiating new activities while a partner's in subspace. Some people have told me they can't even actually safeword when they're in deep subspace; I can't quite relate to this, but I imagine it could happen sometime. I myself have occasionally had trouble safewording in the past, but it wasn't ever just because of subspace, it was because of pride or difficult emotions with the dominant partner. Subspace did complicate things, but I don't think it was the reason I had trouble (though it can be hard to disentangle these things). But maybe someday I'll go under so far that it will be.

I'm not saying it's never okay to push further than you discussed, once they're under — it's just important to be careful, and not to do it unless you're pretty sure you can read your partner... or that they have the emotional wherewithal to deal with it if you push too hard.

Because safety in subspace is a question of emotional safety, more than anything. The vulnerability and intimacy in those moments can be terrifying. The tiniest change in his tone can mean the difference between mindless fear and absolute trust. It's so scary, and so intoxicating, and so weirdly unexplainably glorious.

Come back.

The best part might actually be coming back.

* * *

This can be found on the Internet at:
http://clarissethorn.com/blog/2011/04/22/going-under/

* * *

*　*　*

ORGASMIC "DYSFUNCTION":
[storytime] A Unified Theory of Orgasm

At one point during my blogging career, an editor for the iconic feminist publication Ms. Magazine *got in touch and asked me to do some promotion for them. I asked if they would accept a submission from me, and when the editor said yes, I poured my soul into this long article about my experiences learning how to have an orgasm. The article was rejected by* Ms., *so I went back to my old friend the Internet and got published on the adorable girl-power site OffOurChests.com. Then it was cross-posted in about a million places. I would love to get published in* Ms., *but in retrospect, I'm actually glad that this piece went out on the Internet instead of being trapped in a print publication. I've received an enormous amount of positive feedback for this piece, and I'm certain that most of the young people who tell me it helped them would never have seen it if it were in a print magazine.*

*　*　*

I CAN'T COME.
and it's poisoned
every romance
I've ever had.
masturbating doesn't work. I don't know why. I tried therapy too, but my smart, understanding, sex-positive, open-hearted doctor couldn't help. drugs while fucking? check. I date attentive men who only want to make me happy, but no matter how fantastic they make me feel, I can't get off. and believe me, I like sex. I love sex! how can it feel so good and not end in an orgasm? I tried experimenting, and I sure do love the kink. it feels great. but doesn't get me off. I've tried everything. everything.
now I have the best boyfriend I've ever had. but just like every other one, he can't get me off. big dick? oral sex? tons of foreplay? kink? it's all there. nothing works. I used to lie to my boyfriends and say it was ok that I couldn't get off. then at least they could enjoy sex

without feeling guilty. but then they'd stop trying, of course. and this one is still trying... sometimes. I mean, it's clearly never going to work. so I can't blame him for not having the same passion for trying as he used to. and I keep thinking I should back off. after all, why put pressure on him to "perform"? he'll just resent me if I keep asking for more, even if I'm gentle about it and compliment him and all that. since nothing he does works. it will never work.

and I try so hard not to get frustrated, but I can't avoid the knowledge that I am fucked up, I must be broken. I mean, any normal woman would have come by now. so what do I do? I don't know what I need. do I back off and focus on him? that's what I end up doing, because I can't face asking for a little more attention in bed anymore. what's the point? he'll just resent me when it doesn't work again. so I back off. and I can't help resenting him, just a little, for not noticing how much I'm hurting. and not trying, even if I am broken, and I will never ever come.

* * *

I. *Vaginal Pain*

When I wrote the above, I was actually pretty close to figuring out how to have an orgasm. But I didn't know that. I'd dealt with the anxiety of being unable to come for so long — and I'd also recently begun to understand that my sexuality is oriented towards S&M — and so anguish just flooded out of me, into those words. I craved S&M, but acknowledging the craving made me feel like a "pervert," a "freak." It contributed to my already-overwhelming fear that I was "broken" because I couldn't figure out how to come.

There's one thing I didn't mention when I poured out all that fear and shame: I experience rare vaginal pain — not every time I have sex, not even most times, but occasionally. Medical science has traditionally failed to care about how women experience our sexuality, so very little research has been done on the subject. As a result, it's impossible to say why I get that pain. Is it some kind of physical problem? That seems likely, because my psychological comfort level with a sexual encounter doesn't seem to correlate with whether the pain happens or not. But because female sexuality is often stereotyped as too mysterious and emotional to be worth rigorous medical investigation, I doubt I'll ever know for sure.

For a while I was sure I was allergic to semen, because I read a magazine feature by a woman who said she was. *Aha,* I thought. I stopped taking hormonal birth control pills. I made my trusted monogamous boyfriends use condoms. The pain became less common. Yet throughout that time — continuing through today — I still get the pain occasionally, very occasionally. Sometimes I even feel the pain during encounters that lack vaginal penetration, so it's clearly not about having a penis in me.

I can push through the pain; I can even have an orgasm, a reflex that feels good yet is surrounded by not-good; but I can't get rid of the pain entirely. Whenever I think I'll never feel it again, it sneaks into some sexual encounter.

The semen allergy theory has been ruled out, since I get the pain without semen contact. That doesn't mean that hormonal birth control didn't have an effect, though — the pain was definitely worse while I was taking it. The Pill intersects with sexuality in ways we still don't understand; one common side effect is that it reduces sex drive. Perhaps the Pill affected my sexuality in some physical-medical way, worsening the pain problem.

The long and the short of it is that I experience some vaginal pain; the pain is confusing and hard to predict, and there aren't any good medical resources on the matter. Maybe the pain points to something unusual about my constitution. Maybe there's a reason it's harder for me to have orgasms than the "average" woman.

But the vaginal pain itself is not overwhelming, on the rare occasions that it crops up. And the vaginal pain is not even close to the most central issue of my sexuality — or the biggest influence on my orgasmic ability.

* * *

II. *S&M*

I identify my sexuality as BDSM — a.k.a. kink, leather, fetish, S&M, or B&D. BDSM is a 6-for-4 acronym that encompasses a host of related activities, including bondage, discipline, dominance, submission, sadism and masochism. And yeah, I'm **really** into it: my desires are heavy and overwhelming; I dream of agony, of terrified screams for mercy. I've gone so far as to describe BDSM as my sexual orientation.

Before someone goes leaping to conclusions, there is a definite difference between "good pain" and "bad pain." The occasional pain I feel within my vagina is not good pain; it's not even interesting. It's just annoying. It's not sexy or enjoyable at all.

Some of us in the BDSM community have felt lifelong tendencies towards BDSM. We have conversations ending with thrilled exclamations: "You mean, you tied up your Barbie dolls as a child **too**?!" But BDSM is widely misunderstood and negatively stereotyped, and thus, many of us also went through periods of rejection. We've internalized so much anti-BDSM stigma from society that, at times, we freak out. We deny or erase our BDSM desires.

That's what happened to me when I was in middle school. As my sexuality made itself more and more evident, my anxiety peaked. I'd been producing secret sadomasochistic art and stories without labeling what I was doing, but I stopped. I blockaded my thoughts of violent power-play. I closed it all away as thoroughly as I could.

I still felt sexual desire — I mean, I was entering my teens, so of course I did. Sometimes I felt so much desire, like in the middle of some inconvenient class, that I'd have to rest my burning forehead on the cold desk. I would close my eyes, and breathe deeply, and wait for the erotic shiver to pass. At home, I'd lie around my twin bed and dream about kisses; imagine men's hair and skin and touch.

Yet it was hard for me to trace my desire, to take control of it. I thought I had no problem with the idea of masturbation, but when I touched my own lady bits, I went cold. Vibrators did nothing but bore me.

I had excellent sex education, thank goodness. I went through a Unitarian Universalist sex education program that talked carefully about different experiences, that made space for gay and lesbian and bisexual and transgender and queer folks. I didn't only learn about sexually transmitted infections and pregnancy and condom usage; I was also encouraged to explore my sexuality, to value it. But this marvelous curriculum did not include BDSM and other non-standard sexual identities. Nor did it include much advice on how to negotiate sexual encounters with my partners. So, although I internalized many positive and feminist messages about sex, my own sexuality remained invisible, bewildering and hard to talk about.

When I started having sex around my mid-teens, I liked it — I liked it a lot — but it seemed weirdly lacking. I'd never figured out how to masturbate, so I couldn't show my partners how to pleasure me. And although I occasionally suspected that I wanted something like S&M, I didn't understand how far I wanted to go.

A couple of teenage boyfriends tied me up... but then they acted solicitous and went down on me, which didn't send me over the moon (though it was fun). From this, I concluded that S&M was boring, but the truth is, I hadn't come close to the extremes that form my preferences. It was years later that I released my need for agony, tears, bruises and blood.

* * *

III. *Frigid*

As I got older and had more sex, my apparent inability to orgasm became the most toxic secret I had. Most of my closest friends didn't know. For a while I thought I must be "frigid," and ripped myself apart over the idea that I was a "frigid bitch," even though that made no sense. It was ridiculous to conceptualize myself that way — my sexual desire was undeniable, unavoidable. But I had no other words, no other images or stereotypes, that described a pre-orgasmic woman.

When I did tell my friends, it almost never went well. The best-case scenario was a conversation with anecdotal fragments: "I knew a girl," one friend advised, "who couldn't have orgasms. Then one day she was tripping, and having sex, and she fell asleep, and when she woke up she was having an orgasm."

I also found a book on my father's top shelf, written by a guy who said he could give "any" girl a squirting orgasm. The author claimed that the key was for the woman to be comfortable. He also claimed that the woman had to not know what he was trying to do. In fact, the book explicitly recommended that men prevent their girlfriends from reading it.

Needless to say, it was hard to extrapolate a Unified Orgasm Theory from these tales. The only things that seemed clear were that I somehow needed to both "let go" and to "keep trying." But how?

Every once in a while I made the mistake of telling someone who was convinced they knew the answer — which was: sleep with **them**. When I got drunk with one sexually experienced male friend and asked for advice, he insisted that if I'd just fuck him I'd be sure to come. "Anytime you want," he slurred, "I'll give you an orgasm. Guaranteed!" The fact that I was not attracted to him was, in his view, unimportant.

Worse was my lesbian female friend who declared that I had "issues." She said that I ought to sleep with a woman. Ultimately, she turned out to be right that the problem was one of sexual identity, but she was wrong that I was a repressed bisexual. Her campaign to get me to sleep with her ended in a threesome with a guy I had a crush on. I liked bits of that evening, but most of it was boring — if not distasteful. When I tried to talk to my friend honestly about it later, she insisted that I loved the whole experience. She said that I was merely feeling morning-after guilt. "You were totally into it," she informed me. She was clearly smug with victory, but angry that I resisted her version of events. I felt resentful for years.

I didn't even tell my partners about my orgasm difficulties until I'd known them for a while, because my secret felt like such Restricted Information: I couldn't give it to anyone I didn't trust. I couldn't abide the idea of "everyone knowing" how broken I felt. I couldn't stand the combination of pity and fascination that my problem evoked in the few who knew.

When I did get around to telling my partners, that was most complicated of all. I was quite unpopular in high school, and so I was something of a late bloomer — boyfriend-free until my late teens. It took years before I had any confidence in my boyfriend interactions. And because I had no idea how to come and no idea where to start and little idea of how to communicate about sex, I could not give guidance about what I wanted.

I also felt paranoid that lovers would resent me if they felt I was demanding something too "difficult" during the sexual "exchange," so I downplayed my feelings. I told awful lies like "it's not a big deal that I can't come" — lies that broke my heart as I spoke them, but felt safer than the truth.

I did manage to have one orgasm in my teens — one. I'm still not sure how it happened. It occurred one evening when I was incredibly tired, but went out with friends to get a fudge brownie sundae anyway. When I got back, my boyfriend came over and wanted to have sex, and I let it happen — despite being tired and uninterested and full of sundae — because I had not yet internalized the notion that my boyfriends wouldn't hate me if I denied them sex. I was barely present during the act, but I jolted into awareness when I realized I was having an orgasm. Afterwards, exhaustion overwhelmed me and I fell straight into sleep — so deep that my boyfriend was unable to wake me.

This was puzzling and hard to analyze. What aspects of my singular orgasm should go into my Unified Theory... and which aspects were irrelevant?

The chocolate? Well, chocolate is arguably a mild drug, and drugs help some people come. Also, there were studies that found mild aphrodisiac qualities to chocolate. So maybe.

The position? The position had felt really good but was

somewhat awkward, and I felt weird asking my boyfriend to reproduce it, so I didn't let myself think about the position. (I'm much better at communicating with my partners now.)

What about the exhaustion? It made sense that being very tired might help me "let go." But I hadn't been very turned on or enjoyed the rest of the encounter, mostly because I was so exhausted; and I didn't want to deliberately force myself to have sex while tired. So while the exhaustion might have been a factor, I filed it under "less-than-useful" as well.

I didn't worry about the problem too much for a while, because I figured that now that I'd had one orgasm, surely it would become easy. I didn't tell my boyfriend it had happened, either, because I didn't know how to describe exactly how. I thought I'd figure it out as we went along, and then I would tell him exactly what it took.

Unfortunately, it wasn't that easy. Months and years passed without replicating the incident. Anxiety began seeping back. My Unified Orgasm Theory was not doing well.

My fear of being perceived as "demanding" during sex and relationships was at a ridiculous extreme back then. For example, I'd heard over and over that boys don't like girls who are "high-maintenance," so I told my boyfriends that I never wanted them to buy me flowers. I thought that men would feel relieved that they didn't "have to cater to me," but they were just puzzled. (One responded by buying me fake flowers.)

Because of the awful shaming stereotypes around cunnilingus, I sometimes refused that too. I couldn't believe that the boyfriends who were willing to go down on me were actually enthusiastic about it, enjoying it — and when my anxiety became too painful, I inevitably stopped them. I always stopped them long before I stopped enjoying the act, because I was so scared that they hated it, and hated me for wanting it. I was scared that they resented me more and more, the longer they did it and I didn't come. My fear crept up my spine and twisted around my heart until I **had** to make them stop.

Sometimes I felt trapped between love and disgust, like with the boyfriend who constantly complimented me on how great in bed I was, but who seemed unaware of how much I felt missing. The worst was when he went off on a rhapsodic list of my wonderful qualities ending with: "... and I don't even have to worry about giving you an orgasm!" He didn't see the bind he was putting me in, the awful self-suppression and self-wounding that he encouraged. He seemed unaware that I heard him telling me: "You're great in bed because you are constantly disappearing your own needs, and never asking anything complicated of me!"

In fairness, I wasn't giving him any guidance on how to do better with me. In fairness, I had no idea what kind of guidance to give.

They had their own social programming, and I didn't communicate well. But sometimes I still have trouble forgiving my early boyfriends.

* * *

IV. *The Fight*

Not all my boyfriends were willing to do as little as going down on me. One, in particular, resisted very strongly; never did it at all. This was an especial problem because he was one of the men I've loved most in my life, and our relationship lasted for years. I think well of him when I think of anything other than sex. But when I remember having sex with him, I feel echoes of sick panic and heartbreak.

By the end, every time I slept with him I felt nothing but disgust.

He seemed to prove all my fears: that the men in my life would loathe and resent me if I tried to discuss my confusion and desperation; that they would loathe and resent me if I asked for help with my sexual needs. Towards the beginning of our relationship, I tried asking him (very timidly) to go down on me, and he simply refused. In later conversations he insisted that cunnilingus was "too degrading," an assertion he made with a weird lack of irony, given that I was going down on him regularly.

As the years passed, my frustration deepened and I started thinking about experimenting more sexually, but I was terrified of mentioning it. I didn't know what I wanted to experiment with — I really believed that I'd "already tried" BDSM, and that I didn't like it — but his initial rejection of mere cunnilingus didn't make me feel confident.

Finally, I got to the point of directly asking for sexual experimentation, and we had the worst fight ever.

I recall that our relationship was somewhat rocky already. One of my journal entries from that time contains the sentence, "I can't seem to **not** make him angry when I'm trying to discuss our relationship." For this particular fight, we were sitting in his room reading when I scraped together my courage and asked for his help in figuring out my sexuality. "Well, what do you want me to do?" he demanded.

"I don't know," I said, "but I think there must be some way to find out — I don't know, there have to be books?"

"That's **ridiculous**," he snapped. "I love you, but I'm not going to **read books** in order to figure out how to have sex with you."

It got worse from there. I was crying within the first few sentences. At one point, he outright shouted at me "I don't care about your satisfaction," at which point I said, "You can't mean that," and he repeated it. Eventually, I simply turned around and walked out of his room. I had nowhere to go; it was a long train ride to visit him, and the trains had stopped running that day. It was mid-winter, and freezing cold. Crying, I put on my coat and shoes and exited the house, onto his suburban street.

I walked completely at random. I was hardly able to see. Fortunately, because it was so cold, no one else was out and about. I muffled my sobs by bowing my head into my collar. After fifteen minutes, I discovered my cell phone in my pocket and tried to call my best friend, but she didn't answer. I was still walking around crying an hour later, when she returned the call.

She calmed me down and got the story out of me. It was the first she'd heard about my inability to orgasm, and she didn't know how to advise me because she didn't have the same problem. Also, it was obvious to both of us that trying to communicate with my boyfriend wasn't working. It was obvious that there might be no way to successfully communicate with him on this topic at all.

Eventually, after she'd managed to quiet me into a trembling jellylike mass, my friend said gently, "Okay, hon, you need to hang up and go back inside." She was right. So I did.

When I stepped back into my boyfriend's room, he was still reading. I could sense from the texture of our silence that he felt bad, though. I was exhausted, I felt like a stiff breeze would blow me apart, but I told myself that I had to set a line. I was sure my voice would waver as I made myself say: "If you're going to tell me that you don't care about my sexual satisfaction, then I can't do this anymore...."

"I never said that," he said softly.

I closed my eyes. He would do this sometimes, insist that he hadn't said words I was **sure** I'd heard, and it always made me feel like I had gone insane. I **knew** he'd said it. I'd even responded with, "You can't mean that," and then he'd **repeated** it. But I felt so tired. It had been hard enough to start the conversation. Hard enough to walk around the streets crying for hours.

Maybe I really did misunderstand him somehow; I've been over those moments in my head a million times, and I don't know anymore. Maybe I misunderstood. Or maybe he was falling into a classic pattern of emotional abusers. Maybe he insisted that I was hallucinating in order to confuse me out of protesting: abusers do these things because they work. [1]

What I do know for sure is that when he halted the conversation with a flat denial, I couldn't bring myself to even try to talk about it again. Couldn't bring myself to resume the conversation. But I also couldn't bring myself to break up with someone I loved so much. We talked about other things instead.

And, of course, nothing about our sex life changed at all.

When my best friend called me the next day to check in, I said, "Well, he says that he didn't say what I thought he did."

Her silence echoed with disbelief.

"Maybe I just... didn't understand what he actually meant," I said, but my words sounded weak even to my own ears.

"Maybe," she said doubtfully, but she didn't press the issue.

Even after that fight, I continued dating that man for a long time. I look back now and I can't imagine how I did it.

* * *

V. *Men's Perspective*

The gendered societal pressures that affect men are worth discussing, and worth analyzing, and I often do just that. There is undeniable pressure on men to "perform" sexually, for example. I try to have sympathy for men who feel this pressure — but it is difficult sometimes, because its major effect on **my** life has been to silence me. To make me feel as though I couldn't ask for anything sexually. As though I couldn't express my needs without hurting my boyfriend's feelings or making him angry.

And even now, when I talk about this stuff, I am as vague as I possibly can be about the exact timeline. The last thing I want is for people who know me to read this and know exactly when I started having orgasms. I don't want anyone to know exactly which partners "couldn't perform." Because I know those men might feel it as a social punishment, and as much as I hate the dynamics at work, I can't hate the men who were part of them. They had their own social anxieties and their own blind spots and if I didn't understand what was wrong, how could they?

I recently had dinner with a former partner. At one point we found ourselves having a very explicit conversation, and I mentioned that I've figured out how to come. He looked sad and apologized: "I'm sorry I was never able to get you there." I had no idea what to say.

* * *

VI. *S&M, Redux*

I finally came into my BDSM identity around age 20. At first, when I was faced with the fact that I wanted to be hurt until I cried and begged for mercy, I freaked out. I had no idea what to do about BDSM, no idea how to feel about it. The only thing I knew for sure was that I'd found something I really **needed**. But what did that **mean** for me, when I was also trying hard to be an independent, rational feminist with self-esteem and integrity?

It took me years to parse out my thoughts on feminism and BDSM, to feel comfortable with BDSM, and to talk openly and comfortably about it. During that process, I got better and better at finding partners who were interested in my sexual desires and willing to experiment. I also got to the point of reading sexuality advice books on my own, including books specifically on BDSM. (For recommendations, please check the notes at the beginning of this book.)

And I gritted my teeth, forced down my anxiety, and looked into books about the female orgasm.

One book that came highly recommended from Amazon.com was Lonnie Barbach's *For Yourself.* By the time I was halfway through the first chapter, I was crying because what she wrote felt so true. At the end of the first chapter, I put it down and was never able to pick it up again. Barbach wrote compassionately about experiences very similar to mine — for instance: *[Are you afraid to talk to your partner about your problem] because you're embarrassed to ask for what you want at a particular time; afraid your partner will refuse, get angry, or feel emasculated?*

But she also ended the first chapter this way: *You have to assume responsibility and be somewhat assertive. Our culture has taught us that a woman should depend on a man to take care of her, which means she can blame him for any mistakes. It's nice to be driven around in a car, but it's also nice to be able to drive yourself so you can go where you want to, when you want to. But to do that, you'd have to assume some responsibility.*

It was the same "let go" and "keep trying" advice I'd been coming across for years, except that now it was wrapped up in a nice package of assumptions about me: implications that I wasn't assuming responsibility or being assertive. I felt like she was telling me that I chose to depend on a man to take care of me.

Maybe it would have been okay if the rest of the chapter hadn't been so miserably true, but the combination of reading a bunch of truth about how I was feeling — then being told that I wasn't trying hard enough, that I was choosing to avoid responsibility.... It was toxic.

I also had the bright idea of asking my gynecologist. The doctor rolled her eyes as I spoke, then told me that the problem was obviously my partners. When I insisted that I needed more guidance, she referred me to a center that gave orgasmic dysfunction "evaluations" at $1,500.00 a pop. I was earning $7.50 per hour at the time. I didn't go.

I got up my nerve and talked to my mother, who had been extremely helpful and caring when I came out to her about BDSM. During the BDSM conversation, I'd been scared — then I felt immense relief as Mom told me that there was nothing wrong with me, and reassured me that I wasn't "giving up my liberation." When it came to orgasms, though, she seemed unsure of what to say. She did at least tell me that she, too, couldn't come easily, which made me feel a little better.

Most helpful was the therapist I found on the Kink Aware Professionals list — an online list of doctors, lawyers, and other professionals who believe they understand alternative sexualities such as BDSM. [2] I tried one therapist who didn't seem to get it, but the second therapist I saw was wonderful. He helped me through an enormous amount of my BDSM anxiety. The orgasm problem was thornier, but he didn't make any assumptions, and he did listen carefully, which was more than most people did.

My therapist gently encouraged me to get a second opinion about my how my body worked, from a new gynecologist. Irrationally, I didn't. I suppose I still felt crushed by how the first gynecologist had reacted. I also hoped I'd learn to come as I explored BDSM more — which turned out to be true.

* * *

VII. *Figuring It Out*

In retrospect, I recognize that I went through a brief period where I had orgasms sometimes — weak ones. But the orgasms were hard to hang on to because they happened during sex with my boyfriend. This would be the same boyfriend I described at the beginning of this piece, when I wrote: *now I have the best boyfriend I've ever had. but just like every other one, he can't get me off. big dick? oral sex? tons of foreplay? kink? it's all there.*

Now I see, in retrospect, that **not** everything was there: neither of us had questioned our sexual assumptions, our societally-determined sexual scripts. And one of the biggest sexual scripts is that sex ends with the man's orgasm. That the man's orgasm is the goal.

It's very hard to think around these scripts. It's very hard to even be aware of them. So, since my paramount goal during sex was obviously "satisfying my man," I often pushed my orgasm away due to my focus on him. I knew that if I came then I'd feel tired and less interested in sex (at least for a while). And obviously, if he were to have his all-important manly orgasm, I couldn't go falling asleep on him could I? I couldn't even pause to mentally process my sensations if he seemed to be enjoying himself, now could I? Plus, once he'd come, I certainly couldn't expect him to stimulate me any more than he already had, because he was tired; he'd just had an orgasm!

(These days, one of my #1 judgments of whether a new partner could be good for me is this: if I didn't come before he did, then does he take a moment post-orgasm to catch his breath, and then turn to me and smile and offer to do what it takes?)

In the end, figuring it out was almost anticlimactic.

I saw an online video from sex educator Betty Dodson called "Did I Orgasm?"... and I realized that I'd been occasionally having weak orgasms already. [3] I was also experimenting more and more with BDSM; simultaneously, I put more and more power into the hands of my fantasy men; and once I had compelling private fantasies to feed on, I couldn't help masturbating. Here was the key: initially, I'd felt that masturbating **in itself** involved having too much control over the situation. And that's not how my sexuality worked.

Oh yes, **in practice** I take responsibility for my pleasure; and now I'm pretty good at clearly discussing what kind of role my partners will take ahead of time, describing what they'll do with me. These days, I sometimes take the dominant role, too. But even now, it's hard for me to come if I **feel like** I'm in control.

On some level, even if it's the most tissue-thin fantasy, I usually have to convince my emotional-sexual self that I'm not in charge. It helps if I have an emotional connection with whoever I'm fantasizing about, too. If I don't have an emotionally involved romantic partner, I seem to automatically create BDSM-themed fantasy worlds with hilariously ornate storylines. Years ago, it never occurred to me that I couldn't reach orgasm because my internal characters weren't compelling or my plotlines weren't dramatic enough... but sometimes it's true!

In my case, I believe that BDSM is the key to my sexuality. It is as close to the core of my sexual identity as I can get; close enough that, like some other BDSMers, I occasionally call it my "orientation." But I don't think BDSM is like that for everyone, and I don't even think that's the whole story with me — because during the whole time, this self-discovery process, I was doing things like eating more regularly, keeping a healthier diet, putting some weight on my previously stick thin frame, and exercising more. Health plays a big role in any kind of sex, and it's important to think about. Still, even now I can't come without some thread of dominance and submission, even if it's an entirely internal fantasy that I imprint on whatever is happening.

When women ask me for advice on how to have orgasms, I feel helpless because there is no "one true way." I don't want to fall back on the old "let go" and "keep trying" that I received — it's decent advice, but it's so vague. Perhaps something more useful would be this: first, it really helps to have an idea of what you want. I know this can be hard in a society that soaks us with sexual images designed for stereotypical men, rather than images for women (and especially not for non-normative women like myself). And I feel so aware of how patronizing and useless the "you aren't in touch with your sexuality, that's why you can't come" argument can be. Remember, I had that argument used against me by my lesbian friend. But it was, in fact, kinda true for me — just in a different way: I need BDSM.

If you're not sure what you want, don't panic. Just keep your eyes and ears open, and try to monitor your reactions. It may surprise you. If it does, don't worry — just research it! No matter how unusual your sexuality, there is probably information on the Internet about it. (And even if your sexuality is unusual, odds are it's not nearly as unusual as you think it is.)

I often refer to my personal favorite sex education website in the entire world: it's Scarleteen.com, a grassroots feminist effort with an amazingly comprehensive perspective. Scarleteen has an incredible impact on many, many lives. Sometimes I read it just for fun!

Secondly: it may help not to prioritize orgasms. I am not saying orgasms aren't important; I just don't want the importance of orgasms to wound you, the way it wounded me. For me, it is helpful to imagine sex as a journey. For me, it helps to focus on having fun throughout, instead of doing what it takes to reach the "goal" of orgasm. If you're not taking pleasure in the journey — or at least indulging some curiosity — then why keep going? Why not stop and try something else?

Experimenting sexually in an open-ended way has been, for me, the most productive possible attitude. And in fact, once I knew how to make myself come, I discovered that — though it's helpful to be able to attain that release if I really want to — orgasms aren't actually my favorite part of sex! There are lots of other things I like better.

It's also worth noting that our definitions of "orgasm" are fairly narrow. Some research indicates that there may be other ways to conceptualize orgasms than the stereotypical genital-focused approach. [4]

Thirdly, although it's possible for a person to explore sexuality on her own, relationships can make or break the process. We all make some compromises for romance. But when we compromise, we should know **what** we're compromising, and **we should think about whether the compromise is worth it**.

For me, sexual exploration and satisfaction are incredibly important — but it took ages to develop the courage to put my foot down about them. After my boyfriend shouted at me that he didn't care about my sexual satisfaction, it took me an embarrassingly long time to end things with him; I really was in love, and we'd been together for years. But my sexuality wasn't even close to a priority for him, and breaking up with him was one of the best decisions I ever made.

After ending that relationship, I was able to build my self-confidence and self-esteem with new boyfriends surprisingly fast — and my boyfriends helped me more than they probably know. I owe countless small debts to men who accepted my inability to orgasm, took my anxieties about it into account, and sometimes gently pushed me to try new things.

One particular guy comes to mind: I told him I couldn't come, but that I wanted to experiment with S&M, so we arranged to buy rope and some painful equipment. During our conversation, he gently drew me out on my history, and then he said, "You know what I think we need to go along with this rope? A vibrator."

I blinked and said hesitantly, "I don't know, I've never really liked vibrators." But I was willing to try it again, and that's when I learned that vibrators are awesome. That's when I learned that what I really need is to convince myself I'm not in charge — that once the correct fantasy is in place, vibrators make everything easy.

Even today, few things make me happier than a man who grasps the tension I still sometimes feel about "being demanding" or "asking for too much." I communicate with straightforwardness that amazes most partners, but it's crucial for them to understand that I still have hesitations. That even I, sometimes, need a moment to articulate what I want — or need to be asked whether there's anything he can do.

Lastly, and most importantly: don't let go of your boundaries unless you're sure you're ready. If you really don't want to do something, **you don't have to make yourself do it**. I'm writing this because when I was growing up, all the sex-positive work I read encouraged exploration at the cost of boundaries, and I think that's wrong. There were times when that attitude hurt me — for example, I did things I didn't like because people claimed I hadn't yet gotten over my sexual "issues," like my lesbian friend in college. And I know that attitude has hurt other women, too.

I don't like seeing sex-positive feminism equated with making oneself freely sexually available. Exploring sexuality does not mean you have to ignore your warning bells.

Sexuality is so complicated. Sex cannot be reduced to bodies, or hormones, or psychological stereotypes. Sex cannot be reduced to certainties, to shoulds and shouldn'ts. If I could destroy every force in our lives that drives home ideas of sexual "normality," I would. Which leads to my final piece of advice: **don't let me tell you what to do**. This is just my experience, just my ideas. As with everything, I want you to do whatever feels right for you — as long as it's among consenting adults.

* * *

VIII. *Study Questions!*

Here are some things that might be interesting to reflect on:

1) What questions do you have about your orgasm?
1a) Where have you researched the answers to those questions?
1b) Have you ever discussed those questions with your partners?

2) What questions do you have about your partners' orgasms?
2a) Have you ever asked your partners about their orgasms?

3) What's one thing you wish you'd said in bed to a partner?
3a) What would have made it easier to say it?

4) What are your favorite sexual acts? Are there other ways you could perform them?

5) What's the best sexual experience you remember? What made it great?

6) What's the hottest thing you've seen or read? What made it great and are there ways you could participate?

7) Does anything from this article resonate with you? What?

* * *

Here is a tangential footnote on issues of manliness:

When this article was first posted, a guy grabbed the first comment on the version that I posted to the feminist blog *Feministe*, protesting that I clearly don't get the men's side of this equation. I don't usually get super angry about comments on the Internet, but in that case I did, and I had to take a while to calm down.

There was a mild comment fracas. Eventually, in response to that guy, I wrote:

I worked really hard on this article to try and note both:
A) how men's perspective might make this difficult for them, but simultaneously
B) why men's insecurities aren't actually an excuse for men to treat women badly.
In my experience women are actually extremely aware of men's insecurities. **Women frequently silence themselves and put up with a lot of crap because we are afraid of "emasculating" our man, as I specifically noted in the article.**
Given that this was an article about:
1) a woman's experience,
2) and what it's like to be a woman,
3) and why this issue is difficult to take on as a woman,
4) and why women shouldn't allow men's insecurities to shut us

up...

 ... *can you see why I would avoid putting a lot of text towards describing men's insecurities in loving detail?*

Now. With that having been said....

One of the guys in the Clarisse Thorn Manliness Brain Trust (tm) emailed me with some thoughts in the wake of this article. Once again, I want to emphasize that I don't want anyone to feel that they "ought to" give a crappy partner "another chance" if that partner is treating them badly. I spent **years** giving a terrible boyfriend millions of second chances because I kept telling myself that he was just "insecure." **Walking away from that oh-so-"insecure" man was one of the best choices I ever made.** Nonetheless, I think that the following comment from my Manliness Brain Trust (tm) friend might be useful for some people:

When I first saw this post, my first thought was that I have to pass it on to a couple of the people I'm involved with, who have difficulty reaching orgasm because it's an awesome, awesome article. My second thought was that it seemed like Clarisse didn't really grok the guy's side of this exchange.

Somewhere among 5th, 7th and 9th thoughts, was the notion that I'd be a jerk to raise that point in the comments. This article is a great reference for women working through difficult climax issues and there's no need to drag the conversation off to the guy side of the experience... So I sent Clarisse an email about it instead. Because the thing with Unification theories is that they're never all the way done. And things could have been so much easier for Clarisse if her boyfriends didn't suck. Maybe some insight into why they sucked would help with the ongoing development of the model, or at least provide some eased management strategies.

The thing is, I don't feel attacked or diminished or anything else by this article. Despite the fact that I'm a guy, I have insecurities and I can in some places see a stupid, obnoxious mirror of myself in Clarisse's dumb ex boyfriends — that isn't at all why I thought I should talk about the topic more with the author. It just seemed to me like Clarisse hadn't quite got her head around what the guys were going through with their side of this interaction. Where their insecurities came into play.

In my head, I see a young woman, working through her own issues with orgasms reading this, and seeing her young boyfriend reflected in Clarisse's past relationships. And the take away from Clarisse's experience at the moment seems to be that if your boyfriend is insecure and stupid, maybe he's not the right person to work through this with you. And I'm not sure that's doing anyone any favors. I mean shit, maybe that is what you should take away from reading this — that the guy you're with isn't the right person for you right now if you're struggling with difficulty achieving orgasm. But maybe there are other stories going on as well. Maybe he's insecure about his role and his failings (or his body or whatever) and maybe he could be the right guy to work through this with you, if you're the right person to work through his insecurities with him?

And please, please don't take that to mean let things slide because you don't want to emasculate him. I'm not for a moment advocating putting up with nonsense because he's a guy with a precious male ego. But lots of guys, certainly including myself, have personal insecurities, about masculinity and about sexuality, and attached to the perceptions of masculinity in sexual situations. As a guy, we're all taught that real men don't give head — or at least that it's a private thing that we don't admit too — which is so fucking stupid, but is still really out there in heteronormative western male culture. We're all taught that getting a woman off is our job, and to be a good man, and a good lover, we have to get our partner off before we get off. I don't know a single sexually active guy who has never felt humiliated because he came too early, and too early is largely defined as before our partner gets off. And we're all taught that real men get their partners off with nothing but the awesomeness of our cocks. Hand jobs/digital penetration are fine for highschool or fore play — but our image of a good man, and a desirable lover doesn't integrate with those things. We're coached by pop culture and porn to believe that the guy every woman wants is the one who sticks his cock in and makes her explode with joy from the very first thrust. And any time that doesn't happen, the guy is at fault.

And again, to stress my position here, I think all of those things are stupid, illogical nonsense. But those are the pressures that are on guys. And maybe, if the guy that you're with is struggling to work through your orgasm issues, maybe it's because he's so far under the weight of his own insecurities that he doesn't know how to cope with his own issues, and be a supportive partner to work through yours. But the thing about a good relationship, is that together you're stronger than the sum of your individualities. Maybe as a couple, you can work through his insecurities and your orgasm difficulties at the same time. Nobody's problems exist in a vacuum, and sometimes finding the support you need is easier if you just fix the support you already have.

I posted the comment in response to the other dude's *Feministe* comment, and there was some discussion afterwards — including some guys saying that they never got any memo about cunnilingus being "not manly."

Here's my wrap-up: sympathy is good. Trying to build a better relationship is good. And I understand that some people may have serious, important reasons that they can't or don't want to walk away from their romantic partner. (That's one of the things feminism has always worked towards: giving people many sources of support and safety nets, so people can leave abusive partners if necessary.) But. Seriously, if your partner sucks? Walking away is an option — it's even an option, sometimes, when you think it's not an option. Just remember that.

* * *

This post can be found on the Internet at:
http://clarissethorn.com/blog/2011/10/31/a-unified-theory-of-orgasm/

* * *

***

BOUNDARIES:
[storytime] I'm Not Your Sex-Crazy Nympho Dreamgirl

This was originally published in 2011 on GoodMenProject.com, and it got a lot of attention. I think the feelings I outline in this piece are shared by a lot of people, and that they're one of the reasons people often get angry about porn. But as I said in "BDSM Can Be 'Love Sex' Too," I don't think restricting porn is the answer to these feelings. I think the answer is encouraging people to be honest, yet respectful and flexible about their desires. For many people, mainstream porn seems to function as sex education — and that can be a real problem, because mainstream porn shows a very specific stereotype of sexuality. But if more people had better and more complete sex education, then more people would recognize that mainstream porn is a very limited and particular product, and they'd also recognize that most people aren't interested in actually enacting that style of sexuality. I also think porn probably receives an unfair portion of the blame in these debates. It's possible that the current ubiquity of porn is partly to blame for "sex-crazy nympho dreamgirl" anxieties, but there are plenty of other stereotype sources in our culture — I wish that all the people who talk about banning porn would also talk about banning romantic comedies!

***

There's this cultural image of what it means to be female, and good in bed. The image includes being young and thin and cisgendered of course, and that can be problematic. But it also includes a lot of behavioral stuff: the way you squirm, the way you moan, being Super Excited about everything the guy wants to do, and Always Being Up for It — whatever "It" is. When people think about "good in bed," for a woman, that's often what they think.

Here's a short list of some things I think are totally awesome:
+ Squirming and moaning during sex in a genuine way, out of genuine pleasure!

+ Acting Super Excited when your partner wants to do something you're actually Super Excited about!

+ Being up for sexual experimentation and trying new things, while keeping track of your boundaries and saying no (or calling your safeword) to sexual things you really don't like!

Those things are great. They're great when they happen in all kinds of sex, and I have no problem with how people experience or deal with with those things — whether people get them from vanilla or S&M sex, or porn, or sex with multiple people, or queer sex, or whatever. All consensual sex is fine with me. (In particular, in pieces like the one you're about to read, I often have to make it really clear that I'm not anti-porn. OK? I'm not anti-porn. Got that? Say it with me now: Clarisse Thorn is not anti-porn. Yay, it rhymes!)

What scares me, however — what continuously gets my goat, what still occasionally makes me feel weird about sex — is how easy it is to **perform** those three things I listed above. Because I have always, since before I even started having sex, known exactly **what I was supposed to look like** while I had sex. I don't even know how I internalized those images: some of them through porn, I suppose, or art or erotica or what have you; some of them by reading sex tips on the Internet or hearing the ones whispered to me by friends. But I can definitely assure you that before I had any actual sexual partners, I knew how to give a good blowjob. I also knew how to tilt my head back and moan, and I knew how to twist my body, and I knew what my reactions and expressions were supposed to look and sound like — I knew all those things much better than I knew what would make me react.

There was a while there, where my sexuality was mostly performance: an image, an act, a shell that I created because I knew it was hot for my partners. I'm not saying I was performing 100% of the time — but certainly, when I was just starting to have sex, that's mostly what it was. And, scarily, I can put the shell back on at any time. Sometimes it's hard to resist, because I know men will **reward** me for it, emotionally, with affection and praise. It's much, much more difficult to get what I actually want out of a sexual interaction than it is for me to create that sexy dreamgirl shell: hard for me to communicate my desires, hard for me to know what I'm thinking, hard for me to set boundaries.

And hard to believe that a guy will like me as much, if I try to be honest about what I want. Honesty means that sometimes I'm confused, and sometimes we have to Talk About It; honesty means that sometimes I say no, it means that sometimes I'm not Up For It.

Something in me is always asking: *Surely he'd prefer the sexy, fake, plastic dreamgirl shell?* It's not true, I know it's not true, I swear it's not true — I don't have such a low opinion of men as that. I know this is just a stereotype, the idea that men are emotionally stunted horndogs with no interest in how their partners feel.

So sometimes, I have to fight myself not to perform. But it's worth it — because the hardest thing of all is feeling locked into an inauthentic sexuality. I tell myself, I try to force myself to believe it: even **if** a guy would like me more for faking and holding back and being so-called "low-maintenance" — I tell myself it's a stereotype, but even if that stereotype is true of some men — **no man is worth doing that to myself**. No man is worth that trapped, false, sick feeling.

* * *

Being a sex and S&M writer sometimes increases my performance anxiety. Occasionally I'll meet guys who seem to think I am equipped to give any man the Night Of His Life — and that this is my goal at all times. Sometimes I feel like I should grab certain guys by the shoulders and shake them and say, "**I am not your sex-crazy nympho dreamgirl!** I'm a real person and I have real preferences, I do not exist just as your fantasy fodder!" But if I really like a guy and he's read some of my work, then I feel less irritation than concern that I won't stack up. It increases the urge to go all Sexy Dreamgirl Shell, rather than attempting to communicate.

Being a sex-positive feminist, I also sometimes worry that other women will read my work and it will increase **their** performance anxiety. I worry that writing about some stuff I like will be misinterpreted — that it will lead other women to feel like, *gosh, is this something liberated sex-positive women do? Is this something I "should" be doing?* With some things I write, I get afraid that I've contributed to a nightmare world where women are "liberated" **only in the sense that we can better perform for men**.

I once read a blog post by a radical feminist writer in which she claimed that women always hate fellatio because it's always degrading and disgusting. She wrote something along the lines of, "I say this for the women and girls who believe that they have to do it." Part of me felt frustrated by the way she refused to acknowledge that some women really do **like** performing fellatio (and many other women don't love it, but don't mind doing it as long as they have great sex otherwise). In some ways, it felt like that writer was policing sexuality. But I empathized with her goal: She wanted women who don't like fellatio to relax; she wanted to help them recognize what they don't like. She wanted to decrease their performance anxiety.

I'd like to do the same thing, but I generally prefer to speak from personal experience rather than making claims about others' experience. Accordingly, I've often thought that it would be great if more sex-positive feminists would make lists of Things We, Personally, Don't Like. It's not the easiest project to sell, because one of the big goals of being sex-positive is to destigmatize sexuality and decrease shame. But if we destigmatize sexuality without encouraging good boundaries, then we're not moving forward; we're just creating more bad standards.

So hey, here's an example of a common sexual thing that I don't like: swallowing after giving oral sex. I love fellatio most of the time, and I like it when partners come in my mouth, but I really hate swallowing. In the past I've found a variety of creative ways to deal with this problem, some of which were hot (according to me, anyway) — but usually I just spit it out in the closest sink. (The reason I don't like swallowing is that it makes me physically ill. No, I am not interested in your armchair theories about why this happens; evidence so far implies a physical cause, not a psychological one.)

A more complicated example would be facials. As a sex-crazy nympho dreamgirl, I am supposed to love all facials all the time, to which I say: Bah. I'm occasionally into degradation scenes, and facials feel really degrading to me, so there are circumstances in which a guy can come on my face and it'll be hot — but those circumstances are rare. I've got to **really** respect him and **really** trust him, and I've got to be really turned on and excited about whatever scene we're playing out. And if a guy were to give me a facial without clearing it with me at some point ahead of time? Serious boundary violation. Not cool.

Have I destroyed your image of me as your sex-crazy nympho dreamgirl? Good.

I think that people of all genders receive a lot of unconscious training about how we can damage ourselves in exchange for the attention of the opposite sex. By writing about my own experience, I don't mean to discount the experiences of others. I get that many guys feel locked into acting confident and dominant, and that lots of guys hate that role as much as I hate my Sexy Dreamgirl Shell. I get that many women genuinely enjoy **reclaiming** the Sexy Dreamgirl image, and making it their own; hell, I do it myself sometimes. (Yes, I do it myself sometimes. Sex is complicated.)

People **of all genders** have a hard time figuring out what turns them on. Authenticity is hard — and sexual authenticity gets harder when you're feeling low, or you really like someone and really want that person to like you, or when you feel bombarded with messages about how you've got to "compete" in a harsh sexual "marketplace." I believe that one of the best ways to authenticity is to seek understanding of the pressures on everyone, and to grasp that everyone's got their own nightmare of the Sexy Dreamgirl Shell.

* * *

This can be found on the Internet at:
http://clarissethorn.com/blog/2011/05/27/im-not-your-sex-crazy-nympho-dreamgirl/

* * *

***

BOUNDARIES:
[storytime] Orgasms Aren't My Favorite Part Of Sex, and My Chastity Urge

These two articles were both written and published at OffOurChests.com after I published "A Unified Theory of Orgasm." The first was a followup to "A Unified Theory of Orgasm," and the second wasn't, but when I reviewed the two articles later, I concluded that they deal with fundamentally the same issues and belong together.

Interestingly, when I posted this to my blog, most of the comments didn't come from women; they came from men who agreed that orgasms aren't their favorite part of sex, either.

***

My previous piece "A Unified Theory of Orgasm" was really well-received, and a lot of people have thanked me for writing it. As always, though, there's some mixed feedback too. And I've been worried about one thing in particular: it seems like a lot of people missed the part in my article where I said that, now that I've learned how to have orgasms... **orgasms aren't even my favorite part of sex**. It's a long article, and I can see how people would miss that, but I did say it and I think it's important.

It may be ironic that I spent so much time feeling terrible and broken and depressed because I couldn't figure out how to have orgasms... whereas now I prefer not to focus on them. In fact, **I estimate that *most* of my current sexual encounters don't include my orgasm, and *very few* of my most pleasurable sexual encounters have included my orgasm.**

I'm the first to admit that I don't know everything about sex, and there's a lot that I haven't experienced. Anything might change. But seriously. The best sex I've had in my life has been connective and emotional and, for me personally, has frequently involved intense BDSM. My favorite sex so far? Has also mostly been orgasm-free.

Some people in some sex-related communities have asserted that for maximum amorous power, it's actually best to limit one's orgasms, because then the contained sexual energy ends up channeling into a deeper connection with one's partner. [1] I can see that. For me, another way of thinking about it is that I'm really into being teased — and I'd rather experience hours of being teased without an orgasm, than have a quick encounter that ends in orgasm.

And.... (Oh no, I can already tell this is going to get complicated... but hey, sex is complicated, so I'll give it a shot.).... Especially when I'm doing BDSM, it can actually be hot sometimes if I don't have an orgasm. For example: if I go to sleep so turned on that I can't dream about anything but my partner, and then I wake up in a damp mess, and then my partner makes my life difficult all morning, it's pretty awesome. (Although it's very nice that I know how to give myself orgasms now, because that means that if I'm really feeling overwhelmed by my own sexual energy, I know how to give myself release if I have to. You know, like... if I need to get some work done.)

Aaaaand... here's the most painful, ridiculous, circular irony of all. Ready? Here goes: now that I'm capable of having orgasms, I've found myself occasionally having orgasms **only to satisfy my partner**. How absurd is that? Plus, I know I'm not alone, because I've talked to other women who do the same thing!

I've written before that in the past I've felt trapped by fake plastic ideas of "what hot girls look like during sex"; I've written about how the pressure to "perform" my sexuality can hurt. What has amazed me, as I've gotten older, is just how pervasive that pressure can feel with some partners... and how little pressure there is with other partners. The question of how to create a low-pressure environment for sexuality to flourish is big and complicated, so let me just say here that although I'm all about people giving each other orgasms... it's no good if my partner's desire to give me an orgasm turns into pressure for me to have an orgasm!

Scarleteen, my favorite sex education site, has a great article about "squirting" orgasms and how some women feel pressured to "squirt" for the sake of the sexual "novelty." [2] On a similar note, I'll close this post with an anecdote about a guy I dated a while back who was very focused on giving me orgasms. To his credit, he figured out how to make me come very quickly. But the problem was that — I soon realized — **the biggest reason he wanted to make me come was because he wanted to feel like he could**. Fundamentally, it wasn't about my pleasure; it was about him feeling like "the man."

Let me be clear: he was a great guy, and I was into having sex with him. But it became very obvious to me that if I didn't have an orgasm every time we had sex, then he would be really bothered. So there were definitely a few encounters where, although I wasn't especially interested in having an orgasm, I still closed my eyes and flicked through fantasies with a kind of panic... until I managed to kick-start my body into coming. Isn't that messed up?

One thing I've learned, in years of writing about sex and gender, is that anything — anything at all — can be a tool for limiting or stifling sexuality... just as much as it can be a tool for releasing sexuality. Turns out, orgasms are no exception. Even orgasms can become a difficult duty. **I'm so glad that I know how to have an orgasm now; for me, that was an important step for my sexuality and my self-esteem. But now that I've learned how to do that, I find myself questioning why it's such an important and destructive issue in the first place!**

Sex is a journey. There are so many directions, so many forks in the road, so many stops along the way. There are so many speedbumps and roadblocks, uphills and downhills, free and easy open stretches. Sometimes people stop to rest. Sometimes people double back. Everything is evolving. A lot of people find it most awesome to simply... enjoy the road.

* * *

When I was in my late teens, I had a couple straight lady friends who did this thing where they took a year of chastity... although they had already had a fair amount of sex. It wasn't that they thought sex was bad. It wasn't that they especially disliked sex. It wasn't that they regretted choosing to have sex previously. But these women felt powerfully drawn towards taking a year away from sex, a year where no sex happened in their lives... and I instinctively understood **because I felt the same urge**. In fact, I came up with the idea of deliberately taking a year of chastity on my own, before I heard that anyone else was doing it.

I'm not telling you this because I want to sound like one of the "cool kids"; I'm not trying to say anything like, "I was into chastity when it was underground!" As it happened, I never actually went through with my chastity urge. But I thought about it a lot, and I thought about the fact that other girls I knew were doing it. We didn't have backgrounds that one would normally consider anti-sex. We had liberal backgrounds, liberal parents, liberal educations. Why were we so attracted to the idea of taking a year without sex?

I thought about it a lot, and I concluded this: **We felt like we didn't own our sexuality**. We felt like our sexuality wasn't for us. Or at least, that's how I felt.

Even though on the surface it looked like I was totally in charge of my sexual decisions, there were social pressures and expectations that made me feel overwhelmed and confused. Not always, and not all the time! But enough that there were plenty of times that I just felt like all I wanted to do was **stop** and be done with it... "take my body back" from a world that seemed intent on constantly telling me how I must look, how I must dress, how I must have sex.

I've written about how much easier it was for me to learn how I ought to look and "perform" while having sex, than it was for me to learn what I actually wanted from sex. That, I think, is where the chastity urge came from for me. That, and the way I kept finding myself making out with guys who I had zero interest in because it was "too awkward to say no." Or the way I didn't feel like I could decide not to have sex with my boyfriends; not because I didn't think my boyfriend would listen if I said no, but because his potentially hurt feelings seemed so much more important than my bodily preferences.

So many things about the way I was having sex seemed to have nothing to do with me. And if sex had nothing to do with me... then why was I doing it? I guess I wanted to reassure myself that I could take control of at least one thing: saying no.

Eventually, I got a better handle on my sexual preferences and began to learn how to talk about them. It was a long process, and my sexual journey is far from over (yay!). There were people who showed me what it meant to have a low-pressure sexual relationship; there were people who made it easy for me to talk about sex; and there were other people who made it easy for me to turn them down, sexually, which was just as important.

But one interesting thing during the beginning of my learning process... especially given that I now really emphasize and encourage talking directly about sex... was that I felt like a couple of my boyfriends really, really didn't want to talk about sex. And while sometimes this was clearly terrible and toxic, sometimes it felt good. It felt safe. I wanted to be sexual, but I also felt so much pressure to be sexual that it sometimes felt like a huge relief to just... "not worry about it."

In retrospect, though, I think that the "safety" I felt when I didn't talk about sex with certain partners was a mirage. It was a false safety, sustained by a carefully crafted mutual fiction of the relationship. When we ended up talking about sex later, "giving up that safety" just made the conversation unnecessarily scary and weird. And the independent illusions we each had about our sexual relationship flourished and grew strong within our silence. Those illusions were so much harder to release after months of self-reinforcement than they would have been if we'd dragged them into the light from the beginning!

Occasionally, I wonder how it would have felt if I'd taken that deliberate year of chastity. I wonder which of my early experiences would have changed; I wonder whether a year of chastity would have made me feel more comfortable with my sexuality sooner. I'm very happy with how I feel sexually now. I sometimes feel confused or overwhelmed, but I think I'm okay at handling that and even talking about it. Yet I do wonder how it would have felt to draw such a strong boundary; to say such a strong "No" to the world and its messed-up sexual expectations.

* * *

This post can be found on the Internet at:
http://clarissethorn.com/blog/2012/02/02/orgasms-arent-my-favorite-part-of-sex-and-my-chastity-urge/

* * *

* * *

BOUNDARIES:
[theory] Anger, Fear and Pain

I wrote this post in late 2010. The comments on the online version are especially good, with a lot of people sharing their own experience of these emotions in S&M encounters. So if you have an interest in the topic, this is a good post to review online.

* * *

I like pain. I like submission. What do these things actually mean, though? I don't like it when I stub my toe, for example, and there are quite a lot of authoritarian situations I don't like either. My emotional reactions, in particular, can get really complicated. So I need more precise words than "I like pain" and "I like submission."

This is not a new problem, and around the BDSM subculture there are more precise terms that are frequently used. But when I was first exploring BDSM and didn't yet have access to the community, I started coming up with my own vocabulary for what I liked and what I didn't like. The primary words I came up with — words that I still use a lot in my own head, and that I sometimes try to explain to my partners — were "clean" pain and "dirty" pain.

I think of some pain as "clean" because even if it's intense, I usually... like it. (For lack of a better word.) This is the kind of pain I fantasize about when I'm really craving BDSM. There are certain places on my body that take pain more cleanly — my upper arms, most of my back, my thighs. There are certain types of pain that are inherently more clean — needles come to mind. Wide, deep, blunt bites are good too. Heavy whips made of weighty materials, like suede. Pulling my hair right above the nape of my neck.

On the other hand, I think of some pain as "dirty" because it's... harder to take. I don't think of it as dirty because I see it as scandalous or perverse — rather, dirty pain is complex and hard to process. I never fantasize about it. Pain where my bones are close to the surface of my skin, like my collarbone, is dirty. Pain on top of scars is dirty. Pinches and small, narrow bites are dirty. Pulling my hair anywhere besides the nape of my neck is dirty. Electric shocks are extremely dirty.

But this whole "clean" and "dirty" thing, it doesn't make any sense outside my own body, my own head. It's hard to explain it. It helps that the BDSM community tends to frame pain in terms of techniques and less-subjective adjectives, using words like "sharp" or "sting" or "thud." (A lot of people think of "sharp" and "sting" as the same sensation. I usually separate them a bit more, but I'm not sure how many other people separate them.)

The BDSM and polyamory writer Franklin Veaux defines "thud" as "sensation of heavy, dull impact" and defines "sting" as "sensation of quick, sharp pain." These words are most often applied to floggers (implements for hitting people, e.g.: "this is a thuddy flogger"), but sometimes the words are used for other things too. I've found that I generally prefer thuddy-type pain, for example, but it took me a long time to figure that out, because there are so many specific sharp sensations that I love.

Okay. Now for emotions. This is the really hard part.

A while back I got an anonymous comment on my coming-out story that I absolutely love. Here's a quotation from the comment:

When it came to it, very little about the reality [of BDSM] matched my fantasies. Oh, sometimes what we did matched the way a real-life even can match a fantasy. There were moments that were... Transcendental.

But there were many more moments that... were deeply, deeply conflicted. I NEVER expected to feel that much... anger... toward someone dominating me and inflicting pain. I expected it to be a relief. I didn't expect to wrestle with hatred.

He liked to slap my face. Everytime he did it I would feel this burst of pure hatred. At one point he asked if I liked it. I said, "No. I hate it. But I don't want you to stop doing it."

I can't remember right now if any other "coming out" story I've ever read included such a visceral description of anger. Of course, I think the last time I read one I hadn't experienced it myself. Maybe I never noticed it before, but noticed it this time because it resonated with me. But mostly I remember those stories mentioning fear, shame, worry, and embarrassment.

The events in my coming-out story took place years ago, and my feelings about BDSM are really different now. I remember that I was conflicted, furious, resentful. But at the same time, I have often thought that much of my anger and resentment was due to the fact that Richard — my first intense BDSM partner — was not emotionally available. I needed support that he didn't give me. (To some extent because neither he nor I recognized how much support I needed.) And, of course, much of that anger was due to the fact that I couldn't deal with BDSM. I was fighting back against my sexuality, and felt unable to take ownership of it.

As I settled my feelings and reconciled myself to my sexual identity, my emotional reactions became a whole different ball game. (It helped that I dated a string of men who were more emotionally available and assisted me with emotional processing, too.) It turned out that the rage that I had suspected was inextricable from BDSM was, in fact, entirely possible to separate. I entered a stage where I learned how to avoid that anger. To work around it. I learned to sink myself into fear and desperation, which I love, and which are easier to work with.

I experimented with different types of submissive play. One thing I've learned is that it's almost impossible for me to feel submissive unless someone hurts me. (There have been exceptions, but they were definitely exceptional.) The BDSM community has lots of jargon for interpersonal emotional encounters, but those words usually describe actions or scenarios rather than feelings, like "public humiliation" or "domestic servitude" or "sexual slavery." So I had to learn which emotions are associated with which actions, and that's complicated too, though some things are just obvious. Some people really get off on public humiliation, for example, but that's a strong and instinctive limit for me because it makes me extraordinarily angry. (There have been exceptions, but they were definitely exceptional.)

I got better at calling out my safeword when I had to. Yes, I think it's hard to use a safeword, especially when you're new... for all kinds of reasons: you don't want to disappoint your partner, and sometimes it's hard to realize that you need to safeword, because it's very difficult to keep track of how you're feeling in the moment... but I also think that calling a safeword when you need to stop is a skill that you can get better at, much like other kinds of boundary-setting. So I became fairly practiced at calling my safeword when I needed to. If I started feeling very angry, I got good at halting the encounter, or shifting the emphasis to something else instead.

As I gained a more precise understanding of my physical reactions — clean pain and dirty pain — I figured out that there are differences in emotional reactions, too. Loosely speaking: clean pain makes me feel afraid and submissive, whereas dirty pain makes me mad. (Though this isn't always true. I hate spanking, for example; it irritates me; but it's pretty clean pain. And it might be worth noting how much I hate tickling... but that doesn't hurt.)

If the dirty pain is hard or unexpected enough, I can't seem to control lashing out. I fight back without even thinking about it (which often functions just fine as a way of renegotiating the encounter, in itself, without safewording). If it's mild? I just get annoyed. But if it's intense... I don't just struggle, I attack. I leave marks on my partners.

I learned to avoid dirty pain, usually. I learned to circumvent anger, usually. I had once seen anger, and dirty pain, as maybe being an unavoidable cost of BDSM. I once suspected that I might never be able to have a BDSM relationship where I didn't feel anger, where I didn't feel pain that I didn't want. I was wrong. Those things aren't unavoidable costs. They can be worked around.

But now.... Yes, now! We've reached the part of the entry where Clarisse makes statements about her current self and potential future actions that may or may not be true and should be treated with caution, because she is an evolving and complicated human...!

Now that I've built up all these frameworks, I've had a few encounters lately where I felt... a lot of anger. Sometimes connected to dirty pain; sometimes not. And I didn't stop. I watched how I was feeling and I dealt with it while it was happening, and it was... worth watching. It was hard to take, oh, it was so hard to take. But it was also intense and fascinating.

I've heard from a few other BDSM submissives that they like feeling anger during their encounters, that they need anger in order to get where they want to go.

If I follow the thread of anger, now....

Where will it take me?

* * *

This post can be found on the Internet at:
http://clarissethorn.com/blog/2010/12/26/anger-fear-and-pain/

* * *

***

EVOLUTION:
[theory] Sexual Openness: Two Ways To Encourage It

This was written in 2010, and it amazes me how I've changed since then.

I don't like to talk about people being "further along" in their sexual experimentation than others; people are simply in different places, based on their preferences and experiences. I look at this piece now and I think that maybe it would be better-written if I'd tried to talk about sexual evolution in a more neutral way. However, it's undeniable that when I was younger, I often felt like I was somehow "held up" or "inhibited," and I no longer feel that way about sex. And I do think that in general, lots of people want to explore but aren't sure how to overcome their own hesitance and psychological blocks. Some of them even write to me for advice, and I can only tell them what worked for me: the approach I outlined in this post.

***

I've been thinking a lot lately about the factors that went into my sexual evolution. People have always seen me as sexually open-minded, and I had an extraordinarily liberal upbringing... but at the same time, I think I spent a long time surprisingly buttoned-up.

Part of it was the men I fell in love with, the partners I had. Monogamy felt right to me, and that effectively meant that once I was in a relationship, it was hard to explore sexuality beyond what my lovers were comfortable with. I've often looked back in frustration at sexual shame and inhibitions that I feel were imposed on me by some past partners. But at the same time, **there's no denying that — even when my partners were relatively inhibited — I was with those men partly because I felt comfortable with them.** I recall conversations in which I felt frustrated at a lover's unwillingness to explore or discuss certain things... but I also recall times when I felt relieved that they were willing to leave those things alone.

How did I evolve through that balance and come into the place where I am today, where my sexual boundaries have shifted dramatically? I'm up for trying things just to see what they're like; I routinely have fantasies that would have appalled me in my teens; and I routinely have orgasms as well.... But why is it that, for example, I'm very interested in having multiple partners now, but wasn't at all interested a few years ago? Why did I initially swear I'd never wear a collar, then end up associating collars with profound sexual love? How is it that I initially considered myself solely a submissive but later transitioned into an enthusiastic switch (i.e., both a sub and a domme)?

Here are the **two factors that, I think, facilitate sexual evolution and openness**:

1) *A pressure-free environment*. This is key! A person **can** be pressured into sexual exploration, but in my experience it won't "take." Many people (though not all) who feel pressure react by becoming defensive and unwilling to change; even if they do try the experiment, they're less likely to enjoy it. And someone who has a bad sexual experience will often have trouble enjoying that kind of sex in the future.

Take me, for example — there were a lot of reasons why I felt less willing to experiment with polyamory (multiple relationships) when I was 20, but one of the big ones is that I felt lots of **pressure** to be poly. Because I ran in highly "alternative" social circles, I was meeting "polyvangelists" who argued that polyamory is the "best" kind of relationship and that anyone who doesn't want to try poly is just being selfish or close-minded. **General social pressure exerts an influence, so it helps to have open-minded friends who accept different forms of consensual sexuality** — which doesn't just mean that "vanilla" people would do well to accept those of us who are "non-standard," but also means that even people in "alternative" circles have to accept "mainstream" sexuality.

But in my experience, the actual **sexual relationships are the most relevant aspect of life that must be sexually pressure-free**. They're also one of the most difficult, especially when the stakes are high: if one or both parties are helplessly in love, if they are married, if they have children, if they live together... then it becomes very hard to make the relationship pressure-free. A husband who is afraid that his wife might leave him is more likely to do sexual things for her that make him uncomfortable because he wants her to stay, for example — even if she doesn't ask him to. A girl who is totally in love with her boyfriend is more likely to acquiesce to sex that she's not really into, because of course she wants to please him — but she is simultaneously unlikely to tell him outright that she's not into it.

And then there's the fact that what feels like "pressure" for each person will be different depending on that person's triggers, the relationship, and the time in their life. Today, I feel totally comfortable setting limits and clearly telling my partner "no" if he asks me to do something I don't want to do... but it wasn't so long ago that I'd feel anxiety-inducing pressure to do something if my boyfriend merely mentioned that he liked it. Which brings me to my next point: **there's a fine line between sharing and pressure**. One must be careful when bringing up one's own preferences and desires — which isn't to say one shouldn't bring them up! Merely that it's important to recognize that these are difficult topics, and when we discuss them with people we love or admire, there's lots of potential for accidental anxious pressure.

Okay, I'm talking pretty theoretically, right? So here's some actual concrete advice on how to avoid imposing sexual pressure:

* **Don't demand that people explain their preferences**. A person doesn't have to explain, examine, or "figure out" why they're gay, straight, kinky, polyamorous, or whatever if they don't want to. Even your sexual partner doesn't have to explain why they don't want to do something if they don't want to.

In fact, it may be very helpful if you merely make it clear that your partner doesn't have to explain from the beginning — because they may feel as if they ought to, even if you don't ask. I so clearly remember an encounter I had a few years ago in which my partner asked what I was up for and I said, hesitantly, "Well, I'm not really up for sex tonight... I can't really explain it, I —" and he held up his hand. "You don't have to explain it," he said — and I was totally shocked at the gratitude, relief and comfort that poured through me.

I later felt proud and thrilled to "pay it forward" when I had my first serious encounter as a dominant. Towards the end of the encounter, I asked, "Do you want me?" and my submissive stiffened, saying awkwardly, "Yes, I do, but... I don't want to have sex so soon, it's just one of my own boundaries, I —" and I saw how much the words were costing him. Saw the same anxiety I'd felt once. And immediately I covered his mouth and said, "Shh, it's fine, you don't have to explain it," and I saw him relax with the same terrible relief I'd once felt. And then we made out for many hours and it was unbelievably awesome.

... Of course, **sometimes people will want to examine their**

own preferences, which is obviously fine! But if your partner or friend is examining for their own mental well-being, that's very different from demanding that they examine to satisfy you. Bottom line: they don't owe you an explanation, and asking for one may just make them tense up and feel totally unsexy in all ways.

* **Express preferences gently**. I once attended an incredible BDSM workshop by the author Laura Antoniou in which she offered an outline for bringing up your filthiest, scariest fantasy with your partner: "Buy ice cream. Sit down at the kitchen table and describe your fantasy. Then say, 'Don't say anything now. I'll give you some time to think about it — now let's eat this ice cream and maybe go out for a movie.'" I love this advice because (a) everyone gets ice cream and (b) it's so perfect for lowering tension. And as Laura said, "The worst thing that can happen is that they're not into it."

[Editor's Note: since writing this post, Clarisse went vegan, and recommends eating that frozen Coconut Bliss stuff instead of ice cream. The chocolate flavor is absurdly delicious.]

It's important to emphasize from the start: "This is something I'm interested it, but it's not a requirement and I don't want you to do it if you're not into it." In fact, it might help to begin by saying those exact words.

And if your partner doesn't want to do something now, it's often worth giving time for them to grow into the idea. Perhaps by exploring other sexual angles, they'll come around to yours. I remember that when I was in my late teens, one boyfriend asked me if I'd be up for a certain kind of sex, and I refused. (He asked very gently, and didn't pressure me when I said no, which made me feel much safer and happier with him!) At the time I couldn't imagine ever wanting to do it. Then a few years later — after I'd gained a lot more sexual experience — I ended up asking my boyfriend to try it! I'm convinced that if my previous partner had pressured me, I wouldn't have come around to it so easily years later — and if he and I had still been together, then maybe we would have even done it together.

... But of course, the difficult part here is that sexual needs are important, and can't be put on the back burner indefinitely. If you have sexual needs that are being routinely ignored — or can't be fulfilled — by your partner, then it's obviously not desirable to keep gently saying, "Don't worry, I can do without this." Still, I think that if you're approaching ultimatum territory — for example, if you are tempted to say that "If you can't satisfy this need, then I need an open relationship so I can find someone who can, or else we have to break up" — then it's best to at least state the ultimatum gently, emphasize that you care about your partner and this is difficult, and steel yourself to act quickly in case you have to go through with your ultimatum. And, of course, to understand that this could make sexuality with your partner more difficult if you keep trying to date through ultimatum territory.

Sadly, **sexual pressure can sometimes be simply unavoidable. Sometimes the best we can do is be gentle, understanding, and prepared to face the consequences.**

2) *Exposure to new conceptions of sexuality, sexual mentors, and sex education.* Many gay people say they're "wired" for a certain approach to sexuality, but there's also others, such as some BDSMers, who consider ourselves to be innately kinky. And we often say that we would have come to those sexual conclusions and practices whether we had examples before us, or not. (Even so, it's really helpful to have a community sharing tips and emotional support, especially when it comes to alternative sexuality. It might seem like sex will come naturally and obviously, but sometimes non-obvious things can really trip you up!)

Still, there are lots of sexual ideas are worth exploring and wouldn't necessarily occur to us if we didn't have examples before us: erotica, pornography, friends and mentors, workshops and educational materials. Here's some concrete advice on how best to emotionally access those:

* **Find a good mentor, or at least a friend or social group, to talk about sex with — who you don't want to have sex with**. Being able to honestly discuss turn-ons in a neutral environment is invaluable, as is someone who can guide and advise without inserting their preferences and desires into the conversation. Naturally, it's entirely possible to have a good sexual relationship with a sexual mentor — and sometimes, mentor (or friend) relationships evolve in unexpectedly sexual ways. But it can be very useful to take that element out of at least some relationships.

One piece of advice that I love is for mentors to be the same "type." That is, for example, if you're a heterosexual female submissive, it's awesome to have an experienced heterosexual female submissive mentor if possible.

This post was edited to add the next paragraph: In the comments, Ranai pointed out that it's not always a great idea to have just one mentor — and I agree with her. I think it's helpful to have a range of voices who can give advice, if possible. There's nothing wrong with trusting one person above others, but all humans have their blind spots, and mentors are human too. This is one thing I love about the BDSM community, by the way (or at least, my experience with the BDSM communities I have been part of — not all BDSM communities are the same...). In many BDSM communities, there are many café meetups and other low-pressure gatherings that make perfect environments for getting this kind of advice!

* **Not all BDSM — or porn — or whatever! — is the same**. If you don't like (or are even revolted by) something you see, then you can try watching (or reading, or talking about) something else. Me, I got really excited when I first learned about Comstock Films: Tony Comstock makes documentaries that show real couples having real sex, and his documentaries are much more realistic and comfortably sexual than mainstream porn. [1] And I **really** didn't like mainstream porn. But then I found that I wasn't that into Comstock Films themselves, even though I love the idea so much that I screened one of the movies at my sex-positive film series. So I concluded that I'm just not into porn at all, and that I'd be better off to focus on written erotica.

But **then** I finally saw some porn that turned me on at CineKink, "the really alternative film festival" [2] — and I hadn't even expected it to turn me on! I'd just been watching out of academic interest! And these days, I find that I'm sometimes turned on by watching the mainstream porn I tried so hard to avoid in the first place. The moral of the story is obvious.

The bottom line is that **mere exposure to new ideas about sexuality can bring personal sexual evolution** — and that's awesome. So if you're interested in facilitating your own sexual evolution, the first thing to do is learn about sexuality by whatever means possible.

* * *

This can be found on the Internet at:
http://clarissethorn.com/blog/2010/05/28/sexual-openness-2-ways-to-encourage-it/

* * *

* * *

RELATIONSHIPS:
[storytime] Fear, Loathing, and S&M Sluthood in San Francisco

I originally wrote this and published it at OffOurChests.com in late 2010. If you've read Confessions of a Pickup Artist Chaser, *or any of my posts that refer to "Adam," then I probably don't have to tell you which of these men later turned into Adam. But I'll spoil the mystery for you, and tell you outright that Mr. ThereItIs is Adam. (In this entry, I named him after the post I wrote when I met him: "There It Is." [1])*

* * *

  Since I was small, I've loved the Van Gogh painting "Starry Night." I loved the cypresses in particular: winding spiral trees, hallucination trees. They were so unlike other trees I'd seen that I thought Van Gogh made them up, and so when I first saw cypresses years later, I was stunned: the hallucination trees had been imported into my world. I'd like to think that my world turned a little bit sideways forever, when I first saw cypresses, but I'm probably being melodramatic. (I'm good at that.)
  San Francisco has cypresses, and a lot of other hallucinations, too. The city is full of angles, vantages, transitions, unceasing changing views: it feels, at times, like an unsolvable puzzle. A forested path leads darkly under a bridge, suddenly opens upon a manicured lawn with a white lace conservatory. A cement staircase rises through a narrow outlet, resolving itself step by step into a slice of brightly painted Victorian façade. I walked once with a friend alongside an ocean road, pacing through thick fog, and arrived at a dirt path that I insisted on following; thirty seconds later we stumbled upon extraordinary ruins. [2]
  San Francisco. Halcyon city, heartbreak city. Cypress city. The place I come to recover from being torn apart and, it seems, sometimes the place where I get torn apart again. This is okay with me, because nothing is more fun than overanalyzing strong emotions.

I am not even kidding.

* * *

I returned from Africa recently; paused briefly in my adopted city of Chicago to collect my thoughts; and then went to the Burning Man Arts Festival, thence to San Francisco. This is my version of emotional decompression, and it worked! I feel much more centered now. But part of decompressing, for me, was specifically going out to a **lot** of dates and BDSM parties and pushing my own boundaries, which carries its own potential decompressable risks.

At the time of this story, it had been a couple of months in San Francisco, and I was leaving soon. I'd had an assortment of adventures, but there were two guys in particular who I was excited about. Not necessarily in a long-term way — I'm not in this for the white picket fence and the 2.5 kids (or at least, not yet) — but definitely in a wow-I-have-to-control-myself-or-I'll-come-off-as-kind-of-puppyish way. New Relationship Energy: it is such a mind trick, such a delicious head-trip. *You are the perfect drug.*

I had to control myself less when I first hooked up with The Artist: possibly the most postmodern individual I've ever met, possibly the most creative, who I've loosely been friends with for six whole years, and who has never ceased to fascinate me. It is hard for me to meet people who keep me thinking, but The Artist never disappoints. If anything, our problem was shifting a cerebral connection into a sexual one: the first time we made out, I absolutely **had** to interrupt the proceedings because I'd forgotten to tell him about this great sociology paper. It was okay to show how much I liked him because we'd known each other for so long, it was easier to read the situation, easier to allow investment. Much harder with Mr. ThereItIs, who came out of nowhere, who I barely knew but had awesome chemistry with. In the beginning steps of this game, you can never let them smell your fear.

Saturday morning. I'd spent the night with The Artist, was checking my email while he made breakfast. (He actually likes cooking, which I have trouble comprehending.) I wanted to plan my week, and texted Mr. ThereItIs to ask when we'd see each other. My breath hitched as he texted back: he didn't think it'd be a good idea to spend the night together again, but he wanted to have drinks and catch up. I closed my eyes, made myself breathe. Remembered how many times he'd pulled back, how much anxiety he'd expressed about the BDSM we engaged in. I'd tried to make it clear that he was doing awesomely, but dollars to donuts he was still freaking out about it. I was his first-time heavy BDSM partner. *Why do I keep doing this to myself? Haven't I learned my lesson about vanilla-but-questioning guys yet?[3]*

After giving myself a moment to calm down, I texted back that I was open to getting drinks, but wanted to understand his motives better before doing so. "Feel free to email or text," I wrote, "I can't talk right now," then put down my phone and walked into an intense conversation in the kitchen. There'd been some uncertainty over my last month or so with The Artist, due to surprisingly divergent relationship priorities. We're decently matched in terms of being BDSM-identified, and we have so much else in common, but there were some things I wanted to do that particularly freaked him out, plus he wasn't feeling 100% comfortable with polyamory. Most of all, I've been surprised by his emphasis on settling down.

That Saturday, it ended with him deciding it wouldn't work. "You and I are in such different places right now," he said gently. "You're still focused on having an interesting life. I'm not prioritizing that anymore. I would have been a much better match for you five years ago."

You're one of the most interesting people I've ever met, I wanted to say, *how can you decide this?* The night before, we'd had a conversation in which he'd described how incredibly stable he wants his life to be. Well-designed apartment, respected job, kids, the lot. How much he wants to get away from past days, when he thrived among bizarre subcultures, prioritized art above everything. He doesn't even want to travel! I listened, heart sinking. Trying to understand. "Isn't there anything you can't walk away from?" I asked.

"S&M," he said promptly. "But that bothers me, because I don't know how I can make it fit."

Stability; making things fit. Saturday at breakfast, The Artist mentioned that a friend had compared him to Alex, the main character in *A Clockwork Orange:* in the famous "lost" 21st chapter, Alex decides that it's time to abandon ultraviolence and settle down. [4] Obviously, The Artist was never even close to being the psychopath that Alex is, but it's still an instructive parallel. And I, with all my desire to push and stretch myself, with all the boundaries I'm still seeking to subvert and hack and destroy — I don't work with the desire to settle down. I may never work with that desire.

I understood. Of course I understood. I knew intellectually that it wasn't about me, I knew it was just about the situations at hand, but of course it hurt anyway. Two awesome men, giving me the same message at once: *This is too much, you're too extreme.* A matter of their boundaries. Not about me. Of course it hurt anyway.

"Is there anything else you want to add while we're having this conversation?" I asked The Artist finally, as we wound things up.

He thought for a minute, took my hand. "Well, you're wonderful and beautiful, but you know that."

"Do I?" I asked, and made myself laugh to take the sting from my words.

* * *

An aside:

Occasionally, my mother has tried to convince me that I am at emotional risk in part **because of** the fact that I am forward about my sexuality. Because — I think this is how the story goes, though she's never explicitly articulated it — because it means that men will see me as a disposable toy; the hot edgy girl he likes but would never settle down with; the whore but not the Madonna. Cute enough to catch his attention and passionate enough that he'll call her back but ultimately, not "the keeper," not the girl he'd have any loyalty to in the end. I think my mom is afraid that I'll stumble out the other end of this brilliant razor-edged fluorescent beautiful funhouse that is my "young and attractive" years, that I'll come down like a girl falling through a distorted mirrored sheet of glass. That shards will burst everywhere and I'll collapse, covered in metaphorical blood, and turn my eyes up to the harsh white stars and wonder how I let men use me and why.

This is the stereotype that I think she's afraid of, on my behalf, the one that comes up on occasion when she comforts me through heartbreak. My mother is hardly a conservative slut-shamer, but she loves me and she wants to protect me, so she tells me this. And I'll admit it — I fear it too, I feel those anxieties whispering behind me, thrumming through my veins during times like these. *What did I mean to him? Did I matter, did I make an impression, does he give a damn? Would he be willing to Make A Commitment? He doesn't care, God, I don't matter, and I was just stupid because God forbid I allow myself to like or trust a man that I fuck, when everyone knows that men don't ever have feelings for the women they fuck —*

But actually those fears don't make sense, do they — they don't make any sense at all if I assume that men are complex humans who want to have relationships but aren't always sure about it (much like myself), rather than sex-seeking-stereotype-activated-robots. The fears don't make sense in the context of my own experience, which is full of friends and relatives and lovers who have been caring, self-aware, honest men. The fears don't make sense given the fact that very often, **I'm** the one who prefers not to have a serious relationship right now, or who can only compromise up to a point.

And the fears especially don't make any damn sense if we assume that I want to pursue my own goals, my own dreams, my own pleasures, my own sexuality **on my own terms**. If we **assume** that I have no intention of playing by the rules in a world that tells me women never have our own damn sexual needs; that it's wrong or wicked or dirty for women to negotiate any sexual exchange for pleasure; that women are meant to **trade** sex for "commitment" or "support" (though, bizarrely, never outright for money). If we **assume** that I can get something great from sexual relationships without Being On The Path To Marriage. That I understand and honor my sexual desires, that those desires are worth fulfilling in themselves. And if we **assume** that men have something wonderful they could bring to the sexual exchange; that they aren't always "using" or "exploiting" or "winning" some kind of sick war-of-the-sexes, every single time they fuck.

But even if the fears don't make sense, sometimes they still come out and whisper at the back of my neck... *I'm selling myself short.* As if I should have **bargained** better, should have **traded** my sexuality for far more than "mere" pleasure with someone I "merely" liked, was "merely" attracted to, who "merely" respected my boundaries and "merely" was fun to hang out with. Would some people see it as ironic that I prefer relationships with real emotional heft, even when short-term or casual? Even with that said, though, there is no description of how reasonable, safe, or awesome my relationships are that will matter to our slut-shaming society — or to the fears it's hammered into me. Society, whose judgment of whether a girl is a "slut" can be sudden and devastating, stupid and stereotypical; a lightning strike that lands based on absurd factors like how non-normative or straightforward or aware of her sexuality she is. And once I'm a "slut" — if I dare dance over that ever-shifting line — then I'm beyond the pale. The world always seems to be outdoing itself in finding new ways to tell me that once I'm a slut, no man will ever respect me again.

* * *

I went home. It was raining, all across my cypress city; raining so hard, I had to take the bus instead of walking. The rain struck me as an insultingly obvious metaphor, as did the fact that I was scheduled to attend a wedding that afternoon. It seemed strange that hallucinatory San Francisco would throw such tired tropes at me. (I should have trusted the city more. It was with me, still.)

I was sad. Not devastated. Just sad, and a little bit scared. *I'm such a screwed-up perverted slut, no man will ever care about me.* However, I'm an adult, so I tried to recognize my emotional baggage, give myself some time to process, then eat a proper lunch and get some work done.

I took a very dear, very blunt friend out to dinner recently. (Yes, I paid, and yes, he felt objectified.) Over Indian curries, I tried to explain my fears that All Men (who are of course a monolith) will pigeonhole me as "too much", "too extreme." A "slut." Whatever. My friend listened, savoring his delicious lassi as he thought about what I was trying to say. Then he said, "Look, you shouldn't worry about it. You're extreme. You're also tall. You couldn't be un-tall for a man, and you can't be un-extreme. There are men who will like you just fine for it, so just keep an eye out for those men." I could detect the edge under his words: *Come on, Clarisse, you're the one who always says that People Are Different, why do I even have to tell you this?* A fair point, but I can't help it — stories like this still shake me.

As it happens, though, this story has a happy ending.

I was about to head out to the wedding when I received an email from Mr. ThereItIs:

So my txt was not really well-considered. I was delaying writing you because I've got mixed and confusing inclinations about all this and was hoping I could figure them out before writing. So I spent last night drinking too much and ranting with friends about unrelated topics, which surprise turned out to not have helped me figure my shit out at all.

I'm just feeling intimidated and uncertain about our kinkiness. On one hand I've been feeling "aaa this is weird, run away". But I'm also feeling like this is fun and new and hot and fascinating, and I should get over my bs and try it again. So if you can forgive my impulsive txt and my erratic emotions.... I'm free on your free nights this week.

And if I've spooked you or your schedule has filled up, then I would be disappointed... but I'd understand. Sorry about the drama. I'm usually drama-free, I swear.

It was amazing how much further my internal anxieties resolved themselves upon receipt of this email: it was not only concrete evidence that men are **human beings** who are frequently **just as confused as I am**; not only concrete evidence that men are **different from each other**, and assumptions should not be made about how they're feeling; but also, it was concrete evidence that a man (a vanilla-but-questioning man, no less!) might not inevitably fall into the stereotypes that feed my fears.

I was still a little bit spooked, of course, but I did indeed see Mr. ThereItIs later that week, and it turned out great. And as I was pulling myself together to leave his apartment, I raised my eyebrows at him. "I don't know if I'll ever see you again," I said, fishing. I didn't have any nights open before I was due to catch my plane out of the city, but maybe some other time....

"You'll see me again," he obliged.

I zipped up my backpack. "I wonder why we have so much chemistry."

"I don't know," he said, "but I'll read about it on your blog when you figure it out," and he laughed and caught my wrists when I pretended to punch him. It was such a stupidly adorable moment that I am almost ashamed to write it down, but it was also such a cypress moment, I've got to mention it.

As for The Artist, we went to a charming museum a few days before I left, and had a fine old time. There was almost no tension at all. Right before we parted, we inevitably ended up discussing our brief romance, and the conversation was gloriously friendly. "No hard feelings," I said as I walked him to the bus, and meant it.

I then tried to walk away from the bus, but it turned at the same corner I did and chased me down the street. *Ack,* I couldn't help thinking, *so much for a nice clean exit.* I was suddenly possessed by ridiculous performance anxiety, knowing he could see me, so I paused and took a drag of a passing gentleman's cigarette, and then deliberately zigzagged away from the bus again.

The Artist texted me fifteen seconds later: "That puff of a cigarette looked mighty tasty."

"I needed it to relieve my feelings of being watched from the bus," I texted back, then added impulsively, "Take care, handsome, and have lots of wonderful children."

"You too," he replied. "We'll see if I become okay with poly first, or you gain these 'adult' preferences...."

I shook my head and laughed over my phone, walked home with a spring in my step.

San Francisco had done what I needed it to do.

* * *

This can be found on the Internet at:
http://clarissethorn.com/blog/2011/04/03/storytime-fear-loathing-and-sm-sluthood-in-san-francisco/

* * *

* * *

S&M:
[theory] BDSM As A Sexual Orientation, and Complications of the Orientation Model

The first version of this post was written in 2009. I updated it slightly and reposted it in 2012. There is a lot more that could be said on this topic — at one point, I tried pitching a book about S&M and feminism to some different presses, and my proposal included a whole chapter on various theories of sexual orientation. But as I explain by the end of this post, I think the whole idea is a dead end. These days, exploring it just strikes me as counter-productive.

The online version of this post includes an evolving set of relevant links at the end.

* * *

There's a hilarious sticker that you can buy online at a website called TopPun.com. It shows a list with "Homosexual Agenda" written at the top. The list items are: "1. Spend time with family, 2. Be treated equally, 3. Buy milk." (You can also buy a keychain version.)

I love that because it so perfectly highlights how preposterous all those right-wing accusations about "the gay agenda" are. Actually, gay people just want to live their lives like everyone else; the to-do list for most gay people looks a lot like most other people's.

In a way, that sticker also highlights some problems with the very concept of sexual orientations — the way we sort ourselves into groups based on sexuality and its apparent innateness. Why do people have to insist on being so different from each other? A question that sometimes gets raised in BDSM contexts: is BDSM a "sexual orientation"? And I have such mixed feelings about that question. I feel intense BDSM as an incredibly important aspect of my sexuality, perhaps an innate one, but I don't want us to fall into the same traps that beset homosexuality.

I remember the first moment it occurred to me to consider BDSM an orientation — the first time I used that word. I believe I was writing up my coming-out story at the time; I was discussing the way I freaked out when I came into BDSM, and I wrote: *In retrospect, it seems surreal that I reacted so badly to my BDSM orientation.*

I remember that I felt vaguely electrified at what I was saying, a little scared... but also comforted. At the time, I hadn't had much contact with other sex theorists, and I thought I was saying something radical. I was scared that my words might appear too radical to be taken seriously. Also, since our culture mostly discusses the idea of "orientation" in regards to gay/ lesbian/ bi/ transgender/ queer, it seemed to me that — if I dared refer to it as "my BDSM orientation" — then a comparison with LGBTQ was implied in my statement.

Would the world believe that my BDSM desires could be as "real," as "deep-rooted," as "unavoidable" as the sexual orientation of a gay/lesbian/bi/transgender/queer person? Would I offend GLBTQ people by implying that my sexual needs are as "real," "deep-rooted" and "unavoidable" as theirs?

I later found out that some LGBTQ people do get offended by it, and others don't. Sometime you end up with ridiculous arguments like this one from a comments thread on an incredibly BDSM-phobic blog: one person says, "As a lesbian, I would like to say a sincere fuck you to people comparing BDSM to homosexuality," to which another person replies, "As a queer person myself, I would like to say a sincere fuck you to people who claim that I ought to see my BDSM and my queerness differently." [1] As for me, Clarisse, I'll be frank with you — I've come to the conclusion that I don't have a dog in that fight, and I'm staying out of it. I'm straight as the day is long, but I've also been invited to speak about BDSM at queer conventions and to write about BDSM on queer blogs. So I'll hang out with the people who are cool with me, and everyone else can kick me out of their LGBTQ circles as much as they want.

But I used to feel a lot more worried about how I'd be perceived for talking about BDSM as an orientation. Still, as weird as the concept of "BDSM as an orientation" felt when I first thought of it, it also felt right. When I looked back at my memories and previous actions, it was quite obvious that I have always had these needs, desires and fantasies. Acknowledging this, and applying the word "orientation" to BDSM, helped me come to terms with my BDSM identity.

The "BDSM orientation" idea cleared a mental path for me to think of BDSM as a inbuilt part of myself, like my bone structure or eye color. BDSM became something that it was desirable to accept, come to terms with... even **embrace.** It was a hugely liberating way of thinking about it: **if I thought of BDSM as an orientation, that meant I didn't have to worry about or fight it anymore.**

Since then, I've been so buried in sexuality theory and I've talked to so many BDSM people that — well, now the idea of a "BDSM orientation" seems kinda boring. I am reminded that it's a radical concept only when I talk to people who don't think about these things all the time. I think that the idea of BDSM as an orientation occurs naturally to people who think a lot about BDSM sexuality, because **so many kinksters** either know we're BDSM people all along, or instantly recognize BDSM once we find it. Here's a quotation from an article about a BDSM-related legal case that quotes sexologist Charles Moser at the end, as he very eloquently describes how BDSM can be considered a sexual orientation:

When I talk to someone who is identifying as BDSM and ask them have you always felt this way, and they almost always report that 'This has been the way I was all along. I didn't realize it. I thought I was interested in more traditional male/female relationships but now I realize that I really like the power and control aspects of relationship.'

... They are very clear often that, 'my relationships which were vanilla were not fulfilling. I always felt like there was something missing. Now that I'm doing BDSM, I am fulfilled. This feels really right to me. This really gets me to my core. It's who I am.'

... And so in the same way as someone who is homosexual, they couldn't really change — they somehow felt fulfilled in the same-sex relationship — similarly in a BDSM relationship or scenario, they similarly feel the same factors, and in my mind, that allows me to classify people who fit that as a sexual orientation. I cannot change someone who's into BDSM to not be BDSM. [2]

That's how I feel. Absolutely.

And yet I disagree with Moser on one key point: not all BDSM people are like this. I know that people exist who do BDSM, who don't feel it the same way I do. They don't feel that it's been with them all along. It's not deep-rooted for them. It's not unavoidable, it's not necessary, it doesn't go to their core. They can change from being into BDSM to not doing BDSM, because it's not built-in; it's just something they do sometimes, for fun. There are also plenty of people who have equally strong feelings about their BDSM sexuality, but who have different BDSM preferences from mine. And that's totally okay with me! I will always say that I've got no problem with whatever people want to do, as long as it's kept among consenting adults.

But what does the existence of people like that mean for BDSM as an orientation? Are they somehow less "entitled" to practice BDSM, because it's not as deep-rooted or important to them as it is for, say, me? No, that can't be true. I'm not going to claim that my feelings are "more real" than theirs, or somehow more important, just because BDSM goes straight to my core but not to theirs. They've got as much right as I do to practice these activities, as long as they do it consensually.

So, where does that leave us? It means that BDSM is an orientation for some people, but not for others. I'm fine with that. Does that mean we're done here? Well, no....

... because if BDSM is an orientation for some people but not others, then we're in a bit of a weird place when it comes to societal recognition. In the case I cited above, Charles Moser is claiming that we BDSMers can't change ourselves and that therefore, we don't deserve to be stigmatized for our sexuality.

On the surface, this might seem reasonable, but actually, **whether or not** people can alter their sexual needs, **there's no reason people shouldn't be able to do what they want with other consenting adults**. If any of us phrase the argument as: "I can't change myself, so please don't hate me!" then we are implicitly saying, "If I could change myself, I would... but I can't, so please have pity on me!" In other words, we are implicitly saying: "BDSMers can't 'fix' our sexual needs — it's not 'our fault' — so please don't hate us."

And when we say that, we are accepting and validating the way our culture tries to shame our sexuality. We are fundamentally agreeing with the opposition and begging for an exception, rather than trying to change the rule. We are calling BDSM a "fault," rather than stating that freely exercising sexuality is our "right." **When we make BDSM into an orientation, we are often casting BDSM sexuality as something that we would "fix" if we could. But BDSM is not broken in the first place!**

Also, using the orientation argument leaves the entire segment of the population that doesn't feel BDSM as an orientation standing out in the cold. If we go with the orientation model, and say that it's okay for BDSM-identified people to practice BDSM only because we feel it as a deep-rooted orientation... then we are implying that it's **not** okay for people to practice BDSM if they **don't** feel it as a deep-rooted orientation.

Something like this has happened in some gay/lesbian communities: people who have sex with folks of the same gender, but don't identify as strictly gay or lesbian, have sometimes been stigmatized within gay/lesbian communities or even disallowed from gay/lesbian gatherings. I understand that there are historical reasons that kind of thing happened, and analyzing the phenomenon would take up a whole post. I'm pretty sure books have been written about it. But the point is that when it did happen, it left bisexual people — as well as others who don't fit neatly within the "gay/lesbian orientation" — out in the cold. And I don't want to support that with BDSM.

So I've tended to avoid that kind of language. I think it is important to move away from "I can't help having these needs," and towards "It's fundamentally unimportant whether we can change our sexual desires; the only really important thing is whether or not we practice them consensually."

But...

there's always a but...

I'll admit that I feel anxiety about abandoning the "orientation model." I still haven't taken the word "orientation" out of my BDSM overview lecture, because it is useful for convincing people that BDSM is okay. Many people, at this point, have accepted the LGBTQ orientation as something that should not be stigmatized. The word "orientation" can really help them understand what BDSM means to us and why it's not okay to stigmatize that, either.

Furthermore, there are obviously people out there (like Charles Moser) who are seeking to protect BDSM legally, as a sexual orientation. They want to make BDSM a protected class, so that we can't get fired or have our kids taken away or suffer other consequences for being into BDSM anymore. If talking about BDSM as a sexual orientation means I can worry less about those potential consequences, then is it worth it? Maybe.

And, of course, I don't want to forget how much the idea of an "orientation" comforted me when I was first coming into BDSM. It made me feel so much better to recognize BDSM as an inbuilt part of myself. I don't want to take that comfort away from anyone else.

So, when I try to campaign for general sexual freedom and acceptance — "orientation" or no "orientation" — I imagine that I'll still end up using the word sometimes. But I'll always try to be conscious of it, and I'll always try to speak in ways that support this statement:

It's fundamentally unimportant whether we can change our

sexual desires; the only really important thing is whether or not we practice them consensually.

* * *

This can be found on the Internet at:
http://clarissethorn.com/blog/2012/04/09/classic-repost-bdsm-as-a-sexual-orientation-and-complications-of-the-orientation-model/

* * *

* * *

S&M:
[theory] BDSM "versus" Sex

This was originally published in two parts in 2011. I named the first part "Divide and Conquer," and the second part "How Does It Feel?" But as often happens when I split up my long posts, people were already talking about points that I addressed in the second post while commenting on the first post — before the second post was published. (Unfortunately, my commenters are at least as smart as I am, and they notice when I leave things out.) I've often struggled with length problems as a blogger. If I could write posts that are typical blog length, like 250-500 words, then I'd probably be a lot more successful. But I just can't seem to write short, and since splitting up long posts is a bad idea too, I constantly feel frustrated by blogging... let alone platforms like Twitter! If you have clever thoughts for how I can train myself to be a better short-form writer, email me. Seriously.

* * *

Every once in a while, someone will ask me a question about something BDSM-related that I feel "done with"; I feel like I did all my thinking about those topics, years ago. But it's still useful to get those questions today, because it forces me to try and understand where my head was at, three to seven years ago. It forces me to calibrate my inner processes. I often think of these questions as the "simple" ones, or the "101" questions, because they are so often addressed in typical conversation among BDSMers. Then again, lots of people don't have access to a BDSM community, or aren't interested in their local BDSM community for whatever reason. Therefore, it's useful for me to cover those "simple" questions on my blog anyway.

Plus, just because a question is simple doesn't mean the question is not interesting.

One such question is the "BDSM versus sex" question. Is BDSM always sex? Is it always sexual? A lot of people see BDSM as something that "always" includes sex, or is "always sexual in some way." In the documentary "BDSM: It's Not What You Think!", one famous BDSM writer is quoted saying something like: "I would say that eros is always **involved** in BDSM, even if the participants aren't doing anything that would look sexual to non-BDSMers."

But a lot of other people see BDSM, and the BDSM urge, as something that doesn't necessarily have anything to do with sex — that is separate from sex.

I see two sides to this question: the political side, and the "how does it feel?" side. Both sides are intertwined; **when it comes to sex, politics can't help shaping our experiences (and vice versa)**. I acknowledge this. **And yet even when I try to account for that, there is still something deeply different about the way my body feels my BDSM urges, as opposed to how my body feels sexual urges.** I don't think that those bodily differences could ever quite go away, no matter how my mental angle on those processes changed.

* * *

The Political Side of BDSM versus Sex

"BDSM versus sex" could be viewed as a facet of that constant and irritating question — "What is sex, anyway?" I've always found that **the more you look at the line between "what is sex" and "what is not sex," the more blurred the line becomes**.

For example, recall that ridiculous national debate that happened across America when Bill Clinton told us that he hadn't had sex with Monica — and then admitted to getting a blowjob from her. Is oral sex sex? Maybe oral sex isn't sex! Flutter, flutter, argue, argue.

It is my experience that (cisgendered, heterosexual) women are often more likely to claim that oral sex is not sex, while (cis, het) men are more likely to claim that oral sex is sex. I suspect this is because women face steeper social penalties for having sex (no one wants to be labeled a "slut"), so we are typically more motivated to claim that sex acts "don't count" as sex... whereas men are usually congratulated for having sex (more notches on the bedpost!), so men are typically more motivated to claim that sex acts "count" as sex. (Unless they're Bill Clinton.)

So we already have this weird ongoing debate, about what "qualifies" as sex. And you throw in fetishes such as BDSM, and everyone gets confused all over again. A cultural example of this confusion came up in 2009, when a bunch of professional dominatrixes got arrested in New York City... for being dominatrixes... which everyone previously believed was legal. [1] Flutter, flutter, argue, argue, and it turns out that "prostitution" (which is illegal in New York) is defined as "sexual conduct for money."

But what does "sexual conduct" mean? **At least one previous court had set the precedent that BDSM-for-pay is not the same as "sexual conduct for money"... and yet, in 2009, the Manhattan District Attorney's office decided that "sexual conduct" means "anything that is arousing to the participants"... and then decided that this suddenly meant they ought to go arrest dominatrixes.** It's not clear why the Manhattan DA did not, then, also begin arresting strippers. And what about random vanilla couples on a standard date-type thing, where the woman makes eyes at the man over dinner, and the man pays for the meal? Sounds like "sexual conduct for money" to me. Which could totally be prostitution, folks, so watch your backs.

In his piece "Is There Such A Thing As Kinky Sex?", Dr. Marty Klein says that:

If practicing kinky sex makes you "other," not one of "us," if it has non-sexual implications, if it means you're defective or dangerous — who wants that? And so as "kinky sex" and its practitioners are demonized, everyone is concerned — am I one of "those people"? It makes people fear their fantasies or curiosity, which then acquire too much power. It leads to secrecy between partners, as people withhold information about their preferences or experiences.

... I'd like to destroy the idea of binary contrast — that kinky and non-kinky sex are clearly different. Instead, I suggest that kinky and vanilla sex are parts of a continuum, the wide range of human eroticism. We all slide side to side along that continuum during our lives, sometimes in a single week. We don't need to fear our fantasies, curiosity, or (consensual) sexual preferences. They don't make us bad or different, just human. Some people like being emotional outlaws. They'll always find a way to get the frisson of otherness. But most people don't want to live that way. So ending kink's status as dangerous and wrong, and its practitioners as "other," is the most liberating thing we can do — for everyone. [2]

That's certainly reasonable from a political standpoint. I've made similar arguments. (Some folks, such as the brilliant male submissive writer maymay, also argue against the common idea that "kink" is limited to "BDSM"; they prefer an expansive definition of "kink" that denotes a vaster cornucopia of sexuality. [3])

Plus, **I even suspect that a lot of the distinctions made by BDSMers ourselves are based far more on stigma than sense**. For example, when I was younger, I went through a period where I couldn't stand to have the word "submissive" applied to myself. I insisted that I was into BDSM solely for the physical sensation, and swore I would never ever do something solely submission-oriented (such as wearing a collar). It was like I could only handle BDSM as long as I distanced myself from the power elements; the power elements carried too much stigma in my head for me to acknowledge them... yet.

I also used to carefully separate "BDSM" from "sex" in my head. Part of me felt like, "If my desire for pain and power is sexual, then it's weird. If it's not sexual, then it's less weird." (It looks strange when I type it, now, but I guess that's how sexual stigma works: it rarely holds up against the clear light of day.) It took me a while to integrate sexuality into my BDSM practice. In contrast, I once met a couple who told me that it took them a long time to do BDSM that **wasn't** part of sex. In **their** heads, the thought was more like: "If the desire for pain and power is sexual, then it's not weird. But if it's not sexual, then it's really weird."

I've heard of plenty of dungeons where sex is not allowed — sometimes for legal reasons, but sometimes because there is actually a social standard against it: people are like, "Dude, let's not get our nice pure BDSM all dirty by including sex." (Note: My experience is primarily with dungeons owned by "lifestyle" BDSMers — "lifestyle" being a clumsy word that attempts to denote those of us who are motivated to do BDSM for reasons other than money. While there is some overlap between "lifestyle" BDSM and professional BDSM, the overlap can be surprisingly rare, and professional BDSM is often banned at lifestyle BDSM parties. Lifestyle dungeons are often non-profit organizations, and often function more like community centers than moneymaking venues. I understand that some professional dungeons have a "no sex" rule out of a desire to protect the boundaries of dominatrixes who work there, who may not wish to be asked to engage in sex.)

There are also plenty of cultural groups who do things that look suspiciously like BDSM... who insist that they have nothing to do with BDSM. For example, I've heard of spanking clubs whose members get really mad if you dare bring BDSM up in their presence.

And then there's groups like Taken In Hand, a quasi-conservative organization. Actual testimonial from the Taken In Hand site:

There are lots of websites for people in the BDSM, D/s, DD (domestic discipline) and spanking communities. There are websites for people who belong to religions that advocate male-head-of-household marriage. There are even websites for Christians who are interested in BDSM. But there are very few websites for people who are interested in male-led intimate relationships but who are not interested in all that the above communities associate with this kind of relationship (jargon, clothes, etc.) Some of us don't even like thinking of this as a lifestyle. [4]

Well, my friend, you know what... you can refuse to call yourself BDSM all you want, and you can reject our "jargon" all you want, and you can "dislike" thinking of this "lifestyle" until the end of time... and you have every right to insist that we have nothing to do with you. But when your site has posts that include comments like "When my husband behaves in a dominant manner I basically swoon," or have titles like "Don't forget your whip," well... I'm just saying.

Also, since you mention rejecting BDSM "clothes"? I'll just say that I can be an astoundingly badass domme in a t-shirt. And I have done so. Multiple times.

Personally, I am particularly frustrated by the stigmatizing idea that BDSM has nothing to do with love. Sometimes I encounter this idea that BDSM has to be separated from sex because BDSM has nothing to do with sex, whereas sex supposedly "should" be about love. The truth is that both BDSM and sex are very different for different people, emotions-wise. Although many people experiment with "casual BDSM," the same way many people experiment with "casual sex," a stereotype that BDSMers **cannot** find love in the act is wrong and absurd.

So yeah. Nowadays, many of these "BDSM versus sex" reactions strike me as being born out of pure, irrational stigma. As Dr. Klein noted, these reactions are usually born of the terrible human urge to exclude: to find ways to differentiate ourselves from "those people." Humans apparently love to think things like: "I'm not like **those people**. It doesn't matter if I, for example, write extensive rape fantasy fiction! That couldn't possibly be BDSM! Because I'm not a BDSMer! Because BDSM is dirty."

But we shouldn't necessarily blame people for this instinct to reject and categorize: the instinct is one that comes from being scared and oppressed... because the social penalties for "getting it wrong" are high. Remember, those New York City dominatrixes thought they were "safe" from the law as long as BDSM didn't count as sex. But as soon as someone decided BDSM "counted as" sex, those dominatrixes were arrested.

It's just one more example of how sexual stigma for "different kinds of sex" is constantly intertwined. No type of consensual sexuality can express itself freely until people agree that "among consenting adults, there is no 'should'." The Romans, those ancient imperialists, used to say: "Divide and conquer." When consensual sexualities are scared of each other, we will continue to be conquered. **As long as "vanilla" people are afraid of "BDSM"... as long as "BDSMers" are afraid of being seen as "sexual"... as long as the social penalties for being a "slut" or a "whore" are incredibly steep... as long as sex workers are stigmatized and criminalized... everyone will be bound by these oppressive standards.**

* * *

The Embodied Side of BDSM versus Sex

Although Part 1 was all about how the divide between "BDSM" and "sex" is often nonsensical, or purely political, or socially constructed... **that doesn't mean that the divide does not exist.** I once had a conversation about ignoring social constructs with a wise friend, who noted dryly that: "One-way streets are a social construct. That doesn't mean we should ignore them." Just because the outside world influences our sexuality, does not mean that our sexual preferences are invalid.

Some polyamorous BDSMers have very different rules about having sex with outsiders, as opposed to doing BDSM with outsiders. For example, during the time when I was considering a transition to polyamory, I myself had a couple relationships where we were sexually monogamous — yet my partners agreed that I could do BDSM with people who weren't my partner. **Those particular partners felt jealous and threatened by the idea of me having sex with another man, but they didn't mind if I did BDSM with another man.** Maybe the feelings of those partners only arose because they categorized "BDSM" and "sex" into weirdly different socially-constructed ways... **but those partners' feelings were nonetheless real, and their feelings deserved respect.**

And there are also unmistakable ways that BDSM **feels** different from sex. There is something, bodily, that is **just plain different** about BDSM, as opposed to sex. I often find myself thinking of "BDSM feelings" and "sexual feelings" as flowing down two parallel channels in my head... sometimes these channels intersect, but sometimes they're far apart. The BDSM urge strikes me as deeply different, separate, from the sex urge. It can be fun to combine BDSM and sex, but there are definitely times when I want BDSM that feel very unlike most times when I want sex.

The biggest political reason why it's difficult to discuss this is the way in which we currently conceptualize sexuality through "orientations": we have built a cultural "orientation model" focused on the idea that "acceptable" sexuality is "built-in," or "innate." Some BDSMers consider BDSM an "orientation" — and I, myself, once found that thinking of BDSM as an orientation was extremely helpful in coming to terms with my BDSM desires. But one thing I don't like about the orientation model now is that it makes us sound like we're apologizing. "Poor little me! It's not my fault I'm straight! Or a domme! Whatever!" Why would any of these things be faults in the first place? Our bodies are our own, our experiences are our own, and our consent is our own to give.

The orientation model is one of the cultural factors that makes it hard to discuss sensory, sensual experiences without defaulting to sexuality. As commenter saurus pointed out on the *Feministe* version of part 1 of this post:

Sometimes I think that we have compulsions, needs or "fetishes" that aren't sexual, but lumping them in with sexuality is sometimes the most convenient or socially manageable way to deal with them or get those needs met. They might even physically arouse us for a variety of reasons, but that might be a side effect instead of the act's inherent nature. Which is not to say that every act can be cleanly cleaved into "sexual" and "non-sexual" — of course not. But I think we lack a language around these needs that doesn't use sexuality. I see a lot of groundbreaking work coming out of the asexual and disability justice communities in this regard (which is just to say that I find the folks in these groups are churning out some incredible ways to "queer" conventional dominant ideas about sexuality; not that they never have sex or whatever).

*I think one answer to that is to just open up the definition of sexuality to include these things, but as someone who identifies vehemently not as "sex positive" but as "sex non-judgmental," I know I don't personally want all my shit to be lumped in with sexuality. It just makes me picture some sex judgmental person insisting that "oh, that's **totally** sexual."* [5]

I, Clarisse, can certainly attest that it's common for people to have BDSM encounters that are "just" BDSM — "no sex involved". For example — an encounter where one partner whips the other, or gets whipped, and there's no genital contact or even discussion of genitals. And I'd like to stress that when I have encounters like that, they can be very satisfying without involving sex. The release — the high — I get from a heavy BDSM encounter can be its own reward.

I've also had BDSM encounters where I got turned on...

... but I didn't feel turned on until later, or afterwards, or until my partner did something specific to draw out my desire. For example — I remember that in one intense BDSM encounter as a domme, I wound up the encounter and pulled away from my partner. We had both been sitting down; I stood up and took off the metal claws I'd been using to rip him up. (Secretly, the claws were banjo picks. Do-It-Yourself BDSM is awesome.)

Then I leaned over my partner to pick something up. I had thought we were pretty much done, but he seized me as I leaned over, and he pulled me close and kissed my neck, and I literally gasped in shock. My sexual desire spiked so hard... I practically melted into his arms. And yet if you'd asked me, moments before, whether I was turned on... I would have said "no."

One way to think about it might be that sometimes, BDSM "primes" me so that I'm more receptive to sexual energy. It's not that BDSM is exactly a sexual turn-on in itself; sometimes it is, but that's actually surprisingly rare. Yet BDSM often... gets my blood flowing?... and seems to "open the floodgates," so sexual hormones can storm through my body.

And just in case this wasn't complex enough for you... on the other hand, I've had BDSM encounters where my partner tried to take it sexual, and I wasn't interested. It's almost like there's a BDSM cycle that I often get into, and once the cycle is sufficiently advanced, I can't easily shift out of it.

Sometimes, when I'm near the "peak" of the BDSM cycle, then being interrupted for any reason — sex, or anything else — is absolutely horrible. I'd rather be left on the edge of orgasm, burning with sexual desire, than be hurt until I **almost** cry. The emotion becomes a stubborn lump in my throat; becomes balled up in my chest. At times like that, it almost feels hard to breathe.

A while back, a reporter named Mac McClelland who worked in Haiti made a splash by writing an article about how she used "violent sex" to ease her Post-Traumatic Stress Disorder. I briefly reported on the article for *Feministe,* but at the time, I didn't share many of my thoughts about what she wrote. [6] One thing I did say was that the reporter didn't use any BDSM terminology — at least not that I spotted. She didn't seem to conceptualize her desire for "violent sex" as a BDSM thing at all. Interestingly, a *Feministe* commenter named Jadey, who has experience with kink, also didn't conceptualize the reporter's article that way. Jadey wrote:

I don't think she's bad or wrong, and I don't think her method of coping with her PTSD is bad or wrong.... [Yet] I've got a kink/BDSM background, but that's not what she's describing here. She's talking about something far different, and I can't understand the experience she describes with Isaac. It is... incomprehensible. [7]

I want to stress here that I, Clarisse Thorn, have never been diagnosed with Post-Traumatic Stress Disorder. (And I've undergone plenty of analysis, so I'm sure that if I had PTSD, someone would have noticed by now.) And just in case it needs to be said again, I'll also stress that I have no intention of telling anyone else how to define their own experiences. And just in case it needs to be said again, there is a big difference between consenting BDSM and abuse.

But unlike Jadey, when I read the original "violent sex" article, the reporter's description of her encounter sounded a lot like some of my preferences... indeed, it sounded like some of the BDSM encounters I've had. For example, the reporter writes:

"Okay," my partner said. "I love you, okay?" I said, I know, okay. And with that he was on me, forcing my arms to my sides, then pinning them over my head, sliding a hand up under my shirt when I couldn't stop him. The control I'd lost made my torso scream with anxiety; I cried out desperately as I kicked myself free.... When I got out from under him and started to scramble away, he simply caught me by a leg or an upper arm or my hair and dragged me back. By the time he pinned me by my neck with one forearm so I was forced to use both hands to free up space between his elbow and my windpipe, I'd largely exhausted myself.

And just like that, I'd lost. It's what I was looking for, of course. But my body — my hard-fighting, adrenaline-drenched body — reacted by exploding into terrible panic.... I did not enjoy it in the way a person getting screwed normally would. But as it became clear that I could endure it, I started to take deeper breaths. And my mind stayed there, stayed present even when it became painful.... My body felt devastated but relieved; I'd lost, but survived. After he climbed off me, he gathered me up in his arms. I broke into a thousand pieces on his chest, sobbing so hard that my ribs felt like they were coming loose.

... Isaac pulled my hair away from my wet face, repeating over and over and over something that he probably believed but that I had to relearn. "You are so strong," he said. "You are so strong. You are so strong." [8]

Sounds extremely familiar to me.

Now, it's not like I have BDSM encounters like that all the time; indeed, experiences of that type are relatively rare for me. But the reporter's description doesn't sound "far different" from what I've experienced. Certainly not "incomprehensible." There's only one big difference, actually: I've never had such an intense BDSM experience in which my partner also had penis-in-vagina sex with me. (I'm assuming the reporter means "penis-in-vagina" sex when she talks about "getting screwed," but I could be wrong.)

Honestly, I'm not sure why I would **want** to combine vaginal sex with an experience like that. Vaginal sex strikes me, personally, as kinda incidental to what I'd get out of it. But maybe I'll try it sometime and it'll be the greatest thing in the world; we'll see, I guess.

Sometimes I find that I've still got a "BDSM versus sex" distinction to work out, although I seem to have comfortably settled into the frameworks I've created. One of my very first blog entries, back in 2008, was called "Casual Sex? Casual Kink?", and I spent the whole thing musing about whether I was more or less okay with casual BDSM than I was with casual sex. [9]

These days, I find that I'm kinda okay with both casual sex and casual BDSM, but I much prefer those experiences within intimate relationships. Make no mistake, my friends: BDSM can include a great deal of love and connection... at least as much as sex.

To hammer the point home, let me tell you about what happened after I broke up with a much-beloved ex-boyfriend: Mr. Inferno. It was back when I was very focused on being monogamous with my partners. Mr. Inferno broke up with me, and a month or two later I had the chance to have an overnight BDSM encounter with another man, so I took it. There was no genital contact; the whole encounter was limited to this guy giving me orders, and hurting me until I cried.

But I remember, even as I slipped into the familiar emotional cycle, that I couldn't let go: I couldn't let go because I felt like I was betraying Mr. Inferno. He'd broken my heart, but on some level I felt like I still belonged to him. It was wrong, wrong, wrong for me to cry in someone else's arms. The **wrongness** rang through me like a bell. It was so impossible, unbearable — all I could think was how it should have been Mr. Inferno. I choked on the tears. I couldn't lose myself in them.

Later, I mentioned to my partner that one of my ex-boyfriends (not Mr. Inferno) had trouble dealing with my BDSM desires. "Ah," my partner said. "That explains why you had trouble letting yourself cry." I decided to nod; to let him think he knew what was blocking me off. It seemed simpler.

In the morning, I had breakfast with my partner. We hugged and split up, and I went for a walk until I found a local creek. I sat next to the creek and I closed my eyes and I let the helpless tears slip down my cheeks.

I'd felt (and I'd known others who felt) this way after the dissolution of a sexual relationship. But I had never imagined that such a reaction of intense bodily loyalty could apply to BDSM as well as sex. I hadn't anticipated that I'd feel such heartbreaking, visceral loss just because I let another man hurt me.

So different, and yet so the same.

* * *

This can be found on the Internet in two parts:
http://clarissethorn.com/blog/2011/10/09/bdsm-versus-sex-part-1-political-concerns/

and

http://clarissethorn.com/blog/2011/10/14/bdsm-versus-sex-part-2-how-does-it-feel/

* * *

* * *

S&M:
[theory] BDSM Roles, "Topping From The Bottom," and "Service Top"

I wrote this post in 2011.

* * *

I often say that all **consensual** sexuality is okay. Open relationships? S&M? Same-sex partnerships? One-night stands? Porn? I could care less how people have sex, as long as the people involved are consenting adults. This means that most of the interesting and important questions are about consent: how do we make sure that we always have consensual sex? How do we ensure that we're always respecting our own boundaries and our partners' boundaries? How do we talk about our preferences and our consent? I write a lot about sexual communication for this reason.

Every once in a while, though, there's something interesting to discuss besides consent. (Totally weird, I know!) One of those interesting things is stereotypes. Also interesting: bad dynamics in the BDSM community.

One example of a bad, weird dynamic is the "one true way" thing. Some people act like there are "right" ways and "wrong" ways to do consensual BDSM — as if some consensual BDSM is more legit than other consensual BDSM. Often, people do this via what we call "role policing": they make claims about "real submission" and "real dominance." (Even worse, people will sometimes act like dominant people are socially "better" or "more important" than submissive people. Or they'll act like men are "inherently" dominant, or women "inherently" submissive. It's a clusterfuck! Thomas MacAulay Millar has a great essay about this called "Domism." [1])

Examples of role policing might include:

* "If you were really submissive, then you would be serving my dinner right now instead of having me serve myself."

* "If you were really dominant, then you would pay for my

drinks."

* "If you were really submissive, then you wouldn't be confident enough to write a blog about your sex life." (Not that I'm biased or anything.)

Sometimes these are hilarious light-hearted jokes. But sometimes they're not. Sometimes they're bullshit, and they make people feel as though they're "bad at submission" or "bad at dominance." Also, it gets really silly when we start thinking about switches — people who can feel comfortable in the dominant role or the submissive role, such as myself.

One very common, relevant assumption is that dominant people always enjoy inflicting pain: that sadists and dominants are always the same group. They're not! Sometimes people are into sadism, or into dominance, or maybe they're into a lot of sadism but a little dominance, or whatever. The same thing goes for submission: sometimes people are submissive and like taking pain, but sometimes people are submissive without being masochistic, or maybe they're into a little bit of submission and a lot of masochism, or whatever.

Or maybe they're masochists who like ordering their partners to hurt them. I once threw a memorable party at which my then-boyfriend, a mostly-submissive gentleman, arranged for a bunch of our friends to grab me and hold me down while he ate cake off my body. As he did this, I clearly recall shouting at him: "You better hurt me, or I'm going to safeword on your ass." So he hurt me! It was great.

Because "submissive" and "masochist" aren't always the same thing — and "dominant" and "sadist" aren't always the same thing — the BDSM community uses the terms "bottom" and "top." A "bottom" is a blanket term for a submissive and/or a masochist — the receiving partner. A "top" is a blanket term for a dominant and/or a sadist — the partner who is providing sensation. The point is to have words that indicate who is giving and who is receiving, without making claims about each partner's preferences. (These words can also be used as verbs. For example, if I am "topping," then I am in the dominant and/or sadistic position.)

And yet! **Even though we have these handy terms "top" and "bottom," which are specifically designed to help us avoid making assumptions, people end up making assumptions.** There are two common BDSM community phrases that are often deployed in tones of disgust and irritation. One of those phrases is "topping from the bottom." The other phrase is "service top."

"Topping from the bottom" indicates a person who exercises power in the relationship, despite being in the "bottom" position. There's nothing wrong with doing that, as long as both partners consent. But some people talk about "topping from the bottom" like it's bad — as if power ought to belong to one side or the other; as if the bottom should never express preferences or make decisions about what's going on. Which is ridiculous.

I'll grant that it can be annoying if I'm trying to be a top, and my partner isn't listening or isn't doing what I want. But in those cases, it's important to pay attention to what is actually going on. Is my partner resisting because he actually doesn't want to do what we're doing? In that case, I should respect his preferences. Or maybe my partner is resisting because he wants me to punish him. Or maybe we just have bad chemistry! Whatever. The point is, "topping from the bottom" isn't inherently a bad thing. "Topping from the bottom" doesn't make the bottom into a "bad submissive" or whatever. It just means that either the person is trying to communicate, or the person is looking for a certain kind of push-pull dynamic.

Simultaneously, there's the phrase "service top." It's basically the same thing in reverse. A "service top" is a top who enjoys topping in line with his partner's desires. And once again, some people act like this is a bad thing — as if service tops "aren't dominant enough." But it's not inherently a bad thing! If a service top is doing things just because her partner likes them... then good for her!

I sometimes use phrases like "topping from the bottom" and "service top" to describe dynamics of a relationship: to talk about what is actually going on. But that's because I don't think there's anything wrong with topping from the bottom or being a service top. I try to avoid joking around about it unless I know that the person I'm talking to is not sensitive about the topic. And I really don't like it when people use those phrases while role policing.

BDSM can carry an incredible emotional charge, and a lot of the time, people will want comfort and snuggles after doing BDSM together. Sometimes, part of that comfort and snuggles includes reassuring the partner: "I know you just beat the shit out of me until I cried; I enjoyed it — I still like you and think you're a good person." Or, "I know you called your safeword while I was hurting you; I still think you're a beautiful submissive and you did a great job — in fact I love it when you call your safeword because it helps me understand you better." I think that in these cases it's totally okay to say something like, "You're such a good submissive." But it's so important to keep in mind that there isn't some kind of submission that's inherently "better" than any other kind — or dominance that's "better" — or sadism, masochism, whatever.

And here is the part of the entry where I pull aside the mask and reveal that even though I claimed I wouldn't talk about consent... I was secretly talking about consent all along!

The consent problem here is that **role policing can be used to mess with people's consent**, because role policing can be used to pressure people. If a person wants to feel like a "real submissive," and you tell them that "real submissives" always receive anal sex... then the person might accept anal sex even if he doesn't really want to... because he wants to be a "real submissive."

I have personally witnessed accusations of "topping from the bottom" or "service top" being used to hurt people who were just trying to communicate, or arrange a relationship that they liked. For example: "I thought you were a submissive. Why are you asking me to tie you up? Stop topping from the bottom! I'm the dominant partner, I make the decisions!"

An important facet of consent is trying to create a pressure-free environment, so that all partners feel comfortable talking about what they want. Sometimes, it can be very hard to create that environment, because pressure isn't always easy to see or understand — but if we want maximum consent power, then we have to do our best. One way to create a pressure-free environment is to be careful about phrases like "topping from the bottom" and "service top" and the role policing that can go along with those phrases.

* * *

This can be found on the Internet at:
http://clarissethorn.com/blog/2011/11/12/bdsm-roles-topping-from-the-bottom-and-service-top/

* * *

* * *

FEMINISM:
[theory] "Inherent Female Submission": The Wrong Question

I wrote this post in mid-2011. Perhaps you can tell that I was in the depths of my obsession with pickup artists at the time... those guys talk about "inherent female submission" ad nauseam. Not all pickup artists are evil and misogynist, but the ones who are love to beat this horse.

* * *

I get a certain question occasionally, from straight dudes who've had a number of sexual partners. It goes something like this:
*All the women I've slept with liked pain. They asked me to hurt them or to dominate them in bed. I did it, and enjoyed it; I loved how much it turned them on... it turned them on a lot. But I keep thinking about it now. Why are all women into being submissive and/or masochistic in bed? What does that **mean**?*

They ask me this question in vaguely worried tones. Sometimes they say things like, "It's really creepy." It is obvious that these dudes are rather concerned about this Terrible Truth.

Here's my short answer for those guys: If you know women who are submissive and/or masochistic in bed, that means those particular women like being submissive and/or masochistic in bed. It doesn't mean anything else.

You're still here? Ah, well. I figured that wouldn't satisfy. So here's a longer answer:

Firstly, if you're a straight dude, and you're drawing conclusions about "all women" based on the women you get involved with, then stop. Just stop. Even if you have slept with zillions of women, you don't actually know what all women want, because:

A) **Your experience of women is limited to women who got involved with you.** You are screening for certain qualities, sometimes consciously, and sometimes unconsciously or by accident. If you tend to enjoy the dominant role, for example, or if you use a dominant style of flirtation, then you could be screening for submissive female partners, whether you intend to or not.

B) **Everyone has biases, including you.** I love the old saying: "When all you have is a hammer, everything looks like a nail." If you have a bias towards seeing women as sexually submissive (and you almost certainly do, because female sexual submission is a hugely prevalent cultural trope), then you're more likely to see female submission in places where it does not exist.

C) **Women, like people of all genders, are demonstrably varied.** You really don't think non-submissive straight women exist? Why then, it must be so inconvenient when I point you to the work of blatantly dominant women, huh? [1] It's shocking, I know... next I'll be telling you that queer and asexual women exist! (Not to mention women who switch among roles — from submissive to dominant, from sadistic to masochistic. I primarily go for submissive masochism, but still, I myself play for both teams.)

The thing is, though... no matter how many holes I can poke in these dudes' anecdotal "data," I can't bring myself to worry like they do. Even if a brilliant, well-reviewed study came out tomorrow and proved beyond a shadow of a doubt that 100% of women are submissive masochists in bed, I wouldn't care. (I bet you my left ear this study will never happen, but I'm just saying, even if it did, I wouldn't care.)

Let me say it really clearly: **Even if most women are submissive masochists in bed (and I'm not convinced most women are), there's nothing wrong with that. I don't care.**

Why don't I care? Because all this anxiety and argument about submission — and in particular, what it means for women to be submissive; whether all women are submissive; whether women are "inherently" or "biologically" submissive; whether BDSM is an orientation or not... this is all the wrong question.

I'll note that the research seems to indicate that more kinky women are submissive than dominant. [2] Of course, this doesn't necessarily indicate anything about the tastes of women who don't identify as kinky. And it's probably biased by culture, in that everything from fashion photos to romance novels emphasizes female submission and male dominance. Within BDSM culture, female dominance and male submission are often disappeared, much to the justified frustration of actual female dominants and male submissives. [3,4] When all you have is a hammer, everything looks like a nail — sometimes including our own psyches and sexualities.

Plus, if the only available patterns for kink emphasize something a person doesn't like, then that person will probably avoid kink. Note that in the research I linked to, for example, the percentage of submissive women was higher in samples from within the BDSM subculture than in samples from outside the BDSM subculture... perhaps because many BDSM subcultural gatherings emphasize female submission and thereby alienate women who are primarily dominant. Anyway, regardless... this is **still** the wrong question.

In short, "inherent female submission" is the wrong question.

Certainly, I've fought through a lot of personal fears about what my interest in BDSM meant for me as a feminist... but these days I have trouble understanding what, exactly, got me so upset. I can't believe how long it took me to outthink those fears. Now, it just seems instinctively obvious to me that:

1) **The only reason these conversations happen at all is that BDSM, and especially submission, is seen as broken and problematic and screwed-up and a sign of weakness.** What if we viewed S&M proclivities as a superpower rather than a perversion? What if submission and masochism, in particular, were viewed as signs of strength and endurance and emotional complexity, rather than weakness?

2) **Sexual kinks don't necessarily affect one's performance in non-sexual fields.** A sexually submissive woman won't make a bad CEO (at least, not because she's sexually submissive). I mean, come on, it's not like there aren't sexually submissive men in powerful corporate positions. When I was younger I remember being scared that, in some bizarre way, I was betraying women's liberation by being sexually submissive; this seems ridiculous to me now. That fear can only survive in a culture where people are looking for excuses — no matter how flimsy — to control and disempower women. Because it doesn't make any damn sense on its own.

3) **Rape is still rape. Everyone still has a right to consent, including submissives.** A submissive partner (of any gender) must be able to withdraw consent, and a dominant partner (of any gender) must make space for them to withdraw consent. It's always great when both partners can have an honest conversation about desire, trying to avoid pressure and unfair expectations (whether those expectations arise from sexist culture or from whatever else). Safewords are one frequently-recommended communication tactic for those who have rape fantasies, although they aren't the only tactic. What really burns me about many discussions of "inherent female submission" is that they have horrible overtones of blaming

the victim and justifying rape... much like "she was wearing a short skirt, so she was asking for it." In reality, "inherent female submission" says absolutely nothing about women's right to choose our partners and protect our bodily integrity. Female submissives have made it perfectly clear that we do, in fact, claim that right.

I think most of the dudes who ask this question come to me, a feminist, and they ask this question in hushed and worried tones, because they are decent guys and they are concerned about The Consequences Of This Terrible Truth. I'd venture a guess that they've met other dudes who talk nonstop about how women are *vain and stupid and hysterical and, snicker snicker, why do we let those dumb bitches even vote and, oh by the way, did you know that lots of girls like to be choked and isn't that sooo significant...?* And so these decent guys who are talking to me — they have learned to associate discussions of female sexual submission with anti-feminism, and with attempts to disempower women in other spheres.

Being decent guys, this worries them, because they know that people of all genders deserve equal opportunity. But it is all a red herring! It's a series of illusions thrown up by BDSM stigma; by the idea that sexual kinks always mean something about the rest of a person's life; by people who don't comprehend that everyone has the right to consent; and by blatant, uncomplicated misogyny! Female sexual submission isn't even close to a threat to women's liberation, unless we allow it to be. If we weren't constantly forced to deal with the broken assumptions of a broken misogynist culture, this question would never occur to anyone!

It doesn't matter nearly as much what the cultural patterns are around sexual submission, as it does how we deal with sexual submission. If your partner is submissive, you can respect their desires and also respect them as a person. As I already noted, in BDSM this means communicating carefully, like with safewords and/or other tactics. Some people can have great sexual communication that's totally non-verbal — but I always encourage explicit verbal communication because for many people, it's easier to make intentions and desires clear that way, and tactics like safewords provide a fallback in case there's a mistake.

So: what does "inherent female submission" mean for women, for feminism, for equal rights, for women who work, for powerful women? For housewives? For disabled women? For female rape survivors? For rape survivors of other genders?

Say it with me now: It's the wrong question. The mere act of asking this question implies a cultural context that is seeking excuses

to disempower women. **Female sexual submission means nothing**...
   ... **except what every woman wants it to mean, for herself.**

* * *

This can be found on the Internet at:
http://clarissethorn.com/blog/2011/07/01/inherent-female-submission-the-wrong-question/

* * *

***

MANLINESS:
[theory] *Fifty Shades of Grey, Fight Club,* and the Complications of Male Dominance

I wrote this in early 2012, when everyone and their brother was talking about the amazingly successful fanfiction-turned-BDSM-smut Fifty Shades of Grey *trilogy, by E.L. James. [1] (The online version of this post contains a bunch of relevant current links at the end.) It's one of my rare attempts at pegging an article to a recent news item; I had been planning to write this article for months, but* Fifty Shades *gave me an opportunity to actually do it. My main goal as a sex writer has always been to put forth analysis that's responsive to the conversations I hear a lot, yet independent of the latest craze. For one thing, I almost never care to track what Everyone Is Talking About Right This Minute!!, and I'm irritated to think that I ought to do so. But I've come to reluctantly understand that responding to current news is one of the best ways to get more eyeballs on my work, so I'm trying to do more of that. I've also been encouraged in that direction by employers — most notably the gender-lens website RoleReboot.org, where I took on the role of Sex + Relationships Section Editor in late 2011. A slightly shorter version of this article was originally published there.*

***

Much is being made of the highly successful S&M erotica novel *Fifty Shades of Grey.* People are blaming feminism for making women into submissives, blaming feminism for preventing women from being submissives, blaming women for having sexual desires at all, and a whole lot of other boring and typical stuff that comes up in any conversation about women and S&M. News flash: it's not the feminist revolution that is "causing" women to have fantasies of submission. S&M fantasies have been around since the beginning of time. (And the 1950s S&M-sensation book, *The Story of O,* was much better written than *Fifty Shades of Grey.)*

As an S&M writer, I hear a lot of allegations about how "all" (or "almost all") women are sexually submissive and how this must Mean Something. This is echoed in the coverage of *Fifty Shades of Grey,* in which everyone is demanding to know What It All Means About Women. I've already taken on these questions as they apply to women. But there's another submerged question here — about men. There's plenty of talk and stereotypes about how men are inherently violent, or more aggressive than women, or "the dominant sex."

As I said in my previous article: I think it's quite questionable whether women are "inherently submissive," but my conclusion is that I don't care. It doesn't actually matter to me whether women in general are "inherently submissive" (though I really don't think women are), or whether submissive women's preferences are philosophically Deep And Meaningful (though I'm not convinced they are). What matters is:

1. How women (or any other people) can explore sexually submissive preferences consensually,

2. How women (or any other people) can compartmentalize submissive preferences so that their whole lives are safe and fulfilling and happy, and

3. How women (or any other people) can be treated well in arenas that aren't even relevant to their sexuality — like the workplace.

This is also how I feel about these ideas of "inherent male violence." I don't buy that men are "the dominant sex" or that men are "inherently violent." Based on what I've read, it seems quite clear that individuals with higher testosterone levels — who are, incidentally, not always men — often experience more aggressive feelings. Yet that's a far cry from large-scale generalizations, and it's also frequently irrelevant to questions about how people can best deal with those aggressive feelings. Plus, psychological submission can be a very separate thing from physical aggression levels.

Much of the time, when it comes to aggression, anger management is the answer, the same way a naturally shy or submissive person needs to learn to set boundaries. But there are circumstances where catharsis is completely acceptable. Lots of perfectly decent men have urges towards violent dominance; what do they do about it? How much do they agonize, like Christian Grey in *Fifty Shades of Grey,* and how much do they explore their desires in a consensual and reasonable way?

I always thought that the late-90s movie *Fight Club* was fascinating primarily because of its lens on masculinity and violence. It's not just about the violence men to do each other, but to themselves. Quotes include "You have to give up; you have to know that someday you're gonna die," and "The first rule of Fight Club is: you do not talk about Fight Club." I first watched it before I knew much about S&M, but now whenever I think about it, I think about how the idea of a fight club — where people would get together and fight, for catharsis and community — is so very reminiscent of how a lot of people experience S&M. *Fight Club* even has safewords. Someone says stop, you stop. I obviously don't support the endpoint of the *Fight Club* story (i.e., blowing up buildings), but the idea of establishing a men's community via a fight club seems reasonable to me.

So, what are the practicalities of dealing with aggressive or dominant tendencies in the sexual arena? As an S&M person, I've experimented with dominance as well as submission, but because violence is so associated with masculinity, I turned to some egalitarian male S&Mers for advice. I believe that even for non-S&M people, their perspectives make a really good lens for ideas of gender and violence and power. Of course, the first thing one of my friends told me was: "I'm not sure I really see dominance in general as being particularly masculine. I don't really think it's a gender associated thing."

That gentleman, who comments around the Internet under the name Scootah, went on to add: "I've certainly worried about my kinks in the past. I mean fundamentally, I get really, really turned on by grabbing someone by the hair, throwing them into the wall, backhanding them, etc. That's a pretty disturbing thought for an egalitarian who's worked with abuse victims. I spend a lot of time considering the ethics of my kinks; my partners' enthusiastic consent is a major priority."

Jay Wiseman, author of the famous S&M primer *SM101*, talks about his own early fears towards the beginning of that book. He writes about how he began having sadistic fantasies, and went to the public library to research them. All he could find was portraits of serial killers, which scared the hell out of him. He writes:

I decided to keep myself under surveillance. I made up my mind that I was not going to hurt anybody. If I thought I was turning into someone that would harm somebody else, then I would either put myself in a mental institution or commit suicide. And thus I lived, waiting and watching to see if I was turning into someone that I needed to shoot.

Fortunately, Wiseman found partners who were open to exploring S&M with him, and went on to write extensively about safety and consent and communication within S&M. Trying to communicate in an egalitarian way is arguably the most complicated part of any S&M encounter; as Scootah told me, "There are certainly elements that could potentially unbalance a relationship in my favor. I'm a big reasonably strong guy. I do usually make more money than my partners. I also have this whole sense of position in the local S&M community. I mostly just try to be aware of those things. I try to be very careful about not taking advantage of that and negotiate clearly and not pressure people."

There are lots of ways to do clear negotiation, including asking open-ended questions before any S&M actually happens: "What are you interested in? Could you go into that more?" There's also a huge emphasis on talking through the S&M encounter afterwards, as part of the post-S&M processing we call aftercare. As another gent who goes by Noir said: "It really helped me to have a few great, feminist S&M partners. Having that echo of 'it's OK, I want this,' as well as the honest feedback when I do wrong really helped shape how I experience S&M, and with who. It's meant I learned how better to read and grasp the people in my, er, grasp."

Noir also noted, "I strive to use dominance and submission as a tool for helping my partners become stronger, in ways that also feed my S&M preferences. For example, I tend to form long-term interests with women who want a 'safe space' to extend and explore their ability to be sluts, with all that can imply. But in the process, we also explore how becoming more confident in one's sexuality also can reflect into everyday life. Also, just coming to spaces in the S&M community can be a goldmine of information. All a dominant man has to do is read, listen, open up and understand. One thing I learned was that my fears about reinforcing our messed-up society were shared by women into kink... but also that my ways of approaching the topic, as 'oh, we're so controlled by society!' were themselves pushing too much agency out of women's choices. There's a balance there that we guys who identify as both feminist and kinky have to respect, and that can come from listening to feminist women struggle with these issues, themselves."

The alternative sexuality advocate Pepper Mint (who has his own blog [2]) told me that in terms of putting gender on his experiences, "I am a bit genderqueer, and I personally experience dominance with either a feminine or masculine vibe from moment to moment. Certain activities — like punching — feel masculine, while others — like whipping — feminine in the moment. Also, I switch, meaning that I don't always take the dominant role. Strangely, my most clearly masculine S&M activity is masochism. I always feel very manly while taking pain. I don't think I can clearly explain why these things have attached to gender in my head, though presumably I'm being affected by cultural tropes to some extent."

The consensus in general was that dominance, whether masculine or feminine, is something that happens in an encounter... not outside it. As Pepper put it, "New guys often want to play hard or do hardcore things, and will often boast and swagger. Kinky women almost always recognize this as dangerous bullshit. Learn to chill out and not take yourself too seriously, and learn to start with a light careful touch when playing with someone new. Learn to ask for help and guidance, both from others in your S&M community and from your partners."

Scootah agreed: "The first mistake I see newbie doms make is trying too hard to be some kind of bad ass. Admit your inexperience. Be seen learning. Be modest and have a good time. Learn to communicate well, and to really be friends with your prospective partners."

For me, the bottom line of these conversations is that questioning gender roles, and understanding gender complications, is an ongoing process. People have a lot of urges and preferences that are politically inconvenient and which we will never fully understand. Whether we're shaped by biology or culture, those feelings will still exist for now, and we have to deal with them. There are ways to do almost anything such that people respect each other, though — whatever the implications for gender or power. Violence is complicated ground, but it can be used in balanced and consensual ways that end up bonding people together. *Fifty Shades of Grey* and *Fight Club* are both examples, and I haven't even touched competitive sports!

* * *

This can be found on the Internet at:
http://clarissethorn.com/blog/2012/04/20/50-shades-of-grey-fight-club-and-the-complications-of-male-dominance/

* * *

* * *

ABUSE:
[theory] The Alt Sex Anti-Abuse Dream Team

I wrote this post in 2010 for the high-profile feminist blog Feministe. *If I were to write it today, then I would write it differently. In particular, if I were writing it today, then I would emphasize that there are actually two primary patterns for abusive S&M perpetrators. There are the ones I emphasized in this post, the ones who prey on inexperienced people outside the community... but then there's another category: perpetrators who achieve high status within the community and then use it to get away with non-consensual things. Other BDSMers have been writing about this more and more, and the discussion is really heating up right now, in 2012. My fellow feminist BDSM writer Thomas MacAulay Millar has a particularly long, complex blog series about patterns of abuse in the BDSM community that gives a lot of great reference links to other articles on the same topic. I've mentioned Thomas before; I don't always agree with him, but he's principled and passionate and smart. He blogs at the* Yes Means Yes *blog, and the series is being published post-by-post even as I write this. The first post in the series is available at this link:*
http://yesmeansyesblog.wordpress.com/2012/03/23/theres-a-war-on-part-1-troubles-been-brewing/

* * *

BDSMers face a lot of stigma around our sexuality, and this can be a major problem when BDSMers are trying to deal with abusive situations. I've written a lot about generally negative conceptions of BDSM — they can briefly be summarized as:
* S&M is wicked,
* abnormal,
* a sign of mental or emotional instability,
* inherently abusive,
* or even antifeminist.
Given this climate, it's not surprising that two things almost

always happen when BDSM and abuse come up:

1) People of all genders who are abused are often unwilling to report. **People of all genders who are abused within BDSM relationships tend to be particularly unwilling to report.** Victim-blaming is already rampant in mainstream society — just imagine what happens to, for example, a woman who has admitted that she enjoys being consensually slapped across the face, if she attempts to report being raped. And that's assuming the abuse survivor is willing to report in the first place; ze may prefer not to negotiate the minefield of anti-SM stereotypes ze will be up against, ze may be afraid of being outed, etc.

2) Members of the BDSM community sometimes push back against real or perceived anti-SM stigma by talking about how abuse is rare within the BDSM community. A BDSM blog post and comments over at the awesome blog SM-Feminist claim that **not only is abuse within the community rare, but abusive BDSM relationships seem more likely to happen outside the community.** [1] In fact, if you look then you can find posts from submissive women who found that getting into the BDSM community, being exposed to its ideals and concepts, helped them escape or understand their past abusive relationships. [2]

I tend to think that (2) is a really good point — particularly the bit about how abusive BDSM relationships are more likely to happen outside the community, due in part to lack of resources and support for survivors. For this reason, I tend to stress the role of the community in positive BDSM experiences, and I encourage newcomers to seek out their local community. But lots of people don't have access to a local community at all, especially if they're not in a big city. Plus, lots of people have trouble enjoying their local community for whatever reason, perhaps because they have nothing in common with local S&Mers aside from sexuality, or because they don't have time to integrate into a whole new subculture.

There's also the unfortunate fact that point #2 sometimes reacts with point #1 in a toxic way — that is, it can ironically be harder for abuse survivors to talk about abuse within the BDSM community because the community is pushing back so hard against the stereotype of abusive BDSM. **I've spoken to BDSMers who feel that the S&M community pushes back far too hard, and that survivors are being aggressively silenced simply because the rest of us are so invested in fighting mainstream stereotypes.** I have never personally experienced this, but I would not be surprised if I did. And the fact is that I'm sure there are toxic dynamics in some

BDSM communities — we aren't a monolith, folks — and that even in 100% awesome communities, I'm sure there are at least a few abusive relationships. And **even one abusive relationship in the community is obviously too many.**

As Thomas MacAulay Millar wrote when the most recent abusive BDSM case hit the media, "Our declaration that the abusers are not us has to be substantive." This is something we should be taking action on. But how? [3]

* * *

Dynamics Within the Community

I have personally had excellent experiences within the S&M community. However, I am also pretty thick-skinned (unfortunately, this is partly due to lots of time spent working in a sexist industry); and I have a well developed sense of my own boundaries. I am saying this not to sound self-congratulatory but because I believe that, due to being thick-skinned, I may be less bothered by actual harassment and pressuring dynamics than others are. Also, I am lucky enough that I've never experienced an assault. Therefore, it's incumbent upon me to listen to how other S&Mers — especially female or genderqueer S&Mers — feel about their experiences being pressured within the community.

There are issues that even I have noticed. For example, I think that there is a distasteful tendency to talk about "real BDSM" or "serious BDSM," as if some S&M is more legitimate than other S&M. That's wrong and dangerous because it can make some people feel as though they have to push past their boundaries — do things they aren't comfortable with — in order to be accepted, liked, or seen as "real." On the rare occasions that I encounter this, I try to point out the problems right there and then. **There is no such thing as "more real" and "less real" S&M. The only truly important part about any S&M activity is that it happen among enthusiastic, consenting adults.**

Thomas once wrote to me by email that "I tend to think that the dynamics of abuse in the community are a combination of the desire to avoid washing our laundry in public, patriarchy colonizing our own, and the usual thing in small communities where people's willingness to do the right thing in theory bumps up against their personal friends and loyalties." I completely agree. I'd add that similar issues arise in almost all small communities, and it's not fair to blame S&M in itself for these problems. At the same time, though, **it's incumbent upon all BDSMers to contribute to an environment where people who don't want to participate can easily say "no," and can rely on being supported by others when they do.**

* * *

Existing Anti-Abuse Initiatives in the BDSM Community

Finding existing initiatives is a bit of a piecemeal project, but here's what I've run across.

* **A variety of pamphlets and written statements.** One example was released by The Network/La Red, a rather unique anti-abuse organization for lesbians, bi women and trans people. One panel of the pamphlet shows a picture of handcuffs, and the text says:

*The most basic difference between S/M and abuse is **Consent**. It is not consent if...*
** You did **not** expressly give consent.*
** You are afraid to say **no**.*
** You say **yes** to avoid conflict.*
** You say **yes** to avoid consequences (i.e. losing a job, losing your home, being outed).*
S/M is...
* Always consensual.
* Done with respect for limits.
* Enjoyed by all partners.
* Fun, erotic, and loving.
* Done with an understanding of trust.
* Never done with the intent to harm or damage.
Just because you consent to play does not mean you consent to everything. You have the right to set limits.

(You can look at images of the pamphlet on my Flickr account. [4])

Some SM organizations have also released statements on SM and abuse, such as the national Leather Leadership Conference and New York's Lesbian Sex Mafia. [5] Note that at the bottom of the LSM page, they mention that they've sensitized a local abuse hotline; if I ever get a grant or something to start a pro-sex anti-abuse center, I'll immediately grill the LSM to see how they got in with that hotline and what they said.

* **Kink Aware counselors.** I talk about this all the time, but I think it bears repeating as often as possible. The National Coalition for Sexual Freedom maintains an online list of Kink Aware Professionals, which is a grassroots effort begun by writer/activist Race Bannon and includes doctors, lawyers, and therapists. [6] The list is pretty much open and opt-in — professionals go to the KAP site and offer to list themselves there — and this is one reason it's not a good idea to assume that any given professional will be a great fit for you. Personally, when I was coming into my BDSM identity, I found a Kink Aware therapist to be incredibly helpful — but while I was finding him, I visited another therapist who was not at all helpful.

When people ask me for kink-friendly survivors' resources, I always tell them to seek a KAP therapist first.

* **The annual Alternative Sexualities conference.** This is a comparatively new effort from the Community-Academic Consortium for Research on Alternative Sexualities. They describe it as "a conference for clinicians and researchers, addressing issues around BDSM/Kink sexualities and consensual non-monogamies." 2012 will mark the fifth Conference on Alternative Sexualities. I was on a panel at the 2009 conference in Chicago, and I thought it was pretty awesome, but I am obviously biased.

* **Community workshops.** Most BDSM communities in large cities have educational workshops. These teach SM-related ideas or skills such as community etiquette, how to use various types of equipment, etc. Every SM workshop I have ever attended has emphasized careful negotiation and has, at the very least, mentioned safewords. One workshop — "The Emotional Aspects of BDSM Play," taught by San Francisco's EduKink — gave a detailed list of ideas for how to tell BDSM from abuse, which I wrote down:

1) Consent. BDSM is consenting; abuse is not.

a) Assuming consent was given — was it informed consent? Did everyone know what they were consenting to?

b) Was consent coerced or seduced from the partner? Did everyone feel like they could say no if they wanted? Was anyone worried about suffering negative consequences if they said no?

2) Intent. A BDSM partner intends to have a mutually enjoyable encounter; an abusive partner does not.

a) Did everyone leave the scene feeling somewhat satisfied?

3) Damage. A BDSM partner tries to minimize the actual damage inflicted by their actions; an abusive partner does not.

a) Did the two partners learn what they were doing before they did it? Did they learn how to perform their activities safely?

b) Were the partners aware of the potential risks of their activities?

4) *Secrecy.* Abuse often happens in secret. This is the hardest one on this checklist, because — due to the fact that BDSM is a very marginalized, misunderstood sexuality — BDSM often happens in secret, too. But this is one of the benefits of having an entire subculture that deals with BDSM: we try to look out for each other.

a) Were the two partners involved in the local BDSM scene? Did they get advice from knowledgeable, understanding BDSM people during rough patches in their relationship?

I've heard of one or two workshops specifically focused on "BDSM for Survivors." I've also heard of support groups for BDSM-identified survivors of abuse, but I've never run across one in person. I've said this before, but I'll say it again: I believe that the safest place to have a BDSM relationship is within the BDSM community.

* * *

My Fantasy Sex-Positive, Anti-Abuse Program

You can tell from the above list that relevant community efforts have focused on raising internal awareness, consolidating useful information, and educating. If I were to get a grant or something (ha!), I would certainly look for ways to use it on a dedicated pro-sex, anti-abuse initiative, hopefully more expansive than a hotline, and considerably more extensive than a pamphlet. I've never developed this thought too extensively — I hate to torture myself when I know there's no money for one of my ideas — but I know I'd want my Dream Anti-Abuse Team to have the following qualities:

* BDSM is obviously my main interest, because that's how I identify the core of my sexuality. But I have a strong interest in destigmatizing all forms of sexual expression practiced by consenting adults. Everyone involved in my initiative would emphasize that **people of all genders and sexualities could come for help — whether straight, gay, lesbian, bi, trans, asexual, BDSM, sex worker, polyamorous, swing, or whatever amazing fetish could conceivably come up.**

Ideally, I would personally try to shock the hell out of anyone before I agreed to work with them... because anyone whose face twists up or who gasps at the idea of any kind of consensual weird sex is a person who shouldn't be anywhere near altsexual abuse survivors.

* I'd want **destigmatizing alternative sexuality among the mainstream, especially mainstream anti-abuse organizations,** to be a major focus — so that abuse survivors could feel less anxious about being misunderstood while seeking help. So I'd need people who were willing to go out and charismatically shock the abuse officers at police stations, feminist organizations, college campuses, etc. I'd want us to be running everything from anti-stigma poster campaigns to sex communication workshops.

* I'd want the program to be **well-advertised to the general public, so that people who aren't in the community — yet who are practicing S&M or poly or whatever on their own — could still find us**.

* Of course we'd also do the more traditional work of offering walk-in counseling to abuse survivors, including help making a concrete plan, altsexual-friendly legal advice, and so on.

So.

Anyone willing to fund my Dream Team?

* * *

This can be found on the Internet at:
http://clarissethorn.com/blog/2011/01/16/the-alt-sex-anti-abuse-dream-team/

* * *

* * *

Section 1 Study Guide

A regular reader who goes by SnowdropExplodes suggested that I add "study guides" to the end of each section of this book in order to pull it together, and I thought it was a good idea. (See why I love my readers?) I'm sure that others could find this insufferably patronizing, however; if you're one of them, feel free not to read the guides! I'm just trying to offer questions for further thought, and give some insight on why I organized this book the way I did. This section was intended to pull together the ideas I see as "basic" or "building blocks" for feminist sex, both in theory and in practice.

* * *

1. Have any of these pieces felt relevant to how you communicate with your partners? Have any pieces felt irrelevant or incomprehensible? Can you see any overarching themes that guide which ones felt relevant, and which ones felt incomprehensible?
1a. If you could give your partners one piece of advice about communicating with you, what would it be?
1b. Are there areas of communication that you feel you need to work on? (For example, Clarisse often thinks that she should work on her non-verbal communication, and has occasionally had trouble being direct with her partners about what she wants.)
1c. What ideas about sex and communication do you think you've absorbed from friends, parents, and your larger cultural environment?

2. What stereotypes do you see acting on your sexuality?
2a. Have you come up with any mental tactics for thinking around those stereotypes? What are they? (For example, Clarisse sees the "S&M superpowers" concept as a positive way of framing S&M, so it doesn't feel "broken" or "dark.")

3. Are there any areas of your sexuality where you feel trapped or stalled? Can you think of ways that you want to move forward on

those, or do you think it might be a good idea to take some time off from those activities instead?

4. If you were feeling anxious about a relationship or uncertain about your boundaries, who would you turn to in order to talk about that? Do you have friends (online or offline) or other resources where you could find advice?
4a. Are there unique problems affecting abusive relationships within the communities you frequent? How do sexual stereotypes affect how you and your friends perceive both positive relationships and abusive relationships?

5. What are the overarching patterns that you see within the pieces in this section? How are these disparate topics relevant to each other?
5a. Is consent complicated?

* * *

* * *

SECTION 2:
Activism and Allies

In which we explore activism and other topics tangentially related to S&M feminism — from sex work, to polyamory and monogamy, to the nature of masculinity.

* * *

When I think of this section, I think of:

Abuse of power comes as no surprise.
~ Jenny Holzer

I think of Clarisse as the John Stuart Mills of sexuality.
~ one of my ex-boyfriends

* * *

***

ACTIVISM:
[theory] Grassroots Organizing For Feminism, S&M, HIV, and Everything Else

I wrote this in March 2011 for Bitch Magazine's *Feminist Coming-Out Day Blog Carnival. [1] The goal was to talk about feminist "click" moments, and my entry was predictably wide-ranging and idiosyncratic.*

***

Earlier this month, my sex-positive documentary film series screened *Jane: An Abortion Service.* [2] The film tells the extraordinary story of "Jane," an underground network of women in Chicago who provided thousands of safe abortions in the years before abortion was legal. It was totally inspiring.

Jane was started accidentally by a woman named Heather Booth. Booth was a student at the University of Chicago in the late 1960s when another woman came and asked her — secretly, of course — whether she knew any abortion doctors. Heather Booth found one, and she also found that other women started coming to her for references.

As one woman in the film put it, in those days, women who sought abortions were all "hysterical and desperate and scared": if you needed an abortion, you knew you would have to come up with some fabulous amount of money and take a life-threatening risk. Some women committed suicide when they got pregnant instead. Information about abortion was at a premium.

So Heather Booth began looking for abortion doctors, and better than that, she started **vetting** them. After finding the doctors, she sought testimonials about those doctors. Common problems with abortion doctors ranged from being rude to actually assaulting their patients; some doctors, who already charged sky-high prices, would demand more money at the last minute. Booth kept a list of abortion doctors who didn't do those things. Pretty soon, there were other women who had her list too, and they were vetting doctors and spreading the word as well. The group also provided counseling before and after the procedure, letting the patients know what they could expect — physically and emotionally. They called themselves "Jane": a woman who called them and asked for "Jane" was seeking an abortion.

After some time, the women of Jane figured out that abortion isn't a complex procedure, and they convinced a doctor to teach them how to do it safely. And then they taught each other. So then they didn't have to refer patients to doctors: they did all the abortions themselves, and they did them for whatever the patient could spare rather than charging prices that were out of reach for many women. Jane members continued to provide emotional support, as well: in the documentary, one member reminisces about how she would have patients over to dinner with her kids and talk to them for a while before performing the procedure. It got to the point where doctors and medical students sent women to Jane, rather than getting referrals from Jane.

That is positive activism. That is building the world we want to see.

When abortion was legalized in 1973, the group quietly disbanded. Some members of Jane went on to be involved in other parts of the feminist movement or to found respected women's health organizations.

It's not that Jane had no problems; the organization was not transparent, for example, and it sounds like there was a fair amount of gossip and internal difficulties. These are typical issues within small groups, and the stigma and anxiety of what they were doing can't possibly have helped, but still, it's important to work against those problematic patterns from the beginning. It's worth it, I think; I'm increasingly convinced that the most positive direct change can be traced to small, grassroots, community groups. Which means that making sure your small, grassroots community group is egalitarian but well-organized can have ripple effects all down the line. [3]

Another example of such a group might be Chicago's Rape Victim Advocates. [4] RVA was established in 1974 by doctors and nurses who were appalled by how badly rape survivors were treated in the emergency room. Back then, there was no public understanding of how traumatic rape could be, and little understanding of survivors' experience, even from police and doctors. (An older female friend of mine who was raped in 1970 once told me that she tried to talk to a psychiatrist about what happened. He sighed and said, "Really, do you think that's important?") Rape Victim Advocates has always been a network of volunteers who are on-call to come and talk to rape survivors, but since 1974, it has also developed from a fragile activist group into one with funding and political presence.

And on a somewhat different note, S&M community organizing is really quite good. A lot of people don't realize that most S&M community dungeons (unlike the professional dungeons run by sex workers) are nonprofit organizations, kind of like community centers. (No, seriously.) People don't just go to community dungeons to do S&M — they also go to community dungeons for discussion groups or educational workshops, to learn how to perform certain activities safely.

Much like Jane, the S&M community has also created a network of necessary references: the Kink Aware Professionals list. [5] If you've read my work before, you've probably read about this list, because it had a huge impact on my life and I like to spread the word. S&M activists in San Francisco realized, years ago, that there was a need for lawyers and doctors who understood their lives and wouldn't stigmatize their choices, so they wrote three names on a piece of paper and passed it around. Now, the Kink Aware Professionals list is an international online directory hosted by the nonprofit National Coalition for Sexual Freedom.

Again, it's not like there are no problems in the S&M community; people gossip, people backstab, people fuck up. There's little vetting process for educators or for people who list themselves on Kink Aware Professionals, and a lot of people run kink classes at least as much from a desire for status as from a desire to educate. But still, I think the S&M community is engaging in positive activism... more than a lot of us even realize.

This was a lesson that really hit home for me when I spent a year in Africa working on HIV mitigation. One of the reasons international aid is so complicated is that figuring out how to help a community that's not yours is incredibly hard. A lot of well-meaning Americans (including myself) go abroad with little understanding of how hard it is. The reality is that assisting with, for example, public health in a foreign place entails learning the social fabric of that country in a way that outsiders can only do with tons of sustained effort... and we're **still** unlikely to be as good as someone who grew up there. One of the reasons — maybe the biggest reason — I left was that it was **so obvious** to me that I was a better activist in the USA... even when I wasn't trying to do activism. (When I was there, I received one letter from an American girl asking for advice on how to do African activism. My advice to her can be summarized as, "It's harder than you think, and you might consider staying home where you're awesomer." [6])

When HIV began destroying the gay community, the most effective and important measures to curb it came from people like Richard Berkowitz, the actual gay activist who wrote a safer sex pamphlet on his home typewriter and then distributed it by hand. They saw a need and they did something about it. Just like Jane. Just like S&M educators.

You are probably already part of more communities than you might realize. If you go to a university, you're part of that community. Whether you live in a city neighborhood or a small town, you're part of that community. If you go to particular clubs, you're in those communities. There may be aspects of your identity that could align with a community as well: for example, if you read science fiction there are conventions for that (although of course, identity communities don't always work for everyone with that identity). These are places where your knowledge already makes you powerful... so keep an eye out for needs. (It's also worth considering getting involved in an intentional community. I'm kind of psycho about housing co-ops, for example, because they are awesome. [7] I personally am a member of North American Students of Cooperation, but there are other groups, and there are also independent co-ops that aren't part of larger networks. [8])

We live in an unstable and fast-paced age. I don't know how people in most other countries feel, but I know that here in the USA, there is a quite pervasive and quite justified anxiety among everyone I know in the middle class. Many of our safety nets are evaporating, and it's not at all clear that they will be replaced. But **no matter how much the people in power fuck us over, we'll never be totally screwed as long as we're not isolated and we talk to each other.**

One of the former members of Jane, a white-haired feminist with such powerful energy that she practically glows through the screen, says in the documentary: "Don't stay with people who tell you you're crazy and useless. Don't stay where you're weak." That's what I call an activist click moment: find the other people like you, and organize with them. That applies to feminism, it applies to sexuality, it applies to public health. Go where you're strong and make your people stronger.

* * *

This can be found on the Internet at:
http://clarissethorn.com/blog/2011/03/29/grassroots-organizing-for-feminism-sm-hiv-and-everything-else/

The film Jane: An Abortion Service *is available from the distributor Women Make Movies:*
http://www.wmm.com/filmcatalog/pages/c410.shtml

* * *

***

ACTIVISM:
[storytime] Interview with Richard Berkowitz, Star of *Sex Positive* and Icon of Safer Sex Activism

Richard Berkowitz is an interesting guy. He was active in the gay community in the 1970s and 80s as an S&M sex worker, so he's got plenty of experience with all kinds of sexual history. Not only that, but he also wrote the very first safer sex pamphlet ever, when HIV began storming through the gay community. The pamphlet was called "How to Have Sex in an Epidemic"; Berkowitz literally wrote it at home on his typewriter and then distributed copies by hand. Then he was slammed by his own community for doing so... well, read on and learn more about what happened next.

I was honored to interview Berkowitz in early 2009. I really love it when I get the chance to talk to boundary-breaking activists who were around before I was born, especially if their domain is sexuality. I feel a combination of both exhilaration and despair during these discussions — exhilaration because I learn how far we've come, and despair because I can see how we keep making the same mistakes again and again and again.

***

Our second film at my awesome sex-positive film series was *Sex Positive,* a fascinating documentary about the history of safer sex. I'll be honest: I was psyched about *Sex Positive* from day one, long before I'd even seen it. It was the first film I chose for my film list. In fact, the whole idea for the film series came out of a conversation I had with Lisa (our lovely Hull-House Museum education coordinator) in which I said that I wanted to see *Sex Positive,* and then added, "There are so many sexuality movies I want to see. You and I should have a regular movie night!" She looked at me and said thoughtfully, "You know, I bet people besides us would come to that...."

Sex Positive tells the story of Richard Berkowitz — and how he was one of the first to spread the word about safer sex in America.

Berkowitz, a talented writer, started out as a hot-blooded participant in the promiscuous gay bathhouse culture; later, he became an S&M hustler (i.e., a sex worker). When AIDS started decimating the gay community, Berkowitz was instrumental in teaching his community (and the world) about safer sex. As it became clear to some medical professionals that sexual promiscuity spread AIDS, Berkowitz tried to tell the world about their findings. But there was a huge backlash against him — because in those days, the promiscuous bathhouse culture was seen by many gay men as a huge part of identifying as gay and sex-positive... and anyone who argued against it, or tried to modify it, was therefore cast by many people as sex-negative.

After we screened *Sex Positive*, I reviewed it on my blog, and Richard Berkowitz himself read the review! [1] He left a comment offering feedback, and I was so thrilled and honored to hear from him that I emailed him right away. We talked a little bit, and met in person last time I was in New York City — and I practically begged him to let me interview him by email. Here's the results: a discussion of Richard's history with S&M; what he thinks about advocacy; his feelings about the gay community and its history; and where he finds himself in his life right now.

Clarisse Thorn: In *Sex Positive*, you mention that you didn't initially think of yourself as a BDSM type, but that you had partners who convinced you to do it. Do you think you would have gotten into BDSM if you hadn't had partners pressuring you to do it? Do you think you would have gotten into it if you hadn't been able to make money at it?

Richard Berkowitz: I was filmed talking in three- to four-hour sessions over the course of a year about difficult, often painful, personal history. At times I felt uncomfortable, I made mistakes, so there are moments in *Sex Positive* that I wish I could clarify — but it's not my film. That's why I'm thrilled that you're giving me the first opportunity to address the moments that make me cringe when I see the movie — and what amazed me is that you nailed most of them.

Me pressured into S&M? Hell, no. I stumbled across BDSM porn in college, and was both appalled and more turned on than I was to any other porn. I pursued a few experiences as a novice when I was in college, and I was completely turned off to the scene for years. The few Tops I met were clumsy, distracted by fetishes that bored me, and I was convinced a bottom could easily get hurt — so I walked away.

When I began hustling in NYC, I was an angry activist and it attracted S&M bottoms that were happy to teach me what I could do with my anger that was erotic and consensual. To that I added what I had learned that Tops did wrong — and presto! I got really good at it fast — and I loved it. I was doing two or three scenes a day, but because I could often steer a scene to what turned me on, it felt more like play than work.

If I hadn't had been trained as a Top by older, experienced bottoms who were hiring me, I still would have had S&M experiences on my own. But I doubt that I would have gotten as heavily into the scene if it wasn't for hustling. That's where I earned my S&M PhD.

In 1979, S&M was considered the fallback scene for aging hustlers — it was what you turned to when you were losing your youth. There was such a dearth of good Tops. But I had the raw material to be a great Top at 23, and I built quite a reputation on word-of-mouth referrals and repeats. Many of my clients became close friends.

CT: Where do you place BDSM in your sexual identity and self-conception? Do you see it as deeply part of you, or something you chose? Do you think of your BDSM urges as coming from a place as deep, as intrinsic, as your gay orientation?

RB: I think it's too late for me to answer that question. Turning my libido into an occupation at 23 changed me in both good ways and bad. It would take a book to explain — so let me just say that as a product of gay male sex in the 70s, there was an element of power intrinsic to the sexuality of the times. That shaped me. I don't see vanilla sex and S&M sex as mutually exclusive because I believe in Tops and bottoms — and that's the basis of BDSM. "Tops and bottoms" are not exclusive to BDSM; the terms are widely used for assigning roles of power in sex in general. Gore Vidal said, "There is no such thing as gay and straight — only top and bottom." I believe both are true.

But one shouldn't lose sight of the fact that a third of my living space for the past three decades was a sound-proofed dungeon.

I think that a culture like ours that's based on competition, as opposed to cooperation, can be extremely sadomasochistic. I think bad S&M can be found in many aspects of our daily life, and good S&M is just eroticizing aspects of being human that can enhance sex immensely for some.

CT: What kind of BDSM advocacy have you encountered? What kind of sex work advocacy have you encountered? What did you think of what you saw? Do you have any ideas about how to make those movements effective? Do you have any fears about

those movements? Would you consider being part of those movements?

RB: My only fear about those movements would be if they didn't exist! My neighbor down the hall for the past 25 years built my dungeon and was a co-founder of Gay Male SM Activists, but I always had too much hot sex going on at home to be interested in meetings. [2] Plus, I never stopped feeling like a pariah in the gay community because of the attacks on me and my writing since AIDS began. You reach a point where you just assume people hate you because it's easier than trying to figure out who doesn't.

I fiercely support BDSM advocacy, but mainly from a distance. There's a limited number of body blows any activist can take before we just retreat. I had my fill — but the response to *Sex Positive* and the new Obama era is nudging me out of my shell. I had a breakup a few years ago that devastated me, so I've been out of the scene for almost three years. Now I'm trying to reinvent myself, find one person I can retreat from the world with. I've never lied about S&M being an intrinsic part of my sexuality, and because of my early bad experiences with BDSM, I'm thrilled and inspired by advocates for it. If there had been BDSM advocacy when I came into BDSM, then I don't think I would have had the bad experiences I mentioned earlier. As a BDSM sex worker, I met so many men who had horrible tales of being hurt in scenes, and I did my best to be an antidote for that.

CT: On my blog, you commented that "Of course BDSM was a source of joy in my life but I put it aside when it robs me from having a platform to champion safe sex to the largest possible audience, which BDSM often has." Could you talk more about that?

RB: Smear campaigns are hard to pin down, and there's no way to know how much of the contempt against me or my writing was due to my BDSM, my sex work, my safe sex evangelism or simply me. I'm just a dangling piñata for people who have issues with sex!

There are gay people of my generation who are as uninformed and rabidly anti-BDSM sex as homophobes are about gay sex.

I can't think of anyone who has gone on film with such brutally honest testimony about their radical sexual history as I did in *Sex Positive*. It felt like a huge risk and you can see my anxiety in the film, but to me, this level of honesty is crucial to pro-sex activism. People are so dishonest about sex; many would never talk publicly about their private sexual behavior — and they don't want others doing it either, so it's not easy.

There was a doctor I saw once when AIDS began who heard I was into S&M. As he went to take blood from me, he stabbed the needle into my arm. I bolted out of the chair screaming, and he said coyly, "Oh, sorry, I thought you liked pain." How can I not feel reticent talking about BDSM considering so many people I've met like that? And then I think, how can I not?

I've seen the most courageous pro-sex writers and activists attacked, pilloried and silenced because of their honesty in writing about their kinky sexual histories. I shudder when I recall the vicious smears against pro-sex feminists by anti-porn feminists back in the early 80s. I don't want to invite that bile into my life, especially now, when my circle of gay male friends are no longer alive and here to support me when I go out on a limb with my personal radical sexual issues in public.

So why did I speak out? Why do I still speak out? Because I owed so much to the army of men who loved and supported me over the years and no longer have a voice, and because gay men were dying. It was no time to be squeamish about sex. It still isn't.

CT: Do you have any regrets? — and, concurrently, what are you most proud of? Did the making of the film *Sex Positive* bring any regret or pride to the surface for you?

RB: I have a few regrets about *Sex Positive,* but they pale next to what I've gained. I've been to more cities with this movie in one year than I've been to in my entire life. Young people have been extraordinarily supportive and kind, and it helps me to let go of the past. I've been stuck in the past for so long — it's deadening, but I finally feel that this movie is breaking me free, to finally let go and move on to write about other things. For that, I'm forever indebted to Daryl Wein, the documentary's director.

What I'm most proud of is how much work I did on safe sex that no one even knows about. I'm putting it all on the Internet as a free archive, as soon as I can find or pay someone to help me with the technical stuff. I'm from the age of typewriters.

CT: Is there anything you'd like to add? Please feel free to also respond directly to points I made when I talked about *Sex Positive* on my blog.

RB: I loved S&M hustling before AIDS so much — sometimes, when I talk about it, I become the part of me that tied people up and dominated them; it's like a mental erection. I get lost in the reverie of being an erotic, arrogant Top. I begged director Daryl Wein to delete me saying that clients would tell me that I could do whatever I wanted to them except fuck them, and then I would proceed to do just that. I said that when I was lost in a persona, and it makes me sound like a rapist!

The truth is, my most valued expertise as a hustler was teaching men who were afraid of getting fucked how to relax, how to douche, how to open up, how to explore the intense pleasures of receptive anal intercourse and anal orgasm without any pain. I would never rape or violate anyone's consent — and certainly not customers I wanted to come back! I had tremendous empathy for how difficult it can be to learn how to get anally fucked because I was never able — or had the desire — to do it without being high on drugs. (You have to remember how pervasive recreational drug use was during the sexual revolution. There were articles in the gay press saying how cocaine was good for you. We didn't understand addiction then as we do now. And we paid a heavy price for that innocence and ignorance.)

When I began hustling in NYC, the lesbian and gay liberation movement was ten years old — and about that mature. We grew up in such an intensely erotophobic and homophobic culture — there was no way to escape it, even after we accepted that we were gay. We didn't always treat each other well, and it permeated our sexual expression whether it was vanilla or S&M.

You mention in your blog post that you are wary of how I talk about BDSM as arising from "self-loathing" and "insecurity" and negative cultural pressures on the gay community. Yes — in S&M **and** in vanilla sex — I saw how we brought a lot of the culture's contempt to what we did. But, as I say in *Sex Positive,* many of us came to realize this, and we understood that a lot of sexual fantasies are socially constructed by the times that shaped us. Many of us came to realize that sexual fantasies don't diminish us as people — they can actually help free and enrich us when we understand what we're doing.

I'm reluctant to put myself forward as a role model for BDSM and sex work, because of what happened to me after AIDS when I went back to hustling. I was furious that there was no place in the community for me to do safe sex education. I felt so hurt that some people only saw me as a sex worker/sadomasochist and that political differences got in the way of saving sexually active gay men's lives. You can't imagine the rage I felt that it took two entire years **after** we wrote and published "How to Have Sex in an Epidemic" for NYC to do its first safe sex campaign. I went back to hustling in such despair that I was an addiction waiting to happen, and that's what did.

In the end, though, BDSM and my love for it is part of what saved my life. If I weren't so busy hustling with BDSM before AIDS and safe sex, I would have spent much more time at the baths having high risk sex, and died long ago. I think each of us has a limit to how much sex and how many different partners our spirits can bear. Sex can become an addiction, and when you reach that point, people use recreational drugs to keep that level of hypersexual activity going. If I had found a place in safe sex education, my life would have been a much happier, healthier journey. But I never lose sight of how grateful I am to still be here, or how much joy and pleasure sexual freedom gave me until the world I loved started collapsing all around me and taking the men I loved along with it.

* * *

This can be found on the Internet at:
http://clarissethorn.com/blog/2009/03/23/interview-with-richard-berkowitz-star-of-sex-positive-and-icon-of-safer-sex-activism/

Check out Richard Berkowitz's web site to read more about him and investigate his book (which I admit I have not read), Stayin' Alive: The Invention of Safe Sex:
http://richardberkowitz.com/

And seriously, if you get the chance, watch Daryl Wein's awesome documentary Sex Positive:
http://www.sexpositive-themovie.com/

* * *

* * *

ABUSE:
[theory] Social Responsibility Within Activism

I wrote this post in 2010 for Thanksgiving (the original post had a bunch of "thank yous" at the end, which I removed from this version). The questions here seem to be some of the biggest recurring questions in my life. Later events have taught me a lot about work that has already been done on accountability within communities. In particular, I want to highlight the book The Revolution Starts At Home: Confronting Intimate Violence Within Activist Communities *(edited by Ching-In Chen, Jai Dulani, and Leah Lakshmi Piepzna-Samarasinha), which was published in 2011.*

But there's a lot of other work out there on how to deal with a perpetrator of violence without resorting to our corrupt and violent established prison system. [1] People of color should be credited for much of this work, because communities of color are rarely well-served by the criminal justice system, and thus have particular incentives to seek alternatives. Sometimes, this field is called "transformative justice" or "restorative justice." Here is a post that links to a number of resources on transformative justice: http://clarissethorn.com/blog/2012/01/30/some-transformative-justice-links/

* * *

Tonight I had Thanksgiving dinner with my mother and her boyfriend. Some friends of my mother attended, one of whom is a lesbian who I'll call Kay. Kay attended dinner with her mother, who is unaware of Kay's sexual orientation. One of the reasons Kay's mom doesn't know about Kay's sexual orientation is that Kay's mom has already behaved quite badly towards Kay's elder sister, who is an out-of-the-closet lesbian.

I knew this whole situation going in, and one thing that struck me was how much of a nice person Kay's mom is. I mean... she's **really nice**. I mean, she clearly tries to be a good person. She also tried really hard to help me do the dishes. (I didn't let her because I wanted them all to myself.)

I've been thinking a lot lately about how to engage with people who have done bad things, or who are currently doing things I think are bad (like shaming their lesbian daughters). It wouldn't have been right to throw my sex-positive ideas on the table while talking to Kay's mom — mostly because Kay specifically asked me not to, ahead of time. But. The most powerful tool for getting people to reconsider their stigma against alternative sexuality is personal engagement. Don't I have some responsibility here? Is there something I can do?

Other examples of this are rife. One very intense, very important issue I grappled with this week was having a friend email me to inform me that another friend — someone I like and admire a lot — has been credibly accused of sexual assault by a person who will never press charges. This has come up before in my life... every time it's a little different, and yet so many things are the same: a person is assaulted, the news gets out among friends, the survivor doesn't press charges, there is confusion among the friends about how to act, eventually things die down, and I feel as though I should have done more.

When I was in high school, one of my closest male friends raped a female acquaintance of mine. She didn't press charges and they later had a romance that was, to all appearances, consensual. I pieced events together slowly — he did acknowledge what he'd done, though never directly to me. I didn't know what to do, at the time, and I still feel as though I should have done so much more. He and I were so close. I never had the nerve to directly talk to him about what happened, because — even though we never talked directly about it — I saw evidence that he felt terrible about it, and I was sure that I could devastate him by talking about it more. But still... I should have talked to him.

I also feel as though I should have supported her more, but I don't know what I could have said. There were people who told her that she shouldn't be having a consensual relationship with her rapist. It seemed wrong to tell her that — I felt like it eroded her agency, attacked her right to choose — so I didn't say it. If I had said it, though, would that have been helpful to her? What could I have done to be a better resource for her? Especially given that I was such close friends with him?

I was young(er), but that's no excuse. Then again, what am I excusing? I did nothing. But I should have done more.

Now, again, I have a friend, a good friend, who assaulted

someone. It's a friend in the local S&M community. I don't know the survivor at all. I have to talk to my friend about it, but what do I say, and what happens next? Feminism instructs us that we should listen to the voices of survivors, that community mores and community condemnation are what stops rape from happening. I believe these things to be true; and there are people close to me who have survived rape, and I really want to make sure I'm doing everything I can to ensure that rape stops happening. But I intensely wish that I had more guidance on what exactly to say, how exactly to act, to change the mores.

I emailed my ex-boyfriend Mr. Chastity for advice, because he's got one of the finest ethical minds I've ever been lucky enough to engage with. Here's part of what he wrote back:

I've tried to distill your messages into a few questions, and I ended up with "How does one parse a situation in which a friend, and an otherwise noble person, seems to have done serious wrong?" and "What are a person's moral obligations in this case?"

Nobody is composed of unmixed goodness or evil, no matter how much of a paragon/fiend 1) they seem to be or 2) their principles require. People we respect and love are not forces of nature or avatars of their cause of choice, no matter how thoroughly they embody it to us. I don't say this because I think you haven't considered it, but because I know I've had a lot of trouble absorbing it over the years and think it might therefore bear restating to others, too.

As an individual, a person has a relatively large degree of freedom in action and association. I think where this case becomes truly difficult to consider is when we bring in justice and the community. Because the means of enforcement of the rules of these communities is so interpersonal, one's interpersonal actions take on an unusual role of community-level justice as well as merely justice between two people. I can't see how it could ever be good to allow things like this to just slide. Honestly, I'm not sure what else you can do but (as you suggest in one of your messages) politely ask your friend about their take on the story. If nothing else, it will demonstrate that people are paying attention to this thing and might give you some insight into their character and opinions of the issue.

He's right. I agree. But. What now? How do I ask, what do I say? How can I tell if my friend has dealt with whatever healing has to take place in order for such assaults not to happen again?

* * *

This can be found on the Internet at:
http://clarissethorn.com/blog/2010/11/26/social-responsibility-activism-and-giving-thanks/

It is really worth reading about work that's already been done on transformative justice:
http://clarissethorn.com/blog/2012/01/30/some-transformative-justice-links/

* * *

* * *

BOUNDARIES:
[storytime] Taking Care Of Each Other

This was originally published in 2012 at the girl-power site OffOurChests.com.

* * *

As a sex educator, I think a lot about how to teach boundaries. I try to come up with exercises, stories, maxims that could help people respect their own bodies, minds, and desires; and of course I also think about how to encourage people to respect others' boundaries. But the biggest influences on a person's boundaries have nothing to do with what I teach. Good boundaries are (hopefully) demonstrated by parents, influenced by friends, and encouraged by partners.

Within a community, though, I also think it's really important not to tell people what to do. I believe that it's crucial to be a good resource for the people close to us, without trying to force them to do what we think is best. That way, we can both build trust and foster independence. On the other hand, sometimes it's hard to know how to do that when I know more about a certain subject than someone else. It is so powerfully tempting to tell them what I think they should do!

I was thinking about this recently when, out of the blue, I remembered something that happened when I was 16 or 17. I'd just had a nasty breakup, I was really unhappy about my ex, and I was trying marijuana. I had never smoked before.

There were a bunch of other people my age present — including a guy who'd been flirting with me for a while. When he passed me the marijuana, he kissed me. I kissed back. I wasn't attracted to him, but I felt so empty and hurt, and I guess it was reassuring that someone wanted me, despite the fact that my ex-boyfriend didn't.

Also around was a girl who I'll call Lena. I had always seen Lena as tough and no-nonsense, but I didn't know much else about her. I think she probably considered me a bit naïve. Anyway, Lena watched the situation and my body language; she knew that it was my first time smoking. A few minutes later, she took me aside. I don't remember the exact conversation, but I seem to recall that it went something like this:

"Clarisse," Lena said, "how are you feeling?"

"I'm not sure," I said. Truth be told, I felt a bit numb.

Lena looked directly into my face. "How far do you want to go tonight?" she asked.

I looked away. I felt embarrassed because she seemed so composed. I felt like an airhead compared to her. We were standing next to a wooden wall, and I pretended to study the wood-grain. "I don't know," I said vaguely.

"If you can tell me how far you want to go tonight," Lena said firmly, "then I'll make sure nothing goes past that. Do you want to keep making out? Do you want to do more than make out?"

I traced a knot in the wood with my finger. "Making out," I decided.

"Okay," Lena said, and nodded. I don't remember if she said anything else, but as she took me back to the group I still felt a little embarrassed — and also incredibly relieved.

I wonder if I ever thanked Lena? I should have; maybe I'll try to find her on Facebook or something. Because I really did feel a lot safer that night, knowing that Lena was looking out for me. I made out with that gentleman a little bit more, but after a while I put a stop to it, and nothing else happened.

Maybe if Lena hadn't been there, I still would have had the wherewithal to stop making out with him; or maybe I would have felt so confused, anxious, numb that I let it go further. (And I can tell you for sure that I'm glad it didn't go further.) Or, God forbid, maybe if she hadn't been there then I would have been actively pressured into something that I actively objected to.

Before that, it had never occurred to me to set a clear boundary before I hooked up with a guy. That's an important lesson in itself! Even more importantly, though, Lena didn't tell me what to do. She didn't say anything about how I should be sexual, or who I should do it with. She didn't shame me for what was up. She just asked me what I wanted, and then she offered me her support.

Certainly, Lena is just one small piece in the puzzle of my life. But I still remember her, and I admire and thank her. My parents have offered me a lot of support throughout my life, both in my relationships and otherwise. I've had partners who helped show me what it means to create a low-pressure sexual environment, or who helped me learn clear sexual communication. Still, Lena stands out in my mind — someone I barely knew, yet someone who helped show me what it means to be among women who stand up for each other and help preserve each other's boundaries.

* * *

This can be found on the Internet at:
http://offourchests.com/taking-care-of-each-other/

* * *

* * *

MANLINESS:
[theory] Questions I Want To Ask Entitled Cis Het Men

I wrote this piece in 2009. It was the culmination of years I'd spent thinking about masculinity, manliness, and men's gender role. I was relatively new to blogging, and I hadn't yet established myself. I thought that the most controversial things I would ever write would be about S&M. I was wrong.

I published this in three parts, and it got a huge response. The major feminist blog Alas! A Blog *asked to repost it, for example, but there was a much bigger reaction among non-feminist and anti-feminist men. Some wrote responses with titles like "Answers for an Entitled Feminist." Others actually came over to my blog and engaged me, with varying results. It kicked off a long, dense discussion in my blog Comments section, which lasted for over a year and thousands of comments. I wrote a number of followups, including some that got me labeled "brainwashed by the patriarchy" by other feminist women.*

Some of the guys I was talking to got me interested in the "pickup artist subculture" or "seduction community" — a group of men who trade tips, tricks, and tactics on how to seduce women. Eventually, I did an in-depth investigation of that subculture and wrote the book Confessions of a Pickup Artist Chaser: Long Interviews with Hideous Men, *which contains some of my best work on masculinity, communication, and sexuality.*

One thing I've discovered over the last few years, as I learned more about the history of feminism, is that there are excellent reasons why most feminists are unwilling to talk about men's problems. There's a ton of politics involved, and a lot of very justified fears about the political ground we could lose. We still have a long way to go when it comes to gender equality. But I do believe that those fears are often overblown.

And I've also discovered that there's a subgroup of feminists that's much more likely to be open to talking about men's experience: it's the sex-positive feminists, especially the S&M feminists. To be sure, there are exceptions. Plenty of S&M feminists see no reason to discuss men's experience, and of course, plenty of S&M feminists don't like my writing in particular. But most feminist essays I've found about masculinity were written by women who openly admitted that they were into S&M — Gayle Rubin, author of the pioneering sexuality essay "Thinking Sex," is one good example. Maybe the S&M feminists are the ones most likely to intuitively understand that power is never a one-dimensional picture or a one-way street.

* * *

Part 1: Who Cares?

Why do I care about masculinity?
I'm rather perverted, but not enormously queer. I present as femme, and   although I've been known to tease my sensitive (frequently long-haired) lovers for being "unmasculine" — I fall in love with men. I'm hardly one to go for the "manly man" type, but at heart, I love knowing that I'm fucking a man.

However, because I'm cisgendered and straight, I feel profoundly at a loss when trying to articulate problems of (for lack of a better phrase) "Men's Empowerment." The issues don't feel "native" to me; I've intersected with these questions mainly through the lens of lovers and friends. Watching their struggle is demoralizing, but trying to imagine how I can give them feedback is more demoralizing.

A male friend once wrote to me, "I think you personally find expressions of masculinity **hot**, but you also have no patience with sexism. You've caught on that it's tricky for men to figure out how to deliver both of these things you need, that you don't have a lot of good direction to give to fellas about it, and that neither does anyone else."

So:
How can men be supportive and non-oppressive while remaining overtly masculine?

On top of my limited perspective, there's been an echoing lack of discourse — that is, very little mainstream acknowledgement of the problems of masculinity. The primary factor in that silence is that normative cis men themselves tend to be flatly unwilling to discuss gender/sex issues. Often, their first objection is that the discussion is neither important nor relevant. This is true even within subcultures centered around sexual analysis, like the BDSM world — I once met a cis male BDSMer who said, "Why bother talking about male sexuality? It's the norm. Fish don't have a word for water."

But *if masculine sexuality is water and we're fish, why doesn't that motivate us to examine it more — not less?*

Don't get me wrong: I agree that America's sexual conceptions are centered around stereotypical male sexuality, and I agree that this is damaging and problematic. Believe me, I'm **furious** that it took me many years to reconceive "actual" sex around acts other than good ole penis-in-vagina penetration! But if American stereotypes and ideas of sexuality are male-centered, then surely that makes it **more** useful for us to be thinking about male sexuality — not less.

And those male-centered ideas of sexuality aren't centered around all men — just stereotypical men. LGBTQ men are obvious examples whose sexuality falls outside the norm; fortunately for them, they've created some spaces to discuss that. But there are lots of other non-normative guys who aren't gay or queer, yet feel very similar sexual alienation — and because there's so little discourse about masculinity outside LGBTQ circles, they usually just don't talk about it.

What does it mean to be a cis het man whose sexuality isn't normative? Which straight cis guys don't fit — and hence, feel alienated from — our current overarching sexual stereotypes?

Guys who identify as straight BDSM submissives are one fabulous example of non-normative men who are frequently alienated from mainstream masculine sexuality, but who often don't have a forum. Men with small penises are a second. There are lots of others. In the words of sex blogger and essayist Thomas Millar: "The common understanding of male sexuality is a stereotype, an ultra-narrow group of desires and activities oriented around PIV [penis-in-vagina], anal intercourse and blowjobs; oriented around cissexual women partners having certain very narrow groups of physical characteristics." [1]

Still, that doesn't mean that straight, dominant, big-dicked dudes who love boning thin chicks feel totally okay about the current state of affairs. It just means they tend to have less immediate motivation to question it. They also have less of an eye for spotting gender oppression, because — though they've got their own boxes hemming them in — they're still more privileged than the rest of us, and the nature of privilege is to blind the privileged class to its existence.

A male submissive once told me, "Lots of heteronormative men know something is wrong with the way we think about sex and gender. I can see them struggling with it when we talk. They can't put their finger on it; they have a hard time engaging it. But I engage it all the time; I have to, because my sexuality opposes it."

When is it to a man's advantage to examine and question masculinity and stereotypes of male sexuality? Which men are motivated to do so?

It's tempting to assert that men whose desires fit neatly (or at least mostly) within the stereotype have it made — after all, their sexuality works within the norm so many of us struggle to escape. But I've had this assumption corrected several times, usually by smart "stereotypical" men themselves. At one point, while developing a sexuality workshop, I sent the outline to a bunch of friends. The original draft contained this paragraph: "Our sexual scripts favor a certain stereotype of men and male sexual pleasure, which makes it hard for women to figure out what we really want and what we really enjoy, and also makes it harder for non-stereotypical men to figure that out." One friend sent that paragraph back, having quietly appended: "... as well as for stereotypical men to discover or explore new desires beyond the stereotypical script."

When we discuss the limitations around sexuality from a non-normative perspective, how do we exclude normative people who might develop themselves in new directions if they had the chance? What do normative men stand to gain by thinking outside the box about masculinity and sexuality?

Part 2: Men's Rights

In the 2006 documentary "Boy I Am", a trans man talks about how one of his mental barriers to transitioning was the fact that after transition, he would be a "white male." And, he laughs, the "last thing in the world" he wanted to be was a white male!

A year or two ago, I attended a lecture by Jackson Katz, a rather overtly masculine, cis male anti-abuse educator who lectures in colleges around the country. Bullet-headed and aggressive in stance, he said a lot of valuable things — particularly about how men ought to take ownership of problems we traditionally consider "women's issues." It's certainly true that if we want to end male abuse of women, men must participate in the movement. But although Katz discussed some issues of masculinity, I heard little about how we can make things better for men. His proposition of a men's movement was centered around correcting the things some men are doing wrong.

Although they're often watered down, many feminist concepts

have gone mainstream. For instance, Americans have some consciousness of traditional feminist critiques about how women's bodies are represented in the media. Indeed, that consciousness has become so endemic that, in a grandly ironic twist, marketers now capitalize on it to sell beauty products: the nationwide Dove Campaign for Real Beauty attempts to **use deconstruction of the media's representation of women** to sell Dove soap. Americans are also quite aware of men as the privileged class — sometimes regarded outright as the oppressors.

But this shift in awareness about gender issues faced by women has not been accompanied by a widespread understanding of gender issues faced by men. And that creates situations like an activist working towards a masculinity movement that talks mainly about how men are hurting women, or a trans man who has trouble with the idea of transitioning partly because he doesn't want to be a white man — one of the oppressors.

How can awareness of oppressive dynamics make it difficult for men to own their masculinity? Does male privilege ever make life harder for men? When does male privilege blind us to oppression of masculinity? There's some mainstream awareness of gender issues faced by women; is there any similar awareness of the problems of masculinity?

A good friend of mine first caught my attention by talking about gender. We encountered each other at a BDSM meetup, and when I mentioned that I'd been thinking about the boxes around masculine sexuality, he launched into a rant about oppressive sexual dynamics. He gave me references to complex sexuality blogs and intelligently used words like "heteronormative" and "patriarchy." But a month or so after we started talking, I mentioned his interest in gender issues... and he gave me a puzzled look. "I'm not really into gender studies," he said.

He talks about sex, gender and culture all the time — but he also specifically identifies as highly masculine, and felt that to be at odds with identifying as someone who questions masculinity. As Thomas Millar writes in his aforementioned article: "There's a huge unstated assumption that to even address the question [of male sexuality], for men, is to mark one's self as 'other.' ... cis het men are brought up to fear that their masculinity could ever be called into question. By even opening up a dialog, I think some folks fear that they are conceding that their sexuality is not uncontroversial."

Men currently experience this problem in a way that women do not. In other words, women don't risk being seen as unfeminine as easily as men risk being seen as unmasculine; nor do we have quite the same fears about it. In 2008, a group of researchers published a paper called "Precarious Manhood." Their concluding statement: "Our findings suggest that [so-called] real men experience their gender as a tenuous status that they may at any time lose and about which they readily experience anxiety and threat." Earlier in the paper, they wrote that although "our focus on manhood does not deny the importance of women's gender-related struggles" — "Women who do not live up to cultural standards of femininity may be punished, rejected, or viewed as 'unladylike,' but rarely will their very status as women be questioned in the same way as men's status often is." [2]

When is it to a man's disadvantage to publicly examine and question masculinity? Surely the mere act of questioning and examining gender does not make a man less masculine; how can we work against the perception that it does?

At the same time, though, this isn't a "with us or against us" situation: men who don't choose to identify as non-normative also don't tend to join the "opposition." By "opposition" I mean folks like "Men's Rights Activists" (on the Internet we call them MRAs). [3] MRAs — at least according to my stereotype of them — are conscious of social and legal disadvantages suffered by men, such as the fact that men are at a severe disadvantage in child custody cases; at the same time, they're blind to male privilege. It's a deadly combination. My personal favorite MRA quotation ever is, "White men are the most discriminated-against group in the country." Mercifully, MRAs are a fringe group, but they make a big impression.

My "not into gender studies" friend once told me that although he frequently deconstructs problems of masculinity in the privacy of his own mind, he doesn't like to publicly have those conversations because he doesn't want to sound like an MRA. He said, "A lot of the time, men who want to think seriously about masculinity won't talk about it aloud because we really don't want to be **that**." He later added, "It's very tricky to discuss masculinity yet avoid simply devolving into male entitlement. That's the crux of the problem with the 'Men's Movement' assholes — none of them are addressing the underlying problems of masculinity. They're just whining about not receiving the privileges their cultural conditioning tells them to expect."

How do the current "men's rights movements" discourage men who might, in a different climate, be very interested in discussing masculinity? Assuming men can reclaim the "pro-masculinity movement" from MRAs, do any men feel motivated to do so? Can men occupy the middle ground between MRAs and LGBTQ, feminist, or other leftist discussions of gender — that is, can men find space to discuss masculinity without being aligned with "one side or the other"?

All too frequently in radical sex/gender circles, the theme has been blame. Men in particular are excoriated for failing to adequately support feminism — or criticized for failing to join the fight against oppressive sex and gender norms — but few ideas are offered for how men can be supportive and non-oppressive **while remaining overtly masculine**, especially if their sexuality is normative (e.g., straight/dominant/big-dicked).

There are fragments: some insight might be drawn from the ways in which many BDSM communities create non-oppressive frameworks within which we have our deliciously oppressive sex. With practice, one can get shockingly good at preserving a heavy dominant/submissive dynamic that still allows both partners to talk about their other needs. Surely that understanding of sexual roles vs. other needs could be adapted to the service of gender identity. Yet so many BDSMers still fall prey to the same old gendered preconceptions, and talk nonsense about how "all women are naturally submissive" or whatever. [4]

Don't get me wrong: of course anyone would deserve plenty of blame if they refused to let go of their entitlement, or chose not to examine the ways their behavior might support an oppressive system. But I think men exist who are willing to do those things, yet feel blocked from relevant discussions because participating creates anxiety about their sexual or gender identity. It strikes me as unreasonable to attack them for that. Choosing to present one's sexuality and/or gender identity in a normative way is not **in itself** a sin. It's not fair to expect people to fit themselves into a box that doesn't suit them — not even for The All-Important Cause of better understanding sex and gender.

Where can we find ideas for how men can be both supportive and non-oppressive, and overtly masculine? How can we make it to normative men's advantage to analyze masculine norms? What does it look like to be masculine, but liberated from the strictures of stereotypical masculinity? How can we contribute to a Men's Movement that encompasses all three bases — being perceived as masculine, acknowledging male privilege, and deconstructing the problems of masculinity?

Part 3: Space for Men

I'm about to assert something that makes me nervous, because I worry that people are going to stick me in the "asshole MRA" box. Don't get me wrong: I **certainly** don't think that women have it better, overall, than men do. But I do wonder whether it might be good for feminists to acknowledge that — **although we don't experience nearly as much privilege as men** — there are a lot of advantages women experience that men don't.

Because women aren't seen as threatening, we have an easier time doing confrontational things like approaching strangers on the street. Because women aren't seen as fighters, we stand a lower chance of being mugged than men do. Because women are seen as emotional, we're given a huge amount of social space to consider and discuss our feelings. I can work with and be affectionate with children far more easily than a man could. I can be explicit and overt about my sexuality without being viewed as a creep.

And there are at least a few recurring complaints about how trying to be masculine can suck. First and foremost: that men don't feel they've been taught to process their emotions, or don't feel allowed to display them. Another: that they're perceived as less manly if they don't achieve success through a career, especially if they aren't the main breadwinner for their family. A third: that men are expected to be sexually insatiable, or always to be sexually available.

Of course, it's worth noting that the advantages women experience are almost always the flip side of unfortunate stereotypes. For instance, one might say that women get more social space for emotion because we're stereotyped as irrational and hysterical. But that doesn't change the fact that most of us easily grasp that space, while most men don't. And if we can reject the Oppression Olympics for just one minute and stop thinking about who's got it worse, it becomes clear that the advantages and drawbacks associated with being both male and female are intertwined. The two systems reinforce, and cannot function without, each other. The gender binary may not hurt everyone **equally**, but it hurts everyone. As those beautiful "Every Girl / Every Boy" posters say, the most obvious example is: "For every girl who is tired of acting weak when she is strong, there is a boy tired of appearing strong when he feels vulnerable." [5]

I do suspect that it may not be psychologically realistic to ask people from our underdog-loving culture to embrace an image of themselves as privileged; my thoughts turn again to the trans man who hated the thought of being a white male. But if we feminists can't work productively from a stance that acknowledges our social advantages, how can we expect straight/dominant/big-dicked men to do it?

Could feminist acknowledgment of the women's gender-based advantages help pave the way for more men to acknowledge male privilege? Could feminist acknowledgment of the advantages on both sides of the gender binary help us better grasp what sucks about being a guy?

Am I citing Thomas MacAulay Millar too much here? Well, at least once, he frustrated me. Amongst the comments on one blog post, I thought he was stating his views about stereotypical guys rather harshly. I suggested that it might be better to seek common ground, or at least to explain things gently; he said he wasn't interested — "I think we all work with some people where they are and can't soft-sell our views enough to deal with others." He added, "If I'm going to alienate someone for saying what I think too bluntly, I'll pick entitled cis het dudes." [6]

I won't pretend I didn't laugh when I read that — but I worried about it, too. I've had an enormous number of experiences trying to discuss feminism/sex/gender with men in which the men tensed, bristled, and closed me out. I don't think it was always because those guys couldn't stand the thought of losing their privilege, either. I think a lot of dudes have been led to feel that they have no place in gender discussions — that those discussions will always be about what men are doing wrong, and that no one's prepared to work with them where they are.

All groups have outsiders. Movements inevitably form themselves around oppositional forces. As someone who's spent her share of time feeling feminist rage, I'd say that being filled with feminist rage is totally understandable. And seriously, don't get me wrong: I'm not giving unfeminist guys a free pass. I'm not happy about the fact that so many men are apparently alienated from feminism because us radicals are too confrontational — or too uncomfortably correct — for their fragile masculine egos to handle. (I'm being sarcastic! Mostly.) I'm **really** not happy about the fact that I've got to think about **marketing** anti-oppression — in a just universe, wouldn't anti-oppression market itself?

But at the same time, I'm a realist. I know this isn't a just universe, and I want to use tactics that'll achieve my goals. Which are: I'd really like to find more men at my side in the sex and gender wars. I'd really like to talk to more guys who don't see ideas stamped with feminism as an attack — rather, as an opportunity for alliance. Plus, if we're going to think in terms of cold hard tactics, it's worth noting that normative men hold most of the power in America. (That's part of what we're complaining about, right?) So swelling our ranks with The Oppressive Class means we can ruthlessly use their power for good.

Can we do better at making feminist discourses around gender and sexuality open to normative men, without driving ourselves crazy? How can we make our movement open to, and accepting of, normative men? Put another way, how do we convince normative men to support us?

Maybe we don't need a lot of normative men in the camp of sex and gender radicals; maybe we'll be happier without silly Gender Studies 101 questions clotting our discussions. Still, even if we don't try to "recruit" them, I'd love to see more widespread analysis of masculinity and masculine sexuality amongst normative dudes... if only because getting a sense for their societal boxes might simply make them happier. If only because I think they've got their own liberation to strive for.

So at the very least, I'd like to contribute to an America where serious examination of masculinity and male sexuality can flourish.

That's my final question. *How do I do it?*

* * *

The above entries originally appeared at:
http://clarissethorn.com/blog/2009/10/18/questions-i-want-to-ask-entitled-cis-het-men-part-1/

http://clarissethorn.com/blog/2009/10/20/questions-i-want-to-ask-entitled-cis-het-men-part-2-mens-rights/

http://clarissethorn.com/blog/2009/10/24/questions-i-want-to-ask-entitled-cis-het-men-part-3-space-for-men/

The first followup (plus many many comments) is available at:
http://clarissethorn.com/blog/2009/12/09/manliness-and-feminism-the-followup/

* * *

***

EDUCATION:
[theory] Sexual ABCs in Africa, Part 1: Abstinence

In 2009-2010, I spent a year in sub-Saharan Africa working on HIV mitigation. It was fascinating, frustrating, heartbreaking work. I learned an enormous amount about the possibilities and pitfalls of foreign aid, public health, and global injustice — far more than I could ever summarize in an introductory paragraph. Maybe someday I'll write more about it all, but in the meantime, if my articles leave you with an appetite for more, then I recommend two wrenching books: Letting Them Die: Why HIV/AIDS Prevention Programmes Fail *by Catherine Campbell, and* The Wisdom of Whores: Bureaucrats, Brothels and the Business of AIDS *by Elizabeth Pisani. (Pisani's book in particular gave me so many moments of recognition that I was almost offended. I was like, dammit, Elizabeth Pisani, this is the book I wanted to write!)*

In early 2010, while I was still in Africa, I began writing a series of articles about my experiences. These articles were published at CarnalNation.com and edited by Chris Hall, who is a smart sex-positive writer in his own right. [1] I'm especially grateful to Chris because, unlike a lot of editors, he made the effort to grasp where I was coming from; he always made requests rather than demands, and never changed my work without consulting me. Good editors are hard to come by, and I hope that when I edit other writers' work today, I do credit to the model Chris provided.

I'm sad to report that CarnalNation ceased publishing new articles in late 2010, although you can still read the archives online (and I encourage you to do so). There are a lot of "sex-positive" websites out there that have little real understanding of sex communities, activism, etc. — not to mention, there are websites that hire talented and ethical writers, but then hide truly unethical business practices. But from what I could tell, CarnalNation was the real deal. The list of contributors read like a Sex-Positive All-Stars, and I was proud to be part of it.

So, anyway. This is the first of a bunch of articles that I originally wrote about sex and culture in southern Africa. Like all my writing, it's framed within my own experience. (I'm not republishing all the Africa articles in this book, but they're all available in my CarnalNation archive. [2]) And before we get into it, I would like to note one final thing. One problem with how many Westerners write about Africa is that they treat Africa as "one country": there's little acknowledgment that Africa is a huge, diverse continent full of many different cultures. I try to avoid that, but I also write under a pseudonym, and thus I can't write too precisely about where I was or what I did in Africa. I'm sorry about that, and I hope I don't come off as too much of a colonialist asshole.

※ ※ ※

In the beginning of 2009, I made a name for myself as a sex-positive, pro-BDSM educator in Chicago — and no one was more surprised than me by how suddenly successful I was! I curated the explosive pro-sex, pro-queer, pro-kink documentary film series Sex+++ at Jane Addams Hull-House Museum. I lectured on both BDSM and sexual communication in Chicago, San Francisco and New York. I even fielded a call from Oprah's office! Then, just as my life was going all crazy, I was offered a job doing HIV/AIDS mitigation in southern Africa. I've wanted to do it for years, so I accepted — though not without some soul-searching.

Rather a change of pace, right? I thought I might even give up basic romance by coming here... but not so fast. Only a month after moving, I met a guy I really liked. He's another American, also here to work on HIV/AIDS; we live a bit far apart, but flirted constantly by text message. We discussed etymology, traded literary recommendations, compared religion — I'm Unitarian, he's a Baha'i convert. He lived one summer in Chicago, and we discovered that we'd shopped at the same bookstores.

One night, we found ourselves in the same nightclub. Using a cigarette as an excuse to go outside, we abandoned the music and talked for hours. Our friends came to check on us multiple times, with varying degrees of smirking insinuation; we kept promising to go back in after one cigarette, then neglecting to actually smoke it. The conversation went through homesickness, ethics, roleplaying games, more literature. I lent him a book. He promised to visit me.

His next text message, a few days later, was plainly nervous. Can you imagine someone blurting a text message? That's what he did when he told me that he takes the "no sex before marriage" part of his Baha'i faith seriously. I was stunned — but I had to laugh, too. **Of**

course Miss Clarisse Thorn, pro-sex advocate, just had to fixate on a man who wouldn't sleep with her!

* * *

I did not undergo abstinence-only sex education. My middle school's health teachers were admirably forthright and even hosted condom demonstrations in the auditorium, more power to 'em. I also had the good fortune to be raised Unitarian — so I received incredibly compassionate, complete sex education in Sunday School. [3]

Still, for a long time I was strongly attracted to chastity. In my teens, I decided that I wouldn't lose my virginity until I was much older — I think I picked age 25 — because I wanted to be sure I'd be mature enough to handle it. This resolution didn't last, but after I became sexually active, I occasionally came back to the idea. A few female friends took "time off" — in some cases, full years of abstinence. I considered doing so myself, strongly and for a long time.

Back then, I was terrible at communicating about sex. Reading explicit sex scenes made me feel anxious, perhaps because I felt they set standards I couldn't "perform." Talking explicitly to my partners felt impossible, not least because I had practically no idea what I wanted. Worst of all, I could feel the societal boxes around my sexuality, but I couldn't articulate them. Plus, there were dark undercurrents to my sexuality that simply scared me. Abstinence was the only obvious way around my sex-negative cultural baggage!

Once I adjusted into my BDSM orientation, once I got a grip on how to circumvent some problems with how Americans tend to think about sex, once I experienced mutual sexual communication that was totally trusting and adventurous... my attraction to chastity was greatly reduced. These days, the idea only seems awesome when (a) I've just been romantically burned, or (b) I want more time to myself.

It's tempting to think that Mr. Chastity might be the same way: that he's uncomfortable for similar reasons; that he'll "get over it." Tempting — and offensively presumptuous. Maybe he'll re-examine his motives someday, and maybe he won't. The important thing is to respect his feelings. So when he sent me that text, I did what any responsible sex-positive girl ought to do: I honored his boundaries and thought seriously about whether I could work within them.

I wrote back:
I think it's adorable that you told me the vow thing by text- & on

a serious note, I rather admire you for challenging yourself & social expectations of masculinity. I can't afford exegesis of my sexual history by text; we can talk about it when you visit- which I hope you do, even if you insist on sleeping on the floor. I promise not to push you- though I confess I'm curious about the vow's limits. But I also understand if you don't feel comfortable coming down.

His relief, in our next few exchanges, was palpable. I think a man who wants to abstain has a far trickier journey ahead of him than a woman: America's sexual assumptions may be formed around stereotypical male sexuality — which **really sucks** for women — but it's a very narrow stereotype that limits men too. Men are expected to be insatiable, and preferring not to have sex casts a man's entire masculinity into question. His abstinence can cause anxiety for the female partner, too: after all, given an assumption that men are nigh-indiscriminate sex machines, a woman might feel that there's something terribly wrong with her if a man won't bang her.

Mr. Chastity has dealt with those problems a lot, so my careful reaction and evident lack of anxiety won me lots of points. Since then, I've met up with him publicly twice, and we've even managed to make out! He's still going to visit. Maybe I can convince him to sleep in bed, as long as I promise not to put the moves on him.

And maybe, just maybe, his vow allows him to practice BDSM... a girl can dream, right? But seriously, if we can do BDSM together, then I just might be his dream partner. I'd be happy to focus our sexual time on BDSM and foreplay, and to ignore "actual" sex indefinitely. Plus, some people argue that declining to sate ourselves sexually is the best tactic for prolonging romantic magic. [4] So this could be the way for Mr. Chastity to become the love of my life.

* * *

In Africa, the mantra for HIV educators is ABC: the three things that protect against HIV/AIDS are Abstinence, Being faithful, and Condom usage. But my job is much more complicated than passing out condoms and wagging my finger. The problem isn't so much that people don't know how to avoid HIV, although myths and misconceptions do exist. The problem is that people don't seem willing to change their behavior in order to protect themselves... or that they don't feel they have the power to change their behavior.

People can't just know about condoms — they must prioritize condom usage despite drawbacks like loss of pleasure or pressure from their partners. People can't just know that HIV is sexually transmitted — they must be psychologically open to abstaining from sex despite drawbacks that are, well, obvious. HIV prevention in Africa is less about sharing knowledge, now, and more about marketing: giving people a new perspective on sex, their health, and their futures.

Of course, I'm totally psyched about marketing some of these social aspects, like gender equality. (Gender equality is an HIV/AIDS issue for lots of reasons — the most obvious being that the less power women have, the less they control their own sexual acts.) But others give me pause. Abstinence? Seriously? It sticks in my craw. Obviously, I don't have a problem with people **choosing** not to have sex... but I'm not sure how I feel about actively **convincing** people not to have sex.

In America, I advocate for open, explicit, pleasure-affirming sex education. But that's a radical stance even in America — I'm not sure whether it's possible here! At least I'm spotting a few allies, some in unexpected places: for instance, there's a great high-profile, outspoken sex-positive educator named Agrippa Khathide in South Africa... who happens to be a pastor. I'm starting to think there's room to do fascinating work here, creating culturally appropriate sex-positive education.

Yet abstinence remains the only 100% effective tactic for avoiding HIV. As another educator told me, "I **hate** abstinence-only education more than anything. Seriously. But... here, I think it's a necessary ingredient." Is it responsible for me to avoid promoting abstinence? Even if marketing abstinence means that to some extent, I'll have to tell people sexual exploration isn't worth doing?

I'm still feeling out my approach, but... what if the most effective way to fight HIV is to align myself with values antithetical to free sexuality? Does properly doing my job require me to **promote a sex-negative agenda?** Surely not. Surely there are ways to promote sex-positive abstinence — perhaps a "Vibrators for African Women" program...? (This is a joke. Mostly.)

And that's just one facet of the broader question keeping me awake at night! Which is: given a fatal, incurable sexually transmitted infection; given a population where, in some groups, up to 40% test positive; given a society in which culturally appropriate messages emphatically do not include my pro-sex, pro-queer, pro-kink approach to sex education... what does being a sex-positive educator **mean**?

Maybe I can harvest clues from my own feelings, past and present, about abstinence: clues for how to promote it compassionately, effectively and responsibly; clues for locating my boundaries when I talk about it. And maybe I can harvest down-to-earth advice from my relationship with Mr. Chastity, too. I can work from toxic masculine norms he's had such trouble with, and examine how men in southern Africa might likewise worry about abstinence — if you think American men have tough definitions of sexual manliness to contend with, then try living in a place where the big men have multiple wives and over a dozen children. I also think it'll be hot to be bound against going "too far." Maybe I can learn how abstinence is fun, fun, **fun**!

Hey, at the very least, it'll give me a taste of what I'm telling everyone else to do.

* * *

The original version of this article can be found on the Internet, but please note that I've done some editing for clarity.
Here's the original:
http://carnalnation.com/content/45211/1133/sexual-abcs-africa-part-1-abstinence

* * *

EDUCATION:
[theory] Sexual ABCs in Africa, Part 2: Be Faithful

This is the second in the three-part "Sexual ABCs" series, but I originally intended it to be the last one, because it's the most complicated by far.

* * *

South African President Jacob Zuma has three wives; in a headline-making ceremony, a South African businessman recently married four women at once. King Mswati of Swaziland has thirteen wives, and his father King Sobhuza had 70. (Yes. Seventy.) Here in southern Africa, even those rich men who don't take multiple wives almost always support mistresses. Naturally, local women don't get multiple spouses, and the social penalties for infidelity are much worse for women. In America, feminists often point out that "slut" is an insult while "stud" is a compliment; there's a similar linguistic trend in siZulu, but the English words are mild compared to their siZulu equivalents.

* * *

I rarely practice consensual non-monogamy myself, but I don't hesitate to advocate destigmatizing polyamory and swing in America. True, my primary interest is BDSM, but there's so much to learn from every form of consensual sexuality. Plus, we're basically on the same side — it'd be great if different sex subcultures had more consciousness of a sex-positive "agenda" or "movement"! Although our communities have different emphases and, sometimes, profoundly different values, I see swingers and polyfolk as my brothers- and sisters-in-arms.

But enough of the soapbox! The point is that I've often defended poly — and I've gotten into interesting arguments doing so. One friend noted just how hard it is for poly people to negotiate their relationships. "It's so **complicated**," he complained. "So much communication is required. Doesn't that seem like an argument against it? If polyamory were really a good relationship model, then people wouldn't have to put so much effort into accomplishing it."

"It's only complicated because polyamory isn't our societal default," I replied. "People have to put extra effort into negotiating relationships that fall outside the norm. The same thing happens with BDSM. Kinksters **must** spend a lot more time discussing our sexual relationships, because it's more dangerous for us to make assumptions about where our partners want to go. That doesn't mean there's anything wrong with kink.

"And," I added, "that extra effort can be a feature, not a bug! The fact that kinksters spend so much time isolating different aspects of our sexuality has given us a uniquely fine-grained sexual vocabulary. I think most kinksters tend to make fewer assumptions about our partners' boundaries than vanilla people do. And circumstances have forced us to develop some brilliant strategies for bedroom communication. I'm not saying we're all brilliant communicators, but I think we've got a unique window on it. When I run sexual communication workshops, half the tactics I share are filched from the BDSM subculture; I just rename them for a general audience. Many polyfolk have similar insights about relationship communication."

Being in southern Africa, seeing all these men partnered with multiple women, has brought that conversation to mind. Because the majority of men can't afford multiple wives and some churches frown on the practice, polygyny isn't exactly the default — but it's certainly a well-respected, highly desirable relationship formation. (Polygyny is the most precise term for the type of polygamy that's practiced here, where men can have multiple wives but women can't have multiple husbands. However, a lot of Africans simply call it "polygamy.")

And men who can't go the open route frequently do the same thing discreetly. In the July 2009 issue of *New African Magazine*, Akua Djanie — who moved to England at age 10 and grew up there — observes: "I know very few African men, especially those living on the continent, who keep only one partner. The majority of men I come across are in multiple relationships, sometimes open, but most times on the quiet." She also notes that "in some instances, a man's manhood is judged by the number of women he can keep."

So monogamy is not the default; and negotiating monogamy is difficult, here. But a new factor makes it a matter of life and death:

HIV.

* * *

The basic centerpiece of HIV prevention is ABC — Abstinence, Being faithful, and using Condoms. But the three strategies haven't always received equal airtime. "The Fidelity Fix," a 2004 *New York Times Magazine* article by Helen Epstein, quoted one analyst who believed "partner reduction has been the neglected middle child of the ABC approach." Epstein wrote, "Perhaps the topic seems weighted with moral judgment; perhaps Western advisors in particular feel it would be insensitive to raise it; perhaps they also feel it would be futile to try to change deeply rooted patterns of behavior." She outlined those patterns and concluded, "A fidelity campaign does seem worth a try, even if it might seem overly simplistic and preachy." [1] Another expert, quoted in a 2007 *Washington Post* piece on multiple partners in Botswana, agreed: "There has never been equal emphasis on 'Don't have many partners'.... If you just say, 'Use the condom'... we will never see the daylight of the virus leaving us." [2]

Living in southern Africa now, it seems clear that this recommendation has been taken to heart. I regularly spot posters, stickers and billboards for fidelity campaigns that apparently didn't exist a few years ago. Although cultural pride is a big deal here, locals routinely disparage risky marriage-related cultural practices: for instance, many speak harshly against wife inheritance, whereby a woman whose husband has died is traditionally expected to marry his brother. Many such practices are becoming more and more unusual. However, the larger phenomenon of polygyny seems harder to budge.

I recently sat in on a partner reduction dialogue for one town's church leaders; it was attended by representatives both from churches that allow polygamous marriages, and those that don't. The discussion was quite civil, though one anti-polygamy preacher did make snide comments towards the polygamists. They talked about issues like an absence of marriage counseling, preachers' failure to act as positive role models, and churches' failure to be transparent about HIV. (The all-male group also noted "women's selfish impatience with erectile dysfunction," "women preferring men who last longer," "women preferring men with a lot of money," and "women not loving their husbands enough" as contributing factors to fidelity failure.) The group seemed pleased to work together, and eager to address the problem. The question of members being pro- or anti-polygamy was, apparently, only a side note.

As it happens, there are plenty of polygamy problems that have nothing to do with HIV/AIDS. These divisions would exist without the disease. For instance, some preachers who don't support polygamy will sanction divorce and remarriage. One man told me that "true" polygamous marriage — in which a man has many wives, all supported simultaneously — is slowly being replaced: rich men now often take younger wives, but divorce and cast aside the previous wives first. The "new" approach looks suspiciously like the Western model of "serial monogamy"... except that the women, left with few resources, rarely marry again. (The gender inequality is highlighted when only one partner has HIV: an HIV-positive man will likely be nursed by his wife, while HIV-positive women can fear anything from abuse to abandonment.) Partly because abandonment is getting so common and partly due to doctrinal interpretations, there is yet a third group of church leaders who not only reject polygamy but refuse to remarry divorced people.

Most interestingly, I've noticed that from some perspectives, the current system appears to stack the moral deck in favor of polygyny. A lot of the time, people will claim that there are only three alternatives: (1) abandonment and/or deadbeat fatherhood, (2) cheating, or (3) overt polygyny. If those are the alternatives, then even empowered women will argue in favor of polygyny — though not happily, since they're quite conscious that a system supporting polygamy without polyandry is completely unfair.

For example, in the aforementioned July 2009 *New African* piece, titled "The Sins of Our Fathers," Akua Djanie reflects bitterly upon a father who ignored her mother in favor of his second wife. She writes that she "will encourage [her sons] to have a relationship with only one woman at a time. And if they make the mistake of having children from different women, I will make sure they are responsible for each and every one of them." Then, however, she asserts that "although I myself would never wish to be in such a [polygamous] relationship, I think it can work, does work, and has worked in the past"; that "the issue is not so much with the pros and cons of polygamy, but more with the irresponsible behavior of some men"; and that "African men are still as polygamous as they were in my father's heyday. In fact I believe that polygamy will never go away." Djanie doesn't mention HIV once.

(It's worth noting that Djanie is very aware of Western cultural imperialism; she loathes and deconstructs those who downgrade

African culture in favor of Western. For instance, her November 2009 *New African* piece was about how frustrating it is that Africans usually model Christmas on Western standards, showing images of white children frolicking in Alpine snow. Thus, her argument against polygamy is especially striking.)

Recently, I spoke to some grassroots HIV educators who go door-to-door in their rural villages. They keep a list of different prevention tactics that they discuss with their neighbors. Glancing through, I saw both *Zero Grazing* and *Be Faithful* side-by-side. "I don't understand the difference between these two," I said, prompting the educators to confer amongst themselves in siZulu. Finally, one offered, "Be Faithful is about monogamy with one partner. Zero Grazing is about having multiple wives and not going outside the marriage." The others seemed to agree. Given their limited English and my limited siZulu, I decided not to ask: "Does promoting both strike you as a mixed message?" (I did ask whether they think people listen to their advice. In response, they just looked depressed.)

Clearly, the fidelity fix has arrived. What's harder to determine is how much, and in what manner, the message is being emphasized — not to mention, whether it's actually taking root.

* * *

Given my experience with polyamory, and my nigh-rabid promotion of straightforward communication as the Cure For All Ills, I can't help wondering: would it help to port communication tactics from our polyamorous allies over to southern Africa? But polyamory is fundamentally different from polygyny. Polyamory assumes that both partners have equal footing — equal negotiating status — whereas polygyny assumes that men are entitled to privileges women aren't. Would it be possible to take the lessons of even-handed polyamory, and apply them to polygyny?

What if I choose not to address polygyny — to avoid the whole culturally fraught debate, and just create relationship communication workshops inspired by polyamorous (and BDSM) analysis? (That way, with no one alienated by an overt stance, I may reach the audience better anyway.) Will it work if I teach from a perspective of assumed gender equality? My instinct is "yes"; I've even found a heartening example! The well-known South African Pastor Agrippa Khathide preaches equality for women and sexual pleasure for everyone (as long as they're married first, of course). He gives explicit sermons including technical sexual advice, and has been quoted in interviews asserting things like: "married people should be totally free to express themselves any way they wish in the bedroom," that "they must be willing to experiment, explore and explicitly acknowledge the giving and receiving of pleasure," and that women are entitled to "enjoyment of sex like men."

If he can do that, surely I can do something similar! Surely, then, my inherent egalitarian assumptions would make a positive impact, even if I say nothing direct about irritating male entitlement. Yet I worry that if I focus on relationship communication and don't directly take on the monogamy juggernaut, I will sidestep the heart of these debates. Indeed, not only might I be sidestepping — I might be turning my gaze from the very place I ought to focus.

* * *

Perhaps the hardest part about wrapping my head around a fidelity campaign isn't whether certain tactics are appropriate or inappropriate, effective or ineffective. It's that they can be both, or neither — and while culture matters, it varies by individual. More to the point, while culture affects attitudes towards Abstinence and Condoms, there aren't many ways to interpret the **implementation** of those two dicta.

The people who live here **themselves** are divided about what fidelity means. Be Faithful, or Zero Grazing? Multiple wives, or divorce and remarriage? **They themselves** are working towards gender equality, but have just as many arguments about its implementation as Westerners do. **They themselves** are proud of their culture, and yet there's one anti-HIV slogan that always leaps out at me when I spot it among the myriad of posters and stickers:

There is nothing cultural about dying of AIDS.

* * *

The original version of this article can be found on the Internet, but please note that I've done some editing for clarity.
Here's the original:
http://carnalnation.com/content/45680/1133/sexual-abcs-africa-part-2-be-faithful

* * *

* * *

EDUCATION:
[theory] Sexual ABCs in Africa, Part 3: Condoms

This article followed the previous two articles, published at CarnalNation.com in January 2010. I think a lot of people would like to believe that Africans are "different from us" and that's why HIV has had such an impact in Africa. And it's accurate to say that certain cultural patterns influence the spread of HIV, as I described in the previous piece, "Be Faithful."

But the truth is, also, that people are similar everywhere: we respond to certain incentives, and sexuality is one of our most powerful incentives. The terrifying truth is that Africans are not especially different from us... and given the right circumstances, the West can and will be equally vulnerable to this awful epidemic. And as I learned more and then came home, I began to see just how vulnerable we are. There are poor, marginalized areas of the USA where HIV is reaching the same proportions that it has reached in Africa. And even among privileged young Americans, HIV rates have been rising for the first time in years.

* * *

In America, the common argument against explicit sex education — and promoting condom use in schools — is that it will encourage kids to be promiscuous. The idea is that if we portray it as normal for kids to be having sex and tell them how to do it safely, they'll be more likely to go and have sex. As for the kids who'll have sex anyway... well, they're sinning and don't deserve to know what they're doing.

Some things don't change, even across oceans. I occasionally hear the same arguments against promoting condom use in southern Africa. But here, HIV is ripping the populace to pieces, and it's much harder to speak against condoms when funeral processions wind through your neighborhood every weekend. Occasional religious educators claim that promoting condom usage waters down their message and therefore makes anti-HIV education less **effective** [1];

but most churches I've encountered take a pragmatic, condom-promoting approach. Indeed, one of the best HIV curricula I've seen so far is the "Channels of Hope" workshop, created by the Christian organization World Vision and designed to train church groups. It not only promotes explicit condom education, but urges compassion towards sex workers and homosexuals. **And** it discusses why marital rape isn't okay! I'd venture to say that the majority of liberal, secular sex education curricula in the USA aren't as awesome.

Just the other day, I was surveying a bunch of kids aged 11-13 and they asked how to put on a condom. Cursing myself silently, I had to admit that I didn't have any to show them... at which point one child dashed from the room and returned minutes later bearing both a condom, plus a rather splintery stick from a firewood pile. Condom distribution is in full swing; I can think of three places to pick up free condoms within a ten-minute walk from where I'm seated. Condoms are described in kids' textbooks, and condom demonstrations are welcome in every school. Condoms are lauded by politicians, pop icons, and religious leaders. Take any person off the street and they'll know the HIV-prevention mantra: ABC — Abstain, Be faithful, use Condoms. Yet condom usage rates are still killingly low.

* * *

Though I'm fishbelly-pale, I'm not great at wearing sunscreen, and I live in **Africa**. I try... I mean, I kinda try... I mean it's so annoying to apply, and it feels gross! And this notwithstanding the fact that I literally have ten bottles of top-quality, non-sticky, oil-free sunscreen sitting across the room from me as I type this. On the other hand, I religiously take my malaria prophylactic pill; I've noticed no side effects, and getting malaria would **really suck**.

I recall one recurring conversation between myself and a former boyfriend, whom I dated for years. We'd both had excellent sex education, and yet we used withdrawal as our primary birth-control method. We did it even though we both had boxes of condoms available. We did it even though neither of us wanted me to get pregnant, and — though I'm definitely pro-choice — I wasn't sure I could bring myself to have an abortion. We'd both been tested, and we trusted each other not to cheat, but that's some dangerous trust to extend — and **we knew it**.

One particular moment comes to mind: we were lying lazily in bed together, talking about how stupid we were.

"We should be more careful," he said seriously.

"We really should," I agreed.
"Let's be more careful," he suggested.
I nodded.
We weren't.

Were we stupid? Obviously. Were we normal? Unfortunately, yes. A few months ago, I chatted with another American HIV educator about the situation here in Africa. "They know to use condoms," she complained, "and they have the condoms! I just don't **get** it!"

"I agree that it's incomprehensible," I said, "but hey, **I** haven't always been 100% careful, and I'm a sex educator."

She glanced at me, then away. "Yeah, I haven't either," she admitted. There was a gloomy pause, and then we couldn't help it — we cracked up. "I hate love," she said when the giggles subsided. She shook her head. "That shit fucks with you."

Why didn't I use condoms with that ex? I **still** don't know! When you instruct people to use condoms as often as I do, you get accustomed to the arguments. I hear the same reasons we didn't use condoms — because they don't feel as good, because they interrupt the moment, etc. etc. etc. — I hear them, I smile and I tell the audience, "You gotta use 'em anyway, folks." I'm a hypocrite, but what else can I say?

And there are deeper-rooted objections to condoms — objections that are both rarely stated in public, and harder to confront. One is trust, which I've been struggling with for a long time, since before I got to Africa. I don't think it's good for condom discussions to center on trust, and I wish I had more ideas about how to refocus them. "Use condoms because you can't trust anyone, not even your lover," is an ugly message to impart. Moreover, it only encourages the audience to view **not** using condoms as a gift, or a signifier of trust.

In America, I tend to cast it like this: "Safer sex is normal. It's the baseline. Lots of people practice it. It's an assumption. Act like it." Which, I hope, helps people simply default to safer sex without forcing direct questions about any given partner's integrity. Hopefully, it also distracts attention from seeing discarding condoms as a gift. But the truth is that condom usage isn't always an assumption even in America (witness myself and my ex). And it's less of an assumption here in Africa. How can I avoid validating the viewpoint that not using condoms is the best way to express trust?

The second deep-rooted objection — again, both in Africa and America — is inability to maintain an erection while using a condom. When I was younger, I used to think that guys were just whining when they claimed they couldn't keep it up with a condom, but in my old age I've determined that People Are Different (no way!): while most men deal with condoms just fine, some men genuinely can't. Since people tend to be bad at communicating about sex and especially bad at making space for conversations about non-normative male sexuality, this isn't often acknowledged. Fortunately, the solution is easy: men who have trouble with condomised penis-in-vagina sex gain a glorious opportunity to explore all the other kinds of sex!

People tend to panic when confronted with the idea of a man who can't have penetrative sex. But that's sex-negative nonsense based entirely on the stereotype of "real sex" as penis-in-vagina intercourse. The solution to loss of erection isn't to sit around awkwardly wishing you could be having penetrative sex. The solution is for both partners to start exploring with mouths, hands... and words. But teaching about this means speaking very explicitly, and it can be hard to have those conversations in a conservative society without being run out of town.

* * *

In the Strange Case of Clarisse and Her Condomless Ex, I was at least Being Faithful with a pre-tested partner, and I didn't live in an HIV-rich population. The risks were lower, and it's true that I've never run those kinds of risks outside a long-term monogamous relationship. But the bottom line remains: my ex and I did it even though we knew better.

He and I are both privileged people. Neither of us was dependent on the other for money, for instance. If two highly privileged people who agree that condoms are necessary can fail to use condoms, what about people who don't have that privilege?

In many places across the world, including much of southern Africa, sex workers can charge double for sex without a condom. No businesswoman is likely to insist on a measure that will halve her profits — especially if she already lives on a razor-fine margin, and especially if she's already contracted HIV herself. Likewise, if a girl can't afford expensive school fees and therefore sleeps with her teachers, then she's hardly in a position to demand protection. Many married women quite justifiably fear divorce, violence or murder if they refuse their husbands sex without a condom — in one recent case, a wife tested negative for HIV while her husband tested positive, but when she tried to refuse condomless sex, he killed her.

Some pro-condom campaigns tell the populace that "it's your responsibility: you must respect your body and take the initiative"; but while that works for some people, it's a terribly cruel message for people who lack the standing to negotiate with their partners.

Add to this the fact that, if you know enough people living with HIV — and if your life already seems difficult and directionless — the disease will start to seem like much less of a big deal. A friend reports that one day, sitting in a salon, she saw a man exit with a sex worker. "Don't forget a condom!" she called bluntly. His reply: "I'm not the first to get it, and I won't be the last." (Indeed, there are documented cases of marginal populations **deliberately contracting HIV** when they perceived benefits. For instance, when HIV-positive illegal immigrants in France were offered citizenship as part of a humanitarian initiative, some sought out the disease. [2])

People who ignore prophylactics will always be with us. Some of them will be like me and my ex, or the sex worker's client: despite knowing the risk, transient pleasure trumps absolute safety. There isn't much to be done about that demographic, save ensuring that they (we) truly grasp the consequences we risk with our silliness.

Some people, however, will be vulnerable more because they're female, or young, or poor. In those cases, addressing the root causes — sexism, poverty, abuse — becomes the only solution. Thus, some of the best HIV programs in southern Africa appear to address completely different issues. These include:

* Identifying and supporting income-generating projects for women, so that they have the resources to walk away from abusive partners;
* Sponsoring schools, so that they can educate for free and remove one reason a schoolchild might sleep with a teacher;
* Facilitating support groups, so members can share tactics for negotiating safer sex (or, if already HIV-positive, help each other cope with obligations and treatment regimens);
* Creating strong communities, so people are quite simply more motivated to live.

* * *

It's always tempting to see unfamiliar cultures as monolithic, but we must remind ourselves that they never are. Every society in the world contains its own divides, just like America's culture and subcultures. Because HIV/AIDS functions along the very taboo, very culturally-influenced axis of sexuality, it throws taboo cultural sexual divides into high relief.

In America, one thing the disease's advent served to highlight was stigma towards LGBTQ and other radical sexual subcultures. American HIV mitigation has often sought to redress that stigma. Here, one thing it serves to highlight — one thing mitigation seeks to redress — is mainstream gender and relationship issues. But these splits existed before HIV came along. Although the prevalence of HIV sheds light on and invokes compassion for these divisions, they're more enduring than we like to think.

Still, I can't help noticing the phoenixes arising from these ashes. Firstly, it turns out that the best way to shut down sex-negative arguments against explicit sex education is to invoke the specter of HIV. One 2008 report from a well-respected local organization argued that AIDS prevention efforts should include straightforward lessons on pleasurable acts, such as oral sex or sex toy usage! (Obviously, I hope to work with this organization.)

A 2004 *New York Times Magazine* article on HIV in southern Africa made the case that while "many experts contend that sexual-behavior change in Africa is complicated because women's fear of abusive partners inhibits private discussions of sex, condom use and HIV," the crisis also contributes to a better environment for those discussions. One researcher is quoted pointing out that, "young South Africans are much more likely to talk about sex and are developing 'a vocabulary for discussing feelings and desires.'" [3] Furthermore, southern African movements for women's empowerment invariably cite HIV as a reason change is necessary **now.** Because gender oppression is acknowledged as a driver of the epidemic, gender equality is an explicit goal of both governments and major HIV organizations. Even admirably reasonable laws about sex work are being discussed — considerably more reasonable than most Western sex work legislation. The laws probably won't pass, unfortunately, but at least they're on the radar. [4]

I've got a twisted confession to make. On days when I feel particularly flippant, I find myself thinking: *Thank God for HIV/AIDS!* Without HIV... would women's empowerment be such a given? Aside from bleeding heart feminists like myself, who would care about sex workers' conditions? Aside from sex-positive nuts like myself, who would advocate for explicit sex education?

Here's hoping we can create better social conditions to arrest the pandemic... and keep those conditions going afterwards.

* * *

The original version of this article can be found on the Internet, but please note that I've done some editing for clarity.
Here's the original:
http://carnalnation.com/content/46266/1133/sexual-abcs-africa-part-3-condoms

* * *

ACTIVISM:
[theory] Colonized Libidos

This article was published at CarnalNation.com in early 2010. Anti-oppression theory sure can get out of touch with reality.

* * *

The situation for gay / lesbian rights here in Africa has gotten lots of media attention lately, and I myself have written about meeting a Swazi lesbian activist who was later murdered. [1] So I won't waste your time by talking about how bad it can get to be gay here (although it's worth noting that I've seen at least one interesting argument about how the places in Africa where homosexuality is most heavily punished are also the ones with the strongest national dialogue, and thus arguably some of the best ones to actually be gay [2]). Besides, I've become somewhat numb to the situation's sheer awfulness since arriving last year. What catches my attention these days is unfamiliar cultural angles and arguments.

While reading the local paper, I recently came upon yet another gay-shaming article — but instead of railing about God's will, the article talked about cultural imperialism. Specifically, it argued that gays and lesbians are gay and lesbian **only because of the West**. Gays and lesbians, the theory goes, have been so influenced by the Sodom and Gomorrah that is the West that they've internalized our permissive, scandalous sexual mores. (Those of us who actually come from the West are, of course, a little confused by how our fractured native cultures — still fiercely arguing about homosexuality within themselves — might create such an influence.) An African proud of his or her Africanness, who rejects the colonial West, will therefore not only wear African traditional garb and participate in African traditional ceremonies but will also be straight. (Ironically, some historians have pointed out that much of Africa was much less homophobic before Western missionaries came in. [3])

I got a front-line view of this attitude when I took a newspaper to the Post Office for photocopying. "Another article about lesbians!"

snorted the postmaster — they're getting to know me around there. He took the papers from me and shuffled through my requested pages. "Is it true," he asked, "that President Obama supports lesbians?"

"Yes," I said.

He looked shocked; I wondered if he'd expected me to say no. "What?!" he cried, and took a moment to regain his composure. "Well, that's American culture," he said finally. "It's not African culture."

I took a deep breath and pressed my lips together. I'd be in big trouble with my employer if I kicked up a storm at the Post Office, but oh, man — in that moment, I really, really **wanted** to. "How much do I owe you?" I asked instead, and went home to lose myself in a nice sex-positive book.

Personally, what I find most intriguing about these assertions of cultural imperialism is how they compare to similar assertions in the West. I'm a kinkster and pro-BDSM activist, but I'm also a feminist, which can make for some serious anxiety. A lot of my coming-out process involved both a difficult internal struggle and my observations of arguments between kinksters and anti-BDSM feminists, who often make very similar allegations to these African speakers on "cultural imperialism."

The very articulate BDSM blogger Trinity (who, of late, has sadly decreased her involvement in the blogosphere) has spent lots of time analyzing and participating in those arguments. One of my favorite Trinity posts, titled "Why BDSM?", hosts a radical feminist commenter who writes:

If we lived in a healthy society, the idea of BDSM would not even come up in the first place. BDSM is here, as a manifestation of that unhealthiness, but to try to 'stop' the people who aren't being coerced into it would do more harm than the thing itself....

I am not saying tolerance of BDSM directly causes our sick society, but that it is a very strong symptom of a society were hierarchy, inequality and degradation are seen as the norm of human relations. Accepting BDSM is accepting this status quo. ... by challenging all inequality, including that in BDSM, we are putting forward the idea that other possibilities are available. [4]

In other words: the Patriarchy made me kinky, and if I don't challenge kink then I'm supporting the Patriarchy. I would imagine that Africans pushing the cultural imperialism argument would say something similar: Western colonial influence made you gay, and if you don't challenge homosexuality then you're supporting Western colonial influence.

Well, "with us or against us" arguments are inherently flawed. And then there's the fact that, similarly to homosexuals, many of us kinksters consider our desires to be innate and largely unchangeable. So if our desires can't be changed, then what exactly is accomplished by shaming us through anti-oppressive theory-speak? (And make no mistake — for those of us who take the theory seriously, it really does feel shameful to find others telling us we're in opposition, even within the private sphere of sexuality.) I'm not remotely convinced that our sexuality arose solely because of an oppressive society — but even if it's true, then what am I, or African gay people, supposed to actually **do** in order to challenge the sick status quo? Give up on our desires and never have satisfying sex again?

I tend to think that the idea of sexual orientations or innateness is a red herring — not because I believe that innateness doesn't exist, but because it's not actually relevant to sexual morality. What **should** be important is only the question of whether all involved sexual partners are consenting adults, not whether their desires are innate. Alas, it's clear that across the world, people who are instinctively grossed out by alternative sexuality will always find ways to reframe the question into how our **acts** are just plain wrong and our **consent** is irrelevant — and that's as true of some feminists and cultural loyalists as it is of Bible-thumpers.

* * *

This can be found on the Internet at:
http://carnalnation.com/content/51544/1133/colonized-libidos

* * *

***

VEGAN:
[theory] Confections of a Pickup Artist Chaser

I've been vegetarian since 2009 and vegan since 2011; I wrote this in 2012.

***

There are delicious recipes at the end! Read this article for the recipes!

I feel hyper-aware that this piece may alienate some readers, because it's a post about being vegan, i.e. not eating animal products. Lot of folks are touchy about that. So, I want to do some pre-emptive damage control: I want to clarify up front that **I have no interest in calling anyone an asshole**. If you're not vegan, then I want to try and change your mind... but I don't think you're an Incontrovertibly Bad Person, and I hope we can still be friends.

And, look, I'm not gonna pretend I'm perfect. I screw up all the time, on all kinds of social justice issues, and I'll be learning for the rest of my life.

For me, the hardest thing about being vegan has nothing to do with the food, although I think many foods made from animal products are delicious, and occasionally I have trouble resisting them. For me, the hard part is all about social situations. If I'm at a social event where non-vegan food is served and there are no other vegans, sometimes I just eat it — especially if it will Become A Big Social Problem if I don't eat it. I also sometimes eat non-vegan food that's been rescued from the trash (some of us call this "freegan"). And occasionally, when I'm spending a lot of time with someone who's non-vegan, then I'll sometimes break veganism in front of them in order to reassure them that I'm not judging them. I have vegan friends who consider this an unacceptable level of accommodation; sorry folks.

I am aware that stigmatizing, judging, and attacking non-vegans is one tactic for convincing them to go vegan. Personally, I find it stressful and frequently counterproductive. I'd rather set an example and be welcoming. (Yet I acknowledge that it's possible I wouldn't be able to do this effectively if aggressive vegans did not exist. Aggressive vegans help create the space where I get to look "reasonable" and "welcoming." The blogger Kinsey Hope once wrote a really brilliant activist typology that describes these dynamics [1], and of course, it's worth noting that I'm often characterized as an appeaser by feminists, too [2].)

So. That said? If you think you're going to Get Upset Or Offended by this post, please just don't read it. Seriously. But if you're willing to not freak out for a moment, then here are my two primary arguments for why you should go vegan:

1. It's easy.

Yes, there will be some shitty social situations: awkward moments at restaurants, pushback from your non-vegan friends, and so on. Yes, you will have to avoid some very delicious foods. And food labels will become a whole new world of confusion. But even with all these factors, **veganism really isn't as hard as people make it out to be**.

There's a **lot** of delicious vegan food out there. A number of my favorite foods were vegan before I went vegan, and some of yours probably are as well. (Recipes coming up!) Here is a free online vegan starter guide that includes recipes. [3] Here is a very comprehensive list of vegan cookbooks; they range from "easy" to "incredibly complicated Martha-Stewart-land." [4] I am a fiend for baked goods, and I like *Vegan Cupcakes Take Over The World* by Isa Chandra Moskowitz and Terry Hope Romero. And there's an increasing number of high-quality all-vegan restaurants. My favorite ones in Chicago are Native Foods (delicious cardamom rose cupcakes!) and Urban Vegan (delicious fake orange chicken!).

I won't get involved in appeals-to-healthitude, because I know both healthy vegans and unhealthy vegans, and the science is inconclusive... but I will point that out again: the science is inconclusive. Unless you have an unusual disorder, **modern nutrition has identified *no* conclusive scientific reasons for not being vegan.** Plus: **If you aren't vegan, but you don't pay any attention to eating healthy food, then you're being a hypocrite if you make a "health argument" for being non-vegan even if the science was conclusive, which it's not.** And! If you're really into health, there's a highly-recommended book called *Thrive* written by a vegan professional athlete named Brendan Brazier.

Some of my friends specifically do things like convince people to try veganism for short periods, or run Vegan Weeks at universities or whatever, just to show how (a) delicious and (b) easy vegan food can be. It works surprisingly well. A key ingredient in my own adoption of veganism was knowing vegans, and seeing how simple it was to be vegan. I used to push back really strongly... I think I resisted mostly because it was very hard to acknowledge that by eating animal products, I was participating in an incredibly fucked up system. First I had to recognize that I was doing something really **bad**, that I had been doing so for my entire life, and that most people I love do it too. This is a familiar problem for activists, of course; most people resist acknowledging that they participate in a racist, sexist culture, too. (As one of my vegan friends puts it: "I've found that people usually go through the strongest asshole anti-vegan phase right before they convert to veganism.")

Of all the social-justice acts out there, I actually think veganism is one of the lowest-hanging fruit. It's just so **easy** that the only reason non-vegan culture can possibly persist is through a really high degree of not giving a shit. In a way, that's understandable; I don't have much of a connection to animals myself. A lot of my vegan friends love animals and want to be around them all the time; I don't. If a smelly dog never jumps on me again, it will be too soon. But the fact is, animals have senses and feelings. Interacting with any animal for longer than thirty seconds can conclusively show you that animals like and dislike things, and that they feel something that looks exactly like pain. Which brings me to....

2. *If you care about consent, then veganism is transparently the right thing to do.*

There are environmental arguments and stuff, but I mean, seriously, let's call a spade a spade: when you eat meat, you're eating the murdered body of an animal who died for no reason other than your transient pleasure. As for animal products: many things that happen to animals on factory farms are abominable and obscene, as two minutes of Googling or this website or this video can show you. [5]

Even if you decide to eat animal products that come only from well-treated animals, there's no way to be sure that those animals were actually well-treated unless you're raising them yourself. As this vegan FAQ points out, there's an amazing amount of animal suffering that still occurs on "humane" farms. [6] *(Salon* has written about it, too. [7]) Some of those farms are doubtless fairly pleasant for the animals, but others.... Well, let's just say that calling some "humane" farms more merciful than factory farms is like saying that being burned alive is preferable to dying in a medieval torture device.

Personally, when I went vegan, a lot of the reason it felt easy was because I no longer had to spend tons of mental energy suppressing my empathy. I was amazed at how relieved I felt. Again, I'm not pretending to be perfect about it — I eat non-vegan food sometimes in social situations, sometimes when it's about to be thrown away, and sometimes just when I'm drunk. If you need to make accommodations in order to feel comfortable being vegan, then I'm the last person who will criticize you. I'll just be glad you're taking steps towards being vegan.

It took me a long time to decide to go vegan, and I understand that it might take you a long time, too. I've listed a lot of resources in this post and I hope you'll consider looking at them. Questions are welcome in the comments, although I may not be able to answer them. I wish you luck. And if you're already vegan, then congratulations and high-5!

Now for recipes!

I promise that these recipes are beloved by non-vegans as well as vegans. In fact, even when I wasn't vegan, they were some of my favorites. When I feed these dishes to non-vegans, they are frequently startled that the food isn't vegan. (Sometimes I save the Big Reveal for last. Heh, heh.)

(One of my other favorite gentle pro-vegan tactics is to walk into restaurants and ask if they have anything vegan on the menu. When the answer is no, I smile and thank them and leave.)

Organic and fair-trade ingredients are obviously encouraged. I'm not as good about organic and fair-trade as I could be, mostly because of expense, but I try to do it when I can.

Kickass Vegan Chocolate Chip Cookies

This is a modified version of a recipe that I originally found online [8], and some of the text comes from that recipe.

+ 1 and 1/2 cups of FLOUR
+ 1 teaspoon BAKING SODA
+ 1 teaspoon SALT

+ 3/4 cup of OIL
+ 2 tablespoons COCONUT MILK (or ALMOND MILK or SOY MILK)
+ 1 & 1/3 cups of UNREFINED SUGAR
+ HALF A BANANA
+ 1 1/2 tablespoons VANILLA EXTRACT (I've occasionally used RUM as a replacement; when I do that, I like to add some CINNAMON)
+ 2 1/2 cups OATMEAL
+ 12 oz. of DARK CHOCOLATE CHIPS

Heat your oven to 350 degrees.
Mix FLOUR, BAKING SODA and SALT together. Set aside.
Mix together the OIL and SUGAR. Mix until creamy.
Thoroughly mash the BANANA into the mixture.
Add the COCONUT MILK.
Add the VANILLA.
Stir this mixture until it is a uniform color (this will not take long).
Slowly stir in the FLOUR mixture. Mix this well.
Stir in OATMEAL and CHOCOLATE-CHIPS.
Preheat oven to baking temperature (usually 350 F).
Place large tablespoons full of the batter onto an ungreased cookie sheet (an air filled cookie sheet works best, as the air between the two layers of the sheet keeps the bottom of baked items from burning).
Bake the cookies for about 9 to 13 minutes (ovens vary in temperature). Check them by gently pressing on the top of one of the cookies. If the inside looks moist, but not too wet, they are probably done. It might take you a couple of tries to get the time down, so bake only a few at a time when starting out. Do not, I repeat, do not expect to see them turn slightly brown when done cooking. Without real eggs, they will not get that dark. They will, however, turn a golden tan.
When they are done, remove them from the oven and allow them to sit on the sheet for about a minute or two before placing them on a wire rack. Be careful with them as they tend to be quite delicate until they have cooled.

Kickass Chocolate Cake

I think I modified this recipe from an Internet source too, but I can't find it now.

+ 1 1/2 cups FLOUR
+ 1 cup SUGAR
+ 1/2 cup UNSWEETENED COCOA
+ 1 tablespoon GROUND CLOVES
+ 1 teaspoon BAKING SODA
+ 1 teaspoon CAYENNE PEPPER
+ 1/4 teaspoon SALT
+ 1 cup ALMOND MILK (or COLD WATER)
+ 1/4 cup OIL
+ 1 tablespoon BALSAMIC VINEGAR
+ 1 tablespoon VANILLA (once I replaced this with ORANGE EXTRACT and added some CINNAMON, and the result was amazing)

Preheat oven to baking temperature.

In a bowl beat together the OIL, SUGAR, SALT, SPICES and COCOA until well-combined. Add the remaining ingredients, and stir until well-combined. Pour into a greased enamel plate or cake dish and bake 20-30 minutes. Don't worry if the batter tastes quite spicy — it mellows out a lot, when you bake it so that the end result is more chocolate with a spicy after-taste. Cool.

Then mix the following ingredients together, and pour the resultant icing on top:

+ 1 cup POWDERED SUGAR
+ 1/2 cup UNSWEETENED COCOA
+ 6 tablespoons COCONUT MILK (or ALMOND MILK or SOY MILK)

Tofu Tikka Masala

This is a modified recipe that originated with a friend.

+ 5 tablespoons OIL
+ 2 medium ONIONS, thinly sliced
+ 5 large GARLIC CLOVES, finely chopped
+ 2 BAY LEAVES
+ 1 inch fresh GINGER, finely chopped
+ 1/2 inch CINNAMON STICK
+ 4 CLOVES

+ 4 PEPPERCORNS
+ 1 CARDAMOM POD
+ 2 pounds TOFU
+ 1 tablespoon GROUND CORIANDER
+ 1 teaspoon GARAM MASALA
+ 1 teaspoon GROUND CUMIN
+ 1/2 teaspoon CAYENNE PEPPER
+ 1/2 teaspoon GROUND TURMERIC
+ 14 ounces CANNED TOMATOES
+ SALT to taste
+ 2/3 cup SOY YOGURT

Heat OIL in large, heavy-bottomed sauce pan.

Add ONIONS, GARLIC, GINGER, BAY LEAVES, and WHOLE SPICES; fry gently on medium heat until sautéed.

Add the TOFU, and fry until the pieces are lightly golden brown on all sides. (It's easy to find online tips on frying tofu so it has a light crust. [9])

Stir in CORIANDER, GARAM MASALA, CUMIN, CAYENNE, TURMERIC, TOMATOES, and SALT. Cook for a while (10 minutes works).

Add SOY YOGURT and cook for another while.

As a general rule, the longer you cook a spicy dish like this, the spicier it'll be.

* * *

This can be found on the Internet at:
http://clarissethorn.com/blog/2012/05/14/food-justice-confections-of-a-pickup-artist-chaser/

* * *

***

POLYAMORY:
[theory] In Praise of Monogamy

This post was published in mid-2011, and it got more attention than most things I've written. The reaction was quite mixed. Some monogamists felt that I was damning monogamy with faint praise. Some polyamorists felt that it was problematic for me to write a post praising the culturally dominant Western mode of sexuality, because it's already dominant. On the other hand, the piece was cross-posted at a number of high-profile websites, and I got a lot of positive commentary too.

My favorite comments came from Pepper Mint, a polyamory advocate who commented on this post when it was cross-posted at Feministe. *I really felt like Pepper got what I was trying to do. Here's an excerpt from one of his comments:*

"Monogamy is [perceived as] a hegemonic requirement, not an option that should be advocated. So when people espouse monogamy (which is rare, since it is hegemonic), they do it by claiming that anything else is impossible or they do it by making moral statements. I challenge you to find a mainstream article that actually lists out the pragmatic benefits of monogamy, like Clarisse has done here. I don't think I've ever seen one. Indeed, when monogamy is explicitly discussed in the mainstream currently, it often seems to be in 'is monogamy realistic?' articles.

"Note that this is all to the detriment of monogamous people as well as nonmonogamous people. When I talk to people about polyamory, I get a lot of defensive responses, for the simple reason that monogamous people are often monogamous because they did not know there was a choice, rather than monogamous by inclination or what have you. Discourse that presents monogamy as an actual choice and lists out the pros and cons of that choice is nonmonogamy-affirming in my book, unless it is hugely one-sided.

"We have a problem in the poly communities I engage in, where people new to polyamory spend a couple years unfairly trashing monogamy. This is partly out of anger from their history and partly because they've finally found what they are looking for and everything else looks shabby in comparison. But it creates ill-will where none need exist, it screws up people's approach to relationships, and it bites people later if they want to go back to monogamy.

"So as a polyamory activist I'm very glad this essay was written, and I've posted similar things myself in various forums. It addresses a hole in the discourse that is very important to fill."

Thanks, Pepper.

* * *

There are lots of different ways of approaching non-monogamous relationships, such as:

+ **Polyamory**: Usually emphasizes developing full-on romantic relationships with more than one partner. (I've been researching polyamory since my teens, but only in recent years did I decide to actively pursue it.)

+ **Swinging**: Usually emphasizes couples with their own close bond, who have relatively casual sex with other partners. (Another difference between swinging and polyamory is that swingers tend to be more at home in mainstream culture, whereas polyamorists tend to be geeky or otherwise "alternative." The blog *Polyamory In The News* has a great, long piece on poly culture vs. swing culture. [1])

+ **Cheating**: One partner does something with an outside partner that wasn't accepted or understood in advance. In monogamous relationships, cheating usually involves having sex with an outside partner. Cheating exists in polyamorous or swing relationships as well: for example, a person might cheat on a non-monogamous partner by breaking an agreement — an agreement such as "we don't have unprotected sex with other partners".

Just in case it needs to be said: **I never advocate cheating, ever**. As for the first two, I know both poly people and swingers that I consider totally decent and wonderful folks! I have more personal experience with and interest in polyamory, though.

Yet one thing that often gets lost in conversations about all these options is the **advantages** of monogamy. Of which there are many. Although I don't currently identify as monogamous, I had a very strong monogamous preference for years. I knew that polyamory existed, and I thought about it a lot, because it's interesting — but I just didn't feel like it was for me. (In fact, my most adamantly polyamorous friend used to call me his "reasonable monogamous friend." He said I had examined polyamory enough to reasonably reject it, whereas he felt most people never consider polyamory deeply enough to have a thoughtful opinion.)

And lately lots of my monogamous friends have been getting married. So I've been thinking about the positive aspects of their relationship choices as I dance at their weddings, devour mini-quiches, flirt with their brothers and try to avoid offending their parents. (Okay, I've actually only flirted with one brother. So far.)

A Few Advantages of Monogamy (this is not a complete list)

+ **Jealousy management.** Some people experience jealousy more than, or less than, or differently from other people. Plenty of people in non-monogamous relationships experience jealousy — and plenty of non-monogamous people handle it just fine, through open-hearted communication. (Often, jealousy is managed through very detailed relationship agreements such as a "relationship contract." [2])

But there are also plenty of people who appear to lack the "jealousy chip."

And then there are plenty of people who experience so much jealousy, who feel that jealousy is such a big part of their emotional makeup, that the best way to manage it is simply through monogamy.

Personally, I used to get a lot more jealous than I do now. I think I'm less likely to get jealous these days partly because I've gotten better at finding low-drama men. Jealousy has a reputation for being an irrational emotion, and sometimes it genuinely is an unreasonable, cruel power-grab. But I think jealousy is often quite rational, and often arises in response to a genuine emotional threat... or deliberate manipulation.

There's another reason, though... I've also noticed that some switch in my brain has flipped, and I've started to **eroticize** jealousy. I occasionally find myself fantasizing about men I care about sleeping with other women, and sometimes the fantasy is hot **because** I feel mildly jealous. I cannot explain how this happened. It surprised me the first time it happened, believe me. What's really fascinating is that I think **the same part** of me that eroticizes jealousy, is the part that used to make me feel sick at the thought of my partner sleeping with someone else. Masochism: the gift that never stops giving!

I think it's important to note here that I didn't become less jealous because I felt like I "should," or because I was told not to be jealous.

In fact, I had an early boyfriend who acted like I was a hysterical bitch every time I got jealous... and he made things much worse. With him, I just felt awful when I got jealous; I couldn't get past it. I felt like he was judging me for something I couldn't help; I felt like my mind was fragmenting as I tried to force myself to "think better" without any outside support; and worst of all, I felt like I couldn't rely on him to respect my feelings.

It was the men who treated my emotions like they were reasonable and understandable who decreased my jealousy. It's much harder to be jealous when your partner is saying, "I totally understand," than it is when your partner is saying, "What the hell is the matter with you?" Maybe that's what makes monogamy such an effective jealousy-management tactic: monogamy can be like a great big sign or sticker or button you can give to your partner that says, "I respect your jealousy." Which is not to say that monogamy is always effective for this — we all know that monogamous people get jealous all the time! (Which only adds to my point that monogamy might be viewed as just one of many tactics, rather than an answer, when jealousy is a problem.)

+ **Focus.** There's an oft-repeated joke among polyamorists that "while love may be infinite, time is not." And sometimes, I've found it a little difficult to "switch gears" to a different partner. New Relationship Energy can be a little harder to manage in the polyamorous context than it is in serial monogamy. [3]

I've heard of polyamorous couples who specifically take periods of monogamy when one partner really wants one. This seems like it could be problematic — for example, if my hypothetical primary partner wanted a period of monogamy, and I had a secondary partner (or partners) with a serious emotional connection, then I probably would not be cool with straight-up ignoring my secondary for weeks or months. There'd have to be more of a conversation about it. But regardless, this whole line of thinking makes an interesting showcase of how sometimes, people feel like they just have to focus on one relationship.

Personally, I'm quite interested in S&M games of orgasm denial, though I've never had a chance to mess around with it as much as I'd like. I'm also interested in long-term lust management strategies like karezza, where the partners involved choose not to have orgasms — instead, they maintain a low level of mutual arousal at all times. I have no moral problem with my partners looking at porn or having orgasms on their own, but sometimes when I hear about the effects of choosing not to do those things, it sounds like there's really powerful bonding potential there. [4] Something to keep in mind for the next time I'm really serious about someone, I guess. Monogamy isn't necessary for these things, but it would definitely make doing them less complicated.

+ **Societal acceptance.** Straight up, monogamy is the Western societal default. In some ways this makes monogamy hard to understand and communicate about — because there are so many assumptions and built-in expectations, and folks don't always agree on those expectations! A recent study found that 40% of young couples don't agree about whether or not they're monogamous. [5] That amazes me, because I have never assumed that I was monogamous with a partner until we had a conversation establishing that we were monogamous... but I guess I can see how it happens, if people feel anxious about communicating and fall back on assumptions instead.

Usually, however, being the societal default makes monogamy easier. Heterosexual monogamous people can get married with no problem, for example, and while marriage is obviously contested territory for non-hets, it's instructive that "gay marriage" is such a big political issue (while "polyamorous marriage" is currently nothing more than a specter right-wingers use to scare people about gay marriage [6]). Outsiders usually assume that you're monogamous when you introduce your partner. Romantic comedies exalt monogamy; the media, and many people around us, associate monogamy with love. When you're monogamous, you never have to articulate your weird relationship structure to your parents. You rarely have to think outside the box about relationship problems, and you can go to any Western advice columnist or therapist and be sure that they'll recognize your relationship as legitimate. (Those of you who like privilege checklists might enjoy this monogamous privilege checklist, which is patterned after Peggy McIntosh's classic essay and white privilege checklist. [7,8])

+ **Some people just like it better.** Occasionally, people will toy with the idea of an "orientational" element to polyamory or monogamy: some folks just plain feel aligned with monogamy or non-monogamy. (I have similar thoughts about this as I do about BDSM as a sexual orientation.)

Personally, I always think it's really key, during any sex-positive critique, to emphasize from the start that whatever you like is cool as long as the actions you take are consensual. I know people who act all apologetic for being monogamous, usually because they've been overexposed to "polyvangelists" who argue that non-monogamy is "better" or "more evolved." This is silly! Liking monogamy doesn't have to be justified, as long as you don't turn around and claim that non-monogamy is bad and wrong. And liking monogamy is a perfectly awesome reason for preferring monogamy!

* * *

This can be found on the Internet at:
http://clarissethorn.com/blog/2011/06/09/in-praise-of-monogamy/

* * *

* * *

POLYAMORY:
[theory] My Top Questions About Dealing With Multiple Lovers

I wrote this in early 2011. The comments on the online version are especially good — lots of viewpoints and resources shared. Sometimes my commenters just blow me away.

* * *

I have a lot more theoretical exposure to polyamory than personal experience, but I've been gaining more personal experience over the last year. It's often interesting, sometimes painful.

Some recent experiences are making me think I am not nearly as smart or as on top of my emotions as I like to believe I am. I remind myself that I have to be willing to acknowledge when I don't know what I'm thinking, but that's harder than it looks... I don't always take enough time to understand my feelings before speaking or acting.

Still. Through the stupid mistakes and the understandable ones, though my own failures to be sensitive and the little heartbreaks I've sustained, I've been learning.

One thing I think I've figured out is what I want: I want a number of different relationships that are ongoing, and one or two relationships that are primary, or especially committed. Ideally, in fact, I'd love to eventually have a permanent relationship with a primary polyamorous partner in which we have kids with each other, live together most of the time, etc, but are still polyamorous. That would be a while in the future, though — for now, it's important to me to not feel as though my partners expect me to settle down or stay in one place or anything like that. It seems like any relationship I develop, even during this relatively early time in my life, could become a child-rearing relationship eventually — like, years from now — but if it does, I doubt I'd want to make it monogamous.

I recognize that we don't always get our ideal world. In fact, we usually don't. Although polyamory is a high priority for me, it may be something I eventually compromise on, given that the majority of people in this world identify as monogamous.

Keeping all that in mind, my preference for polyamory presents some challenges, and questions that I worry about. Such as:

1. **What are my responsibilities towards my partners' other partners?** A lot of poly people will tell you that if you get into a relationship with, say, a married polyamorous man, then you must also expect to interact with his spouse. In other words, don't assume that your relationship means you only interact with one half of a couple. I'm totally fine with this, but on occasion I've felt like I was getting sucked into the couple's problems, or like I was expected to have no individual relationship with my partner — that I always had to go through his primary partner.

Yes, it is certainly my responsibility to communicate with my partners' other partners and to be friendly with them. But I need to set boundaries on that too — just dating a poly guy does not make me their relationship therapist, and it doesn't make me best friends with his other girlfriends (or boyfriends, for that matter). I am responsible for what I do, but I'm not responsible for what he does. I am responsible for how I treat his spouse, but I can't be responsible for how he treats his spouse.

But what if I'm already friends with someone, and one of my partners gets involved with that person? Do I have special responsibilities in that case? I'm still figuring that one out.

2. **When is it actually the best time to start talking about polyamory and setting out relationship definitions?** My approach so far has been to put poly on the table during initial conversations, and then talk about it more when the topic of the relationship comes up. But I've been thinking lately that I probably should go into more detail sooner, because people have such different stereotypes of open relationships that I can't be sure they're on board with what I'm talking about unless we've discussed polyamory in-depth.

I feel like I talk to a lot of people who think they want a supposedly "polyamorous" relationship because they see it as a no-strings-attached free-for-all, and that's definitely not what I want. Or I talk to people who back away from polyamory for the same reason. I see polyamory as being about **more** commitment to relationship negotiation, not less. I see it as being about setting individual boundaries, if necessary — it's not about having no boundaries. I see it as being about creating a secure situation for all parties involved — not making anyone insecure, or ignoring anyone's needs. And being polyamorous doesn't make my relationships unimportant to me. Being in love doesn't seem at odds with polyamory for me.

This is a hard thing to communicate in a small dose, though, especially if I'm dealing with someone who has minimal exposure to the concept. On the other hand, having a Serious Conversation about polyamory on the first date is a bit much.

3. **Is it a good idea for me to get involved with guys who ultimately want monogamy?** As I noted earlier, I might compromise to monogamy eventually, but poly is a priority for me. (Who knows, maybe I'll decide it's my ideal relationship formation again someday. This seems unlikely to me right now, but anything's possible.)

But what if I get really into a guy who ultimately plans to be monogamous? Is this a bad call on my part? On the one hand, if I go on a few dates with a 28-year-old guy who doesn't want to get married until his mid-30s but definitely wants a monogamous marriage when he does... I mean, why not have a relationship? On the other hand, I may be setting myself up for heartbreak in such situations, if he basically sees our relationship as "not real" from the start. This brings me to my next point....

4. **Some people see polyamory as a sign of commitment-phobia.** I've made this mistake myself — in fact, the "polyamory as commitment-phobia" stereotype is so strong that I've occasionally reversed it and wondered if my desire for it was a sign of commitment-phobia. But the fact is, my appreciation for polyamory only increased as I became more certain about what I'm seeking in a partner, and as I gained more understanding of how to negotiate that. It's come along with relationship confidence and understanding.

I feel pretty okay with believing in commitment in the context of polyamory. But my potential partners might not be. I already tend towards emotional caginess and am sometimes accused of being way too emotionally controlled — I'm worried that I'll be read as a "player" (or a "slut") by people who write me off as a result. I'm also worried that some may be attracted to me because they see me as an emotionless player, whether they admit it or not — indeed, even if they don't admit it to themselves — and will be annoyed if I turn out not to be that way. Stereotypes and assumptions are tricky to root out whether we're aware of them or not.

Some days, I get nervous that the guys who are going to be willing to talk about and process relationships in the depth that I'm looking for, with a degree of acknowledged emotional commitment, are all monogamous. Then I remind myself of how many awesome polyamorous men I know, and also that I'm falling for stereotypes yet again, just by having these fears.

5. **Other questions:**

How open am I to casual relationships that don't seem to be going in an emotional direction, given that I don't have to give up on more serious relationships to have them?

How does being poly change breakup dynamics?

In the absence of monogamy, are there different signifiers that a relationship is serious — or is getting serious? How can I get better at both giving and reading those signifiers?

What are the other poly stereotypes I've internalized, and how do I act against them? What are the other poly stereotypes I should look out for from others?

6. **Sigh.**

Rereading all my questions and rethinking all my thoughts makes me feel somewhat exhausted. Relationships are hard, and hacking the expected models makes them hopefully more fulfilling... but also so much more complicated. My life seems so weird sometimes; a week doesn't go by that I don't wonder why I'm not getting a nice typical job and settling down with a white picket fence and the monogamous husband and having 2.5 kids. That is not actually what I want, but sometimes the image seems seductively easy.

* * *

This can be found on the Internet at:
http://clarissethorn.com/blog/2011/04/11/my-top-questions-about-dealing-with-multiple-lovers/

* * *

* * *

SEX WORK:
[storytime] One Blurred Edge of Sex Work: Portrait of a Sugar Baby

I published this interview in January 2012 at the gender-lens website RoleReboot.org, where I had just taken on the role of Sex + Relationships Section Editor. Olivia left the business in mid-2012, as you can read in the piece that follows this one.

* * *

Sex work is a controversial and polarized topic, and there are many perspectives on it. My position is complex — but for me, when it comes to how we actually interact with sex workers, one important factor is whether or not they consent to and enjoy their jobs. I am absolutely in favor of giving better options to sex workers who do not enjoy their jobs, and I am horrified by the idea of a person being trafficked or coerced into sex that they don't want to have. But I also know people who have sex for money 100% voluntarily, and I do not want to deny their experience.

My friend Olivia, a 25-year-old graduate student, recently started advertising her services on a "Sugar Baby" site called SeekingArrangement.com. I think it's important for more people to understand these kinds of experiences, so I asked to interview her. Many people have pointed out that once a person starts thinking about the definition of "prostitute," it's a bit difficult to define what exactly a prostitute is. Some of my sex worker friends have asked the question: what exactly is the difference between a person whose partner buys her a fancy dinner after which they have sex — and a person whose partner buys sex with money? Olivia has thought at length about this, and I'm grateful to her for sharing her perspective on that question, and others.

Please note that Olivia is exceptionally privileged. What you are about to read is a portrait of what the sex industry looks like for a person who is very privileged: she comes from a white upper-middle-class background, she is not desperate, she is being paid a lot of money, she does not have a drug addiction. Many other peoples' experiences in the sex industry are very different.

Clarisse Thorn: Hey Olivia, thanks so much for being willing to talk about this incredibly complicated topic. Could you start by defining a sugar baby site? What is it?

Olivia: I use the site SeekingArrangement.com. I don't actually know how many sugar baby sites there are, but I get the sense there's more than one. It's very hard to pin down exactly what it does. I guess it connects people, usually with a big age gap, who are interested in exchanging some kind of material goods or financial resources for some form of companionship that is often sexual — but not always.

As far as I can tell, the site's founder is very against the claim that this is prostitution. He puts out a lot of publicity claiming that this site has nothing to do with prostitution. At first I thought that he was trying to evade legal consequences, but I think he actually probably believes that. The site has a blog that he controls, and you can look at it to get a sense of what he's thinking. One post I think is really interesting is called "Sugar Baby & Sugar Daddy: The Modern Day Princess & Prince?", which compares being a sugar baby to a kind of "happily ever after" princess fantasy. [1]

So far, no one I've talked to seems remotely interested in hiring what they see as a "prostitute." They seem to want to be having sex with someone they find very attractive who is also someone they feel like they can respect, whose intelligence they respect. For example, someone I see occasionally — the last time I saw him, he gave me money at the end and he said that he felt good about giving me the money because he knew I wouldn't spend it on, quote, "a designer handbag." He seems to think that I am reasonably ambitious and have my shit together, and he seems to feel more comfortable giving me money because he knows it goes towards my grad school costs and credit card debt. My ability to write with proper grammar, without overusing emoticons, appears to be my biggest sales point. Men have told me this outright.

That guy also mentioned feeling more comfortable because he thinks I'm from the same social class as he is. There are a lot of class issues coming up in these encounters, I think. Being white and from an upper-middle-class background may help me get clients. My background has also given me a ton of confidence that puts me at an advantage when negotiating. I do not think I radiate "take advantage of me," and I (nicely) tell guys who start doing that to go away.

The guy I was just talking about — he also mentioned that he feels like he doesn't want to have sex with someone that he doesn't feel at least a little bit connected to. There's a distinction between meaningless sex and casual sex. I think these guys want casual sex — maybe they aren't at the point where they want to deal with having a partner, or they're really busy at work, or they already have another partner — they want casual sex but not meaningless sex.

In my encounters with these men, the money does two things. Firstly, it enables them to have a relationship with me that they wouldn't otherwise be able to have. Secondly, it puts them in this position where they can give me something valuable and have that be appreciated. The guys I see really want to feel appreciated.

Clarisse Thorn: Do you feel like this has given you any new insight into gender roles?

Olivia: Hmm.... It's made me feel more powerful. I definitely feel like I am the one with the power in this situation. When I show up, I don't feel like   here is this rich, powerful person who is about to bestow wealth upon me. I feel like — here is this person who is a bit sad and lonely, and maybe I can make their day better.

A lot of the men who are on this site want to feel appreciated, so it's important to them that the woman they're with give off the appearance of appreciating them. So for example, on the website there's a lot of talk about sugar daddies being "mentors" or "benefactors" rather than clients. They seem to want some combination of me asking them about their day, and they also want to feel like they're bestowing knowledge upon me about the world. One of the men I see will always talk about his opinions about money. He has complicated feelings about himself having money because he doesn't come from money, so he's trying to work those out. But he also keeps telling me in a very serious voice that money will not make me happy, that nothing I can buy will make me happy. I tell him that I can buy security and he says yes, that is one thing I can buy.

Other men seem to be having issues with their age. One mentioned that he's just turned 40, and that's really bugging him. Then he flaked out on me a couple times — I don't think he was completely okay with his own decision to be seeing me. But anyway, often, another thing these men seem to get out of it is access to someone who has a bunch of youthful energy and optimism and just plain new ideas. A lot of them have mentioned feeling stuck, or bored, or cynical, or intellectually constrained. So in this sense sex is only one thing I'm offering them — I'm also offering them optimism, hope, energy, and so on. Firstly, the sex is good in and of itself, as most of them aren't getting laid otherwise. But the sex is also a symbol of them getting access to my youthful energy or whatever.

I think the archetypal image of a mistress involves a woman being "kept" so that she doesn't have to work, so that she can be available for sex basically whenever. But I don't think this is what the men I see want. I am more valuable to them because I have other work that I am seriously invested in, and am having sex with them anyway. Again, these men are interested in a woman who they see as more "equal" to them — in this case, defined by earnings potential — and they seem gratified by the idea that they could help me enter their income bracket someday. This is, of course, still kind of patronizing; like I said, they keep using words like "mentor." It's also presumptuous. But I think a lot of them being patronizing and presumptuous can probably be attributed to age and wealth, and only some of it to gender.

I think I've learned more about class and money than I have about gender. It turns out there are people to whom $1,000 versus $3,000 doesn't matter that much, and I finally understand that on a visceral level. $1,000 doesn't mean the same thing to me as it does to most of them. I knew this, but now I *really* know it.

Another thing I've been struck by is exactly how much romantic relationships are worth. I've had several clients tell me they don't feel wealthy, and they feel like they worry about money a lot. I think they were sincere. Of course, my first thought was: don't you think that your $2,000-per-month prostitute is part of the budget that could be trimmed? But I think that maybe it's not, actually. I think *they* think that investing a lot of money in me is a good investment for them if it gives them a release valve so they can deal with the rest of their lives. They're probably right.

Clarisse Thorn: You mentioned that you feel powerful in your relationships with these men. But there are issues of your safety, right?

Olivia: I think there are issues of safety anytime a person meets someone they don't really know, especially if they plan to spend time in private. And especially if you're dealing with topics as sensitive as sex or money. There may be more issues of safety with this because some people really do believe that money can buy them anything. But for the most part, when I meet people they seem very respectful.

Things I do to increase my safety are that I tell my husband and my friends where I'm going to be, I tell them exactly where I am. I'll do things like take down a client's license plate number and text it to my husband. I've been thinking maybe I should look at each client's driver's license too, and text the client's name and driver's license number to my husband. I think some clients might feel threatened by that, though.

The most important thing for my safety is that I'm willing and able to walk away from situations. I'm not desperate — I won't starve or die if I don't do this work. I meet all my clients in public first for a meal, and if someone sketches me out, I leave. I'm not so desperate that I'll get into a situation that scares me.

I guess I am at risk if I meet a really crazy person who wants to chop me up and put me in a dumpster. But I could meet a person like that during a normal night at a bar, too.

The major risks that I see include that I might catch an STD — but I use protection. I might end up alone with someone who believes that the money he's paying actually gives him the entitlement to do whatever he wants to my body, but I've never encountered anyone like that. The thing is, as I said before, I haven't met anyone who I think would actually describe themselves as paying for sex. The terms on which I continue to see these men are probably less explicitly negotiated than an escort's terms would be. I don't have flat rates, for example.

I've heard escorts complaining that people who use sugar baby sites are unprofessional, and I think that from an escort's perspective they probably are.

Clarisse Thorn: If people are unwilling to actually talk about sex for money, it must be hard to negotiate your encounters. Do you have a set of steps for negotiation?

Olivia: I haven't been doing this for very long. It's varied so far. Usually, I meet them for some kind of meal, and we chat. We have a perfunctory conversation, like — "How was your day?" Then one of us will say something like, "Tell me a bit more about what you're looking for. Why are you on the site?"

Then we'll explain our deal to each other. Like, he might say: "I'm divorced, I'm looking for companionship." At some point, money comes up. I am always extremely vague when I talk about money. I've found a good deal of variation in how squeamish people are about money.

For example, one client was saying that he wanted to get married again, but not yet. I said, "Huh, well, if you're interested in a more emotional relationship, how do you feel about involving money?" The way he explained it to me was that people are attracted to each other for all kinds of reasons, probably including money, so why not be up front about the fact that money is attractive. He seemed almost confused about why I asked. With that guy, I ended up sleeping with him before we even talked about money — which was a huge risk, but I thought it might work, and it did. We had the money conversation immediately after we had sex — at some point when we were taking a break, I asked what he was looking for more specifically from this relationship, and he said that he wanted to see me again, maybe once a week. I think I asked him his preference for a monthly allowance as opposed to every time we meet, and he said he'd rather do something monthly. Then when we were getting dressed, he pulled out $1,000 cash and handed it to me, and said, "I'll give you the balance next time we see each other."

With other people I can be more straightforward. Maybe they aren't sure how to set up the relationship, so maybe I talk about another client, like: "I have another client I see 3 times per month for $3,000," and they might say, "That sounds good." But some guys will just negotiate it per encounter. One guy brought it up very quickly after we'd exchanged some emails. He said that he prefers to do a "per meet" of $300 — he called it a "per meet" — I told him that was too low and quoted him $1,000, and he said he'd meet me in the middle. Another guy told me that he would just slip $400 into my purse when he saw me, and that's exactly what he did.

I have one client I've never explicitly discussed money with at all. I had lunch with him, and we didn't negotiate anything, though we talked a little bit about our reasons for being on the site. The next time I saw him — we were deciding where to meet, and he asked if he should get us a room. I said that I would like that, so I met him and we had sex. He knew it was my birthday soon, so as we were getting dressed, he said, "I know we haven't talked about money, so I got you some birthday spending money," and he handed me an envelope with $400. The next time I saw him, he asked about my plans for the evening. I said I was having dinner with a friend, and he handed me $400 in an envelope and said, "Maybe this will help pay for it." I'm lucky that I'm willing to accept $400 — it's my lower bound, but I'm willing to accept it. Imagine if I hadn't been willing to take $400 — that would be super awkward. Probably I should have negotiated that situation more clearly, but it worked out okay.

I've heard about situations where unclear negotiations did not work out okay. There was a *New York Times Magazine* article about the site published in 2009. [2] In that article, there were some examples of unclear negotiations that didn't work out well. But it sounded like that woman didn't really know what she wanted, and didn't really enjoy the work. But I do. And I know other women who do, too.

I have a new client who paid me $3,000 up front to see me 3 times a month. But I haven't heard from him since our first meeting. If I were his girlfriend, I'd call him, but he asked me not to call him. So I don't really know what the deal with that one is. Maybe he's gonna flake out on me, but he already gave me $3,000, so that would be weird.

Clarisse Thorn: So, your husband. You mentioned him briefly. How does your husband feel about this?

Olivia: He does not seem particularly threatened. We already have an open relationship. I think he sometimes feels very visceral jealousy, but that's just like any other time one of us has sex with somebody else. We just have to talk about it.

Part of the deal here is that I'm doing this because I'm broke. My husband really wants to be able to support me financially, but he can't right now, so I'm supporting both us doing this. I think that's a real blow to his ego. To the extent that he gets bothered, I think it's because I'm allowing other men to support me and give me money; he doesn't care about the sex. Even though I see this as work, he sees this as "here's this rich successful guy who just gave my wife a bunch of money, and she slept with him   so probably she's attracted to him."

I am kind of attracted to my clients, and I kind of get off on making them happy, and I happen to think that the age difference is kind of hot. I like having sex with them; it's not unpleasant. I like hearing about these guys' life stories. I think it's interesting. But these guys would never be a threat to my husband. I would never be sleeping with any of them except for the money. And I love my husband. I'm always very up front about the fact that I'm married and I love my husband. My clients accept that.

* * *

This can be found on the Internet at:
http://clarissethorn.com/blog/2012/01/05/one-blurred-edge-of-sex-work-interview-with-a-sugar-baby-part-1/

and
http://clarissethorn.com/blog/2012/01/09/one-blurred-edge-of-sex-work-interview-with-a-sugar-baby-part-2/

* * *

***

SEX WORK:
[theory] A Sugar Baby Leaves The Business

I published this in 2012; it continues Olivia's story. Thanks again to Olivia for being so incredibly generous with her time and her thoughts.

***

Previously on Role/Reboot, we ran an interview with my friend Olivia, a 25-year-old graduate student who had just started having sex for money through a "sugar baby" website called SeekingArrangement.com. In the interview, Olivia covered a lot of topics. She mentioned that she usually feels powerful in her relationships with her clients. As she put it, "When I show up, I don't feel like — here is this rich, powerful person who is about to bestow wealth upon me. I feel like — here is this person who is a bit sad and lonely, and maybe I can make their day better." Olivia also noted that her negotiations can be delicate, because some men are quite squeamish while talking about money. And she explained that she's married — but it was already an open relationship, and she doesn't see having sex for money as different from the other kinds of sex that she and her husband were already having with other people. To deal with it, they're sure to communicate clearly. As Olivia said, "We just have to talk about it."

In the months since that interview, Olivia and I have hung out occasionally to talk about her experience with sex work. She's traveled across the city to meet me, and often bought me coffee; non-judgmental social support for sex workers can be rare, and I've seen more of her since she started the job. Although she really enjoyed the work at first, there were tough times too, especially after the novelty wore off. Recently, Olivia decided to stop seeing clients. We talked it through and she gave me permission to write about it. (She also reviewed this article pre-publication.)

Obviously, there were logistical complexities from the beginning. Taxes were a nightmare. Olivia wanted to pay them, but it's not the easiest proposition. Then there was the question of paying off her debts. Some were simple enough, but then there were loans co-signed by her parents, and there was no way she could make any headway on those loans without talking to her parents... so Olivia had to maintain the fiction that she couldn't pay.

That was nothing compared to the complexities of feelings and communication, though. I've already shown you how hard it was, sometimes, for Olivia to talk about money with her clients. There are other, subtler problems that are hard to handle with empathy: for example, creating the Girlfriend Experience persona.

I've talked to sex workers who enjoy creating a "sexy dreamgirl shell" on behalf of their clients. One of them said to me: "I create that persona for my boyfriends anyway. It's nice to be paid for it." But as a feminist sex writer who's spent years working to understand my own sexual authenticity, this freaks me out a bit. I think it would feel terribly toxic and inauthentic for me.

It often felt inauthentic to Olivia, for sure, and that got harder and harder. "These men are very invested in believing that I'm super into this," she told me once. "I have to keep up the front, and make them feel like I'm interested all the time. It's literally my job to do that. When they tell me how happy I am, or when they inform me that I'm enjoying myself, I can't really contradict them, even if it's not true. Some of them use words like 'magical' to describe me, but the person they're describing is not really me. Sometimes I think these guys pay me because in a non-professional relationship, a woman might push back when he says those things. She might contradict his idea of her too much."

In fairness, Olivia naturally fits one glam stereotype of the middle-class sex worker: the sexually adventurous young student. It's such a widely-promoted stereotype that experienced sex worker activists speak derisively about it, and some escorts lie and say that they fit the profile when they don't. Presumably, clients enjoy believing that a girl is a sexually adventurous college student because it capitalizes on images of "sexy coeds" and convinces the client that she's not being emotionally harmed by the work. (I've often thought that it's way past time for "fair trade prostitution," where sex trade ethics are made into a competitive advantage. I've also thought that the most feminist thing I could ever do would be to open a brothel where all the sex workers are treated well. Too bad it's illegal.)

Of course, SeekingArrangement.com actively encourages the idea that a "real relationship" can emerge from these arrangements.

(In our previous interview, Olivia pointed out the SeekingArrangement blog post "Sugar Baby & Sugar Daddy: The Modern Day Princess & Prince?" [1] Another interesting one is called "Sugar Babies Do Fall In Love." [2]) While some guys on the site really do just want to pay for straight-up sex, some become emotionally invested in the women whose company they buy. And we can tell from Olivia's experiences negotiating payment that a lot of guys don't like thinking about how they're paying for it.

Bottom line: more than one of Olivia's clients were into her for real, and she felt more and more uncomfortable about it as time passed. One man took a surreptitious photo of her and hung it on the center of his otherwise-bare refrigerator. Another client made faux-offhand wistful comments such as, "If you weren't already married, haha...."

Olivia asked my advice on one of these guys, who was clearly falling in love with her from the start. She mentioned that she'd already talked to another sex worker about it. The other worker's reaction was, essentially, "What problem?" As Olivia put it: "She told me that the guy is basically a locked-in regular now, so what am I so bothered about?" But after a while, Olivia couldn't take how guilty and anxious she felt around this guy, what with the feelings she couldn't return. She stopped responding to his messages, but didn't tell him clearly that it was over because trying to phrase the email felt so awful.

"I was so unprofessional about it," she said. "In the end, he sent me this incredibly sweet note asking what he'd done to hurt me so badly. So my husband helped me write a 'it's not you, it's me' breakup email. I still feel bad."

Another facet of emotional difficulty arose when Olivia's husband started taking a medication that decreased his libido. This put the couple in the odd position of Olivia having sex with other men, but not her husband — with her husband's full knowledge and consent. Although her husband tried to reassure her, she began feeling less secure and stable at home. And sex work is stressful enough that home security can really, really matter. Indeed, at one point Olivia mentioned: "One of my friends is tempted to get into sex work. But she says she doesn't think she can deal with it, emotionally, unless she has a partner at home who loves her and will back her up. So I'm not supposed to let her have sex for money until she's in a good solid relationship."

Finally, as Olivia fielded other life stresses, she flatly realized that she couldn't have anything extra going on. What with all the above conversations, we saw signs that the change was coming, but when it arrived it was both sudden and intense. "One day I just knew I had to stop," she told me. "It's bad, because we're behind on rent now, but I had to stop. My husband pointed out, gently, that we need the money. But of course he accepted it when I said I was done. Anyway, I managed to line up a good temp job, so we're okay for now."

I tried to show in the original interview that Olivia is very privileged compared to most sex workers. She's got race privilege for her whiteness, class privilege from her background; she's pretty and young and "valuable," and has tons of education to boot. She doesn't have a drug habit or some other truly debilitating issue. Although she's under some financial stress, she's not desperate.

And that leads me to this question:

If even a woman like Olivia — who was well-treated and made a lot of money and didn't feel trapped; whose life sounded like the glam fantasy of today's high-end call girl — if **even a woman like Olivia** eventually needed a break from sex for money, then what could this imply about the experience of less privileged women? I've got a bunch of sex worker friends, and I would never say that a woman can't be a 100% consenting adult sex worker who enjoys her job. But what I'm trying to get at, here, is that even on the "high end," sex work can be incredibly demanding. Even when sex work is as pleasant as it possibly can be, it's often very hard.

I'd like to see more conversations that acknowledge the reality of sex work as emotionally intense and challenging, a job that can be bad for many people at many times in their lives — without letting go of the fact that some people can and do freely consent to the job. (The sex worker Mistress Matisse has written a fair bit on sex work and emotional labor. [3] And male sex workers don't always have an easy time; the porn star Tyler Knight has written about some of his more difficult moments, too. [4])

The point is not "sex work is bad and should be banned" — but nor is it "sex work is glamorous and fun!" The point is, sex work is often hard work, even for people who are not mistreated or abused. As such, it deserves both respect (from outsiders) and open-eyed caution (from those who consider taking it up).

Olivia's not sure she's done with sex work for good. "The door is still open for future involvement," she told me, last time we met for coffee. "If I do go back, I think I may try for straight-up escorting, but I'm not really sure...." Presumably, working as an escort rather than being a "sugar baby" might evade some of these confusing, strangely-negotiated situations. Would it evade all of them? It's hard to say.

Regardless, I wish her luck.

* * *

After June 1, 2012, this can be found on the Internet at:
http://clarissethorn.com/blog/2012/06/01/a-sugar-baby-leaves-the-business/

* * *

* * *

Section 2 Study Guide

This section was intended mostly to highlight various "other" perspectives that I feel are significant to sex and/or activism.

* * *

1. Do you see your sexual identity as placing you in a community, or is it more private? Or is it a little bit of both?
1a. If you identify as part of a sex community, then are there ways you can contribute to that community? (For example, if you had evidence that abusive relationships were a problem in your community, what could you do about it?)

2. What kind of educational needs do you perceive around sexuality? Is there a way you could contribute to positive sex education?
2a. Does your community have unique needs around sex education?
2b. If you have children, how do you plan to educate them about sex? Specifically, how do you plan to tell them about the stereotypes and limitations affecting the different groups described in this section?

3. How do you look out for and support other members of your community, especially when it comes to sex?

4. What lessons from your sexuality do you think are applicable to people who don't share your sexual tastes?
4a. Are there pieces from this section that feel relevant to you, even if they aren't talking about your experience or preferences?

5. What are the overarching patterns that you see within the pieces in this section? How are these disparate topics relevant to each other?
5a. If some of these pieces are about people you have trouble relating to, can you think of ways you could relate better to those people?

* * *

* * *

SECTION 3:
Making It Complicated

In which we really get into it.

* * *

When I think of this section, I think of:

People's ability to understand their own emotional and physical experiences and sensations is limited by what is safe to ask or know, what systems of interpretation they have received for screening that raw material, and whether they find it possible to connect with anyone who thinks differently about these matters.
~ Pat Califia

* * *

* * *

RELATIONSHIPS:
[storytime] Chemistry

I wrote this in late 2011, while I was finishing up the first draft of my awesome book Confessions of a Pickup Artist Chaser. *I was still processing a lot of stuff I'd learned about pickup artist tactics and pickup artist attitudes, and that's reflected in this piece. But there's a lot more to it, from working out some stuff about polyamory to my feelings about marriage. A lot of these thoughts are developed further in* Confessions.

* * *

It's a long story and a short one, but I guess all of them are.

I'm 27. It's about that age: A lot of my compatriots are getting married lately — most monogamously, some to a primary polyamorous partner. I myself have a stack of relationships in my past. Some were monogamous, some polyamorous. Some have been on-and-off, some short-term, some long-term (5 or 6 years was the longest). Lately I've been processing some tough questions about polyamory, but I'd like to stick with it.

And I've been thinking a lot about what I want in a primary polyamorous partner. The kind of guy I could marry. I wonder if I'll ever get to that point. I wonder if I'd know him if I saw him.

* * *

I met Mr. Ambition at one of the aforementioned weddings. Several people recommended that I talk to him, and we liked each other right away. Mutual friends used words like "zealot" to describe him; let's just say he's got an intense history of dedicated activism. Charisma, integrity, and pure energy pour off him. His words are almost always articulate and challenging. He can socially dominate a room without thinking. He works a challenging job ten hours per day; exercises two hours; socializes several hours; sleeps and eats when he can. He gives hugs easily, laughs easily, hands out compliments like candy.

Mr. Ambition is most definitely not a neutral personality. Of course, neither am I.

At the time, I was just coming out of the worst stage of my research on pickup artists — a subculture of men who trade tips on how to seduce women. Also, I'd just had one of those breakups where I was too busy feeling stupid to properly understand how hurt I was. (Don't you hate those?) You can read all about those Dramatic Events in my upcoming book *Confessions of a Pickup Artist Chaser*. In the meantime, suffice to say that I felt... flattened.

Arguably, I should have had a sign taped to my forehead that read: "Emotionally Unavailable."

I went to dinner with Mr. Ambition later that week. At the end of the meal, he sat back and looked at me. "You're so **authentic**," he said.

"I haven't felt very authentic lately," I said frankly, but his words felt good. Like a balm. Like I was healing.

* * *

We got along excellently, had a lot in common, etc. Typical this-relationship-starts-well stuff. One evening, after we'd been out to eat in a big philosophical group, Mr. Ambition noted the hotness of my intense theoretical bent. "When you were discussing social justice and ethics tonight," he said, "I wanted to reach across the table and grab you."

He mentioned marriage within weeks. "This has never happened before," he told me. "I've never dated someone I thought I could actually marry." *Whoa, tiger,* I thought, but I had to admit that he hit a lot of my Ideal Characteristics as well. Intelligence, drive, charisma, **and** morality: it's hard to argue with that.

Our sexual chemistry was okay, but not climb-the-walls stellar. *We'll develop that,* I told myself. *He's less sexually experienced than I am, and we'll learn each other just fine.* Fortunately he's got some experience with polyamory, but in terms of S&M, he's another of those vanilla-but-questioning guys (I never learn). When we did S&M, I had to monitor the situation extra carefully because it was so new to him.

And for all his intelligence, it was really hard to talk to him about emotions. It wasn't that he was cold or distant; on the contrary, he's one of the most fiery people I've ever met. But he had a lot of difficulty explaining what was going on in his head. Indeed, he told me that he had a lot of difficulty **knowing** what was going on in his head. He did things like laugh when a friend hurt his feelings, then deny that he was hurt, even though I could plainly see the stricken look behind his eyes.

I wasn't surprised that he was more physical than verbal about S&M. Very straightforward: throwing me around, pulling my head back, digging his hands into my skin. He's incredibly strong, and sometimes I called my safeword simply because his strength scared me.

There was one particular S&M encounter... early in the evening, I called my safeword because I wasn't sure he was into it.

"Red," I said, and he stopped. "Is this okay with you?" I asked, and he nodded.

"Yes," he said. "This is good. Let's keep going." His voice was low and slightly rough; a marvel of certainty. He put his hands back on me instantly. My doubts disappeared.

We kept going. I watched my body, felt the lump building in my throat, monitored my breath as it became harsh and fast.

"Red," I said, and he stopped. "You're going to break me," I said, "I'm going to cry. If you don't want to deal with that, then stop."

This, by the way, is a difficult skill that I have learned: this ability to track my S&M reactions so clearly. I would never have been able to do it seven years ago, and I still can't do it during complicated S&M encounters. But now I can do it during simple ones. (Yes, "simple" and "complicated" are in the eye of the beholder.)

I really hate stopping an S&M encounter right when I'm on the verge of tears. It's worse than an interrupted orgasm. But I'd rather do that than break down crying and **then** deal with a horrified partner.

"That's fine," said Mr. Ambition. So we kept going. I cried. He started talking, and I was surprised by how harsh his words could be. *That's more like it,* I thought.

Some S&M encounters have a rhythm to them, a poetry: a beginning and an end that become clear to the participants as they go along. This one didn't — at least not to me. So I didn't rely on him to bring it to a close. After a while, I safeworded out, and took a breath to still my tears.

Mr. Ambition was quiet again. I was having trouble reading him. There was some energy caught inside him, coiled like a dragon, but I couldn't tell if it was violence or something else. I put a halt to my own emotional cycle and tried to focus on him. "How are you feeling?" I asked, but he couldn't tell me. I asked a few more questions, and he just couldn't answer. He just didn't know.

I never got another word from him on how he felt about that encounter. I wondered if I was being too careful in how I asked about it; I wondered if he wanted me to push harder; I wondered if I'd already pushed him too far.

I suspected there were some dramatic feelings trapped in Mr. Ambition. But I wasn't sure I currently had the warmth to coax them out.

* * *

In the past, I've fallen in love so hard that I felt like the world was black-and-white when I was away from my lover; I felt like I only saw color when I was with him. I have dated men where the chemistry was so intense, so obvious, that it hung in the air between us like smoke. I've had sex that felt like telepathy. It's pretty awesome when it works. And it's easier to get that with some people than with others: some guys, I meet them and it's like we speak the same language already.

With some guys, it's not instant, but it also doesn't take long to build our mutual vocabulary.

And then I've dated guys where the learning curve — both sexually and temperamentally — was much longer. It was less instinctive. But it was not impossible. So I know for a fact that **people can build chemistry**. Sometimes it's just there, but sometimes you can create it.

My relationship with Mr. Ambition was definitely polyamorous, but a few weeks in, I decided I was really into him... and I started managing my incentives. There was another guy I saw occasionally, with whom I had stronger instinctive chemistry. This other guy agreed with me that we didn't want a Big Important Relationship. *This other guy will screw up my incentives if I hang out with him too much,* I thought, and I limited my time with him. I set rules with myself: I didn't call him, I didn't text him. I knew: *If I let myself get too intensely into this other guy, that could inhibit my ability to bond with Mr. Ambition.*

I told the other guy that once my relationship with Mr. Ambition was more stable, we might be able to pursue something more intense. By the time we had the conversation, he said he'd already been thinking similar thoughts. That he didn't want to distract me from something that could be beautiful.

Similarly, there are one or two men in my life that I'm attracted to but don't want a sexual connection with at all. So I try not to see them unless I feel inoculated: I don't hang out with them unless I'm sure I can distract myself with my feelings about another man.

A lot of polyamorists say that "love is infinite," that we can love lots of people, etc. I agree with this in theory — but there's also a polyamorous saying that "While love may be infinite, time is not." And hormones aren't infinite, either. I've learned my hormonal reactions, I've seen myself get imprinted by people... I've seen myself develop feelings and fantasies for one guy that made me 100% immune to another hot guy's charms.

Do I have perfect self-control? Absolutely not. That's why I'm trying to influence my own choices so carefully. I know that choice plays a huge role when we build relationships. **Choosing to commit is arguably as big a relationship factor as instinctive chemistry.**

... Arguably.

* * *

When I first got to college many moons ago, my roommate came from a family of immigrants with a tradition of arranged marriages. She and I stayed up late one night, perched on our dorm room mattresses, and I listened in fascination while she told me that her father wanted her to marry a man of her father's choice, rather than her own.

"I'm not sure whether I'll do it," she said. I watched her wave a hand airily. I was mesmerized by her casual acceptance of a custom that struck me as barbaric. "I mean," she said, "I'm cool with this guy that my dad's found for me. But I don't know if we're **that** cool. On the other hand, I can't deny the advantages of arranged marriages."

"Advantages!" I cried. I was so young... (Okay, I'm still young.) "What do you mean, **advantages**?!"

"Arranged marriages are more stable," she said. "Much more stable. I'm not sure I'd ever want to marry for love. That shit goes up in smoke."

From what I understand, there have even been studies about this: people in arranged marriages report being quite happy, quite stable.

I've gotten the it's-not-passion-that-makes-a-successful-marriage message before, of course — often from super-white, super-American Americans. For example, there's that infamous 2008 article "Marry Him: The Case For Settling For Mr. Good Enough." [1] The article is sure to send any woman roughly my age into a panic. It's made enough of an impression that I **still** have conversations about it with other women my age — almost four years after its debut.

I don't like the Settling writer's attitude. She's written with horror and anger about S&M in other venues, for example; and the whole Settling article has a generally conservative bent. But she's articulating some real feelings and important thoughts, and while I don't agree with all of them, I do agree with some. At one point, analyzing television, she notes that:

While Rachel and her supposed soul mate, Ross, finally get together (for the umpteenth time) in the finale of Friends, *do we feel confident that she'll be happier with Ross than she would have been had she settled down with Barry, the orthodontist, 10 years earlier? She and Ross have passion but have never had long-term stability, and the fireworks she experiences with him but not with Barry might actually turn out to be a liability, given how many times their relationship has already gone up in flames. It's equally questionable whether* Sex and the City's *Carrie Bradshaw, who cheated on her kindhearted and generous boyfriend, Aidan, only to end up with the more exciting but self-absorbed Mr. Big, will be better off in the framework of marriage and family. (Some time after the breakup, when Carrie ran into Aidan on the street, he was carrying his infant in a Baby Björn. Can anyone imagine Mr. Big walking around with a Björn?)* [1]

I've never watched *Friends* or *Sex and the City,* but I know the feeling.

Personally, I'm more of a novel girl. The other day, I found myself thinking of my long-ago roommate and her thoughts on arranged marriage while I read Monica Ali's beautiful book *Brick Lane.* Monica Ali is an immigrant to the United Kingdom, and the characters in her novel all come to the UK from Bangladesh. Some of the characters accept traditional arranged marriages, while others make "love marriages" instead — often defying their parents, their whole set of cultural norms, to do so. Towards the end of the novel, one man reflects on the early days of his marriage:

We thought that the love would never run out. It was like a magic rice sack that you could keep scooping into and never get to the bottom. It was a "love" marriage, you see. What I did not know — I was a young man — is that there are two kinds of love. The kind that starts off big and slowly wears away, that seems you can never use it up and then one day is finished. And the kind that you don't notice at first, but which adds a little bit to itself every day, like an oyster makes a pearl, grain by grain, a jewel from the sand.

As you can tell, this character is currently unhappy in his "love marriage." Of course, the grass is always greener on the other side. What's the difference between the big love and the pearl love? Can they even be compared? Is it like apples to oranges?

But couldn't all this be a false dichotomy? Who says it's about arrangement versus randomness — chemistry versus choice? Can we have both? Can we find the big love, and nurture that so it develops into the pearl love, too?

My ultimate conclusion about the Art and Science of Flirting, from my "studies" of pickup artists and also my entire life, is that flirting is all about strategic ambiguity. Deliberate uncertainty. Manipulating ambiguity and uncertainty can contribute to many intense feelings.

Some people learn this, and decide that the only way to have a relationship with chemistry is to include a constant generous dollop of uncertainty about love, loyalty, or something equally important. These people decide chemistry can only derive from little pieces of confusion: tiny mismatches that lodge underneath the similarities that bring people together, constantly unsettling, like a prickly burr. But I don't think that's what I want.

And after all, S&M creates extraordinary feelings too, but plenty of people do S&M in very controlled circumstances: pre-discussed, with safewords and so on. Arguably, S&M is another form of mismatch, of contrast, of uncertainty — but it's a form that can be managed. So I know all about creating intense uncertain feelings in controlled circumstances, and using those to contribute to stable and reliable loving relationships. Don't I?

Eventually, my college roommate caused a gigantic blowup in her family by rejecting arranged marriage. Her father didn't speak to her for a long, long time.

* * *

On my birthday, Mr. Ambition took me out to dinner. Then we went to watch fireflies by the lake. As was inevitable for summer in Chicago, we ran into lots of people we knew. One of those groups contained an on-again-off-again partner of mine: Richard, with whom I have... shall we say, a complicated history. I respect Richard a lot, and I like him, and I'm highly attracted to him... but I'm pathologically wary of him for reasons that will become obvious.

We greeted our friends. "How are you doing?" Richard asked.

"Happy birthday to me, asshole," I teased. "How could you forget?"

Richard sighed. "Jeez," he said, "sorry I neglected to wish you a happy birthday within, like, the first 15 seconds I saw you."

I paused, and took a moment to recalibrate: he wasn't reacting in his usual adversarial, teasing-back manner. On the other hand, history has taught me not to fall for it when Richard seems unexpectedly vulnerable.

"I'm sorry," I said. I kept my tone light-hearted, friendly. "You know I love you, right?"

"Do I?" Richard asked.

I tilted my head at him. Without thinking, I kissed my own fingers, then put my hand gently against his face, as if I were about to stroke his cheek. Or slap him. I guess it was a way of distancing myself and kissing him at the same time. I think he understood that I intended it as an uncertain-but-intimate gesture. But I'm never sure, with Richard.

"Call me," I said.

"No," Richard said. "**You** call **me**."

Hours later, Mr. Ambition brought him up. We were having one of those sweet, intimate, disjointed bedtime conversations. Mr. Ambition was lying back, half-covered by a sheet, and I was admiring the play of light on his chest. "Richard really cares about you," he said.

I stiffened, and sat up. "Maybe," I said. "But I can't trust Richard."

"His tone seemed wistful, when he saw you."

"I can't trust Richard," I repeated. "It's always a game with him. Sometimes I think that we have a real emotional connection, but if I try to talk about it or give him emotional feedback, he just ignores me."

"Maybe he isn't really ignoring you," argued Mr. Ambition. "Maybe every time you say something, or give a little, it makes a tiny bit of difference. Maybe you just have to stay open. Keep trying. These things build up."

"You don't understand," I snapped. "You don't know him! Maybe he really cares, but even if he does, it doesn't matter! Things always end up the same. If I mention emotions, or if I act warm to him, he'll ignore me for a while... and then he'll be cold to me again. I'm telling you, I've been here before, with Richard. It's a trap."

Mr. Ambition didn't waver. "If you're strong enough," he said simply, "then you can walk into a trap."

His words made my heart crack, my breath catch. Made me feel like I've forgotten everything I knew about love.

When I was younger, I thought of my emotional strength like water: an embrace that could make someone I loved feel lighter. Water is a slow, eroding force that pulls beauty from the unexpected. Water makes wood into twisted driftwood sculptures; sharp glass into opaque dim jewels; rocks into soft sand. Water will eventually reveal the heart of everything it touches. If you let it.

I hadn't thought of myself that way in a long time. I felt like Mr. Ambition was calling me out, reminding me of who I wanted to be. Maybe I protect myself better, these days. But vulnerability is not always a bad thing.

I definitely could fall in love with this man, I realized.

"You're really amazing," I said, and threw myself on his chest. He put his arms around me. "So are you," he said.

* * *

As a storyteller, I often look back on my relationships and pick out foreshadowing: the omens. And by now, I recognize the omens even as they're happening... and sometimes I change my behavior, but usually I don't. Perhaps this state is what they call maturity.

One night while we were out, Mr. Ambition sighed in an offhand way. He seemed tired, out of sorts. "I just want someone to take me on an emotional journey," he remarked to me. Then he added, "... No offense."

I mentioned this to a friend, later: "Mr. Ambition says he wants me to take him on an emotional journey," I said.

"An 'emotional journey'? That shit gets old, though," said my friend. I laughed, and agreed with him.

Another night, Mr. Ambition mentioned something about enjoying drama. I was with my best girlfriend at the time; she and I looked at each other. "Careful what you wish for," I said.

My friend said, "Yeah, I'm pretty sure Clarisse knows how to create arbitrary amounts of drama at any time."

"But I'm pretty sure I don't want to," I said.

Later, when Mr. Ambition mentioned that he doesn't usually know how he's feeling, he added: "My friends can often tell more about my own emotions than I can."

"So you basically outsource your emotional processing to your friends?" I asked.

He agreed.

Perhaps the worst omen was when Mr. Ambition told me, "I've never been hurt by love."

"Never?" I asked.

"Never," he said.

His certainty was so great that, in itself, it made me uneasy. Because I have definitely been hurt by love. And my greatest wounds were dealt by men who seemed sure they loved me. A man who seems sure might actually be sure, but he may simply fail to understand himself.... So these days, it's always men who seem certain that make me most uncertain.

There's another great quotation from that Monica Ali novel, *Brick Lane*. Here it is: "The thing about getting older is you don't need everything to be possible anymore, you just need some things to be certain."

* * *

I often felt like I was watching the relationship from a distance. I tried to resist thinking of our relationship using cold, manipulative pickup artist terminology and tactics, but sometimes I couldn't stop myself. I'd rather not talk about that.

I found more and more ways to manage my incentives. I noticed that one of my methods was telling friends and parents that I liked Mr. Ambition a whole lot. I think it was even true.

Most of all, I told myself that the lack of natural chemistry was a good thing, and not a bad thing; the lack of natural chemistry was **why** this relationship could last.

I was quite calculating about it, really, and maybe that was why he broke up with me. On the bright side, I kept my head during the breakup, which was nice, because I didn't keep my head during my last breakup. With Mr. Ambition, I didn't feel like my self-control slipped at all.

"We need to talk," Mr. Ambition said without preamble, when I met him in the foyer of his apartment building. "I'm having some concerns about our relationship." Once we were in his apartment, he said, "To be honest, I don't know how attracted I am to you."

I tried to measure his mien. I got the feeling, again, that energy was coiled tightly inside him. Like a dragon. "Are you breaking up with me?" I asked.

"We're just having a conversation," he said quickly.

We talked about sex for a while. Chemistry. "I don't think I like S&M, to be honest," he said. "I don't feel affected by it."

I thought: *Are you sure?* and *You definitely looked affected by it,* but it's both unethical and unwise to question someone else's experience. So I just said, "You know I don't want you to do anything you don't want to do. Have you felt pressured by me?"

"No, of course not," he said.

We talked some more. He ultimately said, "Look, are you totally satisfied with the sex we're having?"

"I mean..." I said. "It's not the most intense sex I've ever had, but it'll keep getting better."

"I think we should just be friends," he said.

"... Okay," I said. "Um. Is there anything else you want to talk about?"

Mr. Ambition seemed agitated. He seemed barely able to hold still. "I've never dated anyone that I respected like I respect you," he said. "Your charisma, your intelligence, your morality. But... I don't know. I don't feel like we're very authentic with each other. I don't feel like there's much warmth between us."

Maybe you're right, I thought. *But either way, it's too late now.* "Okay," I said. I thought for a moment. "I'm sorry," I added. "I really wanted this to work out." For a moment, tears startled my eyes, but I blinked them back.

"Are you all right?" he asked. He leaned forward. "Is there anything I can do for you?"

I looked at him and tried to think. I knew I was going to be very upset in maybe fifteen minutes. He seemed hurt, and I wanted to say something that would comfort him. I wondered if he wanted me to cry, and beg, and create drama; I wouldn't do that... but maybe it would help if I asked for something simple.

But I couldn't come up with anything, and I wanted to leave. So after a pause, I said, "You can let me go home and cry."

I said it as gently as I could. But Mr. Ambition seemed terribly distressed. "Ohhh," he said, and screwed up his face. He leapt to his feet. "I'm sorry," he said.

"It's okay," I said. "Is there anything else?"

"Sometimes I think men just aren't capable of the kind of commitment women are," Mr. Ambition said. He sounded defensive, even though I hadn't made any accusations. "Then again, you're not like most women.... You're kind of a hardass. You probably have this problem with a lot of the men you date, where you come across as kind of a hardass.... And to be honest, I don't think men really want to date women as smart as they are."

Jesus, I thought, *you already broke up with me; can't you just let me go? Why do you have to rip into me like this?* I wondered how much of what he was saying was about me, and how much was him trying to make sense of his own feelings. But even though I felt sure that he was confused, his words sent an icy spike straight through me. *"I don't think men really want to date women as smart as they are...."*

"I've worked really hard to become less argumentative," I said. "You should have seen me when I was a teenager.... I don't know if I can tone myself down any more than I already do." Even as I said it, I wondered why I was still talking to a guy who'd just said that *men don't want to date women as smart as they are.* I felt like a bad feminist.

"Oh, you shouldn't tone yourself down!" said Mr. Ambition. "It makes you attractive.... Attractive intellectually, I mean."

I sighed. "Yes," I said. "Intellectually."

"I'm sorry," he said again.

"I'm going home," I said.

"We're still friends, right?" he asked.

"Yes, but give me some time to get over this," I said. "Probably about a month."

"What do you mean?" He came after me as I walked to the door. "Like, you don't want to see me at all for a month? You don't want me to call you, or reach out to you, or **anything**?"

I looked at him, again, for a long moment. I regretted his stricken expression. Again, I spoke as gently as I could. "Maybe in a month."

He offered me a ride, which I declined. My fifteen-minute estimate was almost on target: twenty minutes later, I stepped into my bedroom, leaned back against my door and burst into tears.

* * *

I ran into Richard the next evening, and we spent the night together. Richard put a fair amount of effort into convincing me to talk to Mr. Ambition.

"It sounds like he didn't actually mean to break up with you," said Richard. "It sounds like the conversation got away from him. He didn't start that conversation intending to break up with you; maybe he was looking for reassurance, and you approached his questions too logically, and he concluded that you don't care. You really like him. It seems like it's worth trying to make it work."

You may have noticed that both of these men tried hard to convince me that the other man cared about me. I decline to analyze what that means about me and my current approach to relationships.

However, I will say that I tried giving Richard more emotional feedback than I have in a long time; I even told him I missed him the next time he went on vacation. And I did try talking to Mr. Ambition again, and he acknowledged that he hadn't exactly intended to break up with me.

But then Mr. Ambition and I had several of those encounters that I think of as "post-breakup talks". I hate that shit. Every evening ended on a confusing, inconclusive note. He kept saying that he was "confidently ambiguous." We weren't dating, we weren't not dating. It reminded me of a phase I went through with a college ex-boyfriend, back in my monogamous days: my ex and I spent several weeks post-breakup being "exclusive but not together." So preposterous. People are so broken.

Mr. Ambition himself has described uncertainty as an "emotional amplifier"... but sometimes it amplifies in the wrong direction. After a week or so, I got fed up and cut things off. He asked when we would talk again, and I told him I didn't want to talk for a while. A few days later, I broke my neck in a bicycle accident.

It's like a goddamn soap opera, isn't it? Sometimes I can't believe this stuff happens to me.

* * *

Mr. Ambition showed up in my hospital room while no one else was around. I was no longer afraid that I might die, but I was leaden with morphine, and anxious. I awaited the neurosurgeons who would come install a big scary spinal brace, and I felt grateful and glad to see Mr. Ambition. I hadn't been certain he would come, although if he'd had such an accident, I would have moved Heaven and earth to go see him.

"I came as soon as our friends told me," he said. "There are so many people who love you." He said my name, and spoke softly, and the words bruised my heart.

"Thank you," I said inadequately.

"I had to skip out on work to get here," he said, and sat next to my bed. "We're in the middle of important negotiations. A billion-dollar deal."

"I'm sorry," I said. "Maybe you shouldn't have come."

He laughed. "Don't you think you're worth a billion dollars?"

"Probably not," I said.

He took my hand. "Is there anything I can get you?" he asked.

I wasn't allowed to eat or drink before the surgery. "Tell me a story," I requested.

Mr. Ambition retold a story from Dostoevsky's *The Idiot*. It was about a big-hearted man who comes to a small community and befriends an outcast "fallen woman". The big-hearted man gains high status in the community, but when people find out that he's friends with the marginalized sex worker, they become angry. Despite their condemnation, the man stays steadfastly loyal to his friend, and by seeing the way he cares about her, eventually the community accepts her too.

It was exactly the kind of story I expected to hear from him. I thought of the moment, sitting in bed, where he'd said: "If you're strong enough, you can walk into a trap." The moment when I'd realized that I could fall in love with him.

After Mr. Ambition finished the story, the doctors arrived with the brace. This contraption involved using power tools to put four screws directly into my skull, which stabilize seven pounds of metal. For realz. I was awake while they did it, too. Luckily I got local anesthesia, so the screws didn't hurt while they were going in — but I heard the bone crunching, and I felt the pressure building. Also, my neck hurt a lot. It was reasonably horrible.

Some of my friends said later that they arrived at the hospital and tried to get into my room while the brace was being installed, and they couldn't get in, but they heard me screaming. I don't remember screaming, so I deny everything.

I tried to talk normally while it was happening. I felt like the whole affair was probably more taxing for the doctors than it was for me. I mean, at least I had morphine.

"I'm sorry," I said to one of the doctors. "People must say awful things to you while you're doing this procedure."

"One woman told me how much she hated me," the doctor said tranquilly.

I tried not to cry, but I cried. Like I said: soap opera territory.

Mr. Ambition never let go of my hand.

* * *

Mr. Ambition visited me in the hospital for hours every day. He brought me all kinds of awesome vegan smoothies. He met my parents, and got along well with them.

When she got a moment alone with me, my best girlfriend asked what was up with him. "You guys broke up, didn't you? What's next?"

"I'm not sure," I said. "We haven't talked about it."

When I was able to go home, Mr. Ambition helped move me in. My air conditioner had stopped working, which is not fun for August in Chicago, especially for a person wearing a fur-lined brace. He promised to lend me a fan.

I can't turn my head, so when Mr. Ambition arrived with the fan, I didn't realize it was him until he was standing right next to me. I was alone in my room, lying in bed, wearing only the brace and my underwear while I answered text messages. This was not as sexy as it sounds. Unless you're a medical device fetishist. In which case, I guess it was exactly as sexy as it sounds.

The fan was quickly installed next to my bed. I felt awkward because I was half-naked and wearing a complex brace. I felt awkward because I couldn't help with the fan. I also felt awkward because I was racking up unpayable debt to a man who was, to all appearances, my ex. I tried to cover my discomfort by answering some more texts; then I looked up at Mr. Ambition. I couldn't read his expression.

I felt oddly expressionless, myself. I felt wrung out. I couldn't think of any words I wanted to say.

Maybe that was our moment of truth: the moment had no chemistry at all.

I gave Mr. Ambition my hand. "Thank you so much for everything," I said.

"Of course," he said, squeezed my hand, and left.

* * *

After my accident, Richard sent me a quick email, then didn't contact me for over a month. I remembered what Mr. Ambition had said — encouraging me to send more emotional signals — so tried inviting Richard for dinner, and he didn't answer my text messages. When I finally ran into Richard, I asked why he'd been ignoring me, and he laughed. "I knew you'd accuse me of ignoring you," he said. I felt like I'd walked into a trap.

I was hurt, obviously. I was surprised by how hurt I was. The problem with my youthful water metaphor is that water is basically invulnerable, but I am not... and when I was younger and more open, I had much more trouble setting important boundaries.

On the other hand, I had to admit that it was funny, too. I mean, it wasn't like I didn't see this coming. I mean, my coming-out story includes a portrait of Richard at his most difficult. One of the friends I share with Richard made a comment about leopards and spots.

Maybe my life is a soap opera, but it could also be a sitcom with the most amazing characterization ever.

I enlisted a cold, brilliant, evil-hearted friend to help draft my final letter to Richard. The letter was very short. Arguably, it was brutal. It read:

Economists recognize that the most robust relationships are formed through a plethora of implicit agreements. Apparently, these agreements are not present, and probably won't be. Cheers.

Economics arguments in the comments are encouraged. More importantly, readers may feel free to steal that letter for use on whoever is trying to pull their chain.

* * *

I received a couple texts from Mr. Ambition, a few days after he gave me the fan. He said there had been a death in his family. "But I don't want to talk about that, actually," he wrote. "I just want to check in and see how you're doing."

I thought of how he laughed when he was hurt. I thought of how he'd once told me that he wanted drama. I thought of his confusing reactions to S&M. I thought of how he outsourced his emotional labor to his friends. I thought of all the emotion I'd felt in him, coiled and caught and turned in on itself like a caged dragon.

I wondered if he wanted me to push him to talk.

"I'm so sorry," I texted back. "But I understand if you don't want to talk about it. I'm doing fine."

He invited me to a social event a week later, but I declined. I didn't reach out to him for a while after that, and he didn't reach out to me. I heard later that Mr. Ambition asked one of my friends whether they thought he owed me anything.

My friend told him, quite accurately: "No, you don't owe her anything."

If anything, **I** owe **him**. I'm not sure what I owe him, but I'm sure I owe him **something**. A billion dollars? Vegan smoothies? Chemistry?

* * *

This can be found on the Internet at:
http://clarissethorn.com/blog/2011/09/30/storytime-chemistry/

* * *

S&M:
[theory] Start From A Position of Strength

*I wrote this post in 2011, and I wrote it carefully because I was worried that it might be interpreted as putting too much responsibility for BDSM on the submissive partner's shoulders. To be clear, I believe that both partners have responsibilities in a BDSM situation, but I also believe that the dominant partner especially **must** be careful and responsive. I hope that this is a theme in all my work. I really don't ever want to encourage people to blame the victim. However, I think it's undeniable that submissive partners need a sense of themselves, as well as internal strength and resources, to do BDSM — especially very intense BDSM. The goal of this post was to start figuring out what that means.*

* * *

A while back, I attended a workshop run by educator Sarah Sloane on the topic of BDSM and abuse. Sarah centered her workshop on a maxim that I have hereby stolen: "Start from a position of strength, and seek strength in the end."

I've been thinking about this a lot in terms of not just polyamory and BDSM, but sex in general. All types of sexuality are more pleasurable for some people, and less pleasurable for others; emotionally easier for some people, and more difficult for others. I have zero interest in telling other people how they "should" or "shouldn't" deal with their sexuality, as long as what they're doing is consensual. I want to say right now that nothing I'm about to write is intended to tell others how they "should" or "shouldn't" do S&M; it's just my own thoughts on how I might choose and process my experiences.

I can certainly consent to whatever, even if that thing is problematic or scary or difficult or complicated — I can consent. The thing is, if I want to get something amazing and positive out of my experiences, I think it's good to start from a position of strength.

In some ways this is clear. For example, I think that being with a partner who genuinely wants me to have a good experience, who really cares about me, and who wants to see me again — that's almost always a position of strength. Even if I have fairly intense, dark S&M encounters with that person, I can feel confident that he'll treat me with respect; that he'll give me space and lend me strength for emotional processing afterwards.

Also, knowing what I want is a position of strength; understanding how I feel is a position of strength. Being able to recognize my emotional difficulties, hiccups, triggers and landmines is a position of strength. Knowing for sure that I can call my safeword, if necessary, is a position of strength. On a physical level, I prefer to do S&M when my body is in good shape — when I'm well-rested and I've eaten healthy food. That, too, is a position of strength.

In some ways this can become murky. For example: I am rarely interested in one-night stands. There are a number of reasons for this, but one reason is that — especially as a woman — feeling like a "slut" can be scary, difficult cultural territory. And when I don't feel good about myself, my interest in one-night stands is even lower — because I know that dealing with the difficult territory of "sluthood" will be harder with low self-esteem. If I'm feeling happy, strong, competent, valuable, and loved by the world... then one-night stands can easily be fun. If I doubt my worth, or if I doubt how much I deserve love... then one-night stands can be self-destructive.

The same goes for relationships with people who don't care about me. If I'm sure that a guy has no emotional interest in me, then having sex with that guy can be a dangerous emotional proposition for me, and one that I need to feel strong for. This doesn't always end up being true — I've definitely had sexual encounters that left me emotionally unaffected — but sometimes it's hard to predict whether I'll want more emotional investment from a given dude, so I try to keep it in mind for all encounters. (From a polyamorous perspective, I've noticed that less-emotional sex is often easier to handle when I'm already in a solid relationship with someone else.)

A couple I know in the local S&M community will sometimes have encounters that absolutely blow my mind, because they seem so difficult and so psychological. Here is an example: after the pair was married and child-free for many years, the wife realized that she might want children after all. This was a problem for her husband, who married her with the understanding that neither of them wanted kids. It became an ongoing discussion. Then the husband — who is also the sadistic, dominant partner — asked her if they could have an

S&M encounter focused around the topic. She said it was okay.

So, as part of an S&M class that they taught together, the husband used her new feelings about children to rip into her: during the S&M encounter, he told her that she was probably too old to have children, that she'd waited too long. He added that she was too flighty for kids; that she'd be a bad mother. He added that he had always made it clear that he never wanted kids; that she was stupid for marrying someone who didn't want kids, and that this problem was her own fault.

I was not present during this class, but I heard about it from some attendees, and it sounds like it was really intense. He used a genuine and difficult sore spot to put his wife through a psychological S&M wringer, with her consent.

These days, I feel very tempted towards encounters like that: encounters that can tear me apart on a deep level, using important weaknesses and insecurities. I've also received email from other people who want to arrange encounters like that, and who ask my advice. An obvious problem is that such a relationship could easily slip into abusive territory.

So I've thought about this a lot, and here's my conclusion: those kind of intense psychological encounters obey the same maxim as other BDSM — "Start from a position of strength, and seek strength in the end."

Thus, before having such an intense psychological encounter, I should feel that the encounter will ultimately — through the pain and anxiety and tears — make me feel more supported, more capable, more powerful in the world. One angle on this is to trust my partner a great deal, and be sure that he wants the best for me — to be sure that in the end, he wants me to be as strong as I started... or stronger.

It's possible that I might not need so much support from my partner, if I get support elsewhere in my life: perhaps from friends, perhaps from a Kink Aware therapist, perhaps from a great job or a solid diet and exercise plan, perhaps even from another partner. (Of course, if I were planning to get extensive emotional processing support from other people, then I would seek their consent beforehand.)

Still, it seems like the easiest way to get support would be to get it from my partner, who would share more of the experience with me than anyone else. This would also build our intimacy, which is usually a major factor in having intense S&M encounters in the first place.

* * *

This can be found on the Internet at:
http://clarissethorn.com/blog/2011/07/20/slogan-start-from-a-position-of-strength/

* * *

***

S&M:
[storytime] Predicament Bondage

I wrote this in early 2011. Amusingly, after I wrote it, one of the top Google queries that brings people to my blog became the phrase "predicament bondage." I think those folks are probably looking for porn, and I wonder if my article disappoints them.

***

Some people are masochists (who enjoy pain) but not submissives (who enjoy, well, submitting). Some people are really into discipline (with lots of punishment) but not bondage (rope, cages, etc). Some people are sadists (who enjoy inflicting sensations) but not dominants (who enjoy being in control). Some people are switches, who find that they can switch between roles — they can be dominant or submissive; sadistic or masochistic... I am an example of a definite switch.

Me, I get positively bored if someone takes a long time tying me up. For other people, 45 minutes of elaborate knotwork = really hot foreplay. I don't understand this, but that's cool; plenty of people don't understand my preferences and we all coexist quite happily anyway.

So yeah, "bondage" — rope, cages, etc. — is not so much my thing. But there's one phrase I absolutely love: "predicament bondage." Predicament bondage is usually presented in a very elaborate way: for example, a submissive might be tied up with ropes binding him such that his arms are in pain — but if he moves his arms then his legs will be in pain. It's a predicament! And it's bondage! Whee! Predicament bondage!

However, it doesn't have to be elaborate to be predicament bondage. I'm not into rope obstacle courses, but I started loving the phrase "predicament bondage" after a friend went to a workshop run by Fetish Diva Midori and reported back. He said:

Midori had two pitchers of water, or maybe a pitcher and a glass. She told us, "This is the simplest form of predicament bondage," and she had the demo submissive hold his hands straight out at shoulder height. Then she placed the water in his hands. The submissive had to keep holding the water; if he failed, he knew he would be failing Midori. But there was never any threat of "Midori's wrath" if he failed her. In fact, she spoke as if she was on his side, part of his team. In many ways, her sympathy for his plight made it all the more cruel, because she was the one doing it to him.

She explained this. She knew that his sense of disappointment in "failing" her was worse than anything she could actually do to him.

So, the predicament in that case was the submissive's increasing arm agony vs. his fear of failing Midori. For me, that concept is infinitely hotter than a rope obstacle course. Although for me, in practice, I'd also want the pain to be a bit more... um... personal.

* * *

The first time someone flogged me, I had no idea what he was going to do beforehand; he and I had the strongest dominant/submissive dynamic I've ever felt, and I put myself in his hands with almost-total trust. A night came around when I felt that itch under my skin, the dark burn in the back of my mind... I knew I had to go see him. I wasn't hugely experienced, but I knew exactly what that slow burn meant.

It was late. He was in bed, and I lay down next to him. "I think..." I said slowly, "I want you to hurt me. A lot."

I felt him tense beside me.

"Why?" he asked.

I didn't look at him. "Why do you ask me questions when you already know the answer?"

"Sometimes I just want to hear you say it," he said, and stood up. "Take off your clothes and get on your knees."

I caught my breath; did as he said. When I felt the ends of the flogger trail lightly down my back, I wasn't even sure what the soft sensation meant, but I was already trembling anyway. I am surprised by my memory of how much it hurt when he hit me. These days, I don't think of floggers as especially painful, but then again, I seem to recall that he left more marks than I'm used to. (I loved taking off my shirt and examining the bruises in the mirror. I glowed for days, afterwards.) So maybe there was something particular about what he did, or about his materials. Or maybe it's just that it was my first time.

He created the predicament when I started to cry and flinch around. It was very simple. He leaned over me. "For the next three, keep your face down and your hands still," he said. "Promise me."

"I can't," I said. "I can't promise." I said it frantically. I was terrified of failing him. "I can't."

"You have to," he said gently. "So you will."

I cried harder. I sobbed so hard I couldn't speak. He stayed where he was, leaning over me, and kept a merciless silence. "I promise," I finally said, when I could shape words. My back was to him, I couldn't see his face, but I swear I felt him smile.

When he hit me again, I barely moved. After the count of three, he said he wanted to see how much longer I could go, but the answer was that I couldn't — I started to flinch strongly again. Of course, he kept hitting me, if only for that. But at least I hadn't broken my promise. Hadn't failed him.

* * *

I've heard about a game in which the submissive partner stands next to a wall, and holds two coins against the wall — one in each hand. The dominant then does, you know, some stuff. On the submissive's part, dropping the coins spells failure. This sounds pretty hot, and it's one way to make a concrete predicament. But during the above encounter — my first time being flogged — I assure you that it was plenty hot enough without any coins. With only my promise and my awareness to keep me in line.

Sometimes I can't obey the order, no matter how hard I try. My partner may order me not to move, for example, when I can't help moving. If I were in the above scenario, with the coins, I'm not confident that I wouldn't drop them. It's scary — especially if I love him, because then all the emotions are multiplied. But even if I'm not in love — as long as he's got me in the right mental space, then if I fail, I will say "I'm sorry" over and over. I'll be terrified of his anger; I'll feel like I deserve punishment, and if he doesn't keep hurting me I'll feel abandoned.

The more I fail, the more it hurts — more than physical pain ever could. Slamming up against my own limits makes me feel terribly inadequate. It's hot, but it's dangerous; it can rip me apart. At times like that, I often need my partner to tell me after we're done: "I still like you and think you're a good person."

And sometimes I need to hear that especially if I safeword out of the encounter, because sometimes — not always, but sometimes — calling my safeword can feel like the worst failure of all.

* * *

When I trace some of the weirdest and most random situations that get me hot, I see that predicaments come up all the time. For example, I have a terrible tendency to try and make out with a partner right before we're expected to be somewhere. I might be totally cold 30 minutes before we have to leave, but 10 minutes before we have to leave, ding! It's like a switch flips. We've got to leave, but I grab him and now he's turned on, oh no! And now we're late! Whee!

One of my exes pointed out my tendency to make out with him while his car was stopped at traffic lights that were about to turn green. "I know!" I said. "I don't really get why I do that, myself." He responded, "Predicament bondage!"

* * *

Sometimes, when the pain is getting intense, I'll play a little game with my partners. (Kind of a game, except it's also serious, or it feels serious at the time; usually, when I start playing this game, I am not even close to coherent enough to ponder tactics; I'm running on instinct.) I think of this game as the "aren't you scared of the neighbors" game. In the "aren't you scared of the neighbors" game, I start making noise loud enough that I might catch outsiders' attention. Part of me is hoping that my partner is worried about the neighbors; that he'll relent, that I can use my tiny advantage to convince him to pull back. That I can play for a moment of relief, a smidgen of mercy.

Of course, if I'm lucky, my partners will then just order me to be quiet while they hurt me. Which creates a predicament! Because being quiet is actually not at all easy, and it gets more difficult the more it hurts.

And then there's the distraction game. I don't always do BDSM with partners I'm sexually attracted to; even with partners I'm sexually attracted to, I don't always feel sexual during our BDSM encounters. But when I feel very attracted during a BDSM encounter, oh, man. That's when I play the distraction game, which involves attempting to distract him by turning him on. Again, I'm not really coherent enough to be planning strategy at times like this; I'm more going on instinct; instinctively, it's like I'm trying to bargain. *Maybe if I can turn him on, he'll have sex with me instead of hurting me....*

If I'm lucky, he'll recognize what I'm doing; he'll be pleased, amused even, but he won't stop. One recent partner had me handcuffed to a car seat while he was hurting me. (Doing this in his car was not my idea, but at least we weren't moving. Nor were we paused at a traffic light.) I couldn't move too much, so I started licking his hand when he reached for me. Kissing his palm, his fingers — he groaned, and then he laughed.

"You **are** a switch," he said, "trying to control me even now." And he didn't stop.

* * *

"No," I breathed, a few months ago, during an encounter with someone who's really good at this. "You don't get to say no," he replied, so I bit back the word. Had to fight against my own desperate instinct to say it, over and over.

Later, he murmured, "It's so cute how you act like you don't want this," as he leaned in to inflict dark bruises on my shoulder. His words almost brought me to tears. *But I **don't** want it. Do I? How can I want something that hurts like this? But I'm not stopping him — did I really ask for this — I must want it —* Forcing me to face up to my own consent: a predicament?

I fought back when he hurt me, instinctively pushing him away. "Don't push me away," he instructed. "Put your arms around me," and I did. But we moved around, and moved again, so I had my arms back — and again, I couldn't seem to control my instinctive struggling.

And so he stopped for a moment, held my arms in place, and laid down the law. He knows I very much prefer some kinds of pain over other kinds of pain, so he told me this: "If you want the kind of pain you **like**, you have to let me in close." Layer upon layer: he's not just forcing me to take the pain; he's making me complicit. I think there were also practical considerations, in that it was actually difficult for him to control how he hurt me when I struggled a lot, but, still.... It was so hot it made me gasp.

I'm not sure, but I suspect that a few years ago, I might not have been able to handle that level of complicitness: forcing me to acknowledge what I like. Back then, I was too appalled by my own desires. Now, this level of complicitness adds another level of pain — emotional pain; mild pain that I can cope with — which is awesome. But although feeling complicit is a new tactic, it's part of an old game. It's merely another kind of predicament.

Fundamentally, what's hot about predicament bondage isn't the mechanics of what my partner says or does. It's not about the scenario or the equipment or the exact words. It's knowing that he won't stop hurting me, no matter how I fight or beg or scream. It's feeling that every moment, every action reinforces how much I'm in his power.

It's knowing there's no way out.

* * *

This can be found on the Internet at:
http://clarissethorn.com/blog/2011/01/07/storytime-predicament-bondage/

* * *

* * *

RELATIONSHIPS:
[theory] Relationship Tools: Monogamy, Polyamory, Competition, and Jealousy

I wrote this in 2012, but it's the culmination of over a decade of thought. I came across my first polyamory books when I was very young, and I remember that even though I was inexperienced, I felt super frustrated by how most polyamorists discuss jealousy. They were incredibly un-empathic about it; the advice always seemed to boil down to "Get over it," with a dollop of "Stop being so selfish," and without any acknowledgment of how painful and difficult jealousy can be for the person who's feeling it. But at the same time, most monogamists aren't much better about this topic! Many monogamists approach jealousy as something that requires no examination at all.

In this essay, I'm trying to come to a better understanding of all these dynamics. I also seek to integrate them with BDSM theory, which I'm convinced has a much stronger bearing on jealousy than most people will admit.

* * *

Last year, I wrote a piece called "In Praise of Monogamy." I currently practice polyamory in my relationships, but I spent years dating monogamously. I've noticed that when people talk about monogamy, they usually either assume that it's the only way to go... or they assume that it has to be thrown out the window entirely. I think that this either-or approach is completely wrongheaded, so the goal of "In Praise of Monogamy" was to talk about the advantages of monogamy in a more neutral, nuanced way. Different relationship models are all tools in a toolbox, and some people are better with some tools than others.

"In Praise of Monogamy" was probably one of my most successful articles ever — it was republished at a ton of websites, including high-profile venues like *The Guardian*. Simultaneously, the article got a lot of really mixed comments. Some people felt that

I wasn't praising monogamy enough; others felt that I wasn't praising non-monogamy enough; there were lots of other frustrations too. My big takeaway was that these conversations don't happen enough, most people aren't used to having them, and it's really hard to know where it start.

Jealousy is one obvious starting point, because people always bring it up in conversations about non-monogamy. I talked a little bit about jealousy in "In Praise of Monogamy." If you've recently read that piece, then feel free to skip to the end of the following italicized excerpt:

Some people experience jealousy more than, or less than, or differently from other people. Plenty of people in non-monogamous relationships experience jealousy — and plenty of non-monogamous people handle it just fine, through open-hearted communication.

But there are also plenty of people who appear to lack the "jealousy chip."

And then there are plenty of people who experience so much jealousy, who feel that jealousy is such a big part of their emotional makeup, that the best way to manage it is simply through monogamy.

Personally, I used to get a lot more jealous than I do now. I think I'm less likely to get jealous these days partly because I've gotten better at finding low-drama men. Jealousy has a reputation for being an irrational emotion, and sometimes it genuinely is an unreasonable, cruel power-grab. But I think jealousy is often quite rational, and often arises in response to a genuine emotional threat... or deliberate manipulation.

*There's another reason, though... I've also noticed that some switch in my brain has flipped, and I've started to **eroticize** jealousy. I occasionally find myself fantasizing about men I care about sleeping with other women, and sometimes the fantasy is hot **because** I feel mildly jealous. I cannot explain how this happened. It surprised me the first time it happened, believe me. What's really fascinating is that I think **the same part** of me that eroticizes jealousy, is the part that used to make me feel sick at the thought of my partner sleeping with someone else. S&M masochism: the gift that never stops giving!*

I think it's important to note here that I didn't become less jealous because I felt like I "should," or because I was told not to be jealous. In fact, I had an early boyfriend who acted like I was a hysterical bitch every time I got jealous... and he made things much worse. With him, I just felt awful when I got jealous; I couldn't get past it. I felt like he was judging me for something I couldn't help; I felt like my mind was fragmenting as I tried to force myself to "think better" without any outside support; and worst of all, I felt like I couldn't rely on him to respect my feelings.

It was the men who treated my emotions like they were reasonable and understandable who decreased my jealousy. It's much harder to be jealous when your partner is saying, "I totally understand," than it is when your partner is saying, "What the hell is the matter with you?" Maybe that's what makes monogamy such an effective jealousy-management tactic: monogamy can be like a great big sign or sticker or button you can give to your partner that says, "I respect your jealousy." Which is not to say that monogamy is always effective for this — we all know that monogamous people get jealous all the time! (Which only adds to my point that monogamy might be viewed as just one of many tactics, rather than an answer, when jealousy is a problem.)

Now, back to the current article. Jealousy is an incredibly hot-button topic, so I'm nervous about this, but let's focus in on it a little more.

* * *

The Feeling of Jealousy

Jealousy and its cousin, competition, are both things that happen a lot in relationships. Some people are so uncomfortable acknowledging this that they repress those feelings, or ignore the behavior that goes along with them... but I've rarely seen that end well. I believe that some people lack jealousy and competitive urges, but I've also seen a lot of people who feel those things but can't admit it. Not even to themselves.

I dated a guy last year who told me at the start of our relationship that he never got jealous. At first I took him at his word, but I quickly noticed that he changed the subject aggressively when I mentioned past lovers. We had a mutual friend with whom I had a lot of chemistry; when the three of us were together, my boyfriend acted uncomfortable and irritable, and when I specifically acted in ways that made it obvious I was with him — like by giving him Public Displays of Affection in front of the other guy — he relaxed.

I sighed internally when I observed this, and I felt frustrated, but wasn't sure how to talk about it without sounding like I was calling him a liar. Fortunately, he brought it up later. "I think I do get jealous sometimes, and I just don't like to think about it because it makes me feel like a bad person," he said, one night while we were making dinner. In that moment, my respect for him skyrocketed. It's hard for people to keep track of themselves like that, and to shift their self-image when confronted with new evidence.

Some people seem to interpret their lovers' jealousy as a sign of love. Hey, I'll admit that I've had moments of being flattered or pleased when my boyfriends show signs of jealousy — or when they act a little competitive. Sometimes those things are scary, though... or threatening... or frustrating, like in my example above. It's complicated!

However, I often see those dynamics play out in ways that the participants won't admit, no matter how much evidence comes up. I think it gets especially complicated when people experience jealousy as a sexual thing, a turn-on. Most people have a hard enough time discussing their sexuality in the first place. When you add an ingredient as controversial as jealousy, the potential discussions become that much more combustible.

When I was researching pickup artists for my awesome book *Confessions of a Pickup Artist Chaser,* I found a number of discussions in that community that praise competitive feelings because they're seen as making the relationship more fun. A lot of these guys say competition among different lovers within open relationships is awesome because it keeps everyone a little uncertain, and encourages them to be "on top of their game." This contrasts drastically with most polyamorous perspectives; in my experience, poly folks see jealousy and competition as things that should be compartmentalized and managed very carefully, rather than encouraged or exalted. For polyamory theorists, a feeling of safety is often the goal, as opposed to a feeling of competition.

And emotional safety is certainly a concern, because jealousy is one of the most intense and overwhelming emotions out there. It's such a hard feeling to sit with and work through. My worst experiences of jealousy felt like I was choking, like I couldn't breathe, like I was sick to my stomach, like I was terribly obsessed, like I couldn't think of anything but the jealousy and how much it hurt. And yet... I've occasionally felt jealousy that was weak, almost nice, where I felt a little twinge of it and turned to my lover and got reassured... and that made me feel more safe, more cared for, more loved.

The bottom line is that people experience jealousy and competitive urges in many different ways. It's important to acknowledge that and honor it. I don't see it as productive to frame things like "jealousy is bad," or "competition is awesome." **I'd much**

rather frame things like: "Jealousy and competition happen sometimes, and how do we deal with them when they come up so that everyone involved feels comfortable and happy?"

* * *

The Toolkit

I firmly believe that **the primary tools for dealing with jealousy and competitive urges are honesty, good faith and respect**. If you're feeling jealous, then take a deep breath. (I'm pretty sure that most relationship drama could be avoided if more people took deep breaths.) Hopefully, you're dating someone who you like and trust (if you're not, what's the point?). Remind yourself that this person, who you like and trust, probably is operating in good faith and isn't trying to hurt you. Respect that this person has their own desires, which won't always overlap perfectly with your own. Don't assume your partner is obliged to do everything you want — but do be honest about what's hurting you, so you can work it out together.

And, in turn: if your partner is jealous, respect that emotion. Remind yourself that this person, who you like and trust, probably is operating in good faith and isn't trying to control you. Be honest about how your partner's jealousy makes you feel, and think about ways to reassure your partner while protecting your own needs and boundaries.

The **most stable** relationship formation for dealing with jealousy and competitive urges appears to be monogamy. To be sure, I think people have plenty of other reasons for choosing monogamy. But the relationship tool that seems to work most thoroughly, and most often, and for the most people, is simply... being monogamous.

There are many ways of approaching non-monogamy, but the one I'm most familiar with is polyamory. A lot of polyamorists, though not all, organize their relationships into hierarchies: they have one or more "primary relationships," and then "secondary relationships" and other relationships that don't make it to secondary level. Sometimes a primary partner will have "veto power" — i.e., if one partner wants to get a new partner, then the primary partner can explicitly block that partner. This seems to help control a lot of jealousy and competitive behavior.

Some poly folks say that they see hierarchies and veto power as "blunt instruments," and that they prefer to negotiate every interaction case-by-case. This sounds fine to me as long as it works for them, of course. But I would offer this: I think that blunt instruments are sometimes the most useful tool for a given project. And in fact, blunt instruments are **more often** useful than finer-tuned instruments. The whole idea of finer-tuned instruments is that they're useful for precise circumstances... but they're also harder to use, and more fragile. Some people don't have the time or inclination to create a whole new toolkit for every individual relationship. Some people will settle for a slightly less precise, perfect relationship in exchange for a more stable one. Sometimes it's simply easier to use a blunter, but more universally effective tool.

I will also add that I have seen **plenty** of polyamorous relationships in which there were **unspoken** hierarchies, and **unspoken** veto power. This resulted in maneuvering that struck me as both underhanded and unnecessary. I've always felt that it would be better for everyone involved if those dynamics were put out on the surface.

Finally, for people who like jealousy and competition.... If S&M has taught me anything, it's that it's quite possible to play with pain and power **within a safe, loving framework**. The key is to compartmentalize the whole process and discuss it openly. If people are into competitive relationships, then okay. If people like jealousy, then okay. But in that case, they really ought to look for partners who share those tastes, and to find ways that they can deal with them openly and honestly.

In S&M, there's a huge emphasis on careful communication tactics — safewords are the most famous example, but there are plenty of others. There's also a huge emphasis on talking about the S&M encounter and processing it together afterwards; we call this aftercare. If jealousy and competitiveness can be understood as consensual games of pain and power, then I think people who want to play those games would do well to learn about S&M communication tactics. If you're going to have fun making your partner feel an emotion as intense as jealousy, then you might consider giving your partner a safeword.

* * *

This can be found on the Internet at:
http://clarissethorn.com/blog/2012/05/01/relationship-tools-monogamy-polyamory-competition-and-jealousy/

* * *

* * *

EVOLUTION:
[storytime] You Don't Always Know What You're Thinking

I wrote this in late 2010. I have mixed feelings about it now. I think I made important points, but I will also say this: if you don't have a clue what's going on in your head and don't even know where to start, then that can be a bad sign. I think that when people are unhappy, or dealing with situations that are more than they can handle, they often settle into a kind of mental "fog" so they don't have to think about it. (The feminist writer Autumn Whitefield-Madrano has a great article describing how this happens in abusive relationships; she calls it "the fog of abuse." [1])

Yet at the same time, I do believe that we should consciously make space in ourselves for new feelings to emerge, especially when we're pushing our limits. Self-awareness must include allowing new feelings to emerge at their own pace.

* * *

In May 2010, I wrote a post called "Am I Evolving Away From Monogamy?" in which I talked about my urge towards polyamory, and my confusion about that urge. [1] I talked about my previous dislike for polyamory, and I talked about how new it is for me to feel like I want to be polyamorous. I talked quite a lot, really, but a week later, I started feeling like I hadn't covered everything... or like I just wasn't correct about some things I'd written.

But how could I be incorrect? I was, after all, writing about **myself** and **my own feeings**. How could I be wrong about what I myself was thinking?

I guess I realized quickly that I'd claimed things about my past self that weren't quite true. That didn't acknowledge my own complexity. For example, I wrote that although I've toyed with polyamory in the past, my most recent poly leanings came up only because I got my heart broken by a gentleman who I sometimes refer to as Mr. Inferno. I theorized that perhaps I'm just scared of commitment. While it is certainly true that I'm not big on commitment these days, I later recalled that actually — at the beginning of my relationship with Mr. Inferno, I had some doubts about being monogamous. I was monogamous because he was very sure that was what he wanted, but I remember a point when I thought about trying to negotiate something different.

Polyamorous people are stereotyped as being commitment-phobic. I know all about that stereotype — in fact, I have angrily defended my poly friends from it for years! (Even when I was very fiercely monogamous, I got so mad when people who don't know anything about polyamory said ignorant things about my poly friends!) Yet I have to watch out for that stereotype's influence on me anyway. When I forgot that I'd considered polyamory with Mr. Inferno, was I being influenced by that stereotype? Or was I just missing Mr. Inferno a lot that day, and wishing I could talk to him, and maybe therefore remembering him as more influential in my life than he actually was? Or... what?

I'm visiting my father right now; we went out to dinner the other night and talked about relationships. I'm quite open about my parents about almost everything — we don't talk explicitly about our sex lives, but we do have detailed conversations about stuff like polyamory. My dad is not at all attracted to polyamory, and we used to commiserate and theorize about how we just didn't understand polyamory.

Now that I've decided to pursue poly, my dad is puzzled. "I know this is weird," I said to him during dinner, "because we used to be on the exact same wavelength about this," and he nodded. He asks questions, he tries to figure out where I'm coming from — and they're all questions that I have decent theoretical answers for. Answers include: "Well, of course it's possible to love more than one person at a time. Mothers can love multiple children, kids can love multiple parents, friends can love each other, so why wouldn't it be possible for people to have sexual and emotional relationships with multiple people?" Or: "Jealousy can be managed just fine, as long as partners are communicating well and genuinely care about each others' feelings."

In fact, some of my answers are the **same** theoretical answers that he and I discussed back when we were both steadfastly monogamous. Except this time, I'm giving him those answers from the other side; and yet he can't relate any better to them, this time around.

***

I've always spent a **large** amount of time obsessively analyzing my own emotions, and often writing about them. This has been true since childhood. However, one analytical skill I can always improve is this: knowing when to say, "I'm not sure how I feel about that."

Another important skill is staying on top of the stories I tell about myself, the ideas and memes and images and narratives that I'm trying to match myself to. It seems impossible to track all the influences on my psyche, all the different social and cultural and even biological forces. Where am I under all the programming? It's worth trying to figure it out (even if I'll never know for sure)

I don't always know what I'm thinking. I don't believe that anyone always knows what they're thinking. It's important to acknowledge this, because when people don't acknowledge it, they often simply decide to be something that doesn't quite match up with what they want. Sometimes this works fine — if the pattern a person chooses to impose on her self can function, then who cares if it's a perfect match? (I mean, arguably, people are always imposing unmatched patterns on our thoughts and selves.) But although this sometimes works fine, there are plenty of times when it doesn't work fine. Or really at all.

I have a section in my sexual communication workshop for maxims — little slogan-like things. I recently added a new one that I really like: "You don't always know what you're thinking."

***

I've been practicing BDSM for a while, now, and it has been amazing. I've had a lot of very intense sexual experiences and I feel incredibly confident about my sexuality. I feel very far away from my younger self, who realized that she was into BDSM and completely freaked out. However, I used to keep a very detailed (albeit sporadic) personal journal, and this allows me to look into the head of 20-year-old Clarisse. Here's something I wrote only a couple of weeks after I met Richard, my first serious BDSM partner:

On the surface I have a hard time understanding why this has shocked me so much — the fact that I wanted him to hurt me, the fact that even as I was facing down my demons and crying and incoherent I wanted him to keep biting me, scratching me, bruising me, and God, it was bad, but even now I wish it had been far worse... on some level I want to have been physically scarred. He stopped finally because I started saying "no," and couldn't formulate a coherent answer through my tears when he asked me if I was serious. But, of course, although I was serious, I also didn't want him to stop. Of course. Of course I wanted him to hear me saying no and keep going, to be protesting and overridden. And the reason I couldn't formulate a coherent answer wasn't even that I didn't know the answer was, "Yes, keep going." It was that I knew the answer was yes, and when I faced it I started crying so hard I couldn't speak, and he... sensitively, I guess... decided it was time to stop.

How cliché I am. (God, I'm sounding like some naïve ingenue from a random de Sade play or something, just discovering my sexuality or whatever.) How self-conscious. And how humiliated and ashamed. Of all the things I think I expected from myself for this, if it ever came true that this was what I wanted — I never really actually expected to be ashamed.

What I think is especially interesting about those paragraphs is that I felt a certain recognition for my BDSM identity, I felt a certain inevitability about learning what I needed. It made sense to me. "Of course," I wrote, over and over. And at the same time I acknowledged that I had considered BDSM before — but that I hadn't really known what that meant, and I'd had no idea how I would feel if I found it. I knew what I was thinking, I knew what I had been thinking, and yet at the same time I didn't know. I had no idea. I was completely confused.

I'm not so confused anymore. These days.... There are a lot of things I don't know, but there are an awful lot of things I do know, too. I have gotten pretty good at knowing what I want, even when it's hard to figure it out. And I have a very good sense of my boundaries.

But I also keep trying to figure out how to expand them. This isn't just true with BDSM. Arguably, my urge to go to Africa and put myself through extreme culture shock was similar to the urge I feel to expand my head with BDSM. Some of the things I want to do with my life and my body and my self seem almost opaque; totally irrational; a little scary — even to me. I love experiencing and analyzing emotions; experiencing and analyzing personal connections — I want to do more of that, even when there are emotional risks. *What's **past** that emotion? What's under my heart? How much can I feel for another person, and in what ways can I manage that? Which part of my mind will catch me if I end up going over the edge? Will anything?*

* * *

And so, even though I have a good sense of my boundaries, I also occasionally have the sense that anything could happen.

This is not always dramatic. Sometimes it is quite tame, like with my current polyamorous leanings. When I was at dinner with my father, he gently expressed concern about how being polyamorous might affect me emotionally. He wasn't trying to tell me what to do — just that he's having trouble understanding where I'm at. "For me," he said, "sexual relationships encourage emotional attachment," and talked about how he bonds with one person at a time. He added, "I simply find that if my relationship is truly satisfying, I don't want more than one; I can't convince myself to be interested in more than one partner."

I used to feel the same way. Dad knows it, and I know it; we've said these things before. It's not like I don't understand how he feels — I totally do.

And there's no guarantee that, over the course of experimenting with polyamory, I won't bond with a partner in a way that feels monogamous — and then get hurt if they won't be monogamous with me. I'm not convinced that I'll feel completely secure as I continue to pursue polyamory. Recently I had one difficult morning that featured two simultaneous breakups, and that was a bit much to deal with! In short, I'm not certain that polyamory is my ideal. But I'm also no longer certain that it's not. And I'm really enjoying trying it out.

Here's the thing: I'm not sure what I'm thinking... **but that's okay**. I know I could end up getting hurt... **and that's okay**. I could get my heart broken: that's what you risk when you experiment with the alchemy of your own emotions, your hormones, your body, your self. But I'm watching myself and being careful and communicating as clearly as I possibly can, and it seems to be going fine. And if poly really doesn't work out for me, I can go back to monogamy.

And hey, at least if I do get my heart broken, it's something else to analyze obsessively and then write about! That's something to look forward to.

* * *

This can be found on the Internet at:
http://clarissethorn.com/blog/2010/12/13/slogan-you-dont-always-know-what-youre-thinking/

* * *

***

ABUSE:
[theory] Thinking More Clearly About BDSM versus Abuse

I wrote this post in 2011. As I noted in the intro to "The Alt Sex Anti-Abuse Dream Team," other BDSMers have been writing about this more and more, and the discussion is really heating up right now, in 2012. Thomas MacAulay Millar has a particularly good series of posts on the topic, starting with: http://yesmeansyesblog.wordpress.com/2012/03/23/theres-a-war-on-part-1-troubles-been-brewing/

***

Years ago, when I first started thinking about BDSM and abuse, I — like a lot of feminist BDSMers — was defensive.

We get scared of the accusation that "BDSM is always abuse"... and we're accustomed to accusations from certain feminists such as "those of you who pretend to like BDSM just have Patriarchy Stockholm Syndrome and don't know what you really want"... and often, we're also fighting our own inner BDSM stigma demons. We get angry that our sexual needs are seen as politically problematic, or unimportant.

And so, for a lot of people, our instinctive angle on abuse in the BDSM community is: "Shut up! That's not what's going on!" And that's a problem.

Obviously, I don't think BDSM is inherently abusive! Exploring my personal BDSM desires has given me some extraordinary, consensual, transcendent experiences and connections. I also genuinely believe that BDSM has the potential to control, subvert, and manage power. **BDSM can be a place where people learn to understand bad power dynamics in past relationships; it can be a place where people learn to manage or destroy bad power dynamics in their current relationships; it can be a place where people find glory, self-knowledge and freedom by manipulating their own reactions and responses to power.** The sex theorist

Pepper Mint has a great, complicated essay about this called "Towards a General Theory of BDSM and Power." [1] And here's one of my favorite quotations on the matter, from a submissive and former blogger who went by violetwhite:

It's ironic that the most perverse manipulations of power in my life occurred in a past vanilla relationship, where I tolerated tyranny because the normative structure of our relationship obscured the fact that that is what it was.

Still, I've seen things happen in the BDSM community that turned my stomach. Terrible manipulative behavior exhibited by people who have the greatest reputations. Blaming the victim when they try to speak up. Telling "rumor mongers" to shut up when people are trying to talk openly about problematic community members. The BDSM subculture has its own version of rape culture, where "lying bitch" and "drama queen" and "miscommunication" are used against abuse survivors. Miscommunications do happen... but not everything that could be a miscommunication is actually a miscommunication.

Oh yes, rape culture can happen in BDSM just the same way it happens in the "vanilla" mainstream. And there are certainly people in my local community who I would never get involved with, because I do not trust them.

Being defensive about BDSM and abuse won't help; yes, BDSM is stigmatized and stereotyped, but the abuse is still a problem. So after I started blogging, I tried to move past my defensiveness and write more concretely — to write about what exactly the BDSM community does to work against abuse. One of my first posts on BDSM and abuse was called "Evidence That The BDSM Community Does Not Enable Abuse." It highlighted anti-abuse initiatives within the BDSM community. As I learned more about BDSM and abuse, and my perspective got more nuanced, I wrote a more expansive post called "The Alt Sex Anti-Abuse Dream Team." It covered all the information I'd given in the earlier post, and also talked about how I personally would structure an anti-abuse initiative with alt-sex people in mind.

Looking back now, those posts still strike me as defensive. I was making good points, but I also think that I didn't fully understand where some feminists are coming from when they react negatively to BDSM. This past year, I've learned a lot more about abusive gender-based violence, power, and control. And I've concluded that while BDSM is obviously not equivalent to abuse, we need better theory to describe the difference between BDSM and abuse, and we should try to avoid defensiveness while articulating that theory.

I've written before that one thing I think people can do is try to "start from a position of strength, and seek strength afterwards." The overall point of that maxim is that any given BDSM activity can eventually make all parties feel more supported, more capable, more powerful in the world. That's my ideal end goal; that is what I personally would aim for with my BDSM practice. **Perhaps I might do an intense BDSM scene that makes me feel terrible in the moment — or for a lot of moments... but I want to be sure it will make me more supported, more capable, more powerful later.**

That's an awfully vague maxim, though, and one that can be different for every person. I may have found a more concrete focus in a 1984 anti-abuse concept — the Power & Control Wheel:

In 1984, staff at the Domestic Abuse Intervention Project (DAIP) began developing curricula for groups for men who batter and victims of domestic violence. We wanted a way to describe battering for victims, offenders, practitioners in the criminal justice system and the general public. Over several months, we convened focus groups of women who had been battered. We listened to heart-wrenching stories of violence, terror and survival. After listening to these stories and asking questions, we documented the most common abusive behaviors or tactics that were used against these women. The tactics chosen for the wheel were those that were most universally experienced by battered women. [2]

In a BDSM context, a lot of the behaviors listed on the Power & Control Wheel could be part of a consensual encounter — violence, headgames, name-calling, all kinds of things can be BDSM. But this part, this is important:

MINIMIZING, DENYING AND BLAMING:

* Making light of the abuse and not taking her concerns about it seriously.

* Saying the abuse didn't happen.

* Shifting responsibility for abusive behavior.

* Saying she caused it.

(The original wheel uses gendered language, but I'd like to note that although abuse is most often perpetrated by men against women, abuse can happen in any kind of relationship and to people of any gender.)

In the brilliant documentary *Graphic Sexual Horror,* which profiles a now-defunct BDSM porn site, there's footage of a scene with a porn model named S4. The dominant partner slaps S4 across the face, and S4 reacts angrily. She says something like, "We didn't talk about that in advance!" The dominant doesn't apologize; he doesn't take her seriously, and he doesn't talk to her carefully or work to calm her down. Instead, the dominant partner snaps: "We can't talk about everything in advance," and aggressively demands to know whether she's ready to continue. This is an example of minimizing, denying, and blaming.

I have some sympathy for his awkward position — I've made small mistakes as a dominant partner, too, and he's correct that it's impossible to talk about everything in advance. But **the way to deal with those mistakes is by apologizing sincerely and making sure the mistake never happens again**. For example, one of my exes hated being bitten on the lips, and at one point I bit him on the lower lip. And he called me out, and I said, "I'm sorry," and I put my arms around him to offer comfort; I said, "I won't do it again," and I didn't.

My experience of BDSM relationships is that it's best for there to be both communication ahead of time and lots of discussion and processing afterwards. Both partners get to set "hard limits": things they absolutely don't want to do. If one partner has concerns, those concerns get airtime. Both partners acknowledge a role in the proceedings, and blame isn't spread around; even if something goes wrong, the discussion focuses on how to prevent that from happening again rather than making accusations.

And if BDSM is happening, it must be possible to acknowledge it, even if it's subtle. For example, I ran into a partner on the street the other day; he gave me a hug and held me in place for a while, even though I tried to move away. This, my friends, is subtle BDSM. Which was fine with me! But it was only okay because I knew I could call him out on it later and be sure it was acknowledged!

And I did mention it later, and he did acknowledge it, and we both laughed and said it was hot. And if I had told him not to do it, that would have been okay too. And **the fact that I knew I could talk about it, that I knew I could tell him not to do it and he'd listen... meant that I also could have declined to mention it, and I would have felt fine**.

Something else worth acknowledging here is time boundaries. If a person is indeed calling names, controlling what the other person does, etc, then it's often useful for it to be communicated — and also time-bounded. For example: "You can only call me pathetic during this sexual encounter. Otherwise, please don't."

There are BDSM couples that get rid of time boundaries, and have ongoing BDSM relationship situations; there are also BDSM couples that don't use safewords. I think those relationships require a lot of understanding and care from all parties involved. I've never gone without safewords, but sometimes I go without time-bounding, and when I do, I make very sure that I can trust my partner and communicate well with him. (Thomas MacAulay Millar calls safeword-free BDSM "the advanced class".)

The same group that made the Power & Control Wheel has another useful wheel — the Equality Wheel. Here's the text of the wheel:

ECONOMIC PARTNERSHIP:
* *Making money decisions together.*
* *Making sure both partners benefit from financial arrangements.*

NEGOTIATION AND FAIRNESS:
* *Seeking mutually satisfying resolutions to conflict.*
* *Accepting changes.*
* *Being willing to compromise.*

NON-THREATENING BEHAVIOR:
* *Talking and acting so that she feels safe and comfortable expressing herself and doing things.*

RESPECT:
* *Listening to her non-judgmentally.*
* *Being emotionally affirming and understanding.*
* *Valuing her opinions.*

SHARED RESPONSIBILITY:
* *Mutually agreeing on a fair distribution of work.*
* *Making family decisions together.*

RESPONSIBLE PARENTING:
* *Sharing parental responsibilities.*
* *Being a positive, nonviolent role model for the children.*

HONESTY AND ACCOUNTABILITY:
* *Accepting responsibility for self.*
* *Acknowledging past use of violence.*
* *Admitting being wrong.*
* *Communicating openly and truthfully.*

TRUST AND SUPPORT:
* *Supporting her goals in life.*
* *Respecting her right to her own feelings, friends, activities, and opinions.* [3]

All these things ought to be present in a BDSM relationship! Some people do heavy role-play situations where they have specific personas that they don't want to break out of... and they still can make sure that all those elements are included. For example, they can keep simultaneous journals about the relationship, and thereby keep up with each others' feelings and consent without breaking out of their roles.

I also think that the list is especially useful in that **it highlights places where non-consensual control is likely to happen... and therefore, places where BDSMers should be especially careful.** For example, failing to support a partner's life goals would be okay in the middle of an intense BDSM encounter. But afterwards, it might be good to give extra support, just because that can be such an important genuine danger spot.

Just like vanilla people, BDSMers have a lot of unspoken elements of our relationships. For example — the partner I mentioned earlier, who held me in place when I gave him a hug on the street. We didn't negotiate that particular act ahead of time. But we have an established relationship, and we've done similar things before; I knew that if I wanted to talk about it — or ask him not to do it — then he'd listen. And, even more importantly, the rest of our relationship lines up with the Equality Wheel.

* * *

This can be found on the Internet at:
http://clarissethorn.com/blog/2011/08/02/thinking-more-clearly-about-bdsm-versus-abuse/

* * *

***

COMMUNICATION:
[theory] What Happens After An S&M Encounter "Gone Wrong"

I wrote this in late 2011. At the time, I didn't mention another factor that makes it important to talk about S&M screwups: we should do it because talking openly about honest mistakes makes it harder for actual abusers to hide in the S&M community. As I note at the end of this piece, sometimes a miscommunication is a real miscommunication, but sometimes it's a "miscommunication" that's covering for abuse. The only way we can learn to distinguish the two is to talk openly about our screwups. It's an intimidating proposition; for one thing, many outsiders leap to label BDSM as "all abuse, all the time," and none of us wants to give those folks anything that they could use for ammunition. But we have to start talking about this stuff more openly, because the alternative is creating a community where it's much easier to get away with abuse.

In Thomas MacAulay Millar's epic series on abuse in the BDSM community, he's got a whole post dedicated to the various types of miscommunications and mythcommunications that can occur: http://yesmeansyesblog.wordpress.com/2012/04/30/theres-a-war-on-part-5-wallowing-in-the-sl-op/

Otherwise, I hope that this piece is a fairly complete treatment of this incredibly difficult topic.

***

I've often thought that BDSMers should talk more about our "failed encounters." Sometimes the best way to learn is through "failure," or by looking at others' "failures." But when a BDSM scene "goes wrong," it's often highly personal for everyone concerned. So it's really hard to talk about and really hard to write about — both for the dominant and submissive partners. This is just like any relationship, really. After all, people rarely talk about their most embarrassing or awkward or otherwise difficult "mistakes made" during vanilla sex, right?

(I use phrases like "failed encounter" and "gone wrong" and "mistakes" with caution, because I think these situations can often be viewed as learning experiences, and therefore they are successful for a lot of purposes! But certainly in the moment they feel like screwups, and a lot of the time they can make the whole relationship very difficult, and I think that most people who have been through them feel as though some kind of failure happened... whether it was a failure of understanding, communication, empathy, caution, or something else.)

Much of the problem, I think, is that people have such a hard time communicating *after* serious miscommunications and mistakes.

The following quotation is from Staci Newmahr's *Playing At The Edge*, an excellent ethnography of the BDSM community. (I've changed a few jargon terms for the sake of accessibility.)

Sophie had been engaged in a long and intimate S&M relationship with Carl, a friend whom she deeply trusted. During the encounter she describes below, Carl changed his approach, and Sophie subsequently felt that Carl was somehow not quite himself. Sophie and Carl never quite recovered from the incident; though they remained friends and tried to do S&M again, it was, according to Sophie, never the same.

Sophie says: "He was very much a rope top. That was his big thing, was tying people up. And he was excellent at tying people up. And our dynamic was always — I mean, yes, he would absolutely hurt me when the time came for that, but there was also always this element — even when he was hurting me, it was done in this incredibly, like, touchingly caring way. And especially when he was tying me up, it was this soothing, wonderful thing."

Sophie continues, "So one day... Carl starts an encounter with me. Carl had decided in his head, from all the things that he's heard me say about how I play with another partner, that that's what I really want from an interaction, in order for it to be the most gratifying and valuable. So we proceeded to have an encounter where Carl was not Carl. And I didn't stop it because it was so like, I couldn't understand what was going on. I couldn't understand why it felt so horrible. And it wasn't that I didn't trust him, because I trust him completely. [...] I just couldn't figure out what the problem is, I felt horrible through the whole thing. And he was so out of touch with me that he wasn't even aware of how horrible I was feeling. The encounter went on for some time... and the second it was over, I... was just, like, you know, traumatized. And he was like, 'Oh my God, what's wrong?' [and] he carried me into the other room. I said something like, 'Where did my Carly go?' and then he started to cry. [...] He's like, 'I was trying to give you this sadistic experience.'"

In Sophie's story, Carl's risk backfires.... The risks were unsuccessful; each ended up emotionally distraught and distant. Ultimately, they sacrificed the relationship. (pages 179-180)

Man, that description is so intense. Let's talk about it.

The first thing worth noting about Sophie's story is that, while she probably had a safeword, she didn't use it: she says that she "didn't stop it." Sometimes, in really confusing S&M scenes, submissives have trouble using their safewords. This does not mean safewords are worthless... but as Thomas MacAulay Millar put it when we wrote about safewords, "Tops can never be on cruise control." Non-verbal signals matter, and if an S&M partner — top or bottom! — starts reacting in an unusual way, it's great to check in with them even if they haven't used their safeword. **Safewords are a useful additional way of communicating about sex, but they can't replace all communication.**

Note also how hard the situation was on the top partner, not just the bottom. Carl ended up crying afterwards!

Next, what I find myself wondering is whether Sophie and Carl could have communicated past this incident. Sophie obviously trusted Carl, and presumably he trusted her. Could they have talked it out and had a successful relationship afterwards? It would have been hard, but maybe they could have done it.

I've (rarely) had similar experiences myself — where boundaries were severely tested, and afterwards it was difficult for both me and my partner to work through it. It can absolutely have an immense impact on the relationship. I write about this a bit in *Confessions of a Pickup Artist Chaser;* here's a quotation from a section in my book where I'm talking to a dominant partner, with whom I just had such a difficult encounter:

Sometimes, these things happen. One partner pushes a boundary, breaks it; maybe the boundary was unspoken; maybe the dominant misreads signals; maybe the submissive didn't yet realize that the boundary was there. When it comes to S&M, these things can be so dramatic... yet sometimes they're nobody's fault. We find these mental and emotional blocks, and we call them landmines.

My partner didn't hit the landmine on purpose. He wasn't trying to push me as hard as he did. And I didn't warn him off. So the important question becomes — how does one deal with such a situation afterwards?

... *"I'm sorry," he said. "I'm really sorry. I never want to do that to you again."*

"It's okay," I said. "These things happen. But please do be careful. But don't worry...." I trailed off, trying to find words.

It's so hard to know how to talk about this, especially with people who aren't used to discussing S&M. When there's a fuckup, sometimes both sides feel betrayed. The submissive might think: "Maybe I didn't tell you exactly what to avoid, but sometimes it's too much to think about, sometimes it's hard to understand in the moment, sometimes I don't know ahead of time. Okay, so I pushed myself too hard, but I did it because I'm so into you; I did it because, in that moment, I lost track of myself. And anyway, I thought you could read me. I thought you understood me. I thought you knew. You've read me perfectly well before; why not this time? Is it that you don't care?"

Whereas the dominant might think: "Maybe I went too far, but I thought I could trust you to stop me. I thought I could trust you to tell me. I don't want to harm you, I just want to push you; I want to break down walls with you. I want to see your eyes go deep and soft. It's not fair for me to feel like I fucked up, because you fucked up, too. I thought you could take care of yourself. I thought you knew. You've communicated perfectly well before; why not this time? Can I rely on you?"

That particular relationship didn't last, and I think that our most difficult encounter probably affected our trust for each other through the end. Still, I can tell you how we worked on it at the time — and I can tell you that it felt really good. We just listened to each other. And we both assumed that the other person had good intent. By the end of talking it out — which admittedly took a really long time; multiple days — I trusted him more than ever and I felt incredibly close to him.

I've been thinking a lot about classic feminist anti-abuse models, which describe how abusers accomplish abuse. One of the tactics abusers consistently use is Minimizing, Denying, and Blaming their partners. Abusers claim that the abuse didn't happen; they claim it wasn't important; they blame their partners for what happened. A partner who is willing to listen and change will respond openly to criticism and to mistakes: a non-abusive partner will not minimize, deny, or blame.

And those three things are what my ex-partner did not do. He never claimed that our difficult encounter didn't happen; he never put the blame on me; he never insisted that it was no big deal. He didn't even come close to doing those things while we talked it through. He took his emotions and dealt honestly with them, and I did my best to do the same.

Also, in BDSM, we often talk about the concept of "aftercare": that is, what we say and do after a BDSM scene to ground ourselves, bring ourselves back into the world, and connect with our partners. It's important to give careful aftercare after any BDSM encounter, but if the encounter has been particularly difficult, it's doubly important. I have personally had good experiences leaving Super Intense Conversations like the one I describe above until post-aftercare, when all partners have calmed down and dealt with any immediate emotional responses.

I'm writing vaguely, so here are **some concrete suggestions for things to say during the conversation after a difficult BDSM encounter:**

* "I'm sorry."
* "I still like you and think you're a good person."
* "Do you want to talk about this now? If not now, then let's set a concrete time for later."
* "I'm feeling really vulnerable and confused right now."
* "Why do you think that happened? How were you reading me, and what were you thinking as you responded to me?"
* "How do we feel about this now that we've discussed it, and how can we keep it from happening again?"
* "What have we learned about landmines? Are there any particular words or actions that are definitely off-limits from now on?"

I have one final super important caveat to add here: **Not all "screwups" are actually screwups. Some are just plain abuse.** A human-shaped predator **will** use words like "miscommunication" and "mistake" to cover up what they do. This post is focused on honest errors, but there are dishonest and evil people out there. In particular, if a person "keeps screwing up"... that's a terribly bad sign. **It is not an inherent part of BDSM to feel roiled up and confused and alienated after a BDSM encounter; most BDSMers feel more intimate and connected after successful encounters.**

UPDATE, March 2012: I just found some notes that I took during a workshop about BDSM edgeplay that was run by Mollena Williams in late December. (Edgeplay is a term for BDSM activities that feel especially intense for the participants.) Mollena suggests some questions to ask beforehand:

* Have I seen my partner do S&M before? What did they say or

do that made me feel good and comfortable? What did they say that made me have an intense reaction? — *Pass this information on to the partner ahead of time.*

* What does my gut feeling say about this person? — *If you have a bad gut feeling about a person, listen to it!* ***Especially** for edgeplay.*

Mollena also suggested that when BDSMers play at the edge, they "make a contingency plan" ahead of time... not just for the participants, but for everyone watching, since such activities often take place at dungeons. She noted that such a "contingency plan" might contain:

* Honesty and thoroughness, of course
* Each partner giving each other explicit permission to safeword
* Each partner giving each other explicit permission for "things to not be okay" afterwards
* Having someone on hand that each partner can talk to afterwards — not necessarily the same person for everyone involved. This person could be an observer, or might know everyone involved in the scene, or might be relatively separate from it all such as a kink-aware therapist, but the really important thing is that this person can give emotional support in every imaginable scenario.

Thanks, Mollena, for the workshop and the thoughts. I've never made such a contingency plan myself, but I definitely think it's worth considering for people who are planning a heavy scene.

* * *

This can be found on the Internet at:
http://clarissethorn.com/blog/2011/12/09/what-happens-after-an-sm-encounter-gone-wrong/

* * *

***

S&M:
[theory] Aftercare or Brainwashing?

I wrote this in 2012.

***

Yes, it's another article about abuse and S&M, but I'm going to cover a lot more than that. I'll talk about intimacy and bodily reactions and how these things build a relationship — whether consensual or abusive. And I'll talk about how to deal with them, too.

Last year, I received an email from a woman who wanted to talk about sexual desire that exists alongside real abuse. She has been abused, but she is sexually aroused by S&M, and she struggles with boundaries a lot. She wrote to me:

Here's what destroys you: that some of us are designed to shut down and feel terror and horror and arousal and shame all at the same time, to crumple before horrible people, to feel aroused even as they genuinely destroy you. This is not in any one's best interest. It's not hot, it's not awesome. And yet it's there.

The worst pain for some of us, that makes you want to scream and not exist and makes you want to scream to the heavens that you want to die and escape being in your own body is not that you are afraid he will come back. It's that you are aroused by the possibility that he will. And other than destroying your very self, you can't stop it. It is the cruelest of design flaws and the worst people understand it and the most compassionate people don't.

However, the conclusion is **not** that some people want abuse. By definition, abuse is something that destroys you, that leaves you feeling violated and harmed in a way you don't want. And part of that mechanism, that involves the desire for the abuse to continue, is that many of us are designed to want more intimacy once intimacy has been initiated with a person. Many of us don't want to be left.

And the agony of feeling harmed by being left by someone you never wanted to be there in the first place is confusing and can be debilitating.

No one wants to be harmed in this way. Among abuse survivor

communities the arousal involved in abuse situations is often called "body betrayal," but this doesn't seem to encompass how deep the desires can be for some people. At the root, the desires are often the same desires that fit into normal healthy intimate relationships. To be loved, to have an ongoing interaction, to be seen and understood at the root of all your emotion, to be taken sexually and feel the pleasure of another enjoying your sexual arousal. But these emotions have been exploited and manipulated for the gain of others.

For some number of people who have experienced abuse, the greatest split within the self does not simply come from how horrific the acts themselves were but from the feelings of desire and pleasure that can happen in human beings even during horrific unwanted acts. For some of us, BDSM can be a safe way to explore unpacking some of this desire and how these arousal patterns got mixed up with horrific things — or were already hooked up to horrific things and that pre-existing fact was exploited by a harmful person. And for some of us, taking that out and playing with it may not be a necessary part of recovery at all.

But simply knowing this — the fact that your arousal and pleasure systems can be activated by harmful people is ok — it does not mean you want it, it does not mean that it was good for you, or that anyone should have treated you in that way. That can be the greatest healing in and of itself.

I want to thank her for allowing me to publish her words. Her description is so far from how I usually discuss or experience S&M; and yet I see connections, too, and people rarely discuss those connections.

* * *

Aftercare: Intimacy Within Positive and Consensual S&M

A while back, a study came out that established that a consenting, positive S&M experience increases a couple's intimacy afterwards. [1] I cite that study all the time, but I still find its existence kinda absurd; I mean, they could have just asked us how it felt. On the bright side, if S&M is being studied by Real Researchers, it's a sign that S&M is becoming more widely accepted. Yet for all its hormone level measurements and mood surveys, I didn't feel like the study got anywhere near the heart of S&M and how S&M creates such extraordinary intimacy. Why would it? Studies are science, and aftercare is art.

I've previously defined aftercare as "a cool-down period after an S&M encounter, which often involves reassurance and a discussion of how things went." That's a decent quick definition, but there's a lot more to it. Bodily violence sometimes creates a mental malleability and vulnerability that can be used in good ways... but also in terrible ways. I see aspects of this in competitive sports, especially the ones that involve fighting and hurting other people very directly. (Have you ever seen that phenomenon where two guys fight each other and then become Best Friends right afterwards?)

Being together with an S&M partner during aftercare can be used to free people, to make them feel amazing and establish extraordinary intimacy. But it can hurt people too; it can hurt them terribly.

Aftercare, like subspace, is one of the most mysterious parts of S&M. Like subspace, a lot of S&Mers describe aftercare in nigh-mystical language. One excellent page of aftercare advice begins by saying:

Aftercare is the last act of the SM drama. It is the culmination, the pulling together of all loose ends, the finishing touches, the final communion between sharers of the SM ritual, the phase where the participants formally give the fantasy scene a context in everyday reality. Its technical purpose is to transition both players from the elevated states created in a scene [i.e., an S&M encounter] back into normalcy, returning to the motor control and awareness they will need to drive home once the scene is over. But as any good SM practitioner will tell you, it's much more than that. It is the time after the action when the participants come together in mutual affirmation that something special was created and shared. It is when affection and closeness is offered and sought. It is, at very least, the proper time to express thanks to the person who has shared this tiny segment of your life with you. It can be, and often is, the most beautiful part of a scene, and it is part of the scene. To skip it altogether is as rude as having dinner at a friend's house and then bolting once you've eaten your fill. [2]

Aftercare is not always extraordinary, the same way S&M isn't always extraordinary. Not everyone wants or needs aftercare, although I've always felt that if you "don't do aftercare," that's something to warn your partner about ahead of time.

I guess from the outside, aftercare often looks like a combination of snuggling and chatting and giggling — sometimes, crying and/or comforting. From the inside, though, aftercare can feel like... a shot of pure empathy. Blissful connection. Words like "basking" and "glowing" and "transcending" come to mind. As someone said to me when I was first getting into S&M: "Very few S&Mers actually enjoy giving or receiving pain. What they like is where pain gets them."

The Practicalities of S&M Intimacy

I believe that S&Mers should try very hard to put boundaries around our S&M interactions; we should work to communicate carefully, and compartmentalize what we do. Consent, and well-communicated boundaries, are the factors that separate S&M from abuse. I talked about those boundaries in "Thinking More Clearly About BDSM versus Abuse," and I also talked about them in "What Happens After an S&M Encounter 'Gone Wrong.'" I've written about S&M communication tactics that enable communication and boundary-setting, from safewords to checklists to keeping simultaneous journals.

Aftercare is part of that boundary-setting process, but a lot of the time, people have a hard time thinking or speaking clearly right after S&M. Some people become incredibly non-verbal, or vague and confused, or giggly, or all of the above. For this reason, some people include later follow-ups (like a next-day phone call) under the umbrella of "aftercare" — the goal is to allow the post-S&M time to be calming and un-challenging, and then talk things through when everyone's head is clearer. Processing things thoroughly after an S&M encounter is really important, especially if the people involved are planning to do it again. It's important for two reasons: it helps the people involved get a better sense of what they want and don't want; and it helps them learn more about how to communicate with their partners.

Recently, I was privileged to give a partner his first heavy S&M experience. Afterwards, when he was coming out of it, he said to me: "No one has ever touched me so deeply, so fast before." I lay with him, listening. I'm pretty sure I did a good job helping him pick up the pieces, but when I try to figure out **what** I did, I have trouble describing it.

So I wouldn't know how to give a step-by-step "how to" for aftercare, but I can offer some thoughts. For one thing, the person who was dominant during the encounter is usually the person who runs the aftercare, too. When I'm in the dominant position, the message I try to get across during aftercare is along these lines: "I'm here, I'm listening, I care about you, you're safe with me, and you can take all the time you need."

In the submissive position, I'm often too busy processing to think carefully about what message I'm getting across to my partner. But sometimes I do get the sense that he's confused or anxious or needs some feedback, at which point I try to get across a message along these lines: "I care about you and I'm so grateful to you for taking on that power just now. If you need to talk, we will do that when I'm more alert. But for now, let's please just be here together and establish our closeness."

And when I'm switching — or when the power dynamic is otherwise unclear — well. I guess I try to get across a combination of those messages.

The Boundaries of S&M Intimacy

I used to be more willing to do S&M "on the first date," when I barely knew my partner. That's changed for two reasons. Firstly, I've become much warier of doing S&M without a strong foundation to the relationship. I've been lucky, because my partners have treated me so well, even the casual ones. (As more stories of S&M and abuse become public, I realize more and more how lucky I've been.) But I don't ever want to be in a position where I do intense S&M and I can't rely on my partner afterwards; and the best way to build a reliable foundation is to spend lots of time together before we get into anything deep.

Secondly, I've become more aware of how quickly S&M can affect me. It's entirely possible to do excellent, intense S&M with someone I can't trust. And if that happens, then boom: I'll be intensely bonded to him, yet unable to trust him. It's not a good place to be. There are some kinds of S&M that feel light or even impersonal to me, but when I do things that feel intense... the bond forms so fast, and it's so incredibly strong. I swear it's a chemical thing. My body will crave him beyond words, even if my brain knows he's a terrible idea.

I once heard about a woman who won't allow herself to have orgasms during casual sex, because she knows the orgasm itself will bond her to her partner. I don't experience orgasms that way. But when a partner really puts me under with S&M, pulls me in deep, and then he gives me aftercare while I surface? That's where I fall in love.

I've heard of polyamorous S&M relationships in which the primary relationship disallows S&M with non-primary partners. I can certainly understand wanting to reserve that for the primary relationship. I've also heard of polyamorous S&M relationships in which the partners can do S&M with outside partners... but won't allow aftercare with outside partners. I can understand that even better.

* * *

Brainwashing: Intimacy Within Abuse

In late 2010, I cross-posted an article about an intense S&M experience to the blog *Feministe*. In the article, I included these words:

There it was. I felt the tears building, gasps torn from my throat, I felt myself starting to fall apart and reform: around him, around his guidance and force and demands. Almost unable to think. Until finally he relented and said my name, and said softly, "Come back," and ran his hand reassuringly down my hair.

There it was: the reason I want it so much.

In response, a commenter named FormerWildChild wrote:

For some of us, the idea of being hit by another person makes us want to jump up and run out of our skin. It seriously wigs us out. It is not a moral judgment; is a true phobia for another person. It reminds me of when we were at the un-civilized end of Grand Canyon with our children. All that stood between my kids and certain death was inches of loosely packed sand. When we were done sightseeing, I discreetly walked behind the van and threw up until I could breathe again.

I had that same terrified feeling when I read about your account of your last session. I wanted to go wrap a blanket around you, hold you in my arms and feed you tea and cookies until I can finally breathe again.

And my fear is not because I fail to really "get" what you experience. It comes from an absolute recognition of what you describe.

I have experienced what you described at the end of your BDSM session, the breaking and reforming of yourself around someone. I have felt exactly what you are talking about, that feeling of finally letting go, of surrendering, and the other person sensing that you are finally there, and then stopping. I have felt the sweetness of those moments of post-thrashing closeness when tenderness seems to hover in the room. I know the feeling of intense closeness which can follow the next day. The air is filled with a cathartic cleanness, the experience of inflicting pain and of receiving pain has cleared the air better than any southern thunderstorm. I can even imagine coming to crave that feeling in the way that you describe.

But I experienced all of those feelings as a child. What you described is precisely what it feels like when an abuser truly lets loose and keeps going until "it" breaks, until there is that moment of catharsis for both the beaten and the person doing the beating. In my experience, those relationships are like playing along the end of the Grand Canyon: people fall in, and they die.

Now, I am willing to believe two things: one, it is possible that my mother and other abusers are actually engaged in a form of BDSM rape when they beat the people that they love. Just as sex is the overpowering and taking of something that should be beautiful and intimate, so beating a loved one to catharsis might just be the same sort of thing. Perhaps that is something that abuse experts should look at.

I am also willing to believe that you have an invisible fence as you play along the edge of your own personal Grand Canyon. I am willing to believe that you know how to be there without falling into the abyss. But if that is the case — that it is safe for you out there, and that I simply need to accept that. Then I will ask you to accept the fact that I will need to go behind the van and toss my lunch. [3]*

At first I was frustrated by that comment, because all I could see was someone saying "I want to throw up when I read about your sexuality," and I was like: grrr. But now I look at that comment, and I see such important points, points that are utterly crucial to the developing language that distinguishes S&M from abuse.

I will say first that I have never personally survived that kind of abuse. But I have received emails from people asking me to write about this, over and over, and I hope that I can help those folks by offering my thoughts. I have also spoken to some abuse experts who tell me that, behind closed doors, they do talk about this: they discuss how the existence of real desire, real catharsis, and real intimacy within an abusive context can look terrifyingly similar to descriptions of S&M encounters.

Rape survivors of all genders sometimes experience physical pleasure and even orgasm while being assaulted. A paper about this was published in the 2004 *Journal of Clinical Forensic Medicine* [4], and there are plenty of first-person accounts around the Internet. Here's an explicit and tremendously saddening quotation from one of them:

I kept physically fighting him off and telling him that though I respected him as my pastor and as a father figure I wanted him to stop. He pushed me, tore my clothes and raped me. ... The pain was incredible as they were very rough and forceful. After what seemed like forever I blacked out. I remember the pastor shaking me hard and slapping me across the face. He then shoved down my throat ten or so Excedrin (a medicinal mixture of pain killer and caffeine) so that I would stay awake.

One of the most disturbing things that happened that night is that I had an orgasm. Despite years of marriage, it was my first orgasm ever. It really confused me. I thought some part of me must be mentally sick to have experienced the pleasure of an orgasm during this horrific trauma. [5]

Here's the thing about consent: **orgasm is not consent**. Physical pleasure is only the body's reaction to certain types of stimulation. Also: sexual desire is not consent. And **love isn't consent, either**. If I feel sexual desire for my partner, and my body feels good when he touches me, and I love him, yet I make it clear that I don't want to have sex right now... then he's still violating my consent if he has sex with me. (Obviously, if I want to say "no" and mean "yes," then it's my responsibility to negotiate that ahead of time and set a safeword.)

In short: **There can be pleasure, desire, and even love existing alongside real abuse. But that doesn't mean it's not abuse.** This is as true with S&M as it is with non-S&M sex.

I once spoke to a person who referred to himself as an abuser, who told me that he'd read descriptions of S&M aftercare, and that he saw his own tactics within them. He told me when he thought about it, he had always considered it to be "brainwashing."

And I can see it. That's the scary part. I really can see it. I can believe that when we have powerful S&M experiences, we tap into the same parts of our brains that could otherwise be used for psychological manipulation and destruction. S&M shows us how to create and utilize enormous mental vulnerability through violence... and vulnerability can always be abused. In the literature exploring the cycle of abuse, people often write about the "reconciliation phase," in which the abuser is all sweetness and light to their victim [6]; I can't help but wonder how much of the "reconciliation phase" could be recognized as non-consensual aftercare. How much of an abuser's power over their victim might come from the mental malleability that cautious S&Mers learn to respect?

This does not mean that our bodies are broken. The woman whose words I published at the top of this article called it "the cruelest of design flaws and the worst people understand it and the most compassionate people don't." But we don't have to perceive this as a flaw — it's not a flaw any more than orgasms are a flaw. Some S&M instructors compare S&M mental states to "altered states," like being drunk; there's nothing wrong with being drunk, but people should be careful with alcohol. Our bodies are instruments with certain powers and vulnerabilities that we must respect.

This power and vulnerability is one of the biggest reasons I do the writing that I do. Because although they're invisible, I do have a sense of the fences that FormerWildChild talked about when she commented at *Feministe:* the fences that keep S&Mers from falling into the Grand Canyon of abuse. Those invisible fences around the canyon are constructed from self-awareness, self-esteem, respect, and consent.

Building Fences Around The Canyon

How do we build fences around the canyon? We build them by seeking to understand our desires, and talk openly with our partners, and respect our partners' limits. So I write about communication and self-examination and learning to value my boundaries... and I hope it will help people learn what it means to play at the edge, rather than falling into the canyon.

This is scary, loaded, complicated territory. I certainly don't have all the answers. But I have ideas on how we might begin finding answers from here.

Firstly, S&Mers and feminists both need to be aware of this emotional and biological phenomenon. It can create a sense of overwhelming intimacy with unexpected partners. And it can be used as a tool by abusers who groom relationships that started consensually into abusive relationships.

Secondly, we must keep talking about communication and boundary-setting. An important part of this discussion is openly discussing what happens when well-intentioned S&Mers screw up, and how we deal with that. Again, I wrote about that in "What Happens After an S&M Encounter '"Gone Wrong.'" Thomas MacAulay Millar has a great post that lists the mistakes that can happen within S&M. [7] He mentions, for example, that sometimes there are genuine physical "technical" errors; sometimes people also hit "landmines" or unexpected psychological problems. Talking openly about screwups makes it harder for abusers to claim that they "just screwed up."

Thirdly, within our communities, we need to spread the word — especially to people who we believe might be inexperienced or vulnerable or otherwise in a position to have this used against them.

* * *

After June 16, 2012, this can be found on the Internet at:
http://clarissethorn.com/blog/2012/06/16/sm-aftercare-or-brainwashing

* * *

***

COMMUNICATION:
[theory] Feminist S&M Lessons From the Seduction Community

This was originally split into three parts and published in 2011 at GoodMenProject.com. Obviously, it covers some territory that I also cover in Confessions of a Pickup Artist Chaser, *but the book is much chattier and has more fun anecdotes. Also, you should totally buy the book. Okay, I'll stop advertising it now.*

***

There is an enormous subculture devoted to teaching men how to seduce women. Within the last half-decade or so, these underground "pickup artists" have burst into the popular consciousness, aided by Neil Strauss's bestselling book *The Game* and VH1's hit reality show *The Pick-Up Artist*.

Pickup artists — also known as the "seduction community" — exchange ideas in thousands of online fora, using extensive in-group jargon. One pickup artist site lists "over 715 terms, and counting." [1] There are pickup artist meetups, clubs, and subculture celebrities all over the world. There are different ideological approaches and theoretical schools of seduction. Well-known pickup artist "gurus" can make millions of dollars per year: they may sell books; they may sell hours of "coaching"; they may organize training "bootcamps" or conventions with pricy tickets; they may run companies full of instructors trained in their methods. The community even generates its own well-thought-out internal critiques. [2]

I am a sex-positive feminist lecturer and writer. I write primarily about my experiences with sadomasochism, but I have a general interest in sexuality. I first encountered pickup artists when smart ones started attending my educational events and commenting on my blog.

Some aspects of pickup artistry are hugely problematic; many parts of the community showcase and encourage misogyny. While exploring the PUA jungle, I observed things that turned my stomach and brought tears to my eyes. On the other hand, I had to admit that some pickup artist perspectives were very interesting. Some had fascinating insights about gender theory and social power. I also felt drawn by their exploits. Learning seduction, and watching hypothetically-dazzling Casanovas run a courtier-like game, sounded like an extremely fun way to spend my time.

I started my journey by talking to a few pickup artists and reading their fora. By the end, I had given a lecture at a seduction convention, and I had decided against developing my own coaching business. Today, I can offer a quick synopsis of my own history, and why I became so interested in PUAs. I will break down some elementary distinctions among the men of the seduction community. Finally, I will offer a few PUA-influenced thoughts on feminist goals.

* * *

I was an awkward little bookworm of a child, but at least I was creative. I liked to draw, invent games, and run amateur social experiments. When I was in high school, most of my friends were on the Internet; I did not date a real-life boyfriend until college. I was inevitably teased by my peers, but even when treated well, I rarely engaged with the social hierarchies around me. I had difficulty grasping how social mechanics were "supposed" to work. A lot of things seemed obvious to other people that were not obvious to me.

For example, in sixth grade, a female friend of mine teased me about flirting with a boy. "What was I doing?" I asked. "Come on, you were flirting!" she responded. While I thought I almost understood what she meant, I was unsure — so I set out to poll everyone I knew about what constitutes "flirting." Responses were inconsistent. One person said, very definitely: "Giggling." Others cited examples such as "intense looks" or "making jokes."

By the end of this experiment, I concluded that no one seemed able to explain "flirting" in terms of consistent behaviors; there were few commonalities in my final list. From what I could tell, flirting could only be explained in terms of invisible interpersonal dynamics. I found this both entertaining and frustrating.

I sometimes wonder what would have become of me if the modern pickup artist community had existed back then, and I had discovered it. PUAs devote a lot of time to understanding seduction in terms of observed behaviors. They have terms for social tactics that run the gamut from creating rapport, to encouraging trust, to building sexual tension, to shifting social power. But although the purpose of these social tactics is to manipulate emotion, the tactics are typically described as concretely as possible. Some PUA coaches provide long memorized "routines," but it is more common to talk about particular social actions or broader strategies.

One famous PUA tactic is called the "neg." "Neg" stands for "negative hit," and one site defines a neg as "a remark, sometimes humorous, used to point out a woman's flaws." [3] Like many PUA terms, the deeper meanings and usage vary from PUA to PUA — but there is an especially dramatic range of meanings with "neg."

Some PUAs see negs as friendly teasing: a way for the PUA to show that he is paying attention to the girl, without appearing needy or overeager. I can offer a cute example of this approach from my own life. I was sitting in a café with a former PUA, and he gazed deep into my eyes.

"Wait a minute," he said slowly. "Are your glasses held together by epoxy? It looks like you had to repair them at the corners."

"Yeah," I admitted.

He grinned. "Everything about you just screams 'starving artist,' doesn't it."

This made me laugh for quite a while. I think it worked because he understood that I have chosen (for now) to be a broke writer — but he also recognized the tension I feel about that choice. So this gentleman was demonstrating that he correctly discerned my priorities; that he is not bothered by a choice that makes me feel self-conscious; and that he is confident enough to tease me.

Also, at a moment when I thought he might compliment my eyes, the former PUA shook up my expectations by breaking the romantic pattern. Often, effective flirting involves offering the right mixture of confidence plus charming novelty plus paying attention.

Some PUAs see negs more strategically, as a way of passing a woman's "tests" or breaching her indifference. They argue that this is necessary for women who are very high-status, very beautiful, etc. They argue that some women develop a kind of immunity to compliments, and that some women actively prefer feisty, faux-adversarial flirting. Most PUAs only advocate using negs on women who meet a certain "minimum" level of attractiveness, or who seem particularly feisty. Neil Strauss, a famous PUA and author of the bestseller *The Game: Penetrating the Secret Society of Pickup Artists,* once wrote that:

When you give a woman who's often hit on a generic compliment, she will usually either ignore the remark or assume you're saying it because you want to sleep with her.

When you tease her and show her that you're unaffected by her beauty and demonstrate that you're out of her league — and THEN let her work to win you over and ultimately REWARD her with your approval, she will leave that night feeling good about herself. Like something special happened and she connected with somebody who appreciates her for who she REALLY is.

In short, a neg will buy you the credibility you need to sincerely compliment her later.

That said, I don't necessarily advocate negs; they are in many ways a temporary patch to stick onto your personality while you learn to possess real confidence and strength of character. [4]

Although this is a manipulative approach, it is not inevitably harmful. It also is not limited to the sphere of sexual relationships; humans often pretend not to care what other people think, and consistently attempt to be taken seriously by others. Additionally, for many people, flirting involves a certain amount of strategic ambiguity and plausible deniability, and negs are a useful tactic for that kind of game. Not everyone likes playing such tacit and confusing games, but many people do.

However, this is all cute and mild compared to how some PUAs talk about negs: some cite the neg specifically as a tactic to make the girl feel bad.

A well-known PUA who goes by the name of Tyler Durden once wrote that: "You use self-esteem negs to lower the target's self-esteem, and crave your attention to re-validate herself." [5] Similarly, an especially pitiless PUA blogger who is sometimes described as "the Darth Vader of PUAs" writes that:

The best negs are those which are conceivably meant as compliments, but which linger in her psyche for hours afterward, undermining her self-conception and encouraging her to qualify herself to you [i.e. encouraging her to explain why she's worth your time].... [A neg] infiltrates a girl's subconscious so that she spends more mental energy analyzing her worth than she does analyzing yours. [6]

One commenter adds to the above blogger's words that: "So long as you have a woman auditioning for you, power remains where it belongs — squarely in your pocket."

In other words, a person who feels anxious and unworthy will be easier to control. These cruel PUAs have learned the same lesson as thousands of people in abusive relationships.

Here is an especially instructive quotation from the comments on

"Darth Vader's" blog: "[Women] really are insipid, vapid airheads. If it wasn't for the pussy, there would be a bounty on them." [7] That statement is interesting not just because of its hatred but because of its fear. After all, no one puts a bounty on targets that are not dangerous. The most misogynist corners of the PUA subculture not only discuss ways to aggressively manipulate women; they also paint women as selfish, deceitful and hazardous.

The various approaches to negging highlight both the different shadings of opinion across the subculture, and a particularly important distinction among PUAs themselves. Some of these men genuinely do enter pickup artistry out of a desire to connect to women. As one PUA told me, "When I first looked at PUA stuff, I was like, 'This is so sleazy and gross.' But I'd never had a girlfriend, and I kept telling myself, 'Dude, you are lonely and miserable and you don't want to die alone.'" On the other hand, many PUAs become PUAs because they want unilateral power and control over women — and many PUAs attempt to justify this through narratives and jokes that encourage fear and anger against women.

* * *

Aside from the "connection" vs. "control" distinction, there is also a distinction between PUAs who are seeking what is essentially self-help, and those who aren't.

The PUA concept that best illustrates this is "inner game." Inner game is, essentially, genuine confidence and sense of purpose. It contrasts with "outer game" — i.e., the things a PUA says and does to attract women. A "neg" would count as "outer game," for example.

Most successful PUAs reach a point where they decide that, in the words of one coach: emotionless "sport-fucking kinda sucks." (Some PUAs start at this point, but that is a bit unusual.) They conclude that it's time to pull back from the game; to seek longer-term or more emotionally connected sex; to examine their priorities; and to discover interests aside from picking up new girls. Finding themselves in this way can be described as "inner game." The men who discuss inner game often talk about developing their own businesses, exercising regularly, keeping a healthier diet, accepting their own vulnerabilities, pursuing hobbies, and improving their connections with people of all genders.

Most PUAs also realize that women respond well to genuine confidence and sense of purpose. This could be seen as ironic:

notwithstanding the fact that "inner game" emphasizes self-improvement, the concept is still centered on seducing women. However, despite the fact that "inner game" is centered on gaming ladies, its ultimate result is usually to encourage PUAs to think about what they really want from life. PUA coach Mark Manson once wrote that, "You don't end up in the Pick Up Artist community unless you are incredibly unhappy or unsatisfied about something. It may be conscious, it may be unconscious. It may be short-term, or it may be deep-seated and long-term." [8] He later wrote to me by email that: "This is a giant self-help community in disguise." I also once interviewed Neil Strauss himself, who said he hoped that his famous book *The Game* could become "the beginning of a men's self-help movement — because self-help isn't emasculating anymore if you're doing it to get laid." [9]

Interestingly, Neil Strauss also told me that he agreed with feminism in many ways, and said things like: "We still are a patriarchal society." Many feminists felt that my interview with him was full of problematic statements, and his words were picked apart by feminist readers. I do not disagree with many feminist critiques of what Strauss said — but considering where Strauss was coming from, his words were extraordinarily supportive of feminism. One feminist commented to me that, "I don't understand why you're not more critical of this guy." [10] In response, it is worth noting how an anti-feminist writer responded to Strauss's words:

Whether Strauss is an ignorant fool or an opportunist liar who wants to appease feminists in order to avoid negative feedback is anyone's guess, but if his words are anything to go by, we can safely assume that the best-known public advocates of Game are perfectly OK with parroting feminist dogma. [11]

For the few, mild pro-feminist statements Strauss made, some PUAs deride him as either an "ignorant fool or an opportunist liar." (Others hurled particularly misogynist insults such as "mangina.") This is both a demonstration of how vitriolic PUA anti-feminist sentiment can become, and an example of the social shaming that sometimes leads men in the PUA community to avoid associating themselves with anything resembling feminist thought or woman-friendly perspectives.

Clearly, many men view pickup artistry as a kind of therapy. The community can be a support group for self-confidence and self-improvement. Unfortunately, many corners of the seduction community are also a support group for virulent misogyny. Some feminists argue that any man who seeks self-help through the seduction community is effectively embracing misogyny, because so much of the community is misogynist. However, some PUA students could be interpreted as seeking self-help from the only avenue they see as acceptable, if they are coming from a culture that usually defines self-help as un-masculine or anti-masculine. Again, note that Neil Strauss said: "self-help isn't emasculating anymore if you're doing it to get laid."

The most confusing thing about misogyny among PUAs is that although some more-misogynist PUAs separate themselves consciously from non-misogynist PUAs, and vice versa, the groups still overlap a great deal. Even PUA-influenced men who prioritize non-misogyny, and are willing to talk to a feminist writer like me, often seem to soak up misogynist ideas from the rest of the subculture. At one point, I talked to one PUA I thought was committed to being non-sexist... until he expounded quite seriously upon how his favorite PUA blogger thinks the USA would be better off if women did not vote. One goal of my book, *Confessions of a Pickup Artist Chaser,* is to draw clearer lines: to give examples of PUAs and PUA approaches that seem more abusive or inclined towards harm, as opposed to approaches that seem mostly playful, harmless or even positive.

* * *

Although I want to cry when I see statements like, "If it wasn't for the pussy, there would be a bounty on women," I try not to let it distract me from some insights emerging from the seduction community. By focusing empirically and pragmatically on the process of sexual escalation, PUAs are approaching gender norms in a way that many people — including feminists — usually do not. Also, I can relate to some PUAs because some PUAs have the same history of social anxiety that I do.

I have another personal reason for feeling uncomfortable painting PUAs as "the enemy." When feminists criticize how PUAs approach sexuality, I have mixed feelings, because I myself am known for sexual desires that are unpopular with some feminists. As I grew out of being an awkward little bookworm nerd, as I began dating and exploring my sexual needs, I started to understand my sexuality as being heavily involved with BDSM.

Consensual BDSM is a heavily stigmatized type of sexuality, although some sexologists have argued that it might be viewed as a sexual orientation. Many feminists marginalize BDSM just as much as the rest of society does — or more. Famous German feminist Alice Schwarzer once said: "Female masochism is collaboration," and a recent history of *Ms. Magazine* quotes a co-founding editor who recalls that:

I threatened to leave over a manuscript by a woman who was a former editor of ours who was writing about why she was a masochist and trying to make it an okay choice. I would rather leave than work for a magazine that published that. And we didn't publish it. [12]

As a result, notwithstanding my considerable feminist writing and activism, I live in fear of my "feminist card" being revoked because of my BDSM identity.

Yet, simultaneously, my practice of BDSM has greatly informed my feminist understanding. Rape and consent are both very important feminist issues, and much of the BDSM community obsessively examines sexual consent. The dominant BDSM community "mantra" is "SSC: Safe, Sane, and Consensual." Some people debate whether another "mantra" would be better, but I have never heard of someone removing the "consensual" part. Indeed, the ways many BDSMers think of sexual consent overlap dramatically with the ways that many feminists think of it.

Safewords are a famous and high-profile example of careful BDSM communication tactics. They are specific code words that any participant can use to stop the sexual action at any time. Safewords are important in a context where one partner might want to scream "No!" or "Please don't!" or "Mercy!" with no intention of actually stopping the action.

Safewords serve another, stealthier, but equally important function: they bring home the idea that consent is a continuously changing process. Consent is part of the ongoing sexual negotiation that takes place between two people. Here, BDSM consent ideas overlap heavily with feminist consent ideas. For example, one article by high-profile feminist Jaclyn Friedman pushes back against dominant conceptions of consent by stating that "consent is not a lightswitch." As Friedman writes:

Sexual consent isn't like a lightswitch, which can be either "on," or "off." It's not like there's this one thing called "sex" you can consent to anyhow. "Sex" is an evolving series of actions and interactions. You have to have the enthusiastic consent of your partner for all of them. And even if you have your partner's consent for a particular activity, you have to be prepared for it to change. [13]

Safewords are, effectively, a constant reminder that "you have to be prepared for [consent] to change."

BDSMers and feminists tend to teach explicit, straightforward verbal sexual communication — in contrast to the seduction community, which typically teaches non-verbal or playfully tacit sexual communication. For example, the seduction community has an extensive array of discussions about how to initiate flirtatious touching, which PUAs refer to as "kino." The seduction community also places a strong emphasis on developing skill at reading a social situation without asking exactly what is going on; if a PUA is good at understanding implicit social signals, he is described as "calibrated."

For BDSMers and feminists, the sexual consent territory continues to overlap after safewords. Huge factions, if not majorities, within both groups have concluded that the best way to encourage consent is not merely to encourage people to understand that they can withdraw consent at any point — but to encourage open communication and self-knowledge about sex.

Among feminists, an example of this approach is Jaclyn Friedman's brand-new book *What You Really, Really Want: The Smart Girl's Shame-Free Guide to Sex and Safety*. *Salon's* Tracy Clark-Flory notes in an interview with Friedman that:

The book is filled with writing exercises that prompt readers to reflect on everything from body image to sexual assault. It's essentially a guide to writing one's own personal sexual manifesto. [14]

Among BDSMers, an example of this approach is the multi-page checklists that some BDSMers use. (I already wrote about this in my piece "Sex Communication Tactic Derived From S&M: Checklists," reprinted earlier in this book; just in case you haven't read it, I'll briefly describe them.) Checklists are essentially lists of every conceivable BDSM-related act; each act on the checklist looks something like this:

FLOGGING — GIVING _____ O O O O O
FLOGGING — RECEIVING _____ O O O O O

Each partner rates each entry by filling out 1-5 bubbles, with 1 darkened bubble meaning "Not interested" and 5 bubbles meaning "I crave this!" This type of explicit communication is both an excellent way to help partners understand each other's desires — and to help partners understand each other's boundaries. In a way, this sort of thing could be seen as "Master Class" consent communication.

This was the context whence I emerged when I started investigating pickup artistry. I am a feminist, but I'm a flavor of feminist with a troubled history within the movement. I am an advocate for explicit communication, but I believe that no aspect of consent should be ignored, and I am concerned that many feminists and BDSMers give a certain unwarranted privilege to explicit verbal communication over implicit or non-verbal communication.

People seem likely to develop a preference for explicit communication if it seems more necessary. For instance, many BDSMers develop a preference for explicit communication because our desires are unusual and precise, and complicated words will help us get what we want. Feminists develop the same preferences because explicit communication is the clearest way to ensure sexual consent. Accordingly, some people attempt to promote explicit sexual communication by saying: *We should make it necessary.*

Here's an example exchange from the comments on a thoughtful feminist BDSM blog. A male commenter asks:

I once had an argument with a very good female friend of mine about kissing. She was perturbed about a date who asked her if he could proceed to kiss her. She said the man should just know. It should be instinctual and u lose the moment as soon as u ask. I said that was bs, the first move is one of the most nerve wracking things, the very fact that he asked shows his politeness and tact and frankly a lack of presumptuousness.... What do you think? What's the line between politeness and passivity?

The feminist blogger, an intelligent and awesome lady who goes by the name Holly Pervocracy, responds that:

I don't say this very often, but "you lose the moment as soon as you ask" girls really are ruining it for the rest of us.

As far as I'm concerned, they can go without ever being kissed until they wise up.

However, I think (or would like to think? augh) that most girls are not like that, and that you should not plan for girls to be like that. I'd definitely rather offend someone by asking than offend them by not asking. [15]

Holly implies that people who don't like explicit communication should effectively be banned from kissing: she says, "they can go without ever being kissed until they wise up." I have a certain cantankerous sympathy for this perspective, and I have said similar things myself in the past. But my research into pickup artists made me wonder about whether this perspective is tenable, given a world in which most people seem to enjoy and engage in a great deal of tacit communication.

Speaking only for myself, I must admit that I like it when a man can read my unspoken signals well enough that he can tell when to kiss me without asking aloud. Sometimes it can be nice when a guy asks. But if he can read my tacit communication about kissing, that is a signal that he can read a lot of my other tacit communication as well.

Furthermore, if many people really enjoy unspoken social games and strategic uncertainty, then "the game" will never go away. Evidence that people enjoy those things does not only include the pickup artist subculture — romantic comedies and romance novels consistently find a market, after all.

Additionally, part of improving sexual communication means learning more about unspoken communication — not just spoken communication. The pioneering social economist Peter F. Drucker once said, "The most important thing in communication is to hear what isn't being said." This maxim is no less true when it comes to sex than it is in any other area of human endeavor. PUAs have spent years gathering information on tacit sexual communication, so perhaps one feminist goal should be to try and understand what they've learned, such as the characteristics of excellent social "calibration."

Some feminists and BDSMers exist who already think a lot about teaching implicit or unspoken communication. On the feminist side, one webpage about sexual violence features an image of a woman saying: "I stopped kissing you back. I pushed your hand away. I said I wanted to leave. It all meant 'NO'." [16] On the BDSM side, there is often an expectation that BDSM partners will discuss their experience and reactions once they are done doing BDSM with each other, so as to learn more about how to read each other's tacit signals. However, I have never encountered a BDSM seminar on the topic of non-verbal communication, though I've attended several on verbal communication.

My perspective on non-verbal communication is not without precedent among feminist BDSMers, though my willingness to deal extensively with PUAs might be. Still, I believe that non-verbal communication is not taught well, and that feminists and BDSMers in particular do not spend enough time discussing its role in sexual interactions. Given that both communities emphasize that consent and communication are crucially intertwined, perhaps both communities might draw insight from some PUA conceptions of "kino," "calibration" and other ways of examining implicit communication.

I once started a thread about pickup artists on a major feminist blog, to which one feminist responded: "I'm getting so sick of these PUA threads.... So I'll just come out and say it: PUAs rape women through coercion and manipulation. Full stop." [17]

There are a lot of things about pickup artistry that I really do not like. There were points during my PUA adventures when I learned about incidents and strategies that blatantly sound like rape. This is a huge can of worms, and I discussed it at great length in my book. For now I will only note that there is an entire PUA area of inquiry called "Last Minute Resistance" (or "LMR"): that is, what happens when a woman resists having sex. "Last Minute Resistance tactics" ("LMR tactics") are designed to convince a woman who has expressed hesitance, distaste or discomfort to have sex anyway.

"The first two 'no's don't mean much, and should be expected," advises one PUA while outlining LMR tactics. [18] This is exactly the kind of thing that gives the community a bad name. In fairness, some PUAs talk about trying to understand why a girl is uncomfortable, and then addressing the root cause of her discomfort. For example, a PUA might advise asking whether she is menstruating, and then reassuring her that he won't be grossed out by having sex if she is. Some PUAs try to claim that most LMR tactics are harmless and communicative, but this is a difficult claim to defend. I have always been more impressed by the few PUAs who simply advocate respecting Last Minute Resistance, such as David Shade:

Do not push against last minute resistance. You will be like all the other guys who objectify women and do not respect her as a real person. And it will reek of desperation.

... In fact, move things along just slightly slower than she'd like it. Make her wait. It builds that sexual tension, and it makes her think. When she is away from you, she is going to think about it a lot. [19]

Of course, while Shade is advising his clients to respect boundaries, he's advising them to respect boundaries as a tactic for seducing the woman eventually. Another example of this approach comes from Mark Manson, who appears more interested in respecting women for the sake of respecting women, but whose main thrust is still seduction advice:

In [an LMR situation], there's always a fork in the road: you can do the typical freeze-out/high-pressure PUA bullshit to try to manipulate her or annoy her into giving up the resistance. Or you can be honest about the situation and resign yourself to accepting the fact that you may not have sex tonight.

Guys, listen. Always, always, always go with the second option. It may sound counter-intuitive, but you have to go with the second option. Not only because it's the right thing to do. Not only because it's what any respectful human being should do. But because if you make it clear that there is absolutely no pressure for her to sleep with you, if you show her that you can be trusted and that you're OK with whatever she decides (and by the way, you do need to be OK with whatever she decides), then she's going to become ten times more comfortable with you, and therefore is actually more likely to WANT to have sex with you. [20]

PUA frameworks and tactics are often consent-friendly. Many "LMR tactics" encourage pushiness or even outright non-consensual behavior, such as ignoring the woman when she says, "No." Yet things I discussed in previous sections of this article – such as "negs," and body-language "kino" tactics — are clearly neutral: their usage is shaped mostly by the goals of individual PUAs and the social context in which they occur. Discussions of social "calibration" — increasing one's capacity to read social situations — as well as "inner game" and being attractive by improving oneself will generally be a positive good. Indeed, it could be argued that no PUA tactics are inherently abusive, but some are more obviously susceptible to being used badly... the same way a sword is more obviously susceptible to evil usage than a table.

Previous feminist writers have usually preferred to complain about the seduction community's misogyny rather than examining the community deeply. I have been more interested to see whether I could understand and make use of the positive PUA theories. Understanding the "Darth Vader" types might be useful, too. There is a percentage of PUAs who are non-consensually hurting women, and if we learn how those men do it, we might also figure out how to disarm them.

I must acknowledge that I eventually felt that the community was damaging, poisonous, and unhealthy for me — to the extent that I needed to get out and detox. (PUA detox is a recognized phenomenon even among some PUAs... and former PUAs. [21]) However, there are truths within it that are both intriguing and important.

I have never quite erased my fear of having my "feminist card" revoked, although it is not clear how "feminists" — a fractious group if ever there was one — could withdraw my presence in the movement. There is no Central Standards Bureau for feminists. Perhaps inevitably, the feminist reaction to *Confessions of a Pickup Artist Chaser* was quite mixed... although some other feminists appear to agree that there are important and interesting things to learn from PUAs about gender, culture, and feminist consent models.

An overall lesson here might be that thinkers with a lot in common are increasingly isolated from each other through the accelerating Balkanization of detailed, insular, interest-based subcultures. Like the drive towards interdisciplinary research in academia, perhaps a kind of interdisciplinary subcultural approach is being developed by those of us more interested in building bridges than burning them.

* * *

This can be found on the Internet at:
http://clarissethorn.com/blog/2012/02/27/feminist-sm-lessons-from-the-seduction-community/

* * *

* * *

S&M:
[storytime] The Strange Binary of Dominance and Submission

I wrote this in early 2012, and it was originally published at RoleReboot.org. If I had to summarize my relationship with this gentleman today, then ironically enough, I'd say that "it got complicated and I'm pretty sure it's over now." I still like this piece, though.

* * *

It's been a while since I felt simultaneously very into someone, and very sure about him. It's a strange feeling. I've been playing with theories about how "flirtation is basically an exercise in strategic ambiguity" and "insecurity is an integral part of romantic intoxication" and "uncertainty is an emotional amplifier," and I do think that those ideas are true in many ways. But I got so wrapped up in theory that I forgot how it feels to be way into someone... and only a little bit scared.

* * *

I met Mica at a Saturday night party. When I left the next morning, he said he wanted to see me again as soon as possible. "Monday?" he asked. "Tuesday?"
"Monday," I said. "Tomorrow."
He's a smart, creative thinker. There are layers to him, and he practically shines: so why not name him for the mineral Mica? I would love talking to him for those reasons alone. But there's also a kind of certainty to him; a calm presence; an extraordinary quality of attention. Once he's focused on a partner, there's a rhythm behind everything he does. He's so precise that when I'm kissing him, I feel like an awkward puppy.

I observed this very quickly, and something else: that the quality of his attention — often **overtook** him. Controlled him. In a sexual interaction, it's difficult to distract him from catering to me. And since he's excellent at reading my desires, I usually don't **want** to distract him.

It made me think of what I was like, years ago, before I understood my submissive tendencies. Mica hadn't done much explicit S&M before, and when he'd done it, he was dominant. I didn't want to project too much, or make any assumptions about him... but I couldn't help noticing.

The second night I was with him, I asked him to inflict light pain on me. Very light. I didn't want to go further with him, yet. But his instincts for delivering pain and watching my reactions were, as I suspected, beautifully calibrated.

The third night I was with him, he touched my face and kissed me. I felt my eyelashes flutter and my body melt, and he smiled. Then he said, "I'm feeling really gentle tonight. I don't know how much I'm up for."

He doesn't want S&M right now, I thought. Sometimes guys date me and get anxious that I'll be disappointed when they don't want to do S&M. This is understandable, given that I'm an S&M writer. But I hate that, because the last thing I want is for one of my partners to feel obligated... and besides, even I don't want all-S&M-all-the-time. I smiled directly into Mica's eyes and told him I was fine with it.

In bed, I watched him. Watched his extraordinary attentiveness. Eventually we got to a point where I was leaning over him, kissing him. I watched him give up his body to the kiss. *He doesn't want S&M right now,* I thought... *except that his main experience with S&M, so far, is being in charge.*

"Do you trust me?" I asked him.

"Yes," he said. "Absolutely."

I clenched my nails into Mica's side, and his back arched. It was the clearest invitation I'd seen from him and, I suspected, the clearest invitation he knew how to give. If he even knew that he was giving it. It can take a lot of time and experience for a submissive to learn what they want well enough to give good feedback for it. It's one of those submissive skills that people don't think about enough, because for some reason we're always too busy teaching dominant skills. [1]

I kissed Mica again, and tore into his back.

He was ready for it. His breathing fast became irregular; he gasped; he shook in my hands. After a while, I pulled back and simply observed the intensity flooding through him. His body undulated like a wave.

"I knew you were dangerous," he breathed. "In exactly the way that I want."

"Dangerous," I repeated. I hesitated. "What do you mean?" His eyelashes flickered, and I saw that he was too far under to answer me. He probably barely knew what he was saying. (In S&M, we call this state of mind subspace.)

I pushed him a little farther. I only used my nails, but you can do a lot with your nails. I said his name, over and over. He struggled, he fought his own body. I observed the struggle and saw myself in it. "I know," I told him.

Eventually Mica said, quite seriously, that he wanted to stop. I was certain that he could take more. A lot more. I might have been able to convince him to continue, and had him thank me for it later. But he needs to know that I'll respect him when he says to stop. Also, in a somewhat self-interested way, I don't want to set a precedent where his boundaries are entirely nonverbal; where his limits depend on my capacity to see through him. Maybe someday, when we know each other really well. Right now, it would make it too easy to seriously harm him... and for him to hate me afterwards.

So I stopped.

"No one has ever touched me so deeply, so fast before," Mica said, later. And, later later: "This changes **everything**." I lay still, kept my arms around him, listening. "That was total catharsis," he said. "I mean —" a note of doubt crept into his voice. "Do you actually **like** doing that?"

"Yes," I said. I said it fast and hard, because he needs to believe it. I understood why he was asking: I've been there. When I was first getting into S&M, the first time I felt that way, I had a hard time believing that my partner actually liked doing that for me. It felt so incredible. It felt like I couldn't possibly be giving back as much as I received. Sometimes, I still feel that insecurity.

"I'm glad you like it," Mica said. I felt his body relax next to mine. "Because I'm going to want that again."

"I know," I said softly.

I tried not to be afraid. Not only because I like him so much, and it's easy to be afraid. But because someone like Mica, who wants so much to give, can be seriously damaged by a partner who isn't careful to offer him space to be exactly who he is.

And, most of all, because S&M is a complex and fickle mistress. Because I knew that if Mica expected me to be able to do that regularly, he was bound to be disappointed. His tendencies are there, and I can learn them, but this one "total catharsis" depended on a confluence of factors: there had been something close to his surface, something he'd practically begged me to pull out, and it had been his first time.

Plus, S&M also depends on self-maintenance and reasonable expectations and respecting our own failures. An S&M relationship will be much less stable if the people involved can't accept imperfection.

I was scared, scared, **scared** that Mica believed me to be more amazing than I could ever possibly be.

* * *

The next day, Mica was thrilled by his scratches, and showed them off to me. I was pleased by how he eroticized the marks — I do that, too — but I also felt a moment of piercing guilt. "I'm sorry," I said. "I should have been more careful, before leaving marks like that. I should have asked."

Mica met my eyes directly, insistently. "No," he said. "Don't be sorry. Last night was amazing. You knew exactly where I needed to go."

I pushed back my fear — *he expects too much of me* — and answered quietly. I ended by telling him, "S&M can't be that, all the time." He nodded. I hoped he was listening.

Fortunately, he was. The next time we did it, Mica was slightly disappointed that it wasn't mind-blowing — as I knew he would be. But he dealt with it. He articulated the disappointment to me, and he remembered that I'd warned him, and he said that he was prepared to take things as they came. And then, lying on his side next to me, watching me, he asked: "Do you want pain?"

I felt my eyes widen. I felt a spike of fear. I was already so into him. I knew that if I allowed him to get me to subspace, there'd be no going back.

"Yes," I said.

And again, that attention. In a way, sometimes, Mica's attentiveness can be strangely inconvenient. He's almost over-attuned to my desires. Even when I tell him to close his eyes, he can't lose himself that way; he can't make himself keep them closed. The quality of his attention is, however, quite remarkable when he hurts me.

"This is where you could take me apart," I said afterwards, as I surfaced out of that terrible vulnerability.

Mica looked at me, rested his head on me. "I just want to take care of you," he said.

* * *

When I was younger, it took me a while to get around to taking the dominant role. And there's still something I can reach when I'm being submissive and masochistic that I've never reached when I'm dominant. Still, I think of myself as a confirmed switch now: someone who can take either the submissive or dominant role. Yet it's such a strange binary, isn't it? If he rips me apart and then says, "I just want to take care of you," then which of us is in charge?

Mica told me recently that, "When you're hurting me, my favorite thing you say is 'I know.' Because you **do** know. You know exactly what it's like."

By now I'm barely scared. It hasn't been that long, and I'm trying to allow for New Relationship Energy. I know this could still go up in smoke. But we've talked about expectations, and we've talked through what we're both looking for, and we're both thinking of each other in a long-term way.

If I had to point to events that "proved" Mica has serious potential, two things would top the list. First, in the aftermath of his first incredible S&M experience, when he dealt with the disappointment of realizing that S&M can't always be that — dealt with it quietly, sensibly, without drama, by talking to me. And second, when he said, in defiance of most aggressive stereotypical dominant roles: "I just want to take care of you."

* * *

This can be found on the Internet at:
http://clarissethorn.com/blog/2012/02/10/storytime-the-strange-binary-of-dominance-and-submission/

* * *

***

FEMINISM:
[storytime] My Mom's Rape Story, and A Confused Relationship With Feminism

I wrote this in 2012, for Mother's Day. It was originally published at the girl-power site OffOurChests.com.

***

My mother is a rape survivor. In 1970, when she was in her twenties, she came home alone one day with the groceries. As she was opening the door, a man came up behind her and forced her into the apartment, where he violently assaulted her. For years afterwards, my mother had Rape Trauma Syndrome — a type of Post-Traumatic Stress Disorder that affects rape survivors — but neither RTS nor PTSD had yet been identified, and psychiatrists didn't know what to do with her.

Later in the decade, my mother dumped one of her boyfriends. He then came to her apartment one night, broke in, and raped her. As he got in bed, she was in the middle of a flashback. She cried and said "No," and he had sex with her anyway. When she tried to tell him later that what he'd done was unacceptable, he informed her that because she'd pursued him during their relationship — because she was the one who originally asked him out — a rape case would never stand up in court.

My mother met my dad many years after these incidents. Mom first told me that she'd been raped in my late teens, because she was considering telling her story to our church congregation, and she wanted me to know before she did that. The full stories came out during intermittent conversations in my twenties. I love both my parents with the fire of a thousand suns, and let me tell you, I've spent an unreasonable amount of time fantasizing about murdering the men who attacked my mother. I doubt I could find the first guy, but I could probably find the second, and in my early twenties I often imagined shooting him in the head. (Don't worry, Mom, I don't think about that anymore.)

Within the last few years, I started thinking about asking Mom's permission to write about her experiences and my reaction to them. I always shelved the idea because I felt that it wasn't my story to tell. Last year, the topic came up in conversation, and I finally asked permission; she said yes immediately. I double-checked her consent twice this year, and she said yes both times. Still, I was hesitant, and I only got around to it now — for Mother's Day. I also asked her to review this piece, and to feel free to veto anything within it.

I am doing my best not to co-opt or appropriate my mother's story. But her story and her life have shaped mine, intimately — including my views on gender issues, and my course as a feminist activist and writer. A few years ago, a widely-read *Harper's* article by established feminist Susan Faludi asserted that the relationship between younger feminists and older feminists is like a battle between girls and our moms. [1] I read the article with interest, but also with a sense of displacement. As a teenager I fought with my mom all the time, but she and I rarely argue anymore, and we never argue about issues of feminism or sexuality at all. If "young" feminism is about rebelling against our mothers, then I missed that boat completely.

In fairness, my mom's not easy to rebel against. When I was 15, I asked her what she'd do if I ran off with a Hell's Angel. She laughed. "I'd probably be jealous," she said.

* * *

I started blogging in 2008 because I wanted to write about sexuality, particularly S&M. However, I identified myself as a feminist from the start, because I wanted to make it obvious that S&M and feminism are not mutually exclusive. The conflicts of feminism and S&M have been a major theme throughout the Feminist Sex Wars. I tend to repeat myself when I write about this, so I'll just mention my favorite quotation on the matter; it comes from the German radical feminist Alice Schwarzer, who said, "Female masochism is collaboration!"

When I came out of the closet to my mom, I had been freaking out about my S&M identity for a while — but quietly. I told my parents about my sexuality because I wanted to go into therapy, but I wanted a Kink Aware therapist who wouldn't shame me for my S&M preferences. The specific therapist I preferred was out-of-network for my health insurance, which meant I needed help paying for it. My dad was cool with it, but he didn't say much. My mother paused when I told her... and then she explained that S&M is part of her sexuality, too.

I was shocked. I was also incredibly relieved. If my brilliant, independent mother was into S&M, then suddenly I felt much more okay about being into it myself. It turned out that she had explored S&M late in life — and she went through the same anxiety about feminism and S&M that I'd felt. "You're not giving up your liberation," she told me.

Mom also acknowledged the stereotype that S&M arises from abusive experiences. "I once worried that being raped made me into S&M," she said. "But I remember having S&M feelings in my childhood and early teens, long before I was raped. I was like this all along." When she said that, I caught my breath in recognition.

This is another topic I often repeat myself about, but that's because it's important. As it happens, the biggest and best-designed study on S&M found that there is no correlation between abusive experiences and being into S&M [2] There's also plenty of anecdotal evidence within the S&M community that a lot of S&Mers, though not all, feel our S&M identities to be innate (sometimes described as an "orientation"). This is not to say that there's anything wrong with understanding or processing abuse through consensual S&M. The psychologist Peggy Kleinplatz once published a scholarly article called "Learning From Extraordinary Lovers: Lessons From The Edge," which discusses how therapists can help their clients by studying alternative sexualities. [3] Kleinplatz included a case study of a couple whose S&M experiences helped them process their histories of abuse. However, abusive experiences should not be seen as the usual "creator" of S&M desires. (For more on this, check out my article on S&M and the psychiatric establishment. [4])

The stereotype that S&M "comes from" abuse is another reason I worried about writing this article. Basically, this is a prettily-wrapped gift to Internet commentators who enjoy writing posts or hate mail about how fucked up I am, or about how dysfunctional S&M is. I guess there's no help for that.

* * *

"I'm fascinated that you've adopted feminism so thoroughly," my mother told me once. "I never felt like I was into feminism like you are."

"What?" I said. "Are you serious?"

"Well, feminism shaped my life," she said. "I really had my

consciousness raised by some of my experiences. Not just being raped, but by other things, like seeing the anger and resentment among my mother and her sisters. Feminism helped me understand how women compete and put each other down because we're put in that position by men who have power over us. Sometimes, we're like animals who have been starved into fighting for scraps.

"But," my mother continued, "I've never been sure about calling myself a feminist. There have always been a lot of feminist areas I didn't feel welcome. Your dad was a card-carrying member of the National Organization for Women when I met him, and I refused to join. We used to joke about it. And you remember that recent article about the history of *Ms. Magazine* you emailed me? [5] In the article, Gloria Steinem says that anyone could have walked into the *Ms.* office in the 1970s and gotten a job. But I certainly never felt like I could do that. I was actually living in New York when *Ms.* started, and I was even working in publishing... but I grew up on a farm in the midwest, and I wasn't like the women who ran *Ms.* They felt like a club."

My upbringing has not been like my mother's. I grew up with a lot more privilege; my mother used to call me a spoiled "princess" when she was angry, and one of my ex-boyfriends used to tease me by calling me "East Coast Intellectual." Yet in a lot of ways, it took me a while to get into feminism, too. Gender issues have always been a strand of my thinking, but plenty of feminist discourse never impressed me. In university, I felt like everything I heard from feminism was a tortured conspiracy theory. And although I identified as "feminist" from the very beginning of blogging, it was out of a sense of resistance rather than feeling included. I felt like: *Goddamnit, I will* **show you** *that I can be an independent and rational woman who values voting and abortion rights and equal opportunity and consent — and be into S&M at the same damn time.*

As I kept writing, I was looking at other blogs about gender and sexuality, too. The ones whose analysis really spoke to me were usually feminist blogs. And those were also, often, the bloggers who noticed me in return. My work was highlighted by a number of feminist writers who wanted to raise my profile. Talking to them, I began to understand some sophisticated critiques that I'd previously labeled "conspiracy theories." I expanded my understanding of topics like rape culture, as well as "tangential" social justice issues like race and class. My mother said to me, long afterwards: "Feminism really reached out and grabbed you, didn't it."

In 2011, I heard from a feminist friend about organizations that train volunteer advocates for rape survivors. In Chicago and many other cities, when people who have been raped go to the emergency room, the hospital will ask if they want an advocate. The advocate's role is to provide immediate crisis counseling and to help the survivor deal with complexities of the medical and legal system. The minute I heard about advocacy, I knew I wanted to do it.

In 1970, my mother didn't have an advocate, for the simple reason that advocates did not yet exist. Rape Trauma Syndrome was first recognized by feminists in the 1970s, and assault advocacy was developed by feminists during that time as well.

I told Mom all about the advocacy curriculum while I was completing it, and she drank up every detail. "I never got support like that," she said. "My boyfriend insisted that we go to the emergency room, and I guess he tried to advocate for me, but the doctors and nurses ignored me for 20 hours and then sent me home. It was worse that the nurses did. If sisterhood was powerful, then couldn't they reach out to me somehow?" (Rape survivors — at least in Illinois — are now prioritized in emergency rooms, second only to life-and-death situations.)

Mom often regales me with tales about how things used to be. For example, when she became editor of her college newspaper in the 1960s, all the dudes on staff quit because they wouldn't work under a woman. (Some returned later, rather sheepishly.) Other favorites have to do with menstruation. It turns out that back in the day, doctors – who were of course always male — simply refused to accept the existence of PMS. Apparently, it was accepted among doctors that a woman who felt cramps while menstruating was "making it up." (Female nurses who attempted to describe the actual feeling were ignored.) It was understood that a woman who felt unusually emotional or even in physical pain while menstruating was just being moody and hysterical. (You know how women are!) As more women became doctors and feminism gained traction and science advanced with a broader perspective and scientists discovered the actual physical causes of cramps, PMS became recognized as a real thing. Cramps were no longer "typical female hysteria."

Which, of course, makes it all the more ironic that PMS is now often used as an excuse to discount women as hysterical. It makes me laugh, in my cynical way.

It's kind of astonishing that a woman like my mother would disclaim a strong connection with feminism. And yet she does.

* * *

This year I had my first Full-On Internet Feminist Scandal, during which I received hate mail and hate comments from other feminists. (I name the event in capital letters because email from other feminists, some of whom I don't even know, has told me that if you stick with Internet Feminism long enough, it's basically inevitable that you obtain one of these.) The worst of it fell on a holiday when I was visiting my mother. Mom was helping out at church, and wanted me to attend the sermon. I sobbed for hours before leaving home; I managed to make it to church, but I was such a wreck when I got there that she put me in a back room so I could be alone to cry.

To be clear, I definitely think that I've screwed up on some social justice issues in the past, and I'm sure that I will in the future. I am doing my best to keep myself honest and work on the areas where I've been called out. That's a crucial part of social justice work, and it's one I try to take seriously.

But I have to tell you, the piece I wrote that drew the biggest backlash was one that my mother loved. [6] (In the interests of accountability, I'll say that I do think a lot of the critiques are valid and important [7] — and, for those in the audience who are familiar with feminist call-out culture, I can recommend a couple insightful comments from a brilliant *Feministe* commenter named saurus. [8]) When I wrote the initial draft, I felt so uncertain that I asked Mom to review it, and she said: "I think this is one of the best things you've ever written." Yet one key factor in many of these critiques is that I failed to make enough space for rape survivors. I plan to write differently about the topic in the future, but there's real irony in the fact that the most important rape survivor in my life believes that one of my best pieces is the same one that got me hate mail for failing rape survivors. (Of course, I also received incredibly personal comments about my sex life. The Feminist Sex Wars ain't over yet.)

Mom and I discussed it later, of course. She read some of the commentary online, and she came back shaking her head. "The things some feminists are saying about you really floored me," she said. "But I'm not completely surprised. Feminism has always been one of those movements that eats its young. That's one reason I never identified with it. I think there are a lot of people my age who started out living feminist lives, who now wouldn't be caught dead calling themselves feminist. Women who had careers, who raised sensitive, loving sons and strong daughters... who find the baggage of the 'feminist' label distasteful."

I've thought a lot about my mother's comment that feminism "eats its young." One 2009 *New Yorker* article about feminism by Ariel Levy offered an interesting analysis of feminist divisions, but included one offhand claim that isn't explained or justified: "Revolutions are supposed to devour their young." [9] Is that so? Nobody told me. (Perhaps ironically, Levy presents this claim while stating that feminism has actually turned against its elders.)

Some commentators have told me that if I can't take the heat, then I just shouldn't write about feminism. It hurts to think it, but maybe they're right. Somehow, the idea of being "a good feminist" has become utterly tangled up in my identity. It's a weak spot and a sore spot, in a way that I didn't anticipate and don't fully understand. I find social justice criticism to be nourishing when it's generous and constructive, sometimes even when it's aggressive — but sometimes it feels so incredibly destructive. But as I said, I'm not at all the only feminist writer who feels that the community can be internally destructive. How much of the problem is the vitriol within some critiques, and how much is that feminism has become "who we are" rather than "something we do"?

I think we can all agree that it's good to call out other people when they're screwing up — but there has to be a way for us to build a movement without eating our young. Yet from what my mother tells me, we've never been good at that.

On the bright side, I don't have to engage politically with feminism in order to be a feminist, or volunteer for feminist causes, or do feminist work. And it helps to understand that I don't have to be "a good feminist" for my mother to be proud of me. (My dad's another matter.)

* * *

During one of our recent conversations, I confirmed again with my mother that I had permission to write about her experience. Then I asked her if she's out of the closet as a rape survivor.

"I don't know," she said thoughtfully. "I guess so. I don't really think about it. I'm happy with my life now." She paused and drank her tea for a moment. "I don't think of myself as a rape survivor anymore," she added. "By 1980, ten years after the attack, I really thought I was emerging from the cave. And I was, but I was still metaphorically covered in dirt and cobwebs, with grit in my mouth. In the first few years I was with your dad — the early 1980s — I had residual fears. I had become frightened by subways, elevators, and surprise noises, and he helped me work my way through those very effectively. By 25 years, it was simply no longer a part of my current self. I'd say I am wiser and stronger for it, but I think an experience so shocking is a lousy way to build character. And a waste of time! I lost too many years. I hope that things like victim advocacy saves people."

I'm glad that my mother feels good about life today, and I myself don't have the urge to track those guys down and rend them limb from limb. (Much.) Yet I wonder if the men who attacked her ever think about what they did. I wonder if the ex-boyfriend ever understood how thoroughly he brutalized someone he claimed to love, or how male privilege played a role in his actions. These days, I write a lot about masculinity, and I try to understand men's perspective on gender issues. Writing about men and gender is tricky territory, though. What if I end up shoring up the entitlement that led that those assholes to attack my mom?

Mom told me that she Googled her rapist ex-boyfriend. He has three daughters. She wonders whether he ever thinks about it, too.

Naturally, I also think a lot about feminism, and how we can make it both effective and welcoming. What does it mean when people call it a movement that "eats its young"? What does it mean that feminism has become so tied up in identity? What does it mean when a rape survivor who had a career and raised a feminist daughter won't call herself a feminist? What does it mean that taking on the "feminist" label means taking on a host of other associations — associations that even women like my mother are unwilling to accept?

* * *

This can be found on the Internet at:
http://clarissethorn.com/blog/2012/05/25/my-moms-rape-story-and-a-confused-relationship-with-feminism/

* * *

* * *

Section 3 Study Guide

Having established the building blocks of Section 1, and the extra perspectives of Section 2, this section was intended to pull together some seriously multi-layered syntheses.

* * *

1. Is it hard to relate BDSM theory and practice to feminism or anti-rape activism? If so, then how is it hard? If not, then why do some people believe that there are difficulties?

2. Which issues of sexuality do you feel clear about, and which do you feel foggy or uncertain about? How and why?
2a. Do you have a sense of what makes you feel strong and centered in your sexuality and relationships? If so, how do you go about establishing those factors in your life?

3. Did you have a particularly hostile or excited reaction to any of these pieces? If so, why?

4. Are there any binaries or bright lines that you're questioning as a result of reading these pieces?
4a. Could questioning those divisions have an impact upon your identity, or upon the way you act towards others?

5. What are the overarching patterns that you see within the pieces in this section? How are these disparate topics relevant to each other?
5a. Does this stuff really have to be so complicated?

* * *

* * *

Clarisse's Lectures, Workshops and Events

Thank you so much for reading my work. Now for the hustle! I'm not just a writer — I also give lectures and workshops, and organize events. Here's a short list of some of the lectures, workshops and events I offer. I'm available by email at clarisse.thorn@gmail.com, if you'd like to bring me in.

* * *

* **Confessions of a Pickup Artist Chaser.** There's a whole subculture out there devoted to teaching men how to seduce women. Over the last few years, these underground "pickup artists" have slowly surfaced into the popular consciousness, with the help of bestselling books like Neil Strauss's *The Game* and hit reality shows like VH1's *The Pick-Up Artist*. I spent two years doing on-and-off research into these Casanovas. In this lecture I discuss my experiences talking to pickup artists, learning their techniques, understanding their community frameworks and norms, and eventually giving them tips on how to seduce women... all of which culminated in my book, *Confessions of a Pickup Artist Chaser: Long Interviews With Hideous Men*. This presentation was originally created for a lunchtime talk at the Center for Gender Studies at the University of Chicago, and I can deliver it in 90 minutes or less.

* **Leadership in the Bedroom: A Sexual Communication Workshop.** Down-to-earth tips and ideas on how to communicate clearly about sex. This workshop was originally requested by the University of Illinois at Chicago, but I've given versions of it at other venues as well. It was one of the first workshops I ever designed, and I'm currently working on streamlining it and making it more interactive. I can do it in an hour, but it's really better with two hours.

* **BDSM Overview.** Imagery deriving from bondage, discipline, dominance, submission, and sadomasochism (BDSM) is becoming commonplace — and we all know (or think we know) what a dominatrix is — but most people don't have much idea of what BDSM actually involves. Although it is increasingly accepted as an alternative sexual orientation, BDSM remains surrounded by stigma,

scandal and occasional legal action. This presentation covers the basics of BDSM (however, it's not a how-to lecture — you aren't going to learn how to use a whip, though you'll learn where to go to find out!). I prefer to poll the audience to see what they want to cover on top of that — BDSM history? cultural landmarks? BDSM & feminism? legal issues? I've got it all! I have given this lecture more than any other. It can be squished into an hour, but I prefer two hours.

* **Sex-Positivity for Everyone! Including the Mens!** What is masculinity or male advocacy as a movement, and how is it in dialogue with contemporary feminism? Can it be incorporated into feminism, or can the values of the sex-positive feminist community speak to its concerns? What does positive, productive talk about masculinity sound like? I talk about all this in a short lecturette and then facilitate small discussions on kinky male sexuality, men in the pickup artist community, and men who buy sex. This workshop was originally requested by the University of Chicago, and based on feedback from that experience and others, I have been adapting it. It should take about 90 minutes.

* **The Sex+++ Film Series at Jane Addams Hull-House Museum and related film screenings.** I have now overseen many many screenings of sex-positive documentaries, and facilitated followup discussions afterwards. In the past I have done this primarily to accomplish my own activist educational goals or to raise funds for deserving institutions, but I'd be happy to run a screening or two upon request. Please note, however, that I don't own the rights to all the films I've screened, and so if you want me to run a screening for you, you may need to budget extra in order to cover the rights. I started the Sex+++ Film Series at Chicago's Jane Addams Hull-House Museum, and as I write this in 2012, the film series is in its fourth year. You can look at the film series calendar here: http://clarissethorn.com/blog/2011/03/17/the-sex-positive-documentary-film-list-2011-2012/

I would certainly be willing to design a new workshop or lecture upon request — in fact, two of the above events were created at the request of the institutions that invited me.

* * *

***

Footnotes

All these links were last checked in early 2012.

***

Section 1: The Basics

***

S&M: **Love Bites: An S&M Coming-Out Story**

1. Kink Aware Professionals: https://ncsfreedom.org/resources/kink-aware-professionals-directory/kap-directory-homepage.html

***

Education: **Liberal, Sex-Positive Sex Education: What's Missing**

1. The Unitarian Universalist Our Whole Lives curriculum: http://www.uua.org/re/owl/
2. *New Yorker* review of the new *Joy of Sex:* http://www.newyorker.com/arts/critics/books/2009/01/05/090105crbo_books_levy
3. Synopsis of conservative book *Modern Sex:* http://www.manhattan-institute.org/modern/
4. Cuddle parties: http://current.com/shows/max-and-jason-still-up/89557966_first-time-cuddle-party.htm
5. Scarleteen's sexual inventory checklist: http://www.scarleteen.com/article/advice/yes_no_maybe_so_a_sexual_inventory_stocklist
6. *Yes Means Yes* blog on how affirmative communication combats rape: http://yesmeansyesblog.wordpress.com/2009/01/16/the-words-that-come-after-i-want/

* * *

Communication: **Sex Communication Tactic Derived From S&M: Checklists**

1. Example of a BDSM checklist: http://www.thebrc.net/check_list/default.htm
2. Scarleteen's sex checklist: http://www.scarleteen.com/article/advice/yes_no_maybe_so_a_sexual_inventory_stocklist

* * *

Communication: **Sex Communication Tactic Derived From S&M: Journal-Keeping**

1. Submissive journaling prompts: http://bdsm-sexperts.blogspot.com/2010/07/submissive-journaling-prompts.html

* * *

Communication: **Sex Communication Case Studies**

1. The previous post about a really problematic relationship: http://clarissethorn.com/blog/2011/03/01/storytime-how-my-life-wasnt-always-happy-fun-boundaries-are-perfect-land/

* * *

Feminism: **Towards My Personal Sex-Positive Feminist 101**

1. An excellent definition and discussion of the word "cisgendered," by trans activist Asher Bauer: http://carnalnation.com/content/49458/1067/word-day-cis
2. Analysis of the "virgin" shoot at Kink.com: http://missmaggiemayhem.com/2011/01/12/virginity/
3. Most women don't achieve orgasm through penis-in-vagina sex alone: http://www.scarleteen.com/article/advice/i_cant_orgasm_from_intercourse_and_its_ruining_my_relationship
4. Asexual writer discusses sex-positive feminism: http://www.feministe.us/blog/archives/2012/02/07/an-asexual-map-

for-sex-positive-feminism/

* * *

S&M: **S&M Superpowers**

1. Study demonstrates that BDSM desires do not arise from abuse: http://www.news.com.au/top-stories/bondage-lovers-normal-maybe-even-happier/story-e6frfkp9-1111117296864
2. A post of mine on nonsensical stigma, in the context of whore stigma: http://clarissethorn.com/blog/2010/12/17/whore-stigma-makes-no-sense/
3. Psychology paper "Learning from Extraordinary Lovers" by Peggy Kleinplatz: http://www.ncbi.nlm.nih.gov/pubmed/16803770
4. Study finds that consensual S&M increases intimacy: http://www.ncbi.nlm.nih.gov/pubmed/18563549

* * *

S&M: **BDSM Can Be "Love Sex" Too**

1. Rachel Rabbit White's "Lady Porn Day": http://rachelrabbitwhite.com/ladypornday/

* * *

S&M: **Body Chemistry and S&M**

1. Awesome page on aftercare: http://www.leathernroses.com/generalbdsm/chrismaftercare.htm
2. EduKink is a pair of San Francisco S&M educators: http://www.edukink.org/

* * *

Orgasmic "Dysfunction": **A Unified Theory of Orgasm**

1. A tactic called "gaslighting" is a common one used by emotional abusers: http://www.feministe.us/blog/archives/2011/11/21/one-abuse-script-with-many-faces/
2. Kink Aware Professionals:

https://ncsfreedom.org/resources/kink-aware-professionals-directory/kap-directory-homepage.html

3. Betty Dodson's video "Did I Orgasm?": http://www.youtube.com/v/rkCihT1mkmc

4. Our definitions of orgasm are fairly narrow: http://sexuality.about.com/od/anatomyresponse/a/what_is_orgasm.htm

* * *

Boundaries: **Orgasms Aren't My Favorite Part Of Sex, and My Chastity Urge**

1. Deliberately limiting orgasms for a more amorous relationship: http://goodmenproject.com/featured-content/too-many-orgasms/

2. Scarleteen discusses women and "squirting" orgasms: http://www.scarleteen.com/article/advice/squirt_on_female_ejaculation

* * *

Evolution: **Sexual Openness: Two Ways To Encourage It**

1. Comstock Films makes documentaries about real couples and how they have sex: http://comstockfilms.com/

2. CineKink, "the really alternative film festival": http://cinekink.com

* * *

Relationships: **Fear, Loathing, and S&M Sluthood in San Francisco**

1. My blog post "There It Is": http://clarissethorn.wordpress.com/2010/10/28/litquote-storytime-there-it-is/

2. The Sutro Baths, extraordinary ruins in San Francisco: http://www.flickr.com/photos/vicster/2816355231/in/set-72157607093679758/

3. A blog post I wrote on the perils of vanilla-but-questioning dudes: http://clarissethorn.wordpress.com/2010/11/05/bdsm-vs-

vanilla-part-1-why-i-pretend-i-dont-date-vanilla-but-questioning-men/
4. The "lost" 21st chapter of *A Clockwork Orange:* http://www.visual-memory.co.uk/amk/doc/0062.html

* * *

S&M: **BDSM As A Sexual Orientation, and Complications of the Orientation Model**

1. BDSM-phobic thread on a radical feminist blog: http://rageagainstthemanchine.com/2009/02/07/please-somebody-come-and-defend-kinkcom/
2. BDSM-related discrimination case and orientation notes from Charles Moser: http://www.xtra.ca/public/Vancouver/BDSM_lifestyler_unfit_to_drive_a_limo_police-6577.aspx

* * *

S&M: **BDSM "versus" Sex**

1. Definition of "prostitution" shifts and NYC dominatrixes are arrested: http://sexinthepublicsquare.org/ElizabethsBlog/ncsf-statement-on-pro-dom-work-and-prostitution-statutes
2. Marty Klein's "Is There Such A Thing As Kinky Sex?": http://www.sexualintelligence.org/newsletters/issue128.html - three
3. maymay on "kinky" not being limited to BDSM: http://maybemaimed.com/2010/10/05/honor-thy-language-kinky-is-an-adjective-not-an-activity/
4. Quasi-conservative organization Taken In Hand: http://www.takeninhand.com/
5. Comment from saurus: http://www.fcministc.us/blog/archives/2011/10/09/bdsm-versus-sex-part-1-divide-and-conquer/ - comment-397105
6. *Feministe* post on the "violent sex" article: http://www.feministe.us/blog/archives/2011/07/12/violent-sex-writer-compromises-safety-of-rape-survivor/
7. Comment from Jadey: http://www.feministe.us/blog/archives/2011/06/27/the-best-most-disturbing-thing-you-will-read-today/ - comment-373440
8. Mac McClelland's "Violent Sex" article:

http://www.good.is/post/how-violent-sex-helped-ease-my-ptsd/
9. My old post "Casual Sex? Casual Kink?":
http://clarissethorn.com/blog/2008/12/26/casual-sex-casual-kink/

* * *

S&M: **BDSM Roles, "Topping From The Bottom," and "Service Top"**

1. Thomas MacAulay Millar on "Domism":
http://yesmeansyesblog.wordpress.com/2011/05/02/domism-role-essentialism-and-sexism-intersectionality-in-the-bdsm-scene/

* * *

S&M: **"Inherent Female Submission": The Wrong Question**

1. The *Topologies* blog features three dominant female contributors: http://topologies.wordpress.com/2009/11/07/shifting-the-discourse-on-female-dominance/
2. Research on proportion of submissive BDSM women: http://kinkresearch.blogspot.com/2009/10/sex-role-ratio.html
3. The female dominant blogger Bitchy Jones is pissed: http://bitchyjones.wordpress.com/2009/03/14/bondage-awards-not-actually-sexist-on-purpose/
4. The male submissive blogger maymay is pissed: http://maybemaimed.com/2007/08/04/what-sexuality-might-taste-like-if-you-were-a-submissive-man-in-2007/

* * *

Manliness: *Fifty Shades of Grey, Fight Club,* **and the Complications of Male Dominance**

1. The sex writer Violet Blue offers some hilarious *Fifty Shades* commentary and linkfarming: http://www.tinynibbles.com/blogarchives/2012/04/fifty-shades-of-linkbait.html The writer A.V. Flox also did a really great analysis of how badly *Fifty Shades* deals with S&M: http://www.blogher.com/troubling-message-fifty-shades-grey
2. Pepper Mint's blog: http://freaksexual.wordpress.com/

***

Abuse: **The Alt Sex Anti-Abuse Dream Team**

1. The post on *SM-Feminist* about the prevalence of abuse in the community: http://sm-feminist.blogspot.com/2007/11/wut-about-abuuuuuuuuuuzers.html

2. A post on *SM-Feminist* about an abuse survivor who learned to set boundaries and protect herself through BDSM: http://sm-feminist.blogspot.com/2008/01/not-your-usual-bdsm-and-abuse-story.html

3. Thomas MacAulay Millar's article "Not What We Do": http://yesmeansyesblog.wordpress.com/2010/09/21/not-what-we-do/

4. Front image of a pamphlet about abuse in BDSM: http://www.flickr.com/photos/35620214@N02/3488055736/ — Back image of same pamphlet: http://www.flickr.com/photos/35620214@N02/3487239893/

5. Statement on BDSM and abuse from the Leather Leadership Conference: http://www.leatherleadership.org/library/diffsmabuse.htm — Statement on BDSM and abuse from the Lesbian Sex Mafia: http://lesbiansexmafia.org/lsmnyc/bdsm-is-not-abuse/

6. Kink Aware Professionals: https://ncsfreedom.org/resources/kink-aware-professionals-directory/kap-directory-homepage.html

***

Section 2: Activism and Allies

***

Activism: **Grassroots Organizing For Feminism, S&M, HIV, and Everything Else**

1. Bitch Magazine's Feminist Coming-Out Day Blog Carnival: http://bitchmagazine.org/post/feminist-coming-out-day-blog-carnival

2. My sex-positive documentary film series: http://clarissethorn.com/blog/2011/03/17/the-sex-positive-documentary-film-list-2011-2012/

3. Pamphlet on making a group egalitarian but well-organized: http://struggle.ws/hist_texts/structurelessness.html

4. Chicago's Rape Victim Advocates: http://www.rapevictimadvocates.org/

5. Kink Aware Professionals: https://ncsfreedom.org/resources/kink-aware-professionals-directory/kap-directory-homepage.html

6. My advice on activism in Africa: http://clarissethorn.com/blog/2010/01/31/clarisses-advice-column-arises-again-masculinity-african-activism/

7. An general overview I wrote of housing co-ops: http://www.rolereboot.org/sex-and-relationships/details/2012-04-housing-co-ops-arent-just-for-hippies

8. North American Students of Cooperation: http://nasco.coop/

* * *

Activism: Interview with Richard Berkowitz, Star of *Sex Positive* and Icon of Safer Sex Activism

1. My original review of the film: http://clarissethorn.com/blog/2009/02/11/sex-positive-documentary-report-2-sex-positive/

2. Gay Male SM Activists was one of the first S&M advocacy organizations ever: http://www.gmsma.org/

* * *

Abuse: Social Responsibility Within Activism

1. Problems of prisons: http://www.newyorker.com/arts/critics/atlarge/2012/01/30/120130crat_atlarge_gopnik?currentPage=all

* * *

Masculinity: Questions I Want To Ask Entitled Cis Het Men

1. Thomas MacAulay Millar on masculinity: http://yesmeansyesblog.wordpress.com/2009/05/27/things-cis-het-men-are-afraid-to-talk-about/

2. "Precarious Manhood" paper: Vandello et al. "Precarious Manhood." *Journal of Personality and Social Psychology,* Vol. 95, No. 6, 1325 – 1339. 2008.

3. Men's Rights Activists: the "most discriminated against" quotation came from Kuster, Elizabeth. *Exorcising Your Ex.* Fireside, 1996. Also, long after the publication of my blog posts, the politics website AlterNet did a profile of the MRA movement: http://www.alternet.org/teaparty/154617/Leader's_Suicide_Reveals_Frightening,_Violent,_Organized_Misogyny_Movement/

4. Sexism in BDSM: http://maybemaimed.com/2009/10/02/dont-you-fret-sexism-is-alive-and-well-in-bdsm/

5. Seriously, these posters are awesome: http://www.reachandteach.com/store/index.php?l=product_detail&p=50

6. Alienating men with Thomas MacAulay Millar: http://yesmeansyesblog.wordpress.com/2009/01/26/who-is-bidding-on-natalie-dylans-virginity

* * *

Education: **Sexual ABCs in Africa, Part 1: Abstinence**

1. Chris Hall's blog: http://literateperversions.com/
2. My archive of articles at CarnalNation: http://carnalnation.com/users/clarisse-thorn
3. Unitarian sex education: http://www.uua.org/religiouseducation/curricula/ourwhole/
4. Another article on declining sexual satiation and how it can contribute to romantic feelings: http://www.marginalrevolution.com/marginalrevolution/2009/08/against-satiation.html

* * *

Education: **Sexual ABCs in Africa, Part 2: Be Faithful**

1. Helen Epstein's 2004 article "The Fidelity Fix": http://www.nytimes.com/2004/06/13/magazine/13AIDS.html
2. 2007 *Washington Post* article on multiple partners in Botswana: http://www.washingtonpost.com/wp-dyn/content/article/2007/03/01/AR2007030101607.html

* * *

Education: **Sexual ABCs in Africa, Part 3: Condoms**

1. Religious educators saying that encouraging condom usage waters down their message:
http://www.thinkingfaith.org/articles/20090325_1.htm

2. Underprivileged populations "choosing" to contract HIV: Ticktin, Miriam. "Where Ethics and Politics Meet: The Violence of Humanitarianism in France." *American Ethnologist* volume 33, number 1, 2006. Ticktin herself cites an April 6, 2005 National Public Radio broadcast by Nicoli Nattrass, which outlined cases of people infecting themselves with HIV in southern Africa. For an especially haunting and personal account of deliberate self-infection, see also Sylvie C. Tourigny's "Some New Dying Trick: African American Youths 'Choosing' HIV/AIDS." *Qualitative Health Research* volume 8, number 2, 1998.

3. Helen Epstein's 2004 article "The Fidelity Fix":
http://www.nytimes.com/2004/06/13/magazine/13AIDS.html

4. Reasonable laws regulating sex work were being discussed in South Africa around the time of the World Cup:
http://www.guardian.co.uk/world/2009/oct/11/legalise-world-cup-sex-trade

* * *

Activism: **Colonized Libidos**

1. Rest in peace, Pitseng Vilakati:
http://carnalnation.com/content/44250/1133/rest-peace-pitseng-vilakati

2. An argument that the places in Africa where homosexuality is most strongly punished are some of the best to actually be gay:
http://chrisblattman.com/2010/03/10/is-uganda-a-good-place-to-be-gay/

3. An argument that much of Africa was less homophobic pre-Western influence: http://isnblog.ethz.ch/culture/gay-rights---and-wrongs---in-africa

4. The Patriarchy allegedly made me kinky: http://sm-feminist.blogspot.com/2008/10/why-bdsm.html

* * *

Vegan: **Confections of a Pickup Artist Chaser**

1. Kinsey Hope's activist typology: http://genderbitch.wordpress.com/2009/10/03/a-m-o-communication/
2. Characterized as an "Appeaser" activist type, plus tactical discussion: http://www.amptoons.com/blog/2011/02/18/response-to-clarisse-thorns-backlash-2-nuke-and-appease-please-be-a-bothand-blogiverse/
3. Free vegan starter guide: http://www.veganoutreach.org/guide/
4. List of vegan cookbooks: http://vegan.com/cookbooks/
5. Things that happen to animals on factory farms: http://www.veganoutreach.org/whyvegan/ or this video: http://www.mercyforanimals.org/farm-to-fridge.aspx
6. Vegan FAQ: http://vegan.com/articles/faq/
7. *Salon* article on "humane" farms: http://www.salon.com/2005/04/13/milk_3/
8. Oatmeal chocolate chip cookie recipe originally from: http://www.essortment.com/unbeatable-vegan-chocolate-chip-oatmeal-cookie-recipe-13043.html
9. Frying tofu with a nice crust: http://www.tastehongkong.com/recipes/how-to-pan-fry-tofu-with-crust-is-simple/

* * *

Polyamory: **In Praise of Monogamy**

1. Poly vs. swingers at *Polyamory In The News:* http://polyinthemedia.blogspot.com/2009/12/polys-vs-swingers-as-viewed-from-2010.html
2. Polyamory relationship contract: http://www.scarletletters.com/current/021403_nf_rk.html
3. Someone else's blog post on managing New Relationship Energy in polyamory: http://www.adrienneparker.com/2010/07/nre-in-polyamorous-relationships.html
4. How choosing no orgasms can increase couple bonding: http://goodmenproject.com/featured-content/too-many-orgasms/
5. 40% of young couples don't agree whether they're monogamous: http://www.charlieglickman.com/2011/02/new-research-young-couples-disagree-about-whether-theyre-monogamous/
6. The "slippery slope" argument against gay marriage:

http://www.slate.com/articles/news_and_politics/jurisprudence/2004/05/slippery_slop.html

7. Monogamous privilege checklist: http://www.eastportlandblog.com/2011/04/05/monogamous-privilege-checklist-by-cory-davis/

8. White privilege checklist: http://www.nymbp.org/reference/WhitePrivilege.pdf

* * *

Sex Work: **One Blurred Edge of Sex Work: Portrait of a Sugar Baby**

1. The SeekingArrangement blog post, "Sugar Baby and Sugar Daddy: The Modern Day Princess and Prince?": http://www.seekingarrangement.com/blog/?p=5456

2. 2009 New York Times Magazine article on SeekingArrangement: http://www.nytimes.com/2009/04/12/magazine/12sugardaddies-t.html?pagewanted=all

* * *

Sex Work: **A Sugar Baby Leaves The Business**

1. The SeekingArrangement blog post, "Sugar Baby and Sugar Daddy: The Modern Day Princess and Prince?": http://www.seekingarrangement.com/blog/?p=5456

2. The SeekingArrangement blog post, "Sugar Babies Do Fall In Love": http://www.seekingarrangement.com/blog/?p=5561

3. Mistress Matisse on sex work and emotional labor: http://www.thestranger.com/seattle/Content?oid=26113 and also: http://mistressmatisse.blogspot.com/2011/01/im-expecting-bit-of-heat-from.html

4. Tyler Knight on emotional difficulties as a porn star: http://tylerknight.com/2011/12/18/oneironaut-at-wrest/

* * *

Section 3: Making It Complicated

* * *

Relationships: **Chemistry**

1. Infamous article "Marry Him: The Case For Settling For Mr. Good Enough":
http://www.theatlantic.com/magazine/archive/2008/03/marry-him/6651/

* * *

Evolution: **You Don't Always Know What You're Thinking**

1. Autumn Whitefield-Madrano on the "fog of abuse": http://www.feministe.us/blog/archives/2011/08/08/i-can-handle-it-on-relationship-violence-independence-and-capability/
2. My old post "Am I Evolving Away From Monogamy?": http://clarissethorn.com/blog/2010/05/11/am-i-evolving-away-from-monogamy/

* * *

Abuse: **Thinking More Clearly About BDSM versus Abuse**

1. Pepper Mint's essay "Towards A General Theory of BDSM and Power": http://freaksexual.wordpress.com/2007/06/11/towards-a-general-theory-of-bdsm-and-power/
2. The origins of the Power and Control Wheel: http://www.theduluthmodel.org/training/wheels.html — Image of the Power & Control Wheel: http://www.theduluthmodel.org/pdf/PowerandControl.pdf — Text of that wheel, and other relevant wheels: http://www.dhs.state.il.us/page.aspx?item=38490
3. Image of the Equality Wheel: http://www.theduluthmodel.org/pdf/Equality.pdf

* * *

S&M: **Aftercare or Brainwashing?**

1. That study on intimacy again: http://www.ncbi.nlm.nih.gov/pubmed/18563549
2. That awesome aftercare page again: http://www.leathernroses.com/generalbdsm/chrismaftercare.htm
3. FormerWildChild's comment on my post: http://www.feministe.us/blog/archives/2010/10/18/there-it-is/-comment-332491
4. Paper on people who experience orgasm while assaulted: http://www.ncbi.nlm.nih.gov/pubmed/15261004
5. First-person account of orgasm during a rape: http://www.netburst.net/hope/rape_orgasm.htm
6. The cycle of abuse: http://www.uic.edu/depts/owa/cycle_of_violence.html
7. Thomas's post on S&M mistakes: http://yesmeansyesblog.wordpress.com/2012/04/30/theres-a-war-on-part-5-wallowing-in-the-sl-op

* * *

Communication: **Feminist S&M Lessons From the Seduction Community**

1. PUALingo lists over 715 pickup artist terms: http://www.pualingo.com/pua-terminology-list/
2. A PUA internal critique by a dude named Chris. I cross-posted it to my blog, and it's also available as an appendix in my book *Confessions of a Pickup Artist Chaser:* http://clarissethorn.com/blog/2011/04/18/guest-post-detrimental-attitudes-of-the-pickup-artist-community/
3. "Neg" definition: http://www.sosuave.com/articles/neghits.htm
4. Neil Strauss on negs: http://www.neilstrauss.com/neil/what-separates-a-winner-from-a-loser-is-2
5. Tyler Durden on negs: http://www.bristollair.com/2011/pua-seduction-methods/examining-different-pua-methods-pt-2/
6. This guy is a real asshole, and I dedicate most of a chapter in my book to explaining how wrong he is about everything. Roissy on negs: http://heartiste.wordpress.com/2011/09/26/the-subtle-art-of-the-insidious-neg/
7. "If it wasn't for the pussy, there would be a bounty on

[women]": http://heartiste.wordpress.com/2011/08/07/what-are-you-thinking-about/ - comment-267855

8. Mark Manson on miserable PUA dudes: http://postmasculine.com/pickup-artist

9. My interview with Neil Strauss: http://timeoutchicago.com/sex-dating/12914409/neil-strauss-interview

10. Feminist asks Clarisse why she's being generous to Strauss, on a feminist thread deconstructing PUAs: http://www.feministe.us/blog/archives/2011/03/25/i-totally-interviewed-the-worlds-most-famous-pickup-artist/ - comment-357169

11. Anti-feminist doesn't like Strauss either: http://www.inmalafide.com/blog/2011/04/12/kill-your-game-idols-part-2-strauss-schwyzer-and-spengler/

12. History of *Ms. Magazine* includes the erasure of BDSM: http://nymag.com/print/?/news/features/ms-magazine-2011-11/

13. Jaclyn Friedman on how consent is not a lightswitch: http://www.amplifyyourvoice.org/u/Yes_Means_Yes/2010/11/9/Consent-Is-Not-A-Lightswitch

14. *Salon* interview with Tracy Clark-Flory: http://www.salon.com/2011/10/30/a_sex_guide_for_todays_girls/singleton/

15. Discussion of forcing explicit communication on a feminist BDSM blog: http://pervocracy.blogspot.com/2011/07/how-to-not-be-creepy.html?showComment=1310928149621 - c6917844665418677680

16. Feminist site on sexual violence emphasizes non-verbal communication: http://www.uwyo.edu/stop/Get Educated/sexualviolence.html

17. Feminist argues that "PUAs rape women": http://www.feministe.us/blog/archives/2011/03/25/i-totally-interviewed-the-worlds-most-famous-pickup-artist/ - comment-357951

18. PUA claims that "the first two 'no's don't mean much": http://thesocialsecrets.com/2009/04/5-easy-ways-to-over-come-lmr-last-minute-sexual-reservations/

19. David Shade on LMR: *The Secrets of Female Sexuality,* by David Shade. David Shade Corporation, 2007.

20. Mark Manson advises respecting LMR: http://www.practicalpickup.com/the-cheerleader

21. PUA Detox: http://www.practicalpickup.com/the-guide-to-a-

pua-detox

* * *

S&M: **The Strange Binary of Dominance and Submission**

1. An article I wrote about submissive skills, and their value: http://clarissethorn.com/blog/2012/01/16/submissive-skills/

* * *

Feminism: **My Mom's Rape Story, and A Confused Relationship with Feminism**

1. Susan Faludi's article on feminism's "Electra complex": http://harpers.org/archive/2010/10/0083140
2. Study shows S&Mers not more likely to have experienced abuse: http://www.news.com.au/top-stories/bondage-lovers-normal-maybe-even-happier/story-e6frfkp9-1111117296864
3. Kleinplatz's paper on "Learning From Extraordinary Lovers": http://www.ncbi.nlm.nih.gov/pubmed/16803770
4. S&M and the psychiatric establishment: http://clarissethorn.com/blog/2012/05/07/the-psychology-of-sm/
5. History of *Ms. Magazine:* http://nymag.com/news/features/ms-magazine-2011-11/
6. Piece that drew backlash: http://clarissethorn.com/blog/2011/12/22/on-change-and-accountability/
7. Response piece to above: http://www.amptoons.com/blog/2011/12/28/on-change-and-accountability-a-response-to-clarisse-thorn/
8. Brilliant comments from saurus at *Feministe:* http://www.feministe.us/blog/archives/2011/10/17/call-out-culture-and-blogging-as-performance/ - comment-399410 and also: http://www.feministe.us/blog/archives/2011/12/31/on-change-and-accountability-a-response-to-clarisse-thorn/ - comment-424091
9. Ariel Levy's 2009 article on feminist divisions: http://www.newyorker.com/arts/critics/books/2009/11/16/091116crbo_books_levy?currentPage=all

* * *

***

Glossary

As I said in the introduction, I try to keep my writing as accessible as possible. One way I do that is by avoiding jargon and by using terms that I think most people will recognize. I often write "S&M" instead of "BDSM," for example; and when I'm using technical S&M language like "top" or "bottom" or "scene," I try to define the words as I go along. But sometimes I slip into jargon by accident. Also, plenty of S&M terms are super useful, and giving a quick overview of S&M language can go a long way towards describing S&M culture. Hence, this glossary. Many of the terms in the Glossary aren't terms that I used in this book, but you might find it useful or interesting anyway. (I also included a few terms that come from other subcultures, like polyamory or queer studies or feminism, because why not.)

***

aftercare (BDSM): A cool-down period after an S&M encounter, which often involves reassurance and a discussion of how things went. Aftercare is discussed a lot in this book, especially in "Aftercare or Brainwashing" (part 3).
blaming the victim (feminism): The faulty assumption that an assault survivor caused or contributed to the assault.
bottom (BDSM): A blanket term for a *masochist* and/or *submissive*. Not everyone who is a masochist is submissive, and vice versa.
cisgendered (queer studies): A term that means "not transgendered." For example, Clarisse is a cis woman or a cisgendered woman. Here's an excellent essay by the trans activist Asher Bauer describing why the word "cisgendered" is important: http://carnalnation.com/content/49458/1067/word-day-cis
coming out (queer studies): Openly acknowledging one's sexual identity to oneself, one's parents, one's friends, and other parts of one's community.
dominant (BDSM): A person who enjoys being in charge during

an S&M encounter.

dungeon (BDSM): Dungeons can often be split into two types: those owned and staffed by professionals, and those owned by people who are drawn to S&M for non-monetary reasons. There is occasionally overlap between the two groups, but often there's less overlap than one might think. Professional BDSM is frequently banned at non-professional dungeons, and non-professional dungeons are frequently non-profit organizations. Indeed, many non-professional dungeons could be described as "community centers" for BDSMers. They're basically centralized nodes for BDSM support, and they may host lectures, workshops, discussion groups, public parties, or other meetups.

enthusiastic consent (feminism): A standard for ethical sex whereby one is expected not just to have a consenting partner, but an enthusiastic and excited partner.

gender policing (feminism): Gender roles are defined by culture, and when a person steps outside their gender role, that person will often be *policed* or attacked by other members of the culture. For example, a USA man with long hair risks being mocked or beaten up.

heteronormative (queer studies): A term used to describe the cultural expectations of "normal" heterosexual relationships. For example, the expectation that men are the ones to pursue women during romantic interactions is heteronormative.

kink (BDSM): A specific preference. For example, if Clarisse enjoys being whipped, then she has a kink for it. She could also say something like, "I kink on whipping."

kinky (BDSM and others): A lot of BDSMers use "kinky" to mean "into BDSM." However, there are some people who use the term more broadly and include practices that aren't usually considered BDSM, such as *polyamory* or *swing*.

landmine (BDSM): An extremely sensitive psychological spot, sometimes hit accidentally during BDSM play. This is discussed further within this book, in "What Happens After An S&M Encounter 'Gone Wrong'" (part 3).

masochist (BDSM): A person who enjoys receiving pain.

New Relationship Energy (polyamory): The obsessive, irrational joy one feels after starting a relationship with a new and awesome partner. Here's an article about it: http://aphroweb.net/articles/nre.htm

out [of the closet] (queer studies): An adjective to describe a person who is open with people outside her sexual subculture about her sexual identity.

play (BDSM): A verb for having an S&M encounter. For example, if Clarisse was whipped by a gentleman, she might say that she "played with him." Clarisse once saw a display at the Leather Archives & Museum claiming that in Old Guard Leather Culture (i.e, gay men's S&M culture starting around the 1950s), the word was more often "work" than "play" — apparently, even S&M toys were usually called "tools."

play party (BDSM): A party where S&M can happen openly. Some play parties ban sexual intercourse, while others don't.

polyamory: A community to support people who want to have multiple lovers and be honest with everyone involved. Polyamory usually focuses more on an emotional relationship than *swing,* but not always. The writer Franklin Veaux has a good Polyamory 101: http://www.xeromag.com/fvpoly.html And the blog *Polyamory In The News* has a good post on the various distinctions between polyamory and swing: http://polyinthemedia.blogspot.com/2009/12/polys-vs-swingers-as-viewed-from-2010.html

primary relationship (polyamory): A relationship with more commitment and expectations than other relationships. For example, a primary relationship might be one where the participants live together and/or are married. Polyamorists sometimes disagree about whether relationship hierarchies are desirable.

rape culture (feminism): A culture in which rape is prevalent and is maintained through fundamental attitudes and beliefs about gender, sexuality, and violence, including *rape myths.*

rape myths (feminism): Cultural ideas that make it harder to recognize, prosecute, and heal from rape. For example, many people believe that rape usually happens to young, "hot" women... but interviews with rapists show that they usually prioritize targets based on how vulnerable they are, rather than how "hot" they are.

sadist (BDSM): A person who enjoys inflicting pain.

safeword (BDSM): A word that any S&M participant can say at any time to stop the action. Safewords are extensively analyzed within this book, in the "The Annotated Safeword" (part 1).

scene; The Scene (BDSM): The word "scene" is often used to indicate an S&M encounter. For example, if Clarisse was whipped by some dude, she "had a scene" with him (or some would say that she "scened" with him). "The Scene" is also sometimes used to indicate the public S&M community — the *dungeons,* workshops, lectures, discussion groups, and meetups that create an open network of BDSMers in many areas.

secondary relationship (polyamory): A relationship with less commitment and fewer expectations than other relationships. Polyamorists sometimes disagree about whether relationship hierarchies are desirable.

squick (BDSM): A feeling of not wanting to participate in an act, without judging others for doing it. For example, if a BDSMer feels sick at the sight of blood yet doesn't want to express disgust towards blood fetishists, then she might describe herself as "squicked" by blood. The BDSM subculture generally places a high value on recognizing that one can be squicked by an act, without judging it.

submissive (BDSM): A person who enjoys receiving orders or otherwise accepting an experience defined by a partner.

swing: A community to support people who want to have sex with multiple people and be honest with everyone involved. Unlike *polyamorists,* swingers usually don't emphasize developing emotional connections in *secondary relationships,* but this isn't always true. Clarisse is less familiar with swing than polyamory, but some swingers emailed her this Swing 101: http://www.swingersboard.com/forums/faq.php?faq=swinger_faq And the blog *Polyamory In The News* has a good post on the various distinctions between polyamory and swing: http://polyinthemedia.blogspot.com/2009/12/polys-vs-swingers-as-viewed-from-2010.html

switch (BDSM): A person who feels comfortable in either the *top* or the *bottom* role.

top (BDSM): A blanket term for a *sadistic* and/or *dominant* partner. Not everyone who is sadistic is dominant, and vice versa.

vanilla (BDSM): A term to describe people who aren't into BDSM, or sexual acts that aren't perceived as BDSM. Some folks describe so-called "slightly BDSM" people or acts as *french vanilla.* Sometimes, non-BDSM people are offended by being described as vanilla, which Clarisse thinks is silly, but she often avoids the term anyway and says "not into S&M" instead.

ze (queer studies): A gender-neutral pronoun, also written as "xie." The possessive version is "zir" or "xir" or, sometimes, "hir."

Printed in Great Britain
by Amazon.co.uk, Ltd.,
Marston Gate.